Law of Reflection

Law of Reflection

*The Memoirs of a Transformative &
Healing Journey Through Tibetan Buddhism*

Marc Preston Moss

HOLON
PUBLISHING

Copyright © 2021 Marc Preston Moss
All rights reserved. No part of this publication may be reproduced, distributed, or transmitted in any form or by any means, including photocopying, recording, or other electronic or mechanical methods, without the prior written permission of the author, except in the case of brief quotations embodied in critical reviews and certain other noncommercial uses permitted by copyright law. For permission requests, contact the publisher at:

www.Holon.co

ISBN#: 978-1-955342-04-9 (Paperback)
ISBN#: 978-1-955342-12-4 (Hardback)
ISBN#: 978-1-955342-54-4 (eBook)

Published by:

Holon Publishing & Collective Press
A Storytelling Company
www.Holon.co

Cover Art by Scott Allen

This book is dedicated to:

Geshe Jinpa Sonam, my spiritual teacher, friend, and father. Thank you for all the years of guidance and for being the person I aspire to become. I can never repay your kindness of coming to a country whose language you didn't know, having patience for this clumsy fool, and giving me the precious gift of Dharma.

Wyatt White, for being the best friend of this lifetime, an angel in human clothing, for talking me off of countless ledges, and—for being pretty.

Joel Preston Moss, my dad. It took a long time to realize just how amazing you are. Your words of wisdom have soothed and healed so many wounds.

Al, for being an amazing friend when I needed it, and supporting me through this journey.

Andy Turley, for all the hours we dissected life, religion, science, and politics. Thanks for our journey together. It's been a *Whopper*!

Nathaniel Jude, for finding my little meditation spot and starting a journey that's not stopped being amazing... or for continuing one that started long before memory.

The Tibetan people worldwide, for the treasures you safeguarded and the hearts you share. *Bod Gyalo*!

Ama Sonam Drolma and Tenzin Drolkar Gorgotsang (and family), thank you for taking me in as your own and allowing me to call you mine. I love you all very dearly and am blessed to have found you in this lifetime.

DJ, for years of wonderful memories, good and bad, that was the ignition for my spiritual engine. You have no idea how grateful I am for our time together. It profoundly changed everything. I see you as a spiritual teacher who assigned a powerful lesson.

My brother Chris, for being there just when I needed and never judging me, and for showing me another side to this story that my soul needed to hear.

My brother Evan, I love you dearly and I am so sorry that life pushed me away for far too long. I'm glad we're together again!

Craig, for the best friend I could have asked for growing up, and for our celestial connection—proven on April 10, 2007.

Dawa-jojo and Mr. Waiba, for accepting me into your world and guiding me to a lifechanging experience.

My aunt Shirley Smith, for always being the wisdom I needed, and the laugh I love most in the world.

Palden Dorje, thank you for coming into the world and radiating a heavenly light that we all share, and for reminding us what we all can become.

Also, I want to give my deepest heartfelt appreciation to His Holiness the Dalai Lama for not just being the force that introduced me to this tradition of love, compassion, logic, and reason, but for his tireless work spreading the message of brotherhood and sisterhood of all earthling consciousnesses across the planet—a kind of Law of Reflection upon which it is most worthy to reflect.

And to Linda Dale Wasson, my mother. I use your maiden name here as I am certain you'd want it that way. You started this journey, not just by giving me my life, but by so many reasons too many to number. I'll just say, thanks for the Tina Turner album, and thanks for your final message, the right-turning conch shell at my feet in the reservoir park, the place my first spiritual realizations occurred, where I wrote the last page of this book.

Foreword

Geshe Jinpa Sonam, Spiritual Director of the Indiana Buddhist Center;
Translated by Dianne McKinnon

As an introduction to Marc Moss' book, *Law of Reflection*, I would like to offer a few words to you in the beginning. In reading this book, I would like to encourage you to take what is portrayed on these pages as an example that you yourself can model in your own life.

The pursuit to develop oneself as a good person is really of the utmost importance. Regarding this, the great Buddhist master Shantideva said:

So take advantage of this human boat.
To free yourself from sorrow's mighty stream!
As this boat later will be hard to find,
The time you have is now, you fool, is not time for sleep!

Generally, suffering and difficulty often play big a role in our lives. Due to our negative, non-virtuous mental states leading us into destructive patterns and non-virtuous conduct, we experience a lot of trauma and pain. In contrast, when we have positive and virtuous mental states, we follow constructive patterns of virtuous conduct—good and well-intended deeds and actions. Based in positivity, we create and experience happiness.

To develop oneself as a good person requires the ongoing inner examination of these virtuous and non-virtuous mental states within oneself. Differentiating these two, we look to separate from negative intention and harmful action, and focus on good intention and beneficial action. The concentrated and diligent effort in virtue is how we develop this trait.

This focus on being a good or decent person is especially important. His Holiness the Dalai Lama repeatedly mentions that the most important thing we can be in the world is a good, kind human being.

After reading this book, you do not need to become a Buddhist. But what is important is to be a kind person, to be authentic to yourself and others, to lead a meaningful life, and to be happy.

Do not waste this life or throw away your future [lives]. Using your human intelligence well, you are capable of meaningful achievement!

Doug Stout, President, Indiana Buddhist Center

Over 2,500 years ago, when the person we know as the Buddha gave his first teaching, he told his audience something that they knew well, that we are all subject to unhappiness, to stress and strain, and to suffering. Fortunately for them and for us, he didn't leave it at that, and continued with the very good news that this unhappiness and suffering can be brought completely to an end, by understanding its causes and the methods we can apply.

For many people raised in Western countries, there is simply very little exposure to the treasure house of teachings that the Buddha taught in that first discourse, and that great Buddhist masters have shared in the years since. Even after learning about their existence, it's reasonable to wonder if such ancient teachings are still relevant in today's world. In a time when there are greater resources than ever, too many suffer in poverty or live in constant worry that they won't be able to afford the basics of life. While technology has made it easier to interact than ever, many feel a deep and growing loneliness; and while it seems that life presents more possibilities than have ever been available, many fall into depression. In recent years, due in large part to increased availability, Buddhist teachings have been discovered by more and more people in Western cultures. In fact, these teachings regarding suffering and the end of suffering seem more relevant than ever.

In this book, Marc Preston Moss shares his story of how he came upon Buddhist teachings and followed a path that would change his life in ways that he could not have foreseen. Marc presents this journey using the same progression that the Buddha used in his first teaching – the Four Noble Truths – suffering and stress, its causes, its quelling, and the path that leads to the quelling of suffering and stress.

For years, Marc has been encouraging others on their journeys of discovery and personal insight as a principal teacher at the Indiana Buddhist Center. He is known for his energetic and engaging presence, for his deep knowledge, and his ability to clearly explain topics that can sometimes seem difficult to understand and are highly nuanced.

For anyone interested in exploring the world of Buddhist teaching, this book can be of great benefit. Marc gives us the gift of his deeply felt experiences, openly sharing his own suffering and difficulties. He takes us through his story of discovery and transformation, describing the events and challenges all along the way – encountering Buddhist teachings, the search to find qualified teachers, struggling with the esoteric aspects of the teaching, committing to the path, and the personal changes he experienced as a result. May this book be of great help to you on your own journey.

Andy Porter, IBC Member

Who the hell is this white guy in the hoodie and fancy mala, and where are the monks? I thought as class began. There were monks on the website, right? Yeah, I saw them! What is going on?

It was a very typical dreary middle-of-September-in-Indiana Sunday, and the first time I had ever set foot into Indiana Buddhist Center. I had been sober for maybe a month at that point, for the first time since I was about 16. It turns out that when you stop using substance abuse as your only coping mechanism for the first time in 20+ years there is a gaping hole left in your psyche. I had not one way of dealing with the evil carnival that was my mind, and the struggle was as life and death as things that you can do something about can get. Yeah, the AA meetings were great commiseration sessions for me, but the idea that a "higher power" was going to swoop in and take away my suffering seemed, well, silly and illogical. I needed something else. I happened across IBC in a web search for meditation centers, and thought, "These guys have been up to meditation and mindfulness for a few thousand years. Maybe they can help."

The paper in front me read "Introduction to Buddhism by Marc Preston Moss." Ah! A full-namer, I thought. Super! This probably was not the right choice! Then class began. I am fairly sure I had goosebumps within the first five minutes. Not because of what he was saying, either. Turns out the doctrines of Buddhism align well with what I already thought about life, so no huge shockers there (At least in the beginning. Trust me they come). No, it was the fact that as he spoke, he exuded his love for the Dharma he was teaching. He also had the patience to put it in layman's terms, and a sense of both humor and humility that made me feel at ease. I am certain that I was pretty shy for the first couple weeks. I really was not trying to broadcast what had brought me there, but I kept coming back. I was learning, and it was helping me. As the months went by, Marc and I started talking more and more frequently, and not just about Buddhism. I am not sure at what point it happened, but I came to realize that not only had I found a teacher armed with knowledge that would help alleviate my suffering, but that he was quickly becoming my friend as well.

What can I say about the lessons that I have learned under Marc's tutelage, the Dharma? I honestly cannot say enough. Let me put it this way: A few thousand years ago an Indian prince figured out that cessation from suffering is possible for all beings, and he laid out a plan to get there. A very logical and practical path that does not involve blind faith and groveling for forgiveness. If you are willing to study, practice, and act with compassion you can reap the fruits that this path bears. I, like Marc, am living proof of this. I am not—by far—the best practitioner, even in our classes, but I get a little better every day. Life has gotten so much easier. My crazy brain vexes me so much less. My practice gets stronger as time goes on. Had I not sat down in Marc's class on that crappy day in September, I don't know if I would have gotten to the point where I am at today. I am so grateful to have him as a teacher, and ecstatic to call him my friend. I hope his story leads you down a path that helps you as well.

Oh! I almost forgot! I got to meet the monks as well! They are utterly amazing, but that is a whole other story.

Contents

Foreword	vii
Introduction	xiii
PART I – DUKKHA: THE TRUTH OF SUFFERING	1
Chapter One	3
Chapter Two	18
Chapter Three	42
Chapter Four	61
PART II – SAMODHAYA: THE TRUTH OF THE ORIGINS OF SUFFERING	75
Chapter Five	77
Chapter Six	94
Chapter Seven	109
Chapter Eight	126
Chapter Nine	142
Chapter Ten	157
PART III – NIRODHA: THE TRUTH OF THE CESSATION OF SUFFERING	179
Chapter Eleven	181
Chapter Twelve	205
PART IV – THE TRUTH OF THE PATH TO THE CESSATION OF SUFFERING	225
Chapter Thirteen	227
Chapter Fourteen	248
Chapter Fifteen	271
EPILOGUE	289
Acknowledgments	305
About the Author & Illustrator	307
Glossary of Buddhist Terms	308
Further Reading	312

Introduction

I have not had a nightmare in over 15 years. In fact, I laugh myself awake from the craziest dreams quite often. A Tibetan woman who kindly sees me as her own son told me that it is a sign of successful Dharma practice, and I won't deny that I have immersed myself in these teachings with great interest.

I do not say this to pat myself on the back or to brag, but to emphasize the importance of rigorous, devoted study in Tibetan Buddhist philosophy. When one truly practices these teachings, the results *will* manifest. Depression, anxiety, low self-esteem, jealousy, addiction, and all the negative emotions can be diminished or eradicated when one works to transform his or her mind through the various techniques of this beautiful, ancient tradition.

It is also necessary for practitioners in the West to participate in recording the Dharma as we receive it and experience it. Besides the empirical data of science, the Dharma is the greatest study of cause and effect, analyzing three layers of reality: the obvious, the hidden, and the deeply hidden. However, there is the risk that sharing our personal experiences appear as, what Christians would call "witnessing," and the Dharma cannot be confined or owned by any tradition, not even Buddhism.

As Dharma has been translated into English by erudite scholars and philosophers, too many common folks are left behind. The Buddha taught on the level of his students, to each as their capacity could comprehend. Therefore, we need practitioners that have deep, intuitive experience with the path to guide others who wish to follow and overcome a great host of burdens from negative emotions.

In the Tibetan tradition, there are three great scriptural collections: *Kangyur*—the public and private teachings the Buddha gave himself; *Tengyur*—the commentaries on these teachings by great Indian masters who applied them and achieved the results described by the Buddha; and *Sungbum*—the elucidations on the Indian commentaries by the Tibetan master scholars who achieved same such accomplishments. These writings are very much like our modern-day scientific method of observation, experimentation, hypotheses, and peer review, but subjectively applied toward that taboo of the Western world of science: consciousness. The homogeneity of the observations and results of these masters for the past 2,600 years is astounding.

I passionately believe that our contribution of personal experiences with the Dharma has as much to do with preserving the cultures from which they have come to us, as it is assimilating into society tried and true traditions that will quell negative emotions and behaviors that plague our social harmony. American Christianity has been effective in drawing converts through witnessing, and though Buddhism has not emphasized proselytizing, sharing our stories out of love and compassion can act as a beacon for those who've abandoned other traditions. Atheists who still feel a strong sense of spirituality can benefit from the Dharma without the necessity to swear allegiance to invisible entities—though they are readily available in Tibetan Buddhism, they are not entirely necessary.

My own journey has been too remarkable to stash away from the world. The path of Dharma helped me to overcome the habitual negative emotions that were born from a tumultuous childhood in a family torn apart by divorce, years of seeing infidelity in the relationships of friends around me, my own break-up that made me want to take my life, and many other areas, just like everyone else.

We often refer to the Three Jewels—Buddha, Dharma, and Sangha—as the doctor, the medicine, and the nurses and other medical practitioners needed to serve the patient. Just like so many other Westerners drawn to buy book after book without a nearby Dharma Center, I practiced what I call *Over-The-Counter Dharma*. Just reading books as we casually do in America was not enough; I needed to apply these teachings and work diligently with my mind to succeed. I needed a teacher, and thankfully, I found one that deepened my experience, introduced me to other teachers, and guided me through my confusion. Geshe Jinpa Sonam relentlessly advises every one of his students to analyze these teachings with great fervor—and it has been through these serious reflections that I've found the greatest transformation away from a worldview that hadn't been working for me.

That would be enough for anyone merely seeking any small reprieve from the thunderstorm of voices we have habituated to hearing roar through our skulls. But for me, a series of unexplainable coincidences completely changed my position as a material realist. To me, there was so much evidence that it would be unreasonable to dismiss the unseen worlds that the Tibetan and Indian masters describe. I can say without shame now that I believe the mystical and mythical teachings of the Dharma, and that life continues even after the body can no longer be our vehicle.

The greatest spiritual experience of my life came from my mother when she passed away, and she took with her most of my fear of death. I have seen similar anxieties in others begin to dwindle after hearing this story, and so it is my intention to share it as far and wide as possible. Her gift freed a great part of me and put me on a course that would take me to the jungles of Nepal and meet a great being whose very existence defied conventional scientific wisdom.

This is my story, not the words of an expert philosopher, but someone who has devoted himself to the Dharma and committed himself to help improve the happiness and reduce the suffering of those around him. This journey I present to the reader is my interpretation and application of the teachings as I have understood them from my readings, reflections, and reception of instruction from a variety of teachers. It is the story of my great teacher, Geshe Jinpa Sonam and the impact he has had on innumerable lives through his teachings and his genuine love and compassion for every creature. It is the story of the Tibetan people and the gift their culture offers to the world after centuries of safeguarding the holy Dharma. And it is the story of my mother and how what I once saw as just a typical unstable family dynamic may very well have had deeper spiritual influences.

There are people in my journey who, though brought me much pain and anguish, I later learned to see as much my holy teachers as my pantheon of spiritual gurus. My dad, for example, struck fear in my heart as a child and I pushed him away for many years. However, after my mother's death, his words of wisdom healed many wounds that I couldn't. His participation in this journey is equally divine to me, and I have a gratitude for him more than I ever imagined I could so many years ago.

Most importantly, this can be your story, too, if you parallel your own events with those presented here and really apply the methods I try to illuminate as they worked for me. Through so many life experiences and choices, we have wired our brains in such a way to create the framework of the holographic reality in which we move about. By applying great effort, and joyfully enjoying the work involved, we develop a relationship with Dharma in its ancient and preserved form and in its new manifestations in modern scientific knowledge that is healing and whole. And this relationship *won't* cheat on you!

An old monk in Nepal told me that consciousness is like a mirror; It simply reflects all that is placed before it. This was the biggest missing piece of my puzzle upon which numerous quests had been made. The Law of Reflection in physics states that the angle of incidence—the angle from which the light of an observed object moves toward a reflective surface—is equal to the angle of reflection—the angle from which that light bounces to the observer—and since our consciousness is the mirror *and* the observer, everything we see is actually a reflection of ourselves, on many hidden levels.

Master Aryadeva states in his *Four Hundred Verses on the Middle Way*,

> *Those with little merit*
> *Do not even cast a doubt.*
> *Entertaining just a speck of doubt*
> *Tears to tatters the whole of worldly existence.*

The root cause of all of our suffering is ignorance, an erroneous understanding of reality. Master Aryadeva suggests that through the spirit of inquiry and skepticism the illusory nature of appearances is destroyed, and the true nature of reality can be understood. Through reflecting on the Dharma and assimilating its wisdom into our mindstream we can achieve liberation.

PART I
DUKKHA: THE TRUTH OF SUFFERING

What is the noble truth of suffering? It is the suffering of birth, the suffering of old age, the suffering of sickness, the suffering of death, the suffering of separation from loved ones, the suffering of facing unwanted phenomena, and the suffering of not getting what one is seeking. In brief, every aspect of the five aggregates is suffering.
—The Buddha

Twenty-six hundred years ago, in the Indian state of Uttar Pradesh, in a village called Sarnath, the Buddha gave his first teaching to five disciples who had abandoned him when they thought he had given up their austere quest to find enlightenment. He left them for what he believed to be a better path—the middle way—between the extremes of self-cherishing and self-deprivation. After achieving enlightenment, his transformation from an ascetic sadhu to a fully enlightened Buddha is said to have been so noticeable that they asked him if he was divine. He told them that he was awakened, and thus began to instruct what became the core of all of his future teachings, The Four Noble Truths.

These truths are realizations that dawn on the mind of one who has a direct perception of the ultimate nature of reality, a meditative event in the development of consciousness. Until then, the rest of us have to use logic and reason to determine if these are, in fact, absolutes. It requires rigorous study and fervent analysis into these teachings.

The first of these truths is the Truth of Suffering, that all unenlightened life is full of pain, dissatisfaction, and unintended results, and continues through an unending circle of life, death, and rebirth called Samsara. There are three types of suffering: The Suffering of Suffering, The Suffering of Change, and All-Pervasive Suffering.

The Suffering of Suffering refers to our physical, emotional, and mental pains. All beings experience the agonies of birth, sickness, aging, and death. The Suffering of Change refers to the agony we feel when the impermanent nature of the thing or person to whom we are attached reveals itself—the end of our youthful innocence, moving away from home, or a break-up in a relationship, or death. All-Pervasive Suffering is the ongoing subtle cause and effect mechanism that traps us in the cycle of rebirth.

The Buddha taught this truth first as it is the easiest of the four for us to understand as unenlightened beings. We can easily examine these sufferings in our own lives....

✦ Chapter One ✦

Driving away from the setting sun, feeling hopeless, and toward the approaching night sky already engulfing Indiana three hours into the horizon, my hands gently massaged my tears that had fallen onto the soft black fur of my puppy laying quietly in my lap. Everything I owned was packed tightly into my brother's truck, creaking, cracking, and protesting every bump and dip in the road, barely distracting me from the ghosts performing in my memory. My chest ached, and my face was swollen from the constant flow of tears and snot. I felt small and lost, even though I knew my way, mindlessly driving through the golden landscape of the Illinois countryside.

"Why!? Why!?" I pounded my fists against the wheel, howling like a banshee, begging the pieces of my heart to reassemble and reveal that it had all been some kind of cruel joke. The discovery of his cheating, his lies, his betrayal were enough to break my heart in two.

From the western sky behind me, all of the trees, grass, barns, and pavement lost their color and transformed into a monochromatic marvel of the sun, bringing me a moment of pause, even in my pain. The brilliant orange sunset illuminated the cab and reflected through the mirror, turning my tears into molten topaz, and beckoned memories of the first kiss we shared three years earlier. Two sunsets bookended this chapter of my life, I thought, highlighting this period for future reminiscing.

Memories spun, like the truck tires, whirling from our early days of hope and joy then into a familiar feeling of failure and loss—*repeat*. These circles carried me into the night alone, except for the loving canine giving her motionless support on my thighs, for once not competing for attention. Three hours later, I brought the borrowed vehicle to a stop at the home of my business partner who offered his house as a refuge.

"Is she going to pee on anything," Al asked, immovably stationed lying on the sofa. Dropspin darted around the living room, sniffing every bit of cat infested information she could from this new environment. I collapsed into the recliner next to the sofa, a comfortable perch I kept many times years before.

"I'm sorry," I mumbled, curling under the throw blanket he had tossed me, "not much for conversation right now."

Al was an intelligent looking man of his mid-forties, whose socks were always worn through at the heels and delighted in grilling you until you spilled whatever he wanted to know. Tonight, he neglected his usual interrogations and simply drifted to sleep and, so did I, in the recliner where Dropspin eventually came to join me.

Though he could be maddening, Al was generous to a fault, and I loved him for being consistent that way. It was a rare occasion that he wouldn't answer the phone whenever I called and, reliably, was there on the other end listening to my heart shatter explaining my recent devastating discovery. When I told him that I wanted to die, that I was fighting suicidal thoughts, his words quivered—"come home"—through the phone. He responded with immediacy and kept repeating with his perfect Wisconsin accent until I assured him that I'd be there as soon as I could.

I moved my things into the old master bedroom the next morning and was asleep on my futon by early afternoon. Aside from my brother waking me briefly to get the keys to his truck, I tried to hibernate through the shock that I was back in Al's house, recovering from a broken heart—again.

Most of my friends let me rot in my pain. "I'm sorry, Marc. I just don't want to hear about it," one friend, Barry whined. Only Al and my best friend, Wyatt, nursed me with their tireless tenderness. Wyatt had so much patience with me, and so much love. Having been through enough of his own breakups, he understood this circle I was in and allowed me the freedom to spin in it. Depression is a swirling dark carousel that spins you round and round, no change of scenery and no new revelations that can help break the cycle. You start looking for a reset button, a way to bring you back to stasis. But there isn't one, and you can't undo past choices. The lucky ones come to a fork in the road; one path leads to new destinies and new adventures armed with the wisdom gained from the experiences, and the other leads right around into the same life situations constantly burdened with reminders of all the mistakes—back into another circle.

Wyatt soothed the self-destructive inner dialogue that was ready to give DJ a pardon. "We may have desires, but we always have choices," he said, planting a seed in my mind that would germinate and grow for years to come.

Such wisdom was typical Wyatt. He was almost ten years younger than me but wiser than any other gay man his age that I knew. I met him while DJ had been away one summer, and we were instantly inseparable. I sensed in him a genuineness I'd never encountered and wanted to develop in myself. From my experiences with gay men who were oft besmirched with pretention and promiscuity, Wyatt's purity lived up to his family name—White.

Wyatt's wisdom had been forged in the loving household that his parents provided. His mother's short fuse would transform Wyatt Sr. into the *Lori Whisperer*. "You sure are the most beautiful woman I know," I witnessed his hypnosis on her. She would always resist, insistent of her ire but would slowly drain all rage as Wyatt Sr. wrapped his arms around her. There was no bullshit with Wyatt Sr. and Lori White, a working-class couple who were the textbook samples of hospitable backyard barbecue host and hostess. He was an electrician and she worked for the VA. Their years of devotion to every activity in which their children participated was well documented on the walls throughout their home. Each glossy framed photo smiled back at you, convincing you that it was ok to take the beer Wyatt offered. Wyatt Jr. and his two sisters, Lisa and Mattie, were perfect replicas of the best of their parents. Wyatt's voice of comfort was as magically taming to me as his father's was to Lori, and I knew from the first time I witnessed it in their home in Danville, Illinois my new friend would bring me balance.

After he moved to Colorado, we would have racked up a national debt's worth of phone bills had cellular calls not been free. His boyfriend commented that none of his friends had even called to see if he made it to Denver. I was certain it was because they were as tired of his lazy, drunken ass as I was from what I learned of him through Wyatt, who believed he could change Jason's habits with time and love. Wyatt never tired of my calls, and my emotional crisis was certainly a test of his resolve. I'd be damned to let Denver add him to the list of past friends I only heard from on special occasion. Still, Wyatt was physically several states away and I loathed being alone. Whether it was lying in bed and the palpable absence of a spooning partner or driving in my car with a vacant passenger seat, I was left with the worst possible company—me.

Through every bit of personal growth, the reflection in the mirror remained that skinny unpopular red-headed dork, still scarred with the disappointments of his mother, staring back. Even fresh out of the shower with my toned, muscular improvements standing at the vanity, the reflection was still a disapproving echo. Displaying my hard-earned upper arms by wearing tank tops to the dance club, guys would reach out to give an unsolicited squeeze. It was affirming and nice, at first. But that slowly faded the more I recognized that none of them paid any attention to my face. Funny how you can feel so lonely in a tight crowd of wildly dancing people, elbow to side-jabbing elbow.

Loneliness after a break-up is an even more cruel monster. It intercepts your appreciation for those that are still around you, still loving you, and tells you that you're more alone than ever. Even though I knew Al and Wyatt were the best friends they could possibly be through all of this, I took them for granted and maintained my selfishly solitary shell.

This break-up frightened Al. He witnessed my past relationships come and go, none longer than a couple of months and most without interrupting my daily groove. "How're things with Nathan," he asked after a break-up with a long-time friend who shortly afterward became a youth pastor and pretended that we were never a thing.

"Over," I stated simply. Al just sat in his office chair mouth-breathing with a look that begged for more details. I said no more and moved the conversation on to business, thankful that he didn't interrogate, for once, any further.

Believe it or not, designing marching band shows is very time consuming and leaves little extra for a social life outside. In order to make it a livable career, you have to work for multiple schools. Aside from attending rehearsals, there's so much planning and designing that must be done off-the-clock: choreography, costume and uniform design, color coordination, staff meetings, etc. It's far more artsy fartsy than the stereotype of a bunch of misfits bungling around the football field crassly blasting out "Land of a Thousand Dances."

Al, who in his hay day was a front-runner in many circuits nationally was a disciplined model I tried to emulate. During design season—May-August—he'll wake up around 5am, grab a coffee and some toast, sit at his computer planning and designing, and break for lunch and a two-hour nap around 1pm. Afterward, he'll be up at the computer again until around midnight.

After graduating high school, I started working with Al and his first wife, Alice. They both convinced me to join a world class drum and bugle corps, traveling the country and performing in the marching arts on a more professional level.

Al grew to be like family to me, like... distant cousins with straighter teeth and perfect English. He was quick to correct someone's failed grammar, and I was always grateful if I erred. He earned his BA in Business from The University of Wisconsin, which was the wrong tool for romance between him and Alice. She had her unusual endeavors, like being a clown or belly dancing. Constantly hearing, "How much can you make doing that?" from Al added to her list of reasons to leave him. I still haven't accepted them as validation for her cheating on him, though.

Where he excelled in design and finances, he—and his wife—failed in housekeeping. The home had five bedrooms; four were down a hallway in the front of the house and the new master bedroom was part of an extended add-on in the back. Both hallways were floor-to-ceiling with boxes. Though they moved into the house five years earlier, Alice had more excuses for why she couldn't help to fully unpack, and Al knew she'd berate him for where he might choose to put things. There was great delight on Al's face when they came home one day after a weekend get-a-way seeing the halls cleared. Snooping around alone in the house, I found two separate attics! And they had cats. Oh, I do love cats, but they had five—each with their own litterbox. A recipe for getting your own segment on talk shows highlighting bad decisions.

So, there I was at thirty years old, again crying in the same spare bedroom as I had ten years earlier after leaving my mother, carrying the blame she placed on me for the divorce. I was cursed. Every time I tried to make love happen, the causes for its destruction closely followed. Each morning I'd reach my hand to the pillow beside me, often messing it up as if DJ had just gotten up and gone to the bathroom. Try as I did to recreate his presence, my morning tears would not manifest his corporeal form into emerging from the dark master bath. The ceiling above my bed served as a blank movie screen for the projections of my mind. I was loathe to scan through my past, trying to figure out where this pattern of repetition began, the entry point onto the circular conveyor belt that brought me back around to the same life theme again and again—loss.

My friend, Laura, gave me a book before the break-up on how to keep the love you found. It was her secret weapon that succeeded in winning her boyfriend back and becoming his wife. It was a decoction of tools I learned from my college psychology class, of which I took just enough interest to get the grade I needed as a music major and then forgot. As a gay male, Freud's notion that I had some kind of sexual attraction to my mother missed the mark, and I am positive that I didn't have any for my father. Nonetheless, there were many events from my childhood that had a lasting impression on my personality, and the answers to why I kept meeting with disappointments in my relationships *could* be written into my muscles or my DNA. Per the instructions in the book Laura suggested to me, I kept a notebook handy to record my perusals into the past and the lists of characters and their possible infections.

Jotting memories into my journal, one humorous event gave reprieve to my self-pity—my mother dashing into the kitchen one Saturday morning to save her four-year old child, me, from burning the house down. "Mommy, make me breakfast, please." A zombie of a woman before 8am, she mumbled and rolled away from me. So, I went into the kitchen, grabbed an iron skillet from inside the oven and laid it atop the flame, pulled a kitchen chair up to the stove, dropped three eggs onto the oily black surface—shells and all—and moved them around with the spatula, mimicking her. The smoke yanked her out of bed and she burst through the kitchen doorway, whipped me under her arm and to the back door to quickly discard the iron skillet into the snow. That evening, Dad turned me over his knee and spanked me with so much force it stung every day of my childhood and into my teen years, making me fear the man and every small eruption he would ever have again.

Days later, determined to not stay in that house any longer, I trudged through the snow in pajamas and cowboy boots to the Post Office, two blocks away. The postmaster brought me into her office and gave me a stick of bubble gum as a distraction to call my mother and tell her of the young would-be customer who wanted desperately to have himself mailed to Nanny Wasson—my grandmother, Mildred. Nanny was what all her grandchildren called her. Mom arrived a few minutes later, her face peering out of a mass of thick, puffy parkas. She thanked the postmaster whose gift kept me trying to blow a bubble, bundled me in a warm blanket, placed me on the back of a sled, and pulled me home. Upon seeing the driveway, I sprang up with a shriek, determined to get away before Dad could come leave the red marks of his hand on my ass cheeks again.

When my grandmother saw my bottom, she drove me back to the little two-bedroom box of a house in Hemlock, Indiana and proceeded to scream obscenities at him. My aunt Shirley took Nanny and I out on her boat on Lake Mississinewa just a few days later. "I don't ike 'im, I don't ike 'im," Shirley imitated my toddler voice, recalling it for me years later. She said that Nanny pretty much hated Dad from then on. To compensate for what she perceived as neglect she would gift me with money and candy on every visit.

The contrasting personas of my parents made the house of my childhood a chiaroscuro of fun versus fear. Once while Dad was away on a weekend business trip, I escaped my mother's tickling clutches, running down the hallway with her loving laughter close behind. When the phone rang, we began singing, "Who's gonna get the phone?" My hand grabbed the receiver before hers and I sang the words into it instead of an appropriate greeting. Suddenly, every joy was ripped away from me as Dad's scolding voice told me how he'd punish me when he returned. "No!" I screamed, dropped the phone, and ran to my room with tears running down my cheeks. The joy in my young mother's face vanished, replaced with heartfelt concern, and she argued into the phone before coming to comfort me.

After lying there flipping through the photo album of my mind for about a half an hour, I grabbed my coffee and dragged myself into Al's office where he doled out his spiel of reasons to get me back to rehearsals and working. He sat, twitching from Tourette's and did his best to be encouraging, but he didn't have a way with words, and thus it was a repetition of the day before, as if on a laminated script sitting next to his computer. I had a different relationship with money than he, and I resented his admonitions. Sure, he empathized with my situation, since he himself went through an ugly divorce years earlier through which I was his support, but money was the real love of his life. Some mornings he'd turn on the news to see the ticker tape at the bottom of the screen. If the stocks were up, he would be energized and ready to attack the day head-on as if he just received a letter from a hot lover. But if the stocks were down, it could bring him to a full stop, laying on the couch in his living room, eyes closed in complete paralysis, as though he just read a Dear John.

Al tolerated years of my self-searching, which really meant searching for Mr. Right—frequently accepting Mr. Right Now. We jokingly called his house the *Home for Wayward Homosexuals* since the smell of expensive colognes and hair products filled the air from scores of gay visual designers and choreographers who frequented his home office. At twenty, I was fresh meat to the parade of gay men I met there, and I often gave in to the delicatessen, myself. There were also queens who demonstrated the art of rejected retort. "You don't mean anything to the gay community unless you have eight inches or a six-figure income," one of Al's colleagues jealously said as I walked away, uninterested.

Well, I was penniless, not well-endowed, and ridiculously naive. Hell, the only gay presence in my world growing up was Billy Crystal's character on the television show Soap, Boy George and Culture Club, and the waiter at Pizza Hut whose lisp all the kids at my school made fun of. Is *this* the world in which I was doomed to live, I often wondered?

Due to Al's support and encouragement, I went back to rehearsals, punctually—and perfunctorily, at first—with another world of mental imagery superimposed on my mind in every action. As my hands clapped out tempos and commands to my students, I could see DJ's eyes, and a visceral fear that someone else was now looking lovingly into them steadfastly projected everywhere I looked. "*Is this normal?*" I sniffled into the phone, Wyatt patiently waiting to respond.

Most of the daily drives to and from the different high schools were between an hour to ninety minutes of droning the mental script that I memorized to a tee—starting with how I discovered his emails and confronted him with them and ending with the last few words I said before I drove away from the house that ceased to be a home. It was an uncomfortable pattern that drained me of the blithesome character many knew me to be. There was no room to breathe, no space to rest from the exhaustion that depression causes. All I wanted was freedom.

Summoning the strength to call DJ a few times, I hoped to find some closure or resolution from the breakup. He offered none, and clearly didn't want to hear from me. Wyatt begged me to give up. "You're picking at a wound that needs to heal," he'd insist but I couldn't bring myself to relent. More than anything, I needed DJ to tell me that he was done exploring life without me. Yet whenever I would get his voicemail instead of an answer, I angrily imagined he was hooking up with someone new. My face would burn with manufactured jealousy, and I routinely entertained a macabre fantasy of having been widowed. That feeling of powerlessness cuts deeper than loneliness and would return me to thinking that even my own death would be better—could *still* be better.

"What do you see in him, really?" Wyatt asked.

My reddened eyes peered back in the rearview mirror, "I've been with better looking guys, sure," hearing a nasty superficiality come out of my mouth. "But something just clicked, something still retained an innocence about it." I paused, hearing DJ playing the piano in my mind. "It just... wasn't like other relationships."

"That *you've* had," Wyatt implied that some relationships actually worked, and after five more boyfriends in as many years, he proved it with his current partner.

"I don't think it has as much to do with him as it seems," I said pensively, almost hypnotized by the rhythmically passing yellow dashes on the highway. "Gay men are conditioned by a starvation. We can't live as we are and get forced into quick little animal satisfactions, get a quick fix and then back to society's perfect cut-out straight mold as soon as possible, as if nothing happened. They're starving—we, I mean. Eating up these tiny little morsels isn't the same thing as a good home-cooked meal."

"Call me lucky for never having gone through that," he said. It was true that he never had to go through the typical coming-out process with his privy and supportive family. "DJ had a full course dinner with you, Lady, and don't you think otherwise."

I stared thoughtfully at the road as I drove, then said, "Yeah, but sometimes the crumbs taste better, I guess."

DJ's lies and betrayal cut the deepest and were the hardest to heal. Through our hearts together, I remained faithful to him. Had he just broken up with me *and then* dove into promiscuity, at least the rules of the relationship would have been honored—I tried to convince myself. Whenever little signs that caught my attention couldn't be explained away, I would ask, point blank, if he was cheating, to which he would always turn on the charm and coerce me off the ledge—getting himself off the hook by singing "I will never leave you; I will never go away..."

So why did he leave? Why did he go away? What did I lack to keep his attention from wandering? Would these lists of past events and people Laura's book wanted me to make help me find the *why*? I hated nostalgia but obeyed the assignment and continued peering into my past.

The thought of relationships soured me such that every time I looked at another couple, I was sure that one of them was secretly exploiting the other's loyalty and flitting off at every opportunity of a sexual escapade. Every time I saw a couple holding hands in public or sitting together in a restaurant my mind would imagine scenarios of a betrayal waiting to be discovered by one of them.

This became the uncomfortable circle upon which I wandered, day in day out: fall asleep in tears and wake again barely able to start another day like the one before. Though it was freshly happening to me, I witnessed this cycle before in my mother. When Mom discovered that Dad was cheating on her, it set her into vacillating fits of rage, sadness, and misplaced blame. Her words could cut, and she slashed me deep by telling me that Dad left because I kept asking for money for my school activities. The woman almost delighted in announcing how little we had." Marc, do you know how long it's been since I've bought a new bra?" As much pride as my mother had in her large breasts, it's unimaginable that she could've refrained from buying a brassiere if she wanted. Those boobs under which was stashed every dollar I ever requested were never droopy unless she was in her night gown.

We weren't the poorest in our neighborhood, but throughout my teens she had a Depression-Era romance with thoughts that we were struggling to survive. There's an infamous period in our childhood history my younger brother, Chris, and I recall—*Frozen Dinners*. "Why do you buy these if the boys hate them?" Mom, being a stay-at-home wife, gave her best defense of saving hard-earned money, causing Dad to slam his fork into the table, "Linda, I make more money than all the guys on this street!" I was thankful to hear validation that we weren't that poor, and for the distraction he created for Chris and me to sneak the cabbage rolls from our plate to the garbage undetected.

Al listened to the stories of my comical, screwed up family through the years, sitting in his home office, surrounded by walls of framed photos of his favorite marching bands, patiently and sincerely engaged as each of his feline children would take turns being stroked on his lap. "Maybe you need a therapist," he suggested.

"I am not going to spend unnecessary amounts of money and time to sit on some stranger's leather chaise and have them open my skull, pilfer through my cluttered brain, and merely connect dots of different events throughout my life."

"Oh," he laughed, "so I get to do it again for free?"

With the tilt of my head and a raised brow he was immediately reminded of his days of divorce when doctor and patient roles were reversed. "No," I said, turning my eyes downward to the maroon carpet, "I need understanding. I need some *mental medicine.*"

"Well, I'm no Freud, and you've already talked about your mother for years. Have you spent any time thinking about your dad? You haven't talked to him in a long time, and maybe you shut him out of your life for a reason."

"I've considered it," I shrugged. "And I think my reason was a good one."

Not so secretly, I hated my dad, a very intense and short-fused expert on everything. I always feared him—and not out of respect—since that first spanking. He seemed to examine everything I did for an opportunity to assert his power, authority, and punishment. Especially bringing home a disappointing report card. "Refrains from needless talking—*minus?*" he shouted, filling me with terror. When he was home, he sucked the life out of the air and made me his living remote control. I was regularly summoned to bring him a glass of tea and then made to stand at the television changing channels. That very well could be why I've never drank a glass of iced tea in my adult life.

We never attended a church as a family, and with Dad home it made Sundays seem to stretch into thirty-six hours. My younger brother, Chris and I would have tons of chores. Typical. But Dad's list for us was endless: mow the lawn, pull weeds from the flower boxes, clean out his van, organize the garage, and much more. "Should take you about fifteen minutes. Have the rest of the day to yourself." It was *never* fifteen minutes. Mom once popped her head out to check on us as we trimmed the branches of the Russian olive trees bordering the rear of our yard, chuckling as she let us know how far off the fifteen-minute mark it was, proving she was in on the joke Chris and I made of it.

As a child, I swore to everyone that I would marry her one day, so it remained a mystery to me for years how my mother turned from such an archetype of love, beauty, and humor to the witch of my teen life, like the cold, faceless matron of the dead she summoned in our kitchen in front of an audience of prepubescents. All the neighborhood kids used to come to our house on summer nights and listened to her tell ghost stories that started off chilling and scary but usually ended in hilarity.

Once, Mom and I teamed up on my best friend, Craig. She placed a wet washcloth in the freezer and gave it to me just before her ghost stories. My orders were simple: sit under the kitchen table around which Craig and the other kids would be listening, wait until she said the magic word at the end of the story, then lay the cold washcloth on Craig's bare leg—it was summertime, and he was wearing shorts. Mom entered the darkened kitchen wearing a blanket as a cloak; her face illuminated by a flashlight she carried. She took her seat with ghoulish creepiness and began her usual conjuring, "Hilda Bauer, Hilda Bauer! Now it is the witching hour!"

All the kids sunk into their seats as she told her story with dramatic flair, making sudden jumps forward for essential punctuation. When she finally said the magic word, she gave me a gentle kick, and I executed Order: *Chilling Touch*. Immediately, Craig pushed away like terrified lightning, followed by the sounds of Mom's good china crackling against the darkened floor. I jumped out from under the table with urgency and turned on the lights. Craig was sitting there, mouth agape, in a sea of shattered blue and white china.

The other kids dutifully dropped to gather the scattered pieces. I looked at Mom, tears streaming down her reddened face. "I'm sorry, Mommy," I started, "I didn't think about..."

"I'm not crying, Birdy," she said, using my nickname which meant that she wasn't mad. All the kids looked curiously at my mother who was now doubled over in hysterics. Through her laughter, she explained that he had pushed away from the table with great force toward the hutch behind him and into the air. In a flash of foresight, he knew he was about to knock her good china to the floor and, for just a moment, appeared to freeze in midair, looking straight at her before finally succumbing to gravity. "He hovered!" she howled, and the kitchen erupted into a chorus of laughter. Craig had only a small cut on his hand but managed a few chuckles—when he realized he wasn't in trouble.

Craig was my first friend when we moved into the green aluminum sided three-bedroom house that was built for us on Lincoln Street. I saw him playing on his back porch and begged to go meet him. Once Mom approved, I tore across the side yard belonging to the old woman who lived on the corner, dashing through her huge garden that ran the length of Craig's backyard fence. He ran through his mother's fragrant laundry hanging on the line to reach through the chain-links and take my hand.

My younger brother, Chris, was born not long after we moved in, and I was happy to be the guardian big brother. After he learned to walk, we would play in the backyard, and he would laugh loudly as I chased him, both of us barefoot, through the weedless carpet of soft, plush grass.

Craig often joined us in playing *Tag*, and Chris always plopped down on his diapered behind, calling for a time-out to avoid getting tagged.

Craig and I became as close as brothers, never needing to knock or announce our visits. In the summer, Mom would sometimes leave Chris sleeping on the couch with dad so that she could play cards with Craig's parents, Floyd and Geneva, until late. After giving me permission to stay the night, Mom would look at Floyd and say, "Walk me home. I don't want to walk home alone." Though we lived in a small town and the likelihood of any harm coming to her was low, she still felt she needed someone to walk with her in the dark. Floyd walked her home every time.

Craig, Chris, and I used to run through our house, slipping on the linoleum with our wet feet from running through the sprinkler, keeping cool from the summer heat. Mom played records on our large stereo and would often join in the chase, singing Del Shannon's "Runaway" as it blasted in the living room. Summer turned to autumn and she often buried us under fragrant piles of leaves in the front yard. Chris always had a thick dribble of snot mixed with tiny shards of dead leaves under his nose and Craig would take huge flying leaps onto the piles hoping to land on me as I lay motionless, listening to the metal teeth of the rake ring as they dragged in brisk strokes across the lawn. In winter, she boiled pots of cocoa on the stove while we hung our snowsuits in the garage, changing out of our wet socks, sopping from the snow that made it into our boots. In the springtime, the smell of the curtains freshly washed and hung filled the breeze from all the open windows as she let in the fresh spring air. And every April 22, my trio sat at the table and watched me blow out the candles of my birthday cake. They were my best friends—my clan.

Craig's parents—made good money but wouldn't pay for cable television, most likely due to Southern Baptist ideals—allowed him to frequent our living room on weekends to watch scary movies. Being that he was a year older than me and often a bit of a bully, I enjoyed exploiting his fear of the dark, especially when he wanted me to walk him in the night from my house to his back door. At the end of our driveway, I terrorized him, screaming and pointing at things that weren't there.

Being afraid of the dark was at odds with Craig's self-image as an alpha male, and so he challenged me to go into the dark between our houses and try to scare him as he ran to his back door, screaming loudly all the while as to deaden any startling sounds he anticipated. Once, he bet me two dollars that I couldn't scare him and gave me a two-minute head start. I went into the back of their house, walked into the living room to tell his parents of my plans, and listened to them chuckle as I crawled under Craig's bed to wait for him. Just seconds later, the back door banged shut and Craig panted his way into the living room to tell his parents how he made it home without being frightened—and how I would owe him two dollars the next day. Geneva congratulated him and sent him to his room to get ready for bed.

He somehow managed to escape a heart attack from the feeling of my hands quickly grabbing his ankles as he bent over to untie his shoes, letting out the loudest siren of a scream, and breaking one of the hinges on the bedroom door as he tried to run through it. Without pause, he dashed through the living room and out the front of the house back into the night. Floyd stood up so quickly in hysterical reaction that his blanket fell to the floor and he danced on the sofa in his underwear unapologetically. Geneva's face was as red as an apple and she pulled two dollars out of her pocketbook to hand me as I crawled out from under the bed and into the broken doorway that Craig and I helped Floyd repair the next morning.

Another time, standing at the end of our gravel drive after we made it through the first sequel to *Friday the Thirteenth*, Craig boasted that he could make it home on his own through the dark. "Just stand and watch, would you?" he asked me.

Suddenly, a loud roar at the side of the house startled us and I saw my father wearing a pillowcase on his head while holding a chef's knife aloft. The sound of Craig's back door slamming shut almost immediately followed, igniting my mother's laughter as she secretly watched from the bay window. "He set a new world record tonight!" she bellowed.

Her laugh was infectious, and she delighted in pulling pranks on us. We had so much fun throughout the day until she had to make dinner. Afterward, she routinely summoned the demon home from the piano in the living room, tickling the keys with what seemed like twenty fingers. Dad almost always pulled in the drive before she finished "Down at Papa Joe's."

Even Dad had his moments under her power in those days. Once, she went to her room to take a nap and I, being the apple that stayed close to the pranking tree took up the task of making the most memorable popsicles of all time. When she opened the freezer after her nap, she saw my frozen delights and assumed Dad made them from her pitcher of homemade lemonade. One chomp and she knew exactly what they were, then dashed quickly to the bathroom to hang her head over the toilet.

I sat on their bed where she commanded me to wait for Dad to come home, knowing the terror of waiting was almost as bad as a belt to my backside. My body tightened looking up at his inscrutable countenance as he asked, "Son, did you piss in the popsicle molds?"

"Uh-huh," I embarrassingly confirmed.

"Your mother sent me in here to spank you," his smile gave way as he pulled the belt from his waist. "When I hit those pillows, you cry loud enough so she'll hear and think I'm spanking you, got it?"

My enemy extended an armistice and began to slap away at the bed. I was relieved but my poor acting skill made its way to her ear. The door burst open and she threw at us everything she could grab. "It's not funny!"

I never saw that man laugh so hard to this day, and it brightened my attitude as I wrote about it in my notebook so much that I went into Al's office to share the story. As we laughed, I could tell that he was relieved to see my humor emerging from a long period of darkness.

✦ Chapter Two ✦

Sometimes after getting back to Al's late from a rehearsal I'd sit and talk with him—my affordable therapist. One night, as he skimmed somnolently through my notes I took of my self-administered psychoanalysis, I told him that Wyatt asked me what I saw in DJ, and being secure enough in his heterosexuality, he agreed that I had more attractive boyfriends in the past. Superficiality over someone's looks always made me cringe.

"Don't beat yourself up," he chuckled sleepily laying on the sofa. "This house has seen worse nitpicking!"

I pulled a book from my bag and handed it to him. "I've been reading this for a while."

He gave it a biddable glance through his drowsiness, "Is this some kind of self-help book?"

"Kinda," I took it back. "It's relationship psychology. It pretty much says that I should be able to match up personality traits of my parents—*early caretakers*, they call them—from my childhood with just about every love interest I've ever had."

"That's going to be a long list!" he joked. "Have you got time for that?"

"Ha freaking ha," I said with a disapproving scowl.

"And then?"

"I don't know yet. It's got me strolling down memory lane. Have I mentioned how much I hate memory lane?" On that, he started to snore, and I shook my head thinking how often we ended nighttime conversations this way. I followed the cue and went to my room.

Reluctant to enter the world of slumber where my dreams would surely continue to agonize me, I studied the lists in my notebook comparing DJ to Mom and Dad. They seemed like elements to a grand mathematical equation to which I was addicted to finding some kind of answer. He was an amalgam of the both of them, but the truth is that I saw characteristics of all of my family in him in many ways. He played the piano and found humor in the simplest of things, like my mother—the early years. He had a monstrous glare and quick temper when it served as first line of offense, and often held a grudge too long, like my father. He held an unwavering dedication to his interests, like my brother, Chris—and was a spoiled youngest child like my baby brother, Evan.

Though, Evan's rank wasn't the sole reason for my mother's vigilant safeguard. Evan was born cesarean with the umbilical cord wrapped around his neck, had a grand mal seizure during birth and another in the helicopter to Riley Children's Hospital in Indianapolis. As an imaginative ten-year old, I thought that there was something evil happening to the world since the assassination attempt on Ronald Reagan also happened that day. On our first visit to Riley, Mom explained to me what an incubator was as I gently tapped on the glass like I often did on the aquariums in the pet department in K-Mart.

"We have to be very careful with him, Birdy," she said taking the fragile little bundle gently from the nurse."He's going to need a lot of love and gentleness."

She changed. It was demanded. The responsibility and discipline that she needed to have were almost out of her range. Her jokes and pranks faded like a morning mist as she turned her face toward her son with complete devotion. The doctors said that if Evan didn't have another seizure within the first year, he most likely wouldn't have another in his life. He would be special, though—mentally slow, and it was a source of guilt that both Mom and Dad shared.

Every morning she took the bottle of pink liquid from the top shelf in the refrigerator door and carefully administer his dose of phenobarbital. She strictly policed Chris and me, fearing that if we made him cry or caused him to be upset, he might have another seizure, like he was Bruce Banner threatening to become the Hulk.

One Saturday morning while Chris and I were playing *Sock Wars*—using our rolled-up socks as grenades, hurling them at one another all around the house—she poked a heavy-eyed face from her darkened bedroom, "Boys, boys! Please keep it quiet so Evan doesn't wake up. He needs his sleep." After a fleeting truce, our little cotton bombs launched up and down the hallway, an awful din that caused her to burst from her room, slapping aimlessly at us both, while singing "Everybody Was Kung Fu Fighting" at the top of her lungs. We howled at her antics, but she was *really* angry! Our uncontrollable guffaws made her slap harder and sing louder through gritted teeth.

Once Evan started to walk, she became more distant, giving most of her attention to him and the remainder to Chris, with nothing left for me. These were the seeds of my self-loathing, and I cultivated them with a fallacious need to extract everything within me that dissatisfied her. I often stared in the mirror and seethed with hate for the boy staring back, finding fault in every detail of the reflection. When Mom's best friend, Ramona, cooed over my long eyelashes and remarked that they were like those of a girl, I climbed onto the bathroom sink to sit in front of the mirror and angrily clipped them away with my dad's mustache scissors." I'm a boy!" I shouted when Mom discovered my drastic response to what was supposed to have been received as a compliment.

That was around the time that I also became aware of my sexuality and found myself praying to God every night before bed to wake me with the same salacious wont for chasing girls as Craig. Many nights I cried myself to sleep, begging God to not let me become the monster everyone made gay people out to be. "Smear the Queer" was a game guys on the block liked to play in the big field across the street from our house. I never played, fearing that since I was the queer, I would get smeared, whatever that meant.

No matter how often I prayed, I would always wake to find that the same feelings were always there, just waiting for a cute boy to enter my field of view—and there were many in our neighborhood in Greentown. Try as I did, I couldn't help but stare a little longer than I should at the muscular arms of the guys playing basketball on the full-size paved court that the father of two of my friends made just down the street. Their armpit hair aroused me a little, marking the transformation from boys to men.

I was a late bloomer and didn't develop anything under my arms until high school. Craig developed earlier than me, and he was far more vocal about his growing lustful interests. From time to time, he would mention that he thought a certain actress was attractive, and I could play along because they weren't a real flesh and blood female in our presence. In his locked bedroom with REO Speed Wagon's "Keep on Loving You" and his father's cheap aftershave in the air, he taught me how he met his first crush in one of my classmates.

"It's called 'Truth or Dare,'" his voice just above a whisper.

"How do you play it?" I was intrigued but mostly jealous about the party he described that I didn't get to attend.

"Well," he continued. "I say, 'truth or dare,' and you chose if you want to answer a question or do something that I tell you to do."

"Depends on the dare," I was deathly afraid of spiders and wouldn't put it past him to use one as payback for my nighttime frights.

"We played it last night and I got to French kiss Lisa," he rhapsodically explained. I tried to hide my lack of fascination.

"What makes it French?" I asked.

A devilish grin contorted one side of his face. "You get to stick your tongue in their mouth."

The image of Chris's chocolate milk-stained mouth full of Pop-Tarts flashed in my head, "That's gross! Do French people do that?"

"No, it's not," he defended. "It's what adults do." He went to the window to be sure his parents were still away. Aside from posters of a leotard-clad Olivia Newton-John and a motley arrangement of action figures atop his dresser, there was no one watching him turn to me and ask, "Truth or dare?"

"Truth," I said.

He rolled his eyes, clearly displeased with my choice. "Have you ever seen a girl's boobs?" he asked as he plopped next to me on the bed. "Your mom's don't count."

"My cousin, Robin's!" I quickly responded. "They've fallen out of her bathing suit a few times in the pool."

"Ok, your turn," he said.

"Have you?" I asked.

"No, no," he corrected. "You have to say, 'truth or dare' first."

"Truth or dare," I obliged.

"Yeah, in my Dad's Playboy." He mindlessly skipped past the response to pull a magazine from under his pillow. As he lustily flipped through the pages, I was fascinated yet equally disgusted.

"Gross!" I blurted seeing the centerfold.

"Truth or dare?" he asked tucking the magazine back under his pillow. "Just say 'dare!'"

"This better not hurt," I whined. "Dare."

"French kiss me," he said without hesitation. I gasped. He somehow managed to escape my newly discovered radar for cute boys, but those words he just uttered sent a sonar ping bouncing off every awkward muscle in my pubescent body. His eagerness encapsulated us, and I sat... rigidly... in anticipation.

I stared at the darkened peach fuzz above his lip as he drew closer. He paused, "You're supposed to close your eyes."

"Why?" I really wanted to watch.

"Just because," he answered and lunged forward. He stabbed his tongue through my lips, and the tickling of his nascent mustache and texture of his taste buds rubbing across mine caused a tingling in my groin.

After five incredible, immortal seconds he jerked away and started spitting, wiping his mouth with his shirt sleeves. "Ok, yuck!" he said disappointedly. I also feigned disgust and quickly rearranged my pants to avoid detection. That night alone in my bed I tried to recall every millisecond of our exploration, wishing he found more satisfaction with me than Lisa, yanking back and forth... between titillation and shame.

In those days we exploited every moment of independence when our parents left us at home alone. When Craig was at our house and Mom was away, he, Chris, and I played blindfolded Hide 'N Seek. One of us would be blindfolded and the other two would disappear into the few options for cover somewhere in the small three-bedroom house. It was a pretty innocent game for youngsters, as long as all the sharp objects aren't a threat to the one who's *it*. But at the onset of puberty, it was an opportunity for orneriness.

A couple of weeks after that French kiss, I was crawling around my parents' bedroom, blindfolded. I moved toward the sound of someone breathing, on guard to tag whoever it was, sure that it was Craig because his clothes always smelled of Tide and Downy—one of my favorite scents. Suddenly, something was shoved in my mouth and out just as quickly as I yanked the blindfold off. Craig was staring mischievously, kneeling in front of me with his hands in the front of his swollen gray sweatpants.

"What was that?" I shouted.

"Shhh," he whispered. "It was just my thumb."

"Thumbs... have thumbnails, Craig," I countered. I stared at him, knowing what he did.

"Put the blindfold back on," he ordered quietly. I obeyed and got back on my hands and knees with my mouth unusually... but invitingly agape and shortly thereafter discovered my favorite aroma—Tide and Downy—wasn't just in the clothing.

In middle school, boys and girls partnered up as the call of the wild boiled in their blood. Thinking that a girlfriend might cure me from that thing God seemed to ignore from my nightly pleas, I asked a girl out on a date. Mom took us to a roller rink in Kokomo for a

"Roller Dance" put on by our cheer squad. Her name was Tawnee, and her parents were real estate agents that wanted to send her off to Culver Military Academy. While she was a sweet girl, there was nothing about females that interested me. We held hands a few times in the hallway at school, and it always felt awkward. When we talked on the phone after dinner, I sat on my parents' bed flipping through the sports pages to look at the pictures of boys playing basketball, or headshots of cute local quarterbacks getting recognition.

The summer after eighth grade, Tawnee confirmed that she was going to go to Culver for high school. Though I knew I would miss her, it was far easier using it as an excuse to break-up than any acknowledgment of the truth—which had me whirling the pedals of my ten-speed hither and yon throughout Greentown and the surrounding countryside to spend time with boy after boy.

By my freshman year, I started to think that God wasn't real, that all my friends and their families were following a Santa Claus story that just never got revealed. There were many boys who, like Craig, found courage to act upon adolescent curiosity when alone with me—obviously as aware of my sexuality as I was. Whether through a game of Truth or Dare, a request for a back rub while spending the night, or just cornering me with a direct request—followed by a threat to never speak a word of it—I got to know many a classmate in ways their girlfriends didn't. I'm certain it is one of the biggest factors that I never endured gay slurs or bullying walking the halls of school, with so many around me who knew I knew their secret.

Though all of my friends were church goers, seeing the divide between their personal selves and their private selves was taking its toll on my already meager belief—and so were my unanswered prayers. I started to realize that maybe what I was didn't offend an invisible conductor of our reality but was merely something perceived as a social embarrassment that many men never allowed themselves to acknowledge.

No traces of my youthful shame remained as a thirty-year-old lamenting the end of his relationship with a cheating partner. Years after the pubescent explorations with my childhood friends, I found pride and power in my sexual orientation. Craig quickly but quietly took his leave from my life once I accepted the unspeakable label—gay—at twenty-one years old. Sitting in the old master bedroom in Al's house, I compared Craig and DJ, writing down their qualities and feeling the loss of them both.

When we first started dating, DJ wasn't out to his parents, so our sneaking around to be together was a lot like playing Hide 'N Seek all those years ago, crawling around blindly, yearning for something you've been told you can't have. But then you get a taste of it, and you ache from withdrawal symptoms your own nature and nurture create.

DJ had much in common with Craig, as well. For starters, he was the only other guy I met to smell so—ubiquitously—of Tide and Downy. And I shouldn't have been intimate with either of them—a self-identifying straight guy and a closeted homosexual. They both gave me a sense of security when I was with them, and, until DJ, I believed no one else knew me as well as Craig. Wyatt came later, surpassing everyone and genuinely proving to be the best friend of this lifetime.

Most interestingly, DJ had more in common with my younger self than I cared to admit or recognized until conducting my nostalgic analysis. The only difference between the two of us I could find was that I never made a commitment of monogamy to someone else during my promiscuous pursuits. And most of the guys who came to me were simply looking to satisfy a curiosity—I merely obliged.

"That many guys in high school?" Wyatt asked with astonishment after I shared my memories. "I had a couple of experiences but nowhere near twenty-three!"

I almost felt ashamed from the way he said the number but quickly shrugged it off. "You know, I learned a lot about society from them. Males will get off with another guy, a girl, a sock, a glove—anything. But they would never admit it. The fear of embarrassment is pretty powerful."

"And they stereotype us as frightened weaklings," Wyatt laughed. "There's a great reason to allow gays into the military! Just let one of us make a Charlie's Angels tumble pass across enemy lines and pop up in a dashing pose! The straight enemy soldiers would be frozen with fear."

"Nah," I chuckled. "They'd be too busy shifting glances to see if anyone else thought it was fabulous!"

Back on memory lane, I recalled how Mom often snuck off with my brothers from time to time. Whenever I discovered that she got them candy or toys I became enraged with jealousy.

"Marc, they're just children," she defended. "Dad gives you money for things all the time. Don't be ungrateful."

Craig attempted to calm me down, telling me that I was just being paranoid. He loved my mother like his own, and she saw him as her own child, too. He tried to convince me that a mother loves all of her children no matter what, and that my mom loved me. To him, I was making shit up in my head. To me, she treated *even him* better than me!

Then my sixteenth birthday came—Sweet Sixteen! I emerged from my room, dressed and ready for birthday greetings at breakfast, but said nothing, hoping for a surprise or a song. Mom sat on the phone with my Aunt, Shirley, until I eventually and eagerly pushed myself away from the table and headed out the door for school where I thought, perhaps, she planned a surprise. Many of my classmates received balloons and flowers that were delivered to them on their birthdays—but I left school that day with no cards, no flowers, and no balloons.

I sat in front of the TV pretending to watch it, but I was envisioning a birthday party and listening intently every time Mom answered the phone. Dad walked through the door with his usual scent of the bread factory trailing him. He was the one to watch.

For my twelfth birthday, he told me to clean out his van before he went to work that morning. When he arrived at my grandpa's house that evening where we were all waiting, he came into the house in a fury. "Didn't I tell you to clean out that van?" He barked at me and I clinched my ass cheeks fearing he'd hit me in front of my cousins.

"I did," I whimpered.

"You did, did you?" He held the door open and pointed to the van outside. "Go out there right now and show me what you say you did. You look in there, right now!"

If I were a dog I would have crawled under my grandpa's sofa and make a dash for the door before he could swat me. He looked like he was going to kick me as I passed, and I moved with urgency to the back of the van and pulled the doors open. There was a blue ten-speed bicycle standing up inside the usually empty interior, and my family started singing "Happy Birthday," which made me burst with relieved laughter.

But, this year, there was no indication that he had any kind of surprise. He and Mom had their usual boring recaps of each other's day, we ate dinner, and before long I was lying in bed that night staring upward into the dark. My Sweet Sixteen had come and gone and my paranoia was validated. I wanted her to hear me cry but I was afraid Dad would hear me also, so I rolled over and pressed my face into the pillow, crying myself to sleep.

"Oh, Birdy," she put her hand on my leg. "I'm so sorry."

"Two days ago!" I quickly sat up in my bed. It was April 24. "My sixteenth birthday will never come again, Mom." I pushed her hand away and stomped to the bathroom to get ready for school. I stared at myself in the mirror and squeezed a large amount of toothpaste onto my hand then smeared it across the mirror like minty-fresh White-Out, trying to erase the loathsome reflection—tearfully watching.

That memory was like deep, aching scar tissue. "Forgetfulness?" I thought aloud. "No, *neglect*," I nodded as I wrote the word in the list comparing Mom and DJ, then closed the journal and sat it down. I looked at DJ's picture on the table with a similar beseeching gaze I used to give the photo of my mother I kept in a box at the top of my closet. "What did I do? Where did I go wrong? Was any of it real?" The same questions—two different unrelated people. I laid back, holding the picture... like I wanted to hold him.

"How can you go from someone so absolutely amazing and become someone so hurtful, so... wrong?" I fell asleep with the picture against my chest.

Before Evan was born, my mother was on one end of the spectrum and my dad on the other. Now, with that spoiled little toddler in the house they were both on the same dark side—*against me*. Both of my brothers got all of their attention that summer. Evan was Mom's ticking time bomb waiting to rip off his diaper and turn into a massive uncontrollable and deadly tantrum, and Chris—played baseball.

Dad was his team's coach and would often umpire. Mom joined their baseball world and ran the concession stand during games, one of the few social outlets with other adults I ever saw her enjoy. Several other mothers of my friends frequented responsibilities at the ball diamond under her supervision. Watching her interact with the other women gave me glimpses of the entertainer that used to enjoy a kitchen full of neighbor children hanging on her every theatrical word.

Whenever we were at the ball diamond as a family, I considered myself lucky to have her hand me a bag of buttery popcorn. Most often, I stayed home to babysit Evan. As soon as the three of them were out of the drive, I put a video tape of Poltergeist in our VHS player and my terrified youngest brother ran to his bedroom, unnervingly quiet, and remain there until I assured him it was over. At first, it was a magical babysitting tool! I memorized the dialogues in that movie as my baby brother stayed in his bedroom, afraid to come out. "Evan, go into the light, there is peace and serenity in the light," I taunted at the door.

But after about the third time, I felt a little guilty for scaring him and became intent on helping him overcome his fear. I carried him out of his room to force him to sit with me on the recliner and watch it. "It's okay, they're only actors," I held him tightly as he squirmed. "See that woman? She was in *Stir Crazy*!"

He slowly calmed down after recognizing JoBeth Williams, then started to laugh with fake confidence, and perhaps it was then that he began to understand what a movie actually was. By the time Mom came home, he started watching it a second time. "I'm not afraid anymore, Mommy!" She gave me a look that made me wonder if I had just upset her *own* babysitting method.

His fear of horror movies never returned. As the years passed, he came to love that genre of filmmaking and made a hobby of knowing more trivia on the subject than anyone else. He collected horror movie paraphernalia, Freddy Krueger gloves, and all sorts of scary masks. Sitting there together watching Poltergeist I had no idea of the lifelong impact that would have on him—or on myself, as I have tried to always face my fears and come away from them more knowledgeable and wiser.

"Jesus, I was a freaking brat," I said as I recorded my self-reflection into the notebook. Having avoided nostalgia for so long, I was seeing myself in a more objective light... and I didn't particularly like it.

Christmas grew closer and one morning at breakfast while we were alone, Mom told me everything she got the boys—and me. "Hey!" I exclaimed. "You're killing the surprise!" Surely, she was lying, I thought, hoping to make a bigger impact when the wrapping paper started to fly. Sadly, it was all as she told me. By the time Chris and Evan were unwrapping their last gift I could guess what it was by the size and shape of the package. The boys were surprised every time; Evan would jump up and down with nuclear energy radiating through the room, and it made me smile—a little.

But she took something away from me—an innocence, the bliss of ignorance—and replaced it with cold, unfeeling fact. The truth is, my grandmother told me years earlier that there wasn't a Santa Claus, and I never resented her for it. Perhaps Mom assumed that Santa was the illusion and that the surprise didn't matter to me anymore. Even though I received some nice gifts, I was sad that my brothers had far more excitement on Christmas morning than me.

"I swear to you, Craig, when I'm old enough to leave I'm gone and I'm never talking to them again." He was stunned and was trying to think of a reason she would spoil my Christmas like that. "We have... irreconcilable differences."

"You can't divorce your family," he almost giggled.

"*Umm*, tell that to Drew Barrymore," I said with naïve condescension. He was nonplussed. "That was just a movie, dude."

Craig and I started hanging in different crowds. My friend who used to have a crush on Olivia Newton-John, plastering posters of her on his walls, suddenly stopped wanting to get "Physical" and opted to get "Back in Black" with heavy metal imagery everywhere seemingly announcing his emerging manhood. I both resented and adored his testosterone. While I hated the mullet he was growing, I was still attracted to the dark thick fuzz above his lip. Even though we were clearly interested in two different worlds, he still popped in my room unannounced once a week.

Though Craig was much more masculine than me, he didn't play any sports in high school. I wasn't into football, baseball, or basketball myself, but I did start to take interest in show choir, marching band, and cross country. With every new extracurricular activity into which I enrolled myself, Mom would make her protests. "How much is this going to cost us?" she rolled her eyes. I was in every musical from eighth grade until my senior year, but she never bought a ticket. I played bass drum and then switched to trombone in marching band. Not only did she not attend a single performance but complained if I practiced at home. And there wasn't a finish line tape that broke across my chest that she was ever present to witness.

We had a rule that if Mom put the kibosh on a request, the question couldn't be resurrected for Dad. So, when prom came up and she decreed that I couldn't take the car, I summoned my backbone and an audience with the king of the house to plead my case, knowing he didn't share her poverty mentality.

"I'm not going over her head," I began my entreaty, "but can you help me come up with some kind of solution."

My prom date was a swarthy princess that I knew would tickle my dad's pickle, and showing him a picture of her, he sprung up... with an idea.

"Let's rent a limo!" he exclaimed. "Don't tell your mother. Let her see it when it pulls in the drive."

Outsmarting Mom was pretty high on dad's list of favorite things, and the volume of his laughter grew with each slap on the arm from her when she saw the long white car pull into our little drive. I'm sure that her reaction—and a vicarious date with Jennifer—were his real motivations to rent it for me, but I was enjoying the fantasy of being a wealthy playboy too much to investigate those suspicions.

A feeling of great guilt flooded me, and I closed the journal. These memories revealed many moments Dad was so kind and loving, but his rough exterior and regular hard expression made those moments harder for me to accept as a kid. Looking back on them as an adult and far removed from any threat of a belt or a scolding, all the years I shut him out of my life seemed unjustified. For a moment, I sat thinking about him and the many things he did for me through my childhood. But other memories brought me back to the stubborn anger and resentment that seemed to be dearer to me than the man who raised me.

Chris was Dad's favorite son, or at least the one he enjoyed spending the most time with, it wasn't hard to see that. Not only did Chris play baseball and capture my dad's love of the sport, but he loved fishing and was mechanically inclined—neither interested me. One time, before he entered puberty, he took apart our riding lawn mower, which had been sitting in the garage in disrepair, piece by piece and put it back together again. He drew out charts and made lists, and I was blown away at the level of intelligence he had to do it successfully at such a young age. He hugged me tightly as I carried him around the block on my back, bragging about his achievement to all of our friends and neighbors.

We loved each other so much in those days. Sure, we had the typical brotherly fights from time to time, but we were best friends who snuggled together under the same blanket on the sofa every Saturday morning to watch cartoons. Friday nights, Mom would make Jiffy-Pop popcorn and Chris and I would tear through the foil and throw kernels into one another's mouths, then crunch them slowly as we watched spooky movies.

As we got older, I saw the difference in how Dad treated the two of us. Chris could drop "F-bombs" as he spoke, and Dad just laughed. I, on the other hand, got scolded if I merely said, "dang it!" Chris started to notice it, too, and once stood up to Dad just as he was threatening to punish me with his belt. When Chris stood between the two of us and shouted, "*Enough!*" Dad obeyed the little towheaded replica of himself and I ran off to my room.

The spring of my junior year in high school all athletes needed to bring their birth certificate with them for sports physicals. An oversized Bible with a long tear in its old binding that sat unguarded on my mother's dresser was the filing cabinet for all our important documents. "I need my birth certificate for a physical," I said, dashing through the living room to her bedroom, snatching it out of Deuteronomy, and bolting back out the front door.

This little piece of paper is as old as I am, I thought. My eyes carefully investigated the title, "Certification of Birth" at the top, my name, and every detail that was included on this page the day I was born. According to family lore, I popped out in a hospital in Noblesville, Indiana on April 22, 1970 after Mom surrendered to the labor pains while driving home. I ran my hand over the embossed stamp at the bottom, noting that it survived the pressure of the Bible's weight all these years. Examining the impression, one detail stopped me dead in my tracks; It read, Issued September 1975.

Why the hell was my birth certificate issued five years after I was born? My naïve teenage brain wrestled with this, and by the time I got to school I started to lean toward the popular opinion of my classmates that I was, indeed, a bastard. Just what I needed, another thing for the kids at school to pick on me about, I thought.

"What is wrong with you, Marc?" Mom asked me as I stormed through the house after school.

"All those times you called me a little bastard you were being serious!" I shot at her, making a much bigger deal of the revelation than was necessary. Her expression was split down the middle with guilt for being caught and surprise at her little sleuth.

"You and Dad had me out of wedlock, didn't you?" I ran to an end table in the living room where Mom kept the photo albums, remembering a Polaroid of her in a blue wedding dress, cut just below the knee. She remained in the kitchen and said nothing, fighting with the slightest of smirks over my histrionics. After all, her current pissed-off accuser called her an alcoholic when he was eleven years old after he saw her drinking a glass of wine—the only glass of wine he ever saw her drink—so she was used to me blowing things out of proportion.

"It's blue because she wasn't a virgin," my cousin told me years earlier as we looked through the photos together. As a preteen, I didn't know what a virgin was but understood it as those memories came rushing back just before I shoved the picture in her face. Storming out of the house, I zipped away on my ten-speed to the Little League diamond behind the high school to sit alone in the bleachers with memories I had carried but hadn't understood.

I was at that wedding! I remembered watching them smear icing across their faces as they fed each other cake! I was five years old, and I remembered that shortly after the wedding, I was sitting in an office in front of a white-haired man with mutton chops, dressed in a suit and tie—the room smelling of a grandpa's aftershave and a cigarette smoldering on his desk. He asked my parents, "What will his middle name be?"

"Preston," said my Dad—with mutton chops of his own.

I think it's reasonably understandable why I assumed from that memory that everyone went to some office to get their middle name. From that, I had a confident assumption that they tried to hide their embarrassment. With the way society viewed all things unholy back then, she most certainly wouldn't have wanted anyone to know she got knocked-up.

Lisa, a sixteen-year-old girl in our neighborhood, had a baby, and I asked her why the newborn didn't have the father's last name. She told me it was the law since they weren't married. It then dawned on me that I must have been born with Mom's maiden name—Marc Wasson and not Marc Moss! Anything that could disconnect me from Dad excited my heartbeat. Was it possible to change it back, I wondered?

I sat in the bleachers marinating in my thoughts, unable to understand the reason behind such secrecy. Maybe the guilt of it weighed on her over the years and, perhaps, manifested as the growing divide between us. Maybe it was something that got louder in her mind the older I grew, and she was ignoring it by ignoring me. I never stopped hoping the mother I knew before Evan's birth would come back and return things to normal. Perhaps this little bastard could make things right again, I thought as a little hope started to sprout. How I longed for another séance with Hilda Bauer—whoever the hell she was.

"Come with me," she said after dinner, motioning me to follow her down the hallway.

Dad stared at his food. "Go on," he said detachedly.

"What did I do, now?" I followed her into her room, and we sat down on her bed in unison. She removed her wallet from her purse, and I was ready to defend any accusations of stealing money like I had a few times in my pre-teen years. In my defense, I used the money to buy her a twelve-dollar ring—that she wore for years—as a decent cover for the candy bar I bought. Instead, she pulled out a newspaper clipping from behind a photo.

"Marc," she held the little, yellowed paper. "You aren't a bastard."

"Can I get that in writing?" We both chuckled.

"Actually," she handed me the clipping. "It already is."

I read what was a public petition from Joel Preston Moss to adopt Marc Edward Lyon. I had to reread it several times. "What?" I asked, barely audible and thoroughly confused.

"You were born Marc Edward Lyon. I married Eddy at 17 years old to get away from your grandmother. I know you loved her, but she was a witch to live with."

"Apple and the tree?" I said brusquely and raised an eyebrow, but she simply shook her head and continued.

"I wasn't pregnant when I married him. We had you a year after we got married."

I stared at the clipping like it was a Get Out of Jail Free card. I'm not Joe's son? The man who always appeared delighted to see my fear in him, whom I loathed, shared no blood with me. This was like a Christmas gift I would have been pleased for her to reveal prematurely.

"Joe is my second husband, and he is legally your dad." Moments passed almost unnoticeably to me as I repeated my birth name like a mantra in my head. "Say something, please," she implored.

Slowly, I turned to her and drew a breath. "The postal service runs slow but Santa eventually gets his letters."

Her mouth dropped. "Marc!" She scolded.

"Mom, I have lived in fear and loathing of that man in the other room and you're telling me that after all these years he's not my real father? And you want me to have some kind of appreciation for him? No! I will not! There should be confetti and fireworks. I should have this little nugget of relief bronzed!" She said nothing in response, having probably predicted such a reaction. Dad was in his recliner in his usual, disheveled, after dinner pose—pants undone with his undershirt pulled above his hairy, engorged gut—staring at the television when I walked past him to pause at the front door.

"I just want you to know, this changes nothing between us," I said fumbling with my nerves on whether to elaborate as I had in the bedroom.

He didn't look at me, just pursed his lips and gave a nod, eyes fixed on the television. A few minutes later, I asked Craig to take me on a drive away from everything, and as I closed the car door, handed him the clipping Mom gave me. He read it with the same confused look as I had, then handed it back and started the car.

"I told you there was something wrong with the way they've treated me," I folded it up and put it in my pocket. "Drive me as far away from everyone as possible," I requested, and he sped into the country between Greentown and Kokomo to a park I often rode to on my ten-speed.

"Wow," he said, over and over again. "Why wouldn't they tell you about this?"

"Probably ashamed, probably hiding something else. Who knows? And he wouldn't even look at me, like he knew I finally found out that he was the wicked stepmother!"

"Stepfather," he corrected.

"Cinderella reference, Craig. Do I really need to adjust genders to get my point across?"

Back at home in the kitchen the next day, Mom popped open a bottle of Coke and handed it to me. The carbonation burned satisfyingly against my throat, taking several quick gulps before Chris could come in and use his backwash to claim it—a disgusting yet effective method he and I used to steal each other's drinks.

"What was his name again?" my ears eager to hear this new history of my origins.

"Sperm Donor," she laughed. "Just call him the Sperm Donor now. Joe is your dad."

Another swallow of Coke restrained me from a sarcastic retort. "Come on," I begged.

"His name is Ed Lyon. We worked at the same department store, Wasson's, when I was 17." She talked on and on, telling me her side of the story.

I began imagining who my real father could be, wondering about his life, his career, his new family. Why did Mom want Joe to adopt me to keep me from this man, I wondered? What kind of life could I have had if he had taken me and not Mom? My curiosity would always finally win, no matter how much restraint I tried to muster, and I took to her bedroom a few days after she spilled the beans to dial information. She mentioned that the last she heard he was living in Greenwood, Indiana. The operator found a match, read me the number, and I jotted it on a piece of paper towel.

Wondering what to say if he answered, I paced back and forth next to the phone.

"Hello," the man's husky baritone voice greeted. It was the first word I ever heard from my *real* father, I thought, pausing to take it in. "Someone there?"

"Yes, yes! Sorry!" I jolted. "This is... this is Marc."

"Who?" he asked, followed by a brief pause, then," *Oh*! You found me!"

"How are you?" I winced right after asking. *That's the first question I'm going to ask the father I've never seen?* Our brief conversation was nothing exceptional, merely small talk. Not really different than two strangers carrying on at a bus stop or at the mall. Then, he told me that he would be in Kokomo that Saturday and invited me to meet him for dinner. He said he was a novelties distributor and had business in Kokomo; I had no idea what that was, but it sounded important to my seventeen-year-old naïve ears. We agreed to meet at a grocery store in Kokomo.

"Linda be ok with it?" he asked. I was certain Mom would be pretty angry, so I needed to find a way without her knowing.

"She's so excited, she's driving me there herself," I lied.

My bike never zipped faster through Greentown as I pedaled wildly to my cousin Deana's house. With uncontrollable excitement I burst through the front door and dashed into the kitchen. "*Oh, my god!* You will never guess who I talked to on the phone just a few minutes ago," I said, trying to catch my breath.

Deana, a dead ringer for Julia Roberts mocked me with a smidgen of anticipation, "Oh, my god! Who?"

"Ed Lyon!"

"Ed... ?" Her bright red lips made a perfect circle as she gasped. "Does your mother know?"

"Please, please, please don't tell her! And don't tell your mother! He wants to meet me in Kokomo Saturday!"

As she handed me a soda from the fridge, the purpose of my visit became obvious. "You need a ride, don't you?"

"Please?" I asked, taking a swig from the can.

"Linda is going to kill us both!"

Saturday came and I lied to Mom about my plans. I headed out the door for Deana's, pounding the pedals round and round. She was waiting for me, as if she were in a getaway car ready to take me to safety. "Are you excited?" she asked as we drove toward Kokomo.

"Of all the questions in the world, Deana," I replied, shaking my head.

From Deana's car to the doors of the grocery store I carefully rehearsed in my head how I would ask for the Novelties Distributor. Would he have to be interrupted by a secretary, I wondered? Just inside the vestibule a man filling the coin operated candy dispensers looked at me, "Marc?"

"Yeah?" how did that guy know my name. Then... my heart dropped—all fantasies destroyed. I figured it out.

"Look at you," he reached out and shook my hand. I was ready for the obligatory hug, but apparently—we weren't *both* ready for it. He stepped back examining my skinny body top to bottom. "Do you ever eat?"

"Mom complains that I eat her out of house and home," I tried to keep the look of surprise from my face, but I couldn't. He was a candy stocker and not a rich CEO—on top of that, he was bald.

We stepped outside and walked over to his van where he pulled out a bag of candy and tossed it to me. He talked on and on for about ten minutes, about relatives I never met, people I didn't know, and events from my past that never registered in my infant brain. "Let's have dinner tonight after I get off work," he invited. "I can stick around Kokomo for a little bit. Wanna ask you mother to join us?"

I gleefully imagined the heat emitting from her red angry face. "Absolutely!"

Waving at Ed as I closed the door to Deana's car, I whispered "Drive fast, drive fast." She looked surprised as she turned the key and I stopped her from any questioning. "He's a bald candy stocker. Drive!"

"Shirley!" I called out as I walked in the back door of my aunt's house. "You'll never guess what just happened!"

"Well, Marcus Wellaby," Shirley greeted, addressing me by the nickname she gave me years ago, an intentional mispronunciation or clumsy bastardization of the name of the titular character of a 70s medical series. "What did you think of Eddy?" she asked, and I turned to shoot a disapproving glance at Deana.

"I need you to call Mom for me," I started my plea. "He wants to have dinner tonight." Deana and I sat down at the kitchen bar. Shirley furrowed her brow as she looked at me and picked up the phone. "With both of us," I added.

She quickly winced like something had just pinched her. "Lordy, Marc, she's going to be pissed," she warned and started dialing.

"I'm counting on it," I said under my breath.

The look she shot me when she arrived to see her first husband standing next to me was dessert ahead of the meal. But she was an

Academy Award winner at dinner, smiling like she was delighted for the reunion. They took turns answering my questions, telling me stories of how they met, never mentioning why they split. The one time I queried about it, Ed seemed to intentionally deflect with a surprise memory of a toy chest he made for me. "Do you remember that chest, Marc?" Mom asked, apparently picking up the baton of distraction Ed handed her. I shook my head, not in response to Mom's question, but to their ignorance of smooth segues. "There's a picture of you sitting on it as we're carrying it upstairs at our apartment."

"We lived in an apartment?" I had no memory.

"The first year after Ed and I divorced," she explained. "It was more of a townhouse, really. Eddy used to come and visit you there until you were three."

They went on and on about events I didn't remember and a never-ending onslaught of names I didn't know, followed by "Do you remember him?" or "You have to remember her," including a half-brother who was apparently excited that I reappeared after all these years. It almost had me regretting my curiosity.

Then, Ed cleared his throat and leaned forward on the table, looking me dead in the eye, "Just to be clear, I'm not going to be trying to catch up with past Christmases and birthdays or any future college plans, got it?"

That came from out of the blue! I thought. I took a deep breath—sensing Mom's usual inward retreat in the presence of an assertive man—and let it fly. "Let's not get this mixed up," I responded slowly and deliberately, leaning in to meet him. "Today was not about you. It was about me discovering where I came from and the truth about my history. I'm not looking for a father because a capable one stepped to the plate when you left." For just a moment, I had a little appreciation for Joe Moss, even as it was intentionally weaponized at the man across the table. "So, don't worry about Christmas or college." I pulled myself from the booth, glanced back at Mom, then looked at Ed and said, "But you will pay for this damned dinner." And I walked out of the restaurant, head held high—but fuming mad.

In the car, Mom held her composure as we pulled out of the lot and onto the road. This was her way, waiting to react to something until we were safely out of sight.

She finally burst into her loud, percussive cackle. "Birdy, I'm so proud of you!"

"It's really not mutual, Mom! Your taste in men is

confirmed—questionable!"

Mom shot a quick offended expression, then looked back to the road, laughing. "Eddy's bald!"

I never told Dad about that dinner, and after a couple of days I realized Mom didn't want to talk or think about it herself. She must have told him, though, since there were noticeable tensions growing between them, little biting responses to one another that neither Chris nor I missed. And I think Chris was paying close attention to them after I told him that we weren't fully brothers—he never held me tighter than that night, crying against my shoulder.

My journal was full of pages of my sloppy handwriting of key considerations from my recollections. Uncertainty coupled with my frustration as these memories would always take me to an unconformable place, but I needed to know my past from my adult vantage point. Instead of helping me find some kind of resolve or hidden catharsis, I just felt helpless and overwhelmed. But Laura assured me that it was this book that got her down the aisle. With a meager yet hopeful faith in her evidence, I continued my voyage down neural networks covered in cobwebs.

Craig graduated and went to Tennessee to spend time with extended family for the summer, barely spending any time with me before he left. In late July, Mom announced to my brothers and me that she and Dad were getting a divorce. Chris broke into tears, while I tried to look upset. I didn't want Mom to suffer—but surely, she would eventually recover with Dad gone, I told myself to alleviate my marginal guilt.

One day, she burst into a fit of rage about something without provocation as we drove through town. She started bitching about how I never clean up after myself—which wasn't true; my bedroom met standards I learned from my grandmother, who I heard remark to Mom that it must skip a generation. Then she criticized me for never showing Dad any appreciation. I'll admit, it's hard to want to be around someone you don't love, let alone send them undeserved gratitude. "Gee, thanks for the belt whacking, Dad!"

Then she pulled out the zinger—"That man wouldn't be leaving us if you hadn't nickel-and-dimed him to death at every turn."

"What?!" I snapped back, engaging in the fight she had been fishing for. "He's cheating on you!"

"You just had to be in the musical and that took money!"

"Another woman has nothing to do with..." I tried to interject.

"Cross Country, that took money!"

"And you never went to a..."

"Track, more money!" A crack in her voice betrayed her restraint. "You just wouldn't stop, and you wouldn't get a job."

"Mom," I tried to calm my volume. "You won't let me drive. I still don't have a driver's license. That's on you."

"You need to get a job to get a car," she was resolute.

"In this little town, the jobs are all taken. Should I walk ten miles to Kokomo every day?"

"Just find one, shovel shit if you have to!" she shouted with a desperation in her voice I had never heard from her. "You're spoiled rotten—rotten to the damned core." At the next intersection, I jumped out of the car and ran off. With no objections, she drove away and never circled back.

At the end of summer, band camp rescued me. There was little air in the house to breathe between them during the divorce process. Most nights I waited until I was certain that Dad was asleep and snuck in through the back. Mom was always entranced in front of the television and never acknowledged me.

At the beginning of my senior year, she told me that the house was on the market. "We're moving in January. You'll go to Kokomo High School."

"I am not going to a new school for my very last semester, Mom," I rebelled.

"Yes, you will, by God!" she said firmly.

"That's bullshit," I shot back. "I won't know anyone there! And it's only for four months. I want to graduate with my friends that I've known my whole life."

"You can want in one hand, shit in the other," her words stabbed at me.

As the first semester of my senior year progressed, the house became a dumpster of packing boxes. Soon, the walls became bare and covered in fresh, white paint—except the kitchen wallpaper she refused to remove since it was the last project she and my late grandmother completed together. My homework suffered because to me homework was... work you do at home—and I didn't have one anymore.

Was I really so stubborn?—I wrote in my notebook then closed it, chagrined and ashamed. The realization that I caused her as much suffering as she caused me was glaringly obvious now in a way that I had simply ignored for years. A sense of regret sat in my stomach and I wished I could go back in time and remove my contribution to the pain Mom was going through as her family crumbled around her.

Mom and the boys moved to Kokomo during Christmas break. I refused to help. I was determined to finish my schooling at Eastern. She didn't care what it meant to me, and it didn't slow her down getting out of the house where so many memories could haunt her—and I didn't care what that meant to her. Once I convinced her that my friends and I had arrangements for me to stay with them throughout the weekdays and that she wouldn't have to drive back and forth between Greentown and Kokomo, she gave in. While we were registering for my last semester of school, she looked at me and said, "By God, you're stubborn."

"Who do you think I got it from?" I asked bitingly.

"Well, you perfected it," she bit back.

The mother of one of my classmates realized that I had only two pairs of pants and five shirts and took me shopping one day. It was embarrassing. Mom made sure the boys had lots of new clothes for school, though, and I saw it as the many great lengths she took in our apparent competition of stubbornness. The Superintendent found odd jobs for me to do to pay for my cap and gown after I told him that Mom wouldn't give me a dime. It wasn't the regular paycheck she thought I should have, but I didn't care. I was going to get that diploma from Eastern High School.

Finally, graduation came. I needed to reserve tickets in advance, but Mom didn't put a single dollar in my hand that whole semester, not even to take to someone else. So, I instructed her to show up early enough to pay herself, otherwise the tickets would go to a friend's mother, Sharon, who I lovingly called *Ma*, as if I could have myself adopted by someone who better understood the job description. I looked to the door frequently as I stood in the hallway among my friends, all in our graduation regalia. As the time edged closer and she hadn't shown up yet, the hope that she'd prove me wrong slipped hopelessly into oblivion. Eventually, my friend's mother walked into the gymnasium with her ticket and found the chair next to mine. Sharon appeared to be prouder of me than the Walking Womb that raised me—a short-lived nickname I tried out to pair with Sperm Donor.

Walking to my seat during "Pomp and Circumstance," I saw her, sitting next to Dad at the top of the gym. She waved down at me with so much saccharine that I nearly got diabetes watching. It was fake, and surely just a display for any onlookers. Afterward, we met in the hallway for pictures to be taken. "Let's get this over with quickly, shall we?" I glanced her up and down, embarrassed... and sad.

A friend drove me to Mom's, and I changed clothes as quickly as I could, but she returned before I was out of there. As I headed to the door to leave again, she told me she had iced a cake and sat it on the kitchen table for me. "I'll have some later," I said dismissively, barely audible, and hastened away.

I went to several open houses that day, enviously watching the interactions of my friends' families and wishing that I had been raised with such normalcy. The finality of graduation hit me as I realized my friends would be gone by summer's end, off to college or the military, and I didn't have a clue if I'd ever see any of them again. I also had a slight sense of accomplishment, making it to the end of the school year with these people, feeling like I triumphed over hurdles Mom had placed in my way.

On the way to the last open house, Dad intercepted me and asked me to take a drive with him, noticeably upset, and though I wanted to resist and ignore him, I acquiesced and got into the car. "You want to tell me why you couldn't even be bothered to have a slice of cake with your mother today, young man?"

"If you can tell me why my damned mother couldn't be bothered to show up on time," knowing he wasn't my real father gave me a boost of courage I never had before the newspaper clipping. "Those tickets went to Will-Call, Dad!" I pounded the syllables against the dash with my fist. "I warned her."

His jaw dropped. "Wait, you couldn't save two tickets for her?" He apparently heard a different version of events.

"Dad, I told her! She didn't listen! So, just add this disappointment to the long list: my sixteenth birthday, every Christmas for the past four years, not coming to a single marching band contest, I could go on. I don't know what the hell I did to that woman to make her treat me this way." I paused, then sighed. "And you want me to have a piece of cake?"

He stopped the car in the driveway of my friend's house, almost on cue. In fairness, once he had all the pieces to a puzzle, he could shift gears, indicated by a slow nod and pursed lips. "Things make a bit more sense now," he said, then pulled out a twenty from his wallet and extended it. "I'm sorry, son." I stared at it for a few seconds and considered refusing it.

"Thank you," I exhaled. Finally, someone heard me, I thought. After leaning over and customarily kissing him on the cheek, I jumped out of the car and headed toward my friend's front door. Dad didn't pull away immediately, though, and I looked back wondering why he paused. Staring at me from behind the wheel, he looked like he was about to step out and tell me something else. But then, he shook his head, waved, and backed out of the drive.

Chapter Three

Al was thrilled that I was finally doing rehearsals again, and I did my best to ignore my desire to just lay in bed, staring at the ceiling. Five days of driving per week and organizing with which school I would spend my Saturdays are what pulled the sheets off of me each morning. Also, if I stayed in bed too long, he would rap on the door and shout, "Rise and shine, Sunshine!" Incessantly.

It didn't take too long to get myself back into a rhythm. Wyatt would call and we would talk for the forty-five minutes it took him to get to work, then I'd spend an hour, alone, spinning away as I showered and prepared to leave. "I'm off," I'd say coming down the hallway. Then I'd smile, and with gleeful artifice wave to Al on the couch as I'd walk out the door to my car, all the while feeling as though my blood had been replaced with concrete.

Aside from Wyatt, two things gave me my daily dose of energy: First, coffee. Surprisingly, I didn't start drinking it until I was twenty-six. I figured I should make use of all the annual coffee mugs Al gave me—a non-coffee drinker—as a Christmas gift. He wasn't exceptionally astute to another's interests and needs around the holidays, but I had plenty of experience with yuletide disappointments. And second, the students—watching kids grow and develop self-worth is the greatest heavenly elixir that I've discovered. Every year, I get letters and gifts from graduating seniors thanking me for their personal development in one of my ensembles. I've never thrown a single one away and am sure that one day I'll use them to create some work of art that would make Martha Stewart proud.

The best part of my job is that it isn't a job. I genuinely love what I do. Though it's hard work putting a show together, driving all those miles, and getting all those high school kids to stay focused on a common goal, the work is rewarding when it all comes together.

"We all come from different backgrounds, have different dreams and worldviews," I usually start a season with a pep-talk. "But we put all that aside for the good of the ensemble."

Actually, that's not the first thing I tell them. I usually let the mushy stuff come at the end of my introductory spiel. "This is not a democracy, it's a benevolent tyranny! Just do what you're told and trust that your staff has your best interests in mind."

I was blessed to have been taught by some of the best in the industry, brilliant educators who said pretty much the same thing I tell my students, then guided us to the world championships in my last season eligible for drum and bugle corps. It's my lifeblood being able to give those lessons to new students, year after year. The greatest teacher who taught me the reason for teaching was a most ineffaceable lion among educators.

John Aylsworth was the embodiment of love and compassion for his students and working for him was like interning for God. He was a giant of a man—intellectually and spiritually. Though he was confined to a wheelchair and could never demonstrate to his students how to march, he zipped back and forth like lightning across the parking lot on which his band rehearsed. He saw and trusted something in me as a twenty-two years old instructor, and he successfully fine-tuned the fire this red-headed Taurus had for winning, though long after I stopped working for him.

John understood his students, their families, and their stories, and he never had an ounce of judgment toward any of them. One morning, one of the kids stood up and started defending a mistake he made on his mellophone, and stormed out of the band room, yelling obscenities. When he returned the next morning, head hanging low with a barely audible apology, John gave him a short lecture about the importance of anger management and a hug. The boy was back out with the band as if nothing happened. A few days later, like déjà vu, it happened again. John met the boy with tenderness and forgiveness the next day.

"How long will you let James get away with that?" I asked him.

"As long as his face is always red with regret. The Bible says to forgive seven times seven times."

That tenderness touched me, and I wanted that. I wanted to be that—a teacher who could inspire his students with radiant love and shake more out of them by simply saying, "I'm disappointed." John shaped my mind and my heart in his every word and deed with his students by simply being... him.

At one competition, he introduced me to a friend, another band director from Dubois County. "This is Marc, my secret weapon.

He's a genius." It surprised me, having never received such a compliment—if that's what it was—but I shook the man's hand firmly with flattered confidence.

Later, I said to him, "John, thanks for the kind words, but I'm no genius."

He stopped his wheelchair and turned toward me to be emphatic. "Marc, I've had some of the best in the industry come work with my kids. You give my program something the other professionals with their secret bags of tricks won't—retention."

True, I believed that a good teacher strives to make his students his equal, to become peers. The lesson is lost if the student is unable to synthesize the information independent of the teacher, and the teacher cannot take them to new levels. So, yes, I give them retention, but that isn't grounds for a descriptor that puts me in the company of Einstein who played a violin—not a fitting instrument for the marching field, I thought.

"That doesn't make me a genius, John, does it?" I asked, a little smugly overcome with flattery.

"I mentor intelligently gifted students, Marc." His sincerity wasn't lost on me, even though I often shied from compliments about intelligence. He turned his chair and continued, and I followed shortly after.

I only visited John at his home once, and on the deck that surrounded the house were nearly a hundred bonsai trees. It was his hobby, and I realized that this great teacher saw each student like he viewed his miniature creations—pure perfect potential.

The stream of memories paused as I pulled into the parking lot at Southport High School just moments before rehearsal. I felt a desire to call and thank Al for introducing me to this side of the marching world and its inhabitants. Memories of John gave way to wholehearted appreciation, a welcome break from the DJ Circle. Short, chance occurrences that might not have happened can ripple through time and rewrite an entire destiny. I started to dial Al's number but floated away in a current of memories of my early days with him and his first wife.

I did summer stock theatre after graduation and had dreams of becoming an actor, but I didn't land any stellar roles. Nonetheless, I was away from Mom, making my own decisions. In the fall, however, I conceded and lived with her. I auditioned for the local civic theatre and got several parts in various musicals, including the lead in *Little Shop of Horrors*—to which Dad came and loved. I also worked at

McDonald's during the day, and that should have made her happy, yet nothing I did seemed to bring out an ounce of pride—or a word that she believed I'd amount to much more than the drive-thru window. She belittled my dreams of acting, so I stopped sharing them. I would punch the clock in the daytime and dash to the theatre in the evening. Life around thespians is good for the soul.

During rehearsals for *Show Boat*, a short, loud Latina with a peculiar limp stepped out of the elevator next to the dressing rooms one day, a laundry basket overflowing with bunched up costumes in her hands. As she stepped out, a bra fell on the floor between us. She looked at me and said, "Oh look, a hat for Siamese rabbis!"

Her name was Alice, she was Al's wife, and I remembered she accompanied him once to one of my high school band rehearsals. Al and Alice were quite a pair of polar opposites. She was high strung, loud, funny, and creative; Al was subdued, quiet, serious, and logical. She was so charismatic, filling a room with her alto-ranged laugh everywhere she went. I was drawn to her, and for once in my life there was an adult who verbalized their appreciation for my uniqueness. She loved referring to herself as a hippy. Many barriers society erected in my brain tumbled to dust under her influence. I first learned of biblical errancy from the shelves of books on the topic in Alice's office—which doubled was the family laundry room, overflowing with piles of clothes and costumes—and carried that interest as my defining hobby for many years.

She was the one to serve me my first taste of Chinese, Greek, and real Italian food. Greentown was small with a family diner on one end and a drive-thru ice cream shop on the other. Everything in between was the bland, salt-as-a-spice dish in any household that might have invited you in for dinner. Any opportunity to expand my palate beyond my small-town influence delighted her, and she found plenty of opportunities.

She would often take me with her to a Greek restaurant in Indianapolis where she performed during dinner as a belly dancer—excuse me—danseuse Orientale, as she insisted on referring to the craft. Admittedly, my westerner ignorance found it fitting that she and all of the women who came to practice with her had lots of belly to dance!

Her teacher and mentor, a gorgeous Egyptian lady named Faten once noted to Alice about me: "Yazmeen," she called her by her stage name. "This Marc, I think... he is a gay." It wasn't long before I came out of the closet and Alice was there as my official hag. She treated me like her little brother—her gay, white, redheaded brother. We joked that we would have our own talk show one day, The Marc and Alice Show, and had our own song, acting out episodes in the car.

Al and Alice met as members of competing drum corps. After they married, she became a decent choreographer, working with schools for whom Al designed. I started accompanying her to marching band rehearsals around the state when she would have to go teach. My dance background I accumulated through musical theatre made me her perfect companion, she mentioned.

One night she, Al, and I were returning home from a rehearsal and they wooed me into the world of drum corps. Hearing them refer to their fellow corps mates as 127 brothers and sisters and the lasting bonds they all maintained lured me. I watched the world championships of drum and bugle corps on PBS several times—the Olympic level of marching band. Al and Alice described a richer history, a deeper world of this activity than was exposed on television. I made up my mind and auditioned for the Star of Indiana, in Bloomington. I never auditioned for an instrumental ensemble before, having only played a brass instrument for three semesters in high school. But I had nerves of steel when I would audition in theatre, and I took that confidence into the small room at Brown Elementary where the auditions were held.

Drum and bugle corps, also called drum corps, are independently run competitive organizations, not affiliated with schools or colleges. Individually, they meet one weekend a month throughout the winter and then spend a couple of weeks learning their shows after moving into the corps' hall at the end of May before taking it on the road and touring the country. Most corps will compete sixty times a summer, travel 15,000 miles, culminating in the world championships in early August. For the average outsider, drum corps looks like marching band. A key difference is that there are no woodwinds; that means that there are no flutes, no clarinets, no saxophones—no problem! Brass instruments can be louder without having to balance to the breakable reeds of the woodwinds trying to match volume. In the Star of Indiana, we played a welcome back concert for the troops with Styx and we were just as loud as their electronic amplification!

My audition earned me a member position in the corps. I wore my pride—literally. I bought my member jacket in May, and a week before moving in for the summer went to show it to my friend, Mike,

Sharon's son. Due to my lack of seniority in the high school band, it was no surprise that he beat me out for drum major—disappointing, nonetheless. He told stories about his week at drum major camp every damned day that whole school year, and I wasn't the only one maddened by it. Parading around in my proof of trumping his week with an entire summer of marching arts participation would be the perfect turd into which I could rub his nose.

"If you had all those stories after a week of drum major camp, can you imagine what I'll have after three months?" We never spoke again—my stubborn vindication always came with a price.

From the seat of an air-conditioned coach that wreaked of sweat and hairspray, I got to see America that summer. If we weren't traveling or taking time off at a laundromat, we were in the summer sun on a football field for sixteen hours, frying to a crisp. This redhead actually tanned! Except for the crusty burnt shoulders, earlobes, and nose, my body was practically bronze.

It was the most demanding work I ever did, and most people are unaware of the physical exertion of playing an instrument with controlled exhalation while jazz running in perfect formation with others. One of the guys in the tuba section, a hairy and muscular tower of manhood, was previously in the military and swore to me that drum corps was harder than basic training.

Fitter than ever, I returned after that summer to my mother's house and continued working fast food and rehearsed local marching bands. Disappointingly, my schedule became too full for theatre. Besides, I got a taste of teaching and wanted a full banquet. Al and Alice became the waiters, serving me school after school.

Mom couldn't care less for my fascination with marching bands. In fact, she almost seemed jealous anytime I would walk through the door with a new story. I felt like that damned WB frog that will dance and sing and entertain the right audience, but in front of the wrong company gives out a plain old *ribbit*. In front of my mother, I always croaked.

One afternoon before she left for work, she told me that she was dating a guy she met at a bar for the past week and that he told her that he wanted to marry her. "After a week?" I disapproved. "That's not healthy."

"You can't be happy for me, can you?" she replied, offended.

After a couple of weeks of dating Elton, she said to me, "We're thinking about getting married in May."

I only saw him once, a short troll-like creature with salt and pepper hair, dressed very much like you'd expect of a former pastor.

"That's pretty soon," I said, but quickly changed tone to avoid arousing any ire ."But it's enough time for all of us to get to know each other, to help you make a decision."

She turned to me, arms akimbo, "I don't need anyone's help, Marc." She walked out of the kitchen and said, "A husband means more to me than my children."

I stood in disbelief, trembling with growing anger. "You're serious?"

She turned around and started to answer what I knew would be something I didn't want to hear. We stared at each other, no words, for a few moments before I walked out the door and away from the house.

She came to breakfast the next morning, her eagerness to speak couldn't be missed. "We decided last night to move the date of the wedding to February," she said with a synthetic pride.

"Mom," I started, but she stopped me.

"You hate it, don't you? It just pisses you off that I have found someone who wants to be with me!"

"No, Mom," I insisted. "You don't really know this guy. He could be—anyone! You don't know how Chris and Evan will get along with him. Forget about me. I don't plan on staying here forever."

"The boys will be a hell of a lot more supportive than you," she said. I couldn't argue with that since they delighted in joining her in jabs whenever they could. "And where do you think you're going, working at McDonald's."

Did she really chide her nineteen-year-old son for not having a flourishing career yet?

I drew a calming breath, then said, "Will I come home this week to you flashing me a wedding ring and saying, 'Guess what we did today.'" Sure enough, by the end of the week it happened. Mom and Elton came home and dropped the news to Chris, Evan, and me that they went to the courthouse and gotten married. I shook my head, not out of disbelief but at the fact that I pretty much predicted her actions.

"How irresponsible, Mom."

"Hey," snipped the brand spanking new father-in-law. "Don't talk to your mother like that."

Springing out of my chair, I got right in his face. "No, no little man," I yelled. "You do not get to tell me what to do, wedding ring or not."

The house erupted into a cacophony of shouting from everyone in it. Mom and Elton finally walked out, and I picked up the phone and called

Al and Alice. "Can you come get me, please?" I begged into the phone.

The three of us sat around their dining table and discussed me coming to live with them for a while. "We're old school drum corps folk," Alice explained. "We take care of each other." I had two more summers to participate in drum corps, and they wanted to facilitate that. Al and I got in his car and went to my mother's.

Had Mom not been there, the boys wouldn't have even noticed me as they were transfixed to the television. I carried a few boxes and a duffle bag out to Al's car, where I instructed him to wait to avoid any possible verbal explosions. Mom just sat in the kitchen with a smirk, assuming I was up to my familiar theatrics. "You won't be gone for long," she said. "You'll be back."

"That's all you've got to say to me?"

The boys came to life and followed me outside jeering. I looked at Chris and said, "You're the scapegoat now."

I closed the door and never went back. Al and Alice had a futon upon which I cried at night for a couple of months, scared and lonely. Mostly, I felt defeated.

Chris called me from a pay phone that December, crying after a fight he had with Elton which prompted him to run out of the house and into the snow without any shoes. Borrowing Al's van, I drove quickly to Mom's where Dad's car was in the drive, still running. He was inside telling Mom that she could fight him in court if she wanted but that she was not fit to look after his children. My face was covered in "I told you so"—she knew it—and thus didn't speak. Chris and Evan carried their bags past me and went to live with Dad. Mom and Elton eventually moved two hours north.

For the next two summers I toured and competed with the Star of Indiana again. Performing the music of Ottorino Respighi, we won the coveted world championship in 1991, my last eligible season at twenty-one. One of my instructors in those last two years shaped me more than anyone else. George Zingali was a brilliant, theatrical mind and a genius designer who shaped the artistry of the marching arts. I never met such a magnitude of personality, intentionally flamboyant and expressive. He sometimes called me Carrot for my red hair, and other times he'd call me Marquestra. I wasn't officially out of the closet and the feminine nickname concerned me, until I realized I wasn't special at all. Everyone got a drag name from George, even the most masculine guy in the drum line!

I often called George on the phone in the off-season to get advice to improve my teaching skills. "Let the kids be your teacher," he said to me in his thick Boston accent. Much of the mannerisms in my own teaching style I attribute to him and his brilliance. Shorty, one of our head brass instructors and the best trumpet player I ever personally knew, used to be one of George's students. Sitting with Shorty one day when we took a break from rehearsing to do laundry, he shared with me a story about George that moved me to tears. Shorty's last eligible season, he toured the summer with a corps from New Jersey, and had little money of his own. George saw him outside a convenience store and asked if he had eaten anything. "I don't have any money, George," he said. George came out of the store with a huge bag of food, nearly in tears, and told Shorty to never be ashamed to come find him if he needed anything. After hearing that story, I imagined myself being like George for my future students.

The night of our victory, the corps director placed a winning medal around the neck of each of his students. "Congratulations, Marc," Mr. Mason said. "You're a world champion... and nothing can take that away from you!" I finally accomplished something amazing—a world championship—with 127 other people I called brother and sister. In Mason's embrace, I wanted the gratitude of my soul to enter him.

There were so many amazing people involved with Star—students and adults—that influenced me endearingly. In fact, my friend Laura who gave me the relationship psychology book I was using was a member of the corps with me. After we aged out, she came to my apartment from time to time and was the bartender for entertaining evenings drinking blue margaritas, and we'd dance throughout my kitchen as the blender whipped her frozen delight with "Low Rider" playing on the stereo.

Most of my corps mates were music majors in college, and their stories made me dream of higher education. That mixed well with the reward I reaped from my instructing experiences with marching bands. One friend encouraged me to apply to college, but I was scared I wouldn't be able to afford it. I learned as much as I could about loans and grants, but I still needed financial information from my parents and, thus had to reveal to Mom this secret I tried to keep from her.

"If you're so talented, get there yourself," she said and hung up.

The university accepted my request for emancipation from my parents and upon settling in my dormitory a few days late after my final world championship, I made copies of my acceptance letter and notifications of my grants and financial aid and put them in a manila envelope with a Post-it note attached and sent it to her. The Post-it read, "Guess I'm talented enough!"

I fell in love with learning and, finally, excelled in academics. Participating in Student Government showed me the power of politics, and I became the On-Campus Caucus Chair. I still managed to find time for a few marching bands during the Fall.

Mom called my sophomore year and told me she wanted to leave Elton. It was all I could do to not laugh at her and hang up. She was more frustrated than sad. And after a while of listening to her beg me to help move her out, I felt the tug from my heart strings and told her I would. I brought my friend, Kent with me—very tall, very opinionated, very intelligent, and very gay! She took to liking him immediately, as well-spoken people often found a soft spot in her heart. Kent told her an amusing story about correcting a woman he saw on an elevator talking baby talk to a child in a stroller. "Ma'am, that infant brain is trying to learn the English language and you're really fucking it up right now."

She let out a big guffaw. "That sounds like something you'd say, Birdy! I like you, Kent!"

As we drove closer to the house, Mom worried how we would succeed getting her things out to the U-Haul past her stepson, Aaron, while Elton was working third shift.

"Let's have a code for all of us," I voiced an idea. "Kent and I won't know what's yours and what's theirs. Your things we'll refer to as 'first trip,' and theirs as 'second trip.' If Kent or I grab one of their boxes you simply say, 'that's second trip stuff,' and we'll know to put it down and Aaron will be none the wiser."

Mom's approving smile gave me a spark of pride.

Without a hitch, and with the olive branch Dad extended, we moved her things into his barn two hours away. Mom agreed to drive us back to Muncie the next morning on the proviso that Shirley come with us for company on the hour drive back.

In Muncie, Kent exited, and Mom thanked him for the help, but I know she was more entertained by his stories about being gay. "That's a nice fella, Bird."

"Well, here we are!" I said outside my dormitory. "Come on up and take a look."

"Marc, I'm tired and just want to get back," she hung on the steering wheel, and I sensed that I wasn't going to coax her off.

"What? Linda!" Shirley snapped. "Go see your son's room, for Christ's sake!"

Mom wouldn't budge, and I wouldn't fight. I was exhausted, too. It was a somewhat unexpected hit in the gut that after all that time helping her flee the little elf, she couldn't give me ten minutes of pride. To her credit, she eventually apologized.

Coming out of my daze of memories and intent to get to work, I walked over to the practice field at Southport and watched the kids coming out of the building to get into their stretch block. The band director waved at me, indicating I should get things started without him as he was inundated with a small group of parents. By his expression, it was the same unnecessary bombardments of parent questions I've seen in every band director with whom I've worked. It's one of the biggest reasons why I withdrew from college after the first semester of my junior year, not having an alternative major to switch to. As I waited for the last of the kids to get out of the building, I remembered that year vividly.

I took Mom shopping shortly after withdrawing and spent four hundred dollars on clothing for her, making sure she got a new bra—several. She stopped at the cosmetics stand and I put my hand on her shoulder, "Get whatever you want, Mom." She protruded her bottom to jokingly pout. I grabbed her chin, "Except blue eye shadow."

We ate lunch, laughed, and had a good time without an argument. Good things never last long, they say, and a few weeks later at my aunt's house Mom started in about me dropping out of college. No matter my reason, she kept pestering me about being a drop out.

"Are you kidding me with this?" I yelled. "I'm the first person in this family to even make it to college!"

I surrendered. I didn't want to keep volleying like we did over the years. Walking out of Shirley's house, I resolved to keep her at a distance. For a couple of years afterward, we barely spoke at all, only twice and they were both short and cold. On my 26th birthday, she called and sang to me. After I thanked her, she became quiet. I thought we got disconnected. Then, I heard her sniffling, and after a few moments she drew a deep breath.

"Oh, Birdy," she cried. "What have I done to you."

I froze, completely paralyzed. I listened to her sniffles turn into heavy, vocal whimpers. "What do you mean?" I asked.

"I am so sorry I treated you so badly."

My lips tightened at her apology. I switched off long ago—the stubbornness that I got from her would not surrender.

I interrupted her, "Well, those years are behind me, and I really don't want to open any wounds right now... just so that you can feel better about yourself." I hung up and my fake strength vanished into a very messy cry. I was so angry with myself for treating her that way. After all, the sincerity of her apology was clear. John Aylsworth would have been disappointed. I wiped my snot and looked for a tender memory, some kind of emotional salve. Then, I chuckled into my handkerchief as I recalled the day that I came out to her.

"There's something I need to tell you," I said, holding my 19-year-old posture with pride.

"If it's what I think it is, you don't have to." She said, and I recalled that years ago, she asked me if I was gay after finding a letter I wrote to a classmate. I denied it, and she dropped it. Now, I had the opportunity to acknowledge it openly.

"Yeah, I know. But shouldn't you make this just a little difficult for me." We both laughed.

"Well, as your mother I should probably ask you if you're sure you just haven't met the right girl yet?"

"I could ask you the same thing," I quipped.

"I probably should be a lesbian with the husbands I've had."

I put my arms around her. "Nah, you suck too badly at softball."

I was actually blessed that of the problems I experienced throughout my childhood, my sexuality wasn't one of them. Both of my parents separately inquired during my mid-teen years but didn't press after hearing my denial. We weren't religious by any sense, never having stepped into a church together. Dad grew up a Jehovah's Witness and abandoned it after his own brother, Bruce, disowned him publicly for accepting draft into the military. Mom believed in a higher power, but she didn't think humans could ever piss off an immortal. They weren't hippies, but they weren't prudes either. And as I sat there crying after a shameful burst at my mother's apology, an overwhelming sense of gratitude came over me.

As the kids at Southport took a five-minute water break, I excused myself and took a walk around the stands and stared off at the parking lot of cars. Despite the fact that I saw countless football stadiums across the country, and due to the fact that my self-conducted psychoanalysis became an obsession, my mind drifted into the memories of the most memorable experience I had in a football stadium parking lot.

My dad was the one who started my healing process from the pain with which Mom inflicted me during the divorce. At one of my drum corps performances in the parking lot at IU Memorial Stadium in Bloomington he handed me a care package from the trunk of his car. "That's for the rest of your summer," he said as I opened the box filled with loose bills, disposable razors, candy bars, and condoms. "Let's take a walk," and he pulled me out of earshot of the boys and his new wife.

"Marc, I learned what your mother told you." My muscles braced themselves. "You had nothing to do with any of it." It was a moment of which I was fully aware would resound throughout my life.

"We just fell out of love," he continued. "She stopped being my partner and started acting like a mother to me. And you know, son... that's just not very romantic."

It made sense to me, and I wanted to forgive him. But he cheated and married the woman for whom he left Mom. I even got coaxed into attending the wedding. There she was in that parking lot, talking to Chris and Evan as if she raised them herself. Soon after seeing them in Bloomington, everything festered in me, and I stopped talking to Dad altogether. It took more than fifteen years before we spoke again, and another nine before we would be face to face. Even after giving me the precious pardon in the parking lot I cut him out of my life for all the years for which I thought he should pay. Regretfully, I truly perfected the stubbornness I inherited.

When I was twenty-five, Alice divorced Al and moved to Chicago, leaving him a shell of the man I once knew. I grew to not like her much, living with someone can do that. She had a different best friend every few months and there were a few of us in the discard pile that compared notes with one another. Underneath all of her charisma and charm was a motherlode of contradictions and self-absorption. This woman who spent more money than she put back into the coffers and caused her husband financial stress had the audacity to try to teach me—TNSTAAFL—which means, *There's no such thing as a free lunch.* After she left, a part of Al was gone forever, and his designs began to suffer. Though I was busy seeking my own relationship, boyfriend after boyfriend, I did my best to be a caring presence for him as he did his best to recover. It was my familial duty to him for all he had been to me.

Having pushed my own family away, I dove into the marching

arts for comfort. In front of an ensemble of students I was confident, far from the skinny high school unpopular kid from Greentown. Many of my students told me that I was intimidating, but never questioned my devotion to them. They became the family I lacked. For the most part, I learned early on to keep my romantic separate from my professional. I watched many couples who met on a staff somewhere, straight and gay alike, pair up for a while and end in an ugly split, most often out of jealousy of one or the other's success. But there were also successful marriages made in band, and many were the directors who married a former student, like John and his wife. I tried to keep from mixing those two worlds because the rules were always different for gay instructors—angry sarcasm intended. Nonetheless, I had some moments of weakness, but I rarely succumbed.

That's where DJ came in. He was the drum major for a band I worked for and after he graduated, I gave in to the chase. Now, let me note that right after college I read the *Male Couple's Guide* by Eric Marcus, and in it he found over years of researching gay relationships across the country that the longest lasting of them were couples with considerable differences in age. Plus, my grandmother was seventeen when she married my grandfather—who was thirty-three. So, I didn't feel a bit of shame for finally relenting to him. Besides, he was the first guy to make me feel wanted for more than a half-hour, and I knew we already had much in common.

One day, he helped me move some new furniture into a duplex I was renting. When we finished, we fell back side by side onto my new sofa as the sun set through the back door, wide open, setting the interior ablaze. Slowly we turned toward one another, and the second most memorable kiss of my lifetime drew me in. After a few minutes, I stopped and pulled him up from the sofa and guided him, hand-in-hand toward the hallway.

I stopped at the front door and grabbed the doorknob. "I think you should go."

He was shocked, frozen. "I'm sorry," he could barely get it out.

"Don't be," I leaned in and kissed him. "I have a lot to think about and this doesn't need to escalate into something it shouldn't so quickly."

He smiled and stepped outside. "Don't worry," I assured. "This is a better response than you realize." I watched him pull away, staring at me all the while. As he drove off, I couldn't wait to see that car pull back into the drive again one day. If we went to the bedroom as I was habituated to do on too many first dates, I doubt we would have had much more to do with one another after that—an all too reliable trait in men after crossing the sexual finish line too soon.

A little white van honked as it passed, snapping me out of my chain of memories and reminding me to head back to the rehearsal that restarted without me. I walked down the service drive next to the bleachers and paused, watching a memory of my mother's van, much like the one that had passed, pull into my driveway, as she did at least once a year, unannounced with Chris and Evan. Sometimes she'd take us to lunch, other times she just wanted to drive around with her boys, blasting "Sweet Caroline" from the stereo. I nearly always kept my guard up and refused to take any bait—but I joined in singing from the top of my lungs as we cruised through the countryside.

For my thirtieth birthday I prepared a strategy for the phone call I knew would come. Mom's annual tradition was to call to sing to me, have some conversation, then begin crying and try to apologize for my childhood before we hung up. Since the call would leave us both upset, I decided it was time to introduce her to a technique I secretly used since college. As a sophomore at Ball State University, I sat in a small audience in our student center and listened to the comedy of Kathy Buckley, a deaf comedian I saw on a news segment on television. The Student Union planned the evening with her, and I was excited, knowing it wouldn't be a large crowd.

I volunteered at the event, hoping that would get me closer to an autograph. She had a very inspiring story, besides doling out self-deprecating jokes that were always followed by an eruption of laughter. She also had the blessing of rewriting the painful parts of her past with humor. Toward the beginning of her set, she said, "When I was young, I was put in a school for retarded kids for two years before they realized I actually had a hearing loss... and they called me slow!" I laughed so hard I cried. Even though the audience was about fifty students, Kathy performed with a fire like it was a sellout crowd of thousands.

After the show I volunteered to take her to the room the Student Center reserved for her, grabbed her bags, and walked behind her. Her ability to make fun of herself was something I admired and hadn't yet learned. Within just a few minutes of being with her, she somehow homed in on that and made me take myself a lot less seriously.

"I really loved your performance tonight," I said. "I learned so many new things about you."

"Ain't you sweet," she said as she gave a quick glance to my Gamecocks tee shirt that simply said COCKS on the front. "Hey, mind me asking, but are you gay?"

"Guilty," I said, hoping I had correctly identified the playfulness in her voice, but she mentioned the Holy Spirit in her set, and I wasn't too sure how this would go.

"Damn, Kathy," she shrugged. "Not getting laid tonight." I laughed. "Oh well, want to get a pizza?" And that's how it went.

She invited me into her room, and I got on the phone and placed an order with a decent parlor down the street that would deliver. I didn't want to leave this room for nothin'!

"You already heard enough about me. What's your story, kiddo?" she asked then sat next to me on the bed.

First, I fumbled around, not feeling adequate in the presence of the biggest personality I ever met, even bigger than Alice and George, and that was saying a lot for me at twenty-three years old. So, I told her about my three years in drum corps—and the world championship—thinking that might help me feel a little less small. But then the funny lady opened up a whole new presence, and all fears of judgment vanished. I started talking about my childhood and the difficulties with my mother.

"Ain't life the shit?" she got up and pat me on the back. "It'll get better, I promise."

"How did you do it, Kathy?" I watched her walk across the room and retrieve something from her bag. "After everything *you* went through, how did you keep finding the will to fight."

"It wasn't a fight," she walked back to my side. "Not from me, anyway."

Kathy is known as America's first deaf comedienne. In her act, she told her story of being born HR negative and having spinal meningitis which led to her hearing loss. Then, in her late teens she was run over by a lifeguard Jeep while lying on the beach, causing her to be quadriplegic for five years. When she could finally walk again, she was diagnosed with cancer. Her performance was as much about triumph and the human spirit as it was a night of uncontrollable laughter. "When they told me I had cancer, I just laughed," she said. "I said, 'God, I give up. I'm done."

She reached over and placed a wallet size photo in my hand, the face of a little girl smiling back. I stared at it for a while then gave Kathy a confused glare. "That's me," she smiled, then gently punched my arm.

"Can't you tell? I'm not that old that you can't recognize me!"

I looked back down at the photo. "And?"

She relaxed back against the headboard. "At that moment I realized that I had been carrying the little girl I used to be with me my whole life, disappointment after disappointment. I said to myself, 'Kathy, you are the only one who can take care of that little girl now, babe.'"

She told me that she often would have special days in which she would go do things she would want to have done as a little girl, fittingly called her Little Girl Days. She might sit at a restaurant, for example, and ask for a table for two, even ordering two meals—one for her, and one for her imaginary child. It sounded like such a beautiful practice and touched my heart. "I carry that picture with me always, and I look at it when I get down and remember that I have to keep going for her because no one else will."

"So, I need to take care of my little boy," I said, already thinking of the picture of my five-year-old self I would carry with me.

"Bingo!" she explained.

"Thank you, Kathy."

"You just needed someone to listen to you, babe. Everyone does." She gave me a warm, healing embrace. "But why they always come to the deaf broad?"

Ever since that night I got to spend with Kathy I carried a picture of myself at five years old. It's a black and white of me sitting on Mom's lap in a photo booth. When times get rough, and they have many times throughout the years, I follow Kathy's lead and pull out the picture and remind myself for whom I need to keep going.

Mom called and sang to me, as I expected. I pulled that picture out of my wallet as we spoke. After I sensed that the conversation was drawing to a close, I knew what I needed to say. "Mom, it's about that time in our conversation where you start the waterworks and apologize for my childhood and I get angry. So, I want to impress upon you how much you need to never apologize again. There is nothing—please hear me—nothing you will ever be able to say that will erase the hurt experienced by that little boy I used to be."

I paused for a moment and drew a deep breath, knowing she was listening intently.

"The reason, Mom, is because you're not the woman that little boy I carry inside me needs to hear the apology from. She doesn't exist anymore. So, please know that I love you and I don't want you to hurt anymore, either. I'll take care of that little boy, but you now have to take care of your little girl."

There was a long pause on the other end. After a few sniffles, she asked, "Where did you get so wise?"

"You, Mom," I replied, and I could hear her gentle sobs. "You weren't a bad mother. I learned to care about others, to treat people better than they treat me by watching how you treated everyone you met. When Evan was born with so many problems, you gave all of your energy to his needs. I just got pissed and selfish when it couldn't be me you poured your attention into anymore. But that didn't stop me from seeing those things, Mommy... all that love, all that care. It's what made it worse... because I wanted that... again. You were so focused on Evan that I felt I had to say stupid shit to get you to see me, and it always made you snap, like any mother would. My stupid stubborn mouth just wouldn't shut up! And then when you found out that Dad was cheating... I," my voice cracked, and I paused to keep myself from breaking down. "I was too selfish at the time to see that you needed me more than I needed you. It's all as much my fault as it was yours." I took a breath, and exhaled, hearing her crying. "But most of all, you taught me to laugh. And you and I need more of that between us from now on."

"I love you, Birdy," she cried. And for several minutes I joined her, knowing that we both had just experienced a miraculous union of our souls.

"Marc?" a voice snapped me out of my daydream. "Are you ok?" It was Southport's drum major, sent off to find me and get me back to rehearsal.

"I'm fine, I'm sorry," I said, reaching in my pocket for a tissue. I went and finished the rehearsal, then drove home with a car full of ghosts.

At home in my room, Wyatt patiently listened to me complain into the phone. "I don't think this analysis of my past is bringing me anywhere," I moped. "I can't find any connection to my childhood and how I ended up with someone that put up a really good façade for three years."

"Well, I think everything happens for a reason," Wyatt tried to soothe. "Maybe you should see a professional. I know what you're thinking, but they're living, breathing people. A self-help book can't see you or tell you what you need."

"I know, but I can't afford that, Wyatt," I said quietly. "And maybe there's nothing wrong with everyone else and it's just been me—through everything. Maybe it's just a matter of time before it happens between you and me, too."

Wyatt sat pensively silent for a moment. "I think you need to take a break from all these memories, kiddo. It's all in the past anyway. Nothing's going to change that. And don't worry about me, I'm here for the long haul. I don't know anyone who's done more self-reflection after a break-up than what you're doing. Is this healthy or is it an obsession—are you just trying to find a way to get him back?"

"No," I started to sniffle as I mindlessly flipped through the pages of the notebook. "I wouldn't take him back."

"Are you sure you mean that?"

Closing the journal, I sat back in a slump with the phone against my ear. "I think I mean it. But to be honest, Laura's story of how she used this book to get her boyfriend back—who is now her husband—I guess really has been an underlying reason to make all these lists and try to remember all this stuff. Turns out, it's been more of an exercise of studying my own suffering than anything else. It's bad enough to have gone through this break-up, but to be obsessively scouring through my memories and trying to identify some kind of cause that led me to DJ... well, it's just like salt... actually, salt and lemon juice, both, on a big gaping wound."

"Pain is part of healing, darlin'," Wyatt said. "And everyone needs a doctor to prescribe them effective medicine. Everything has a cause, and surely a psychologist could find connections you can't, maybe even use hypnosis to unlock forgotten memories."

"Hypnosis... like regressive hypnosis," I said thoughtfully, slowly rekindling thoughts to which I had been introduced just a year earlier. "What if all of this goes much, much farther back?"

✦ Chapter Four ✦

A breeze caresses my skin and swirls out across a brilliant green grassland, swinging long stalks gently around. To my left in the distance, a long staircase leads down a steep, stony cliff to a beach where waves crash lightly against pure white sand. There's a faint, slow melody in the air.

"Where is this?" I am asking. I hear my voice, but my mouth doesn't move.

"Home," a clear voice turns my head. A beautiful white donkey with a red silk bow around its neck walks slowly toward me. Its eyes are pale blue, and I can feel myself in their gaze. "You'll come back when you're finished."

It is the loveliest vista I've ever seen. The sky is clear, and there is a great feeling of peace and a palpable sense of love all around, but from whom or where I don't know... and am not concerned.

I stand up from the chair inside a golden gazebo and am overcome by a great sense of awe, as if seeing the ocean for the first time. The sunlight is different, it causes everything to shimmer like burnished gold mixed with the sparkle of the clearest diamond.

"But where is this?" I step out from the gazebo onto clean, carefully placed cobblestone.

"You'll know and remember," the voice has changed. A white goose spreads its wings where the donkey had been, wearing the same ribbon around its long throat.

"I want to stay here," I feel a longing that isn't shallow but full of compassion. The field of grass suddenly has flowers of all colors and I feel myself ready to run through them. "This is a magical, beautiful place," I say, looking down in my hand, the goose transformed. "Where I can hold a white mouse wearing a little red bow..."

DJ shook my body back and forth and I opened my eyes through tears. Though in my dream there was only the most warm, loving sensation, I must have been crying in my sleep.

"Are you ok, Jellybean?" he put his arms around me.

"I'm fine. I don't know why I'm crying."

DJ kissed my forehead and rolled back to sleep. Trying to remember every detail of the vision I was gifted, I spent the rest of the night until dawn in the dark on the front porch.

The next day I met my friend, Amber, for lunch, and I carried a book she had given me the week before. "Oh, thank you," she put it in her bag. "What did you think?"

"It's interesting, though I'm not sure if I think it's true, I do want to know more." The book was about a psychologist's experience with a client who discovered many of her past lives through regressive hypnosis. Amber gave it to me to read after we discussed how swiftly we became friends.

While DJ was in the musical theatre building preparing for an audition one day at the beginning of the semester, Amber walked up to where I was sitting and just started talking. There was a familiarity between us in that introduction that I never experienced with anyone else, and we carried on for a couple of hours as if we always knew one another.

"I don't know what to say," I continued about the book. "Perhaps it's real. Until I see some science, it's a leap of faith. Like, I've always criticized religious fanatics for saying that."

She was sipping her straw and nodding as I spoke. "So, I think we might have known each other in a past life."

I smiled, studying the porcelain white face with cartoonishly large blue eyes. "Maybe," I couldn't commit to something with which I had skepticism. Surely, there was a scientific reason yet to be found. Still, I let Amber have her way and keep the topic up as long as she liked, and I entertained the fantasy with her.

DJ and a tall, thin guy—reminiscent of an ugly blond flamingo—walked through the patio doors of the restaurant. I studied their body language.

"Marc, this is Sergio," he introduced. "We're going to work on some choreography tonight. So, I'll be home after dinner."

My eyebrows remained stone as I raised the corners of my mouth, trying to hide the spark of jealousy that fired inside me. He leaned in and kissed me on the top of the head, and as he stepped away, I pulled him back and rose up to plant a kiss on his lips.

"Jealous?" Amber read me after the boys disappeared into the restaurant.

"Maybe a little," I said, sinking against the back of the chair. "I just get feelings. Probably nothing, but I've never had a relationship last this long."

"Be careful. Your thoughts could create a reality you don't want." She grabbed her glass of water and raised it as if to toast. "Power of positive thinking."

That night, DJ quietly walked through the front door, cautiously, in case I was asleep. Seeing that I wasn't, he dropped his bags, took off his shoes, and stepped in front of the television to block my view and get my attention.

"What was that?" he asked aggressively.

"I was going to ask you the same thing—*that?*"

"Sergio is a nice guy," he defended. "You don't need to get jealous." He put his things on the floor by the bed and after undressing slipped under the sheets.

His arms slipped around me and his lips met the side of my neck. I sighed. "I'm sorry, Babybear," I rolled to face him. "I just don't like feeling like I'm competing. I'll never win in a looks competition."

He play-slapped my arm, then kissed me. "You're cute, Jellybean. And didn't you tell me about winning an underwear competition in Indy on your 26th birthday?" Dropspin began to whimper from the floor below. "Not now, little girl," he said, tossing her one of her favorite toys, "your daddies are about to get busy."

After DJ fell asleep, I stepped out onto the porch and sat on the front steps. Thoughts of the dream and the idea of past lives filled my head such that I couldn't fall asleep. I read Amber's book twice, actually, and was so absorbed in it—the wish for it to be true—that I zipped through it in one day... then decided to read it again. After all, it was written by a credible, well-educated psychologist, and that swayed my disbelief—a little.

I fantasized about the lives I might have had—exciting and lavish lifestyles in exotic lands. But the more I pondered, if rebirth was real I more than likely had a boring string of lives. Among seven billion people on the planet, not everyone can claim to have been Cleopatra.

Mom called more frequently after I moved to Decatur with DJ. Sometimes, she called when our favorite movie, *On Golden Pond* was on a station she knew I would have. We'd sit and watch together on the phone, intermittently quoting throughout. "That son of a bitch happens to be my husband," we would say along with Katherine Hepburn.

When I feared that DJ was cheating, I called her. "I don't tell you this to put you down, Mommy," I paced with the cordless to my ear. "I just don't want to have inherited your codependency. Your stubbornness is already too much."

"I wish I didn't have it to pass on," she chuckled.

"How do I know for sure? What if he is cheating? How did you find out about Dad? What do I do? I picked up everything and moved here because he asked."

"Slow down, Birdy," she tried to interject. "Joe and I are another story for another time. Let's just focus on you and DJ. These are just suspicions, right?"

"I got a real estate license for him and made a home for us." I was too frantic for tears until I looked down at Dropspin. "I even got a dog to keep me company when he's gone." It was true I got a real estate license, though it was too expensive to put it to use. It was a sense of pride to pass the state exam with a perfect grade, particularly since a woman with a local realtor predicted I'd fail. She taught the class for licensing and her two best students failed twice each. Who was I to do any better having only taken a correspondence course?

Mom summoned her mother-power to soothe through the phone. "Birdy, you're better than this. Stop worrying until there's certainty to worry. Men aren't worth it." Though I didn't address the irony of her being on her fourth marriage, I exhaled and thanked her for trying to make me feel better.

DJ went back to his parents' house for Christmas break and Amber moved in since the college apartments were closing. Without DJ, there was plenty of room for her and her synthesizer keyboard. The only rent I requested was that she play often.

We spent two weeks together, drank lots of wine and looked up everything we could about past lives. I was fascinated, but Amber was fanatic. Whenever she found a new story, she'd flail her arms about as she'd speak, and I joked that all of her stories came with choreography and required back-up dancers. Stacks of printouts lay beside the computer, and out of guilt she bought several reams of blank paper.

We happened upon the works of Dr. Ian Stevenson, a psychiatrist who researched past lives through the stories of children. He had an impressive body of evidence that suggested reincarnation should be taken seriously. I was fascinated, but I wasn't quite a believer like Amber. Though I was sure there had to be a scientific explanation, I surrendered myself to Amber's excitement. She talked about it more than musical theatre, which was her major in college. But, by the time she left the day before Christmas, I was just a bit ready to reclaim my solitude.

Not a day passed that I didn't spend considerable time thinking about the dream. If there was another side awaiting us at death, had I somehow stumbled across a memory of it? I hadn't died in my sleep, but the imagery in the dream compared well to various stories of near-death experiences Amber and I read.

Flipping through the channels on television was a buffet of psychics, infomercials and guest spots on talk shows. It was easy to get sucked in. After dismissing religion shortly after high school, I spent considerable time studying biblical errancy, and thus wanted to be able to debunk these various mediums and ghost whisperers. After all, they were all asking for money, and that didn't sit well with what few spiritual inclinations I did have. If psychics were real, why didn't Linda Georgian warn Dion Warwick about the eventual bankruptcy of *The Psychic Friends Network*?

I remembered a small house in a town nearby with a sign in the front yard that read, TAROT-PSYCHIC. There would be no harm in making a trip and getting a read, I thought. The most I'd be out was twenty bucks and time—cheap for a little investigation into the spirit world.

The door opened and a thin, pale skinned creature with long jet-black hair invited me in. She certainly looked the stereotypical part. I wanted to ask if she was Hilda Bauer.

"You want card read or tea leaf?" her thick accent added to the persona.

"Cards will be fine," I followed her to a table with two large black candles.

There was a fragrance in the air, flowery sweet and it would've given me a headache if I were to stay too long. She sat across from me and shuffled a deck of cards. They were regular poker cards and not the traditional tarot I had seen before, causing me to briefly wonder why she was using them.

"Sorry," she said as she watched herself shuffle.

"Excuse me?" I asked.

"Poker cards no offend Christian visitor. Tarot card devil they think."

"Wow," I said quietly. Did she read my mind? "What kind of Christian would visit a psychic anyway?" I asked. She didn't respond. The cards were laid slowly, one by one and she examined them, humming quietly.

"I see you have a problem with love," she caught my attention.

"Really? What problem?"

"No worry, problem going away soon." I was intrigued, but

certain that this was a generalization she used often.

"Yes, someone coming back to you. A love you have been missing." The back of my neck began to tingle. She couldn't be talking about DJ coming back from break, could she? She hummed a little bit as she laid a few more cards down. "Going to be very happy for long time."

I knew I was probably getting my hopes up, but I wanted to believe that this was real, and she had a mystical gift. I wanted this to be assurance DJ and I would last.

"Very beautiful, yes," she cooed over the cards.

Beautiful? Who describes guys as beautiful? I think he's cute, handsome, attractive. I wasn't going to give her an English lesson, so I waited for more.

"Yes, yes," she looked up at me with certitude. "She's beautiful, long blond hair, big boobs."

"She? Big boobs?"

"Yes, trust me. Beautiful lady from your past coming back. Long romance, long life together. Very nice boobies."

Every muscle in my face collapsed. "Ma'am, I'm gay."

Her hands quickly swept the cards toward her. "Whoops."

"Yeah, big whoops!" I sprung up and stormed out.

With the disappointment of that experience and Amber gone, I let the paranormal fade out of my interest over the next few months. DJ went home nearly every weekend and I sat in the window on Sundays waiting for him to return, always wondering how my mother's trait of codependency surface in me after scores of other boyfriends failed to reveal it. Each weekend he got back later and later, and it was emotionally frustrating. I tried to keep it bottled up, but would often blurt out an aggrieved protest to which he always offered a plausible excuse. To abate my unease, I started working with a couple of high school marching bands nearby, which took up two weekdays and every other Saturday and I planned to give them more time once summer began while DJ was on tour.

He left at the beginning of May. I had Dropspin to keep me company, but she lacked sufficient conversation skills, so I took to the computer to see if there were any social outlets I could explore. I signed up for an account with an LGBT chat site and started scrolling through the different usernames. Thankfully, there were no porn advertisements on this site, though there were plenty of personalities to make up for it. I had no idea how to go about meeting someone with purely platonic intentions on a chat site yet tried starting up conversations with random usernames. They never lasted long, or they turned explicit quickly.

Then, a username I instantly understood jumped out at me—Portquad—a type of rifle catch in color guard, so I assumed that this person was also involved in the marching arts. I named my dog Dropspin, which was also a color guard term—a flag maneuver. This would be an easy ice breaker, I thought!

That's how the best friendship of my life began, in a gay chatroom—of all places. Wyatt and I messaged back and forth for nearly an hour. I invited him over, and though it was after dinner and getting late he agreed to come. After a shower and a bowl of ice cream, I sat on the sofa awaiting his arrival. Danville, Illinois was just about an hour and a half away and looking at the clock I realized it might not have been such a great idea to meet on a weeknight so late. Everything would be closed, so we'd just have to make really good conversation, I thought. Staring at the television, my eyes got heavier, and heavier.

The sunlight from the window shone in my eyes, and I slowly stretched then sat up for a moment, feeling like there was something I should be doing. Suddenly, the realization that I fell asleep waiting for Wyatt hit me. If he showed up, he could have knocked on the door and I wouldn't have heard it. People have kicked me in the head while I'm sleeping, and I easily snoozed right through. I dialed his number hoping he would tell me that he had a sudden change of plans and stayed home last night.

"Yeah, I stood outside and knocked for a while," Wyatt recalled with a suspicious tone.

Oh, shit! I thought. I apologized and explained how I could sleep through an atomic bomb. Coaxing him with gas money for a second try he agreed and was at my doorstep two hours later.

"It's nice to meet you," I opened the door. "I promise I'll stay awake!"

The six-foot-two lean wire of a man with what could pass for an afro walked in and bent over to give Dropspin the attention for which she adorably barked. "I figured you must've fallen asleep, and I was afraid to knock on that window because I wasn't sure whose it was."

We sat down and started the usual small talk. He had also been in a drum corps, the same one that DJ was off touring with—a perfect ice breaker—and I was certain it was the reason he gave me a second chance. After about an hour, I led us to the kitchen and threw a quick meal together. He ate so quickly I was afraid he'd pass out from asphyxiation. I noticed his overbite as he talked and chewed, and he had the biggest cleft in his chin I'd ever seen. He was quite attractive, and the warmth of his personality was off the charts.

When I started to clear the table, he went to the sink and started washing the plates. "You don't have to..." I started.

"Nonsense," he interrupted. "You cooked so it's only right that I clean up."

We went into the front yard with our color guard equipment and started showing each other what we could do, throwing our flags and rifles in the air with impressive choreography underneath. He was very skilled and graceful, and was surprised that I never participated as a color guard performer, just a musician. Later, we took Dropspin for a walk, and I learned that he had a black toy poodle, as well. He loved that I named her Dropspin. "I should have named my dog Flagpole, or Trumpet instead of Buddy."

Wyatt was instructing color guards himself at several other schools. As he talked about his students and his philosophy, his face lit up like a Christmas tree. "I'm fiercely competitive, don't get me wrong," he said, "but at the end of the day it's just a bunch of musical instruments on a grass field. We're not curing cancer. So, for me the most important thing I think I do is give those kids a self-esteem and a good work ethic so they can go on in life and tackle anything that comes their way."

"That's one of the best ways I've ever heard it expressed—not curing cancer," I raised my glass. "Can I steal that from you?"

"Sure," he said, clanging his glass with mine. "It'll cost ya, though!"

Wyatt was the kind of person that actually talked his punctuation. If he wanted a word to be bold, it was. He'd tilt his head to italicize and used rabbit ears frequently. The best was when he would create a dramatic pause to represent a dash. But he would always speak out every ellipsis—*dot, dot, dot.*

By the end of the evening, I decided I wanted him to come work with me, and he was excited at the opportunity. The next morning, I called the three band directors for whom I worked and told them about him and, because they trusted me were ready to hire him immediately.

He wasted no time jumping in at our first rehearsal and we had an immediate chemistry playing off of one another as we instructed our students. His keen eye and charisma put me at ease with him, and that's saying a lot for a control freak of an instructor like me. The kids loved him, too. He'd add a touch of humor after demanding more out of them. "And just remember, if you drop your equipment, you work like hell to catch back up like it never happened! Then catch your breath, relax, and think 'Wyatt's pretty,' and you'll have a perfect show!"

We drove to Alton, Illinois to see DJ perform at the first contest of the season, and I got to introduce them to one another. That night on the way home, a very thick fog rolled in after midnight, and I tried to stay awake but failed as Wyatt was talking and white knuckling the steering wheel. He kindly chose not to mention it the next day.

By the end of the summer, Wyatt met a guy named Jason and their relationship moved surprisingly quickly. They made plans to move in together after just a month of dating. I thought it was quite a bit rushed but made no scolding as it wasn't my place. Gays often joke that on a second date gay men bring a U-Haul. I thought I was justified in my concerns when I asked Wyatt to do something with me one evening, to which his decline is famous among our friends:

"I can't," Wyatt said. "I'm going out with that guy."

"What guy?" I had no idea who he was talking about.

"You know," he was trying his hardest to remember. "That *one* guy."

I just stared at him. He started snapping his fingers, hoping to call to mind the name that was escaping him. "Oh, come on. The guy I'm going to move in with."

"*Jason?*" I asked in disbelief. "Wyatt, you can't remember your boyfriend's name and you're going to move in with him?"

"Child," his insouciant response began, "you're going to find out how absolutely shitty I am with names."

"But a boyfriend?" I wasn't buying the excuse.

"Seriously, I can remember almost every phone number I've ever been given and can remember just about every note I've ever played on a trumpet. But if that trumpet's name is Larry, I'll forget it even if I've played it for a decade."

And that was truly the case. Wyatt couldn't recall names very quickly, taking some moments of pause to get them out of his mouth. It's something quite interesting about him and continues to this day. For someone I have held in such high regard for his near perfection in my eyes, this is the only flaw—it's adorable.

Wyatt took me to his home in Danville often, and once when I flew to Denver to work with a marching band for a weekend, he took

DJ. There wasn't a shred of jealousy in my bones when I talked to them both on the phone, and they were sitting in the hot tub drinking cocktails. If ever there was ever a time to be jealous, it would be when my lover was saucing it up in a hot tub with another gay man.

When Wyatt and Jason finally moved to Colorado, DJ and I just started to fall apart. Wyatt moved in with DJ and me for a few weeks prior to the move, bringing with him an incredible dynamic to the house that inspired us to get along better than ever. Wyatt brings out the best in people, as long as he's not dating them. His boyfriends have always been *fixer-uppers* he thought he could reform or change. And he's not a fool—he knows just when to collect his losses, send them packing, and shake it off.

The night Wyatt and Jason left town I felt the absence immediately. Our time together hadn't been that long, but we managed to create three competitive shows together and made a lifetime of memories. I knew that I would miss him and worried that we'd eventually drift apart with only occasional phone calls and emails.

My suspicions that DJ had a secret life intensified. When he went away, his cell phone would be switched off, something he never did in my company. And when he returned from a trip to Indianapolis, I found in his pocket a phone number with a name beside it—Mark.

I called the number, confident that if there had been a one night stand this Mark wouldn't have had enough time to memorize DJ's voice—we were often mistaken for the other, even by our friends, over the phone. "Hey," the voice on the other end turned my stomach, but I was committed.

"I think I left my wallet at your house," imitating DJ as best I could.

"Let me look," Mark said. Confirming that DJ had been there. "Nope, I don't see it."

"That's okay," I said. Then, instead of hanging up the phone, impulsively asked, "Was I good last night?"

There was a pause. If nothing happened, he would be trying to figure out what I meant. "Yeah, I enjoyed myself. We could do it again sometime." My tears were given a green light, and I hung up the phone.

DJ was in the shower when I made the call. I cracked open the bathroom door and said, "I'm gonna go get us some lunch," then grabbed his keys—since my car was in the shop until the next day—and darted out the door. I drove to a nearby park and shut the car off, slumping onto the steering wheel in a flood of tears. I cried for about ten minutes, feeling jealous anger and intense loneliness then looked around the inside of his car for anything to wipe my nose on. There were some napkins under a notebook that I used, and as I sat the notebook down, on the backside was an email address that made me freeze with instant understanding. DJ adopted my love for two brilliant choreographers: Martha Graham and Bob Fosse. Seeing their conjoined last names as an email address, I instantly surmised that this was an account that DJ created without telling me... and I assumed there was good reason.

"Where's lunch?" DJ asked as I trudged through the doorway and collapsed in a chair, no possibility for him to sit beside me.

"Who's Mark?" I asked simply, the tears in my eyes indicating to him that I found the phone number. I said nothing else, giving him all the rope with which to hang himself.

He stared at me for a moment, then realized what was going on. "There you go again, Jellybean," he tried to sound soothing. "Making the worst out of something innocent."

"Explain," I didn't let on that I had called.

"He's just a guy I met with some friends over the weekend. We had some pretty amazing conversation about a musical theatre conservatory, and he gave me his number so we could share information about auditions and stuff."

I studied his face. He wasn't a good actor in the theatre department, could he be that good of a liar? The realization that I never asked Mark about sex directly, made my conviction weaken, and I found myself apologizing—for the time being. I still had that email address and was certain that I could figure out the password.

The next day while DJ was in class I sat at the computer and closed my eyes. I heard him say on many occasions to our friends that I knew him better than he knew himself. There I was, about to see if that was true—and it only took me three attempts to figure out the password and gain access to his emails. I read each and every one. They were messages to different guys nearby, sixty different men looking for sexual encounters—no other topic to anyone else, just hook-ups. Each message had phone numbers, directions to homes, and explicit messages to one another that were difficult to read. The dates spanned more than two years... since the time we had moved to Decatur. I printed out every single email and logged out of his account, hoping he wouldn't try to log in while on campus. He regularly came home for lunch, so I took the stack to the front porch where I could see down the street, giving me ample reaction time.

Then, I called them all. Every single phone number that was in those emails revealed everything. The suspicions I had over the past two years were not unfounded. I had been lied to and betrayed. Why on earth would someone do this when it's just as easy to be single and not destroy someone emotionally in the process? I wasn't rich, so the sugar daddy answer was a resounding "no."

While talking to one of the men, he was angry that DJ lied about his relationship status. He said that he'd like to be with me during the confrontation, and I agreed so that I could have a smoking gun that DJ couldn't explain away. That evening while we were home together, there was to be a phone call that hung up as soon as I answered—a signal that this guy had just crossed the railroad tracks two blocks away. That's when I was to start the interrogation.

DJ and I were sitting beside each other on the sofa when the call came, and it happened so quickly that there was no reason for DJ to ask anything. I counted to thirty in my head before speaking. "Are you sure you want to be in a relationship with me," I started. "After last night's accusation, and pretty much every time I've been accusatory?"

"I'm sure, Jellybean." He tenderly took and stroked the back of my hand, then leaned to kiss my cheek. "You're the only one I want."

"Are you absolutely sure?" I asked, trying to hide the anger that wanted to punch him square in the face.

"Honestly, Marc you're it. I love you and I will do anything to prove it to you."

The doorbell rang and DJ walked to the window. After peering through the curtains, he quickly turned to me with a look of horror and said, "I'll get this, stay right there."

"Who is it, DJ?" I asked percipiently.

He bolted into the vestibule, opened the door, and asked, "What the hell are you doing here?"

I took DJ by the wrist and pulled toward the living room, "It's okay, I invited him."

DJ huffed back into the house and sat angrily on the chair next to the sofa. "Would you like to introduce me," I asked with an anger that bypassed my heartbreak. He said nothing but stared at the floor. I went to the cushion upon which DJ was sitting just moments ago, turned it over, and withdrew the stack of emails I printed. "You should look at these," I threw them at him. "Might jog your memory."

The surprisingly unattractive guy just stood in the doorway. In a brief glance, I felt gratitude and disgust for him. I sized him up against me, wondering why my partner would have any encounter with him in my absence, other than as a customer at some filthy gas station he surely attended. I turned to him and said, "I'm sure seeing you standing there is enough confirmation, right DJ?"

"I just don't want to be in a relationship anymore," DJ said, eyes red with tears, surely from the fact that he got caught and not out of remorse for what he did to me. I motioned the guy away and he obliged.

"Who the hell are you?" I asked. "Do you remember what you just said to me only a few minutes ago? Do you?"

He sat in shock, unable to muster a word. I stood there, arms crossed and waiting for anything to be said or to happen—nothing. He had no song to sing to try to smooth it over. And I, for once, didn't back down as I exorcised the demon into plain sight. The tears running over my steel expression were the only betrayal to the pain I managed to withhold. There was no reason for us to continue any discussion of all that had been clearly revealed—it was the end. Grabbing my jacket, I dejectedly walked out the door, climbed into my car, drove off and slept in the park on a picnic table.

Almost hourly for the next two days, I called Al, crying into the phone. He practically commanded me to pack my things and get to his house immediately. I called Chris, having never asked him for anything since I moved out, and begged him to let me use his truck to move my belongings. He was the most kind I ever knew him to be. We met halfway to trade vehicles, and he gave me a long, consoling embrace.

A couple of hours before dinner, I was putting the last of my things into the truck when DJ returned from classes. I met him on the front porch and could see by his expression as he looked at the truck that he knew what was going on. "Come," I motioned for him to follow me through the house.

The place was bare. I placed all of DJ's things in the corner of the living room and only a few of my things still remained. Everything we had bought together was mangled in a pile in the dumpster, and I was certain he understood the symbolism. He walked to the kitchen and opened the cabinets. "One plate, one bowl, one cup?" Then quickly opened the drawers, "One fork, one spoon, one knife?"

"You didn't think I'd accommodate any dinners for two without me, did you?" I quickly shot back.

After an hour, I finished my packing. "This is it," I said, knowing there would be no goodbye embrace.

"Yeah," was all he could get out of his mouth. Staring at him as we were bathed in the orange glow of the sunset much like the one from our first kiss, I was hoping that he would miss me, that he would feel so much guilt that it would consume him. But he didn't. I shook my head and turned to leave.

"His fucking name was Mark!" I cried out with my back to him. "Didn't that sound familiar?" I knelt to gather my strength, crying harder than any other time in my life. Without any compassion, he refused to budge and didn't utter a sound. He was just ready for me to go.

So, I did.

PART II
SAMUDAYA: THE TRUTH OF THE ORIGINS OF SUFFERING

What is the noble truth of the source of suffering? It is craving which produces rebirth, and which is accompanied by passionate desire, and which is total delight with or attachment to this and that.

—*The Buddha*

The second truth that the Buddha taught in Sarnath was the Noble Truth of the Origins of Suffering. Throughout his teachings about the origins of our suffering condition is an exhausting examination of cause and effect. From our ignorance that fails to see the ultimate nature of reality, we create karma, which means actions of body, speech, and mind, that result in equal and opposite reactions that can be pleasant, unpleasant, or neutral.

To put it simply, any unpleasant experience that we have is a result of an earlier cause. Somewhere, somehow, we are responsible for the negative events that we experience. Thankfully, we are also responsible for the joyful events and relationships in our lives. This is often difficult to accept because what we observe to be happening on the level of appearances actually may have richer, more detailed relationships on more subtle levels.

Tibetan Buddhist philosophy breaks reality into three basic layers: obvious, hidden, and deeply hidden. On the obvious level, our senses suffice. Throwing a rock at a window and shattering it into hundreds of pieces of broken glass can be seen by anyone with healthy, functioning eyes. Hidden reality requires a line of reasoning, like deducing the presence of fire from seeing smoke, or that sound is non-static or impermanent. Deeply hidden phenomena are those that require a kind of faith in authoritative texts or speech of the enlightened words of a Buddha or someone considered to be valid sources of information. The location of a hidden treasure, the existence of other dimensions, or the subtle workings of cause and effect are examples.

Padmasambhava, a Buddhist saint of the ninth century, said,"If you want to know about your past lives, look at your current situation. If you want to know about your future lives, look at your current actions." Modern psychology looks for early childhood causes for mental disturbances and phobias that we experience in adulthood and attempt to work them out by facing them and understanding them. Reflecting on our past life experiences that are the causes of effects we experience later in life help us understand how to make better decisions and avoid unwanted results.

✦ Chapter Five ✦

The morning sun shone through the half-window of my room with a failed attempt to cheerlead me out of slumber. Through the relationship I grew accustomed to opening my eyes in the morning to look over at DJ, deep in sleep, and stare at his face, memorizing the soft curves of his cheeks, the stubble on his chin, and the airtight eyelids that curtained the dark green circles whose power to entrance I had fallen into many times. Months after it ended, I would wake unevolved feeling like I did the day it happened. My hand caressed the space he used to occupy, wanting him there more than wanting him out of my life. The freshness of morning, the blankness of the page upon which we are to write the destiny of the day hides histories that slowly emerge as the blood quickens, like the invisible ink on parchment slowly becoming visible from a close lit candle, and my tears began their morning ritual of remembering the reason for the vacancy at my side.

After a quick stretch, I grabbed the notebook to write some details I remembered from the night before while reflecting on meeting Wyatt and the last days of the breakup with DJ. Every time I recalled those final events, it was like ripping stitches from a fresh suture still healing. It said in Laura's book that it usually takes people about half the time that a relationship lasts to get over it once it dissolves. So, I had a little relief that several months into it the feelings I had were textually verified. I considered Wyatt's advice that a vacation from all of my compounded stresses was needed and decided to visit a familiar little get-a-way.

A free day from rehearsals and competitions allowed me to steal away to the park in the country between Kokomo and Greentown where I would sit by the Wildcat Creek Reservoir, spinning around in the DJ Circle. As a kid on my ten-speed, I often rode there in the predawn hours, weather permitting. Nestled among Hoosier cornfields, a long entryway led away from the country road and to a grassy haven, complete with picnic tables and a church with its reflection on the water, reminiscent of paintings by Andrew Newell Wyeth.

When the water was low, I walked the shoreline and found little memoirs from fishermen past, little trinkets and trash the locals discarded recklessly into the reservoir. I often invented histories in my mind of how these things found their way into the mud—a story of a little girl, for example, whose elephant charm bracelet slipped from her tiny wrist and disappeared under a disappointing splash.

The park had a large, wooded area beyond the parking lot with an adjacent inlet. About a half-mile walk around what I called "the lagoon" led to miles of trails in the woods that I could explore for hours, through the aroma of each season—perfumes of spring, humidity and my sunburnt sweat of summer, decaying leaves of fall, and in winter, hints of wood burning stoves in the air coupled with the cold salty snot from my nose. Mornings there were among the quietest I've found in Indiana. I saw countless sunrises alone, aside from the occasional retiree with their dog on the trails. This was my refuge through the years, my escape from a busier world where I could take in a clean breath and leave my troubles at the gate.

The breakup stole my smile, and it made me less trusting of anyone new. In social events and staff meetings I remained quiet—hoping I'd appear pensive. But gossip spreads quickly in the small world of the marching arts, and my fake appearances failed.

One morning after a shower, I heard a high-pitched laugh coming from my bedroom. The Dalai Lama being interviewed on a morning talk show momentarily charmed the weight from my chest. I knew almost nothing about him, though I hadn't missed the "FREE TIBET" stickers on nearly every Jetta I saw.

"We are same human being," he said again and again with a voice that danced a wide range of pitch. "We are social animal, we need more compassion, more warm-heartedness." The first smile in months started to stretch across my face, momentarily chasing away my usual gloom. But at the commercial break the smile quickly vanished. "Probably like all the other religious whackos—*money, money, money.*" I turned off the set and went about getting dressed.

Several days later, a kiosk in the bookstore dedicated to the Dalai Lama easily grabbed my attention through its life-sized poster of him standing on top; no one could miss it. That joyful smile coaxed my own again, and I said to myself, "Alright, what do you have to offer besides incense and bonsai trees?" I picked up one of the books from the variety on display. *There is a disparity between the way things appear and the way they actually exist*—were the first words I read. "Yes, yes," I said to myself." Like a lover who appears loyal but is actually a cheating whore."

I stood skimming the pages, intrigued that there wasn't some message of salvation if we just give ourselves to the holy church of *Boo-dah*. In fact, there wasn't a single familiar characteristic of what I knew of religion and worship. It was a small book, devoted to the core philosophy of Buddhism, the *Four Noble Truths*, and I opened up to a section explaining the origins of suffering—according to Buddhism.

> *Once we appreciate that fundamental disparity between appearance and reality, we gain a certain insight into the way our emotions work, and how we react to events and objects. Underlying the strong emotional responses we have to situations, we see that there is an assumption that some kind of independently existing reality exists out there.*

Reflecting back on the relationship, had I seen the reality of who he was and his behaviors from the beginning, would it have changed my emotions? Would I have reacted differently to what the reality was? I wasn't sure that was the case... and what did *out there* mean.

> *"... although certain types of mental or emotional states seem so real, and although objects appear to be so vivid, in reality they are mere illusions. They do not really exist in the way we think they do."*

These words jolted me, causing me to reread it several times. My eyes began to dart around at every sight in my vision, checking to see if everything was still there. Illusions? A moment of simultaneous understanding and terror flashed through my mind, ever so briefly, but compelling. It was as though someone had just shone a light in a darkened room, then abruptly turned it off. Quickly paying for the book and dashing out to my car, I read almost half of it right there in the parking lot, as enthralled as a scientist on the verge of a discovery. I had poured through the book Laura gave me, unsuccessfully analyzing everything in my history to find causes that I could connect to my current situation. But this book was pointing out to me the biggest key factor that I never considered—there's something wrong with the way I think!

Back at home, I memorized that statement and recited it aloud in my room many times, pacing back and forth just the way I did when I would rehearse my lines during my thespian years. But this was beyond portraying an O'Neil character, or a singing florist with a man-eating plant; it was a complete shift in my worldview, as if I was looking at the world through backward binoculars and someone kindly just came and turned them around! An article in a Buddhist magazine I found online elaborated this concept further. Things that we see and experience that we think are *out there*, are really holographic images our brain uses to engage them. In other words, our poor little brain, the actual *us* that controls our experiences is trapped behind the confines of our protective, bony skulls.

This is what religion should be, I thought. If there was a divine plan it wouldn't be to create a world of door-to-door pamphlet pushers and get angry for nudity after sending us all here naked! *No!* This was a manual that was showing me exactly how my mind worked, and for the first time I saw that the world *out there* is really the world *in here*, infected by my own past experiences that I project onto it. If there had been a Buddhist priest nearby, I would have converted that very day!

Aside from Angela Bassett as Tina Turner teaching the world *nam-myoho-renge-kyo* in *What's Love Got To Do With It*, I knew little about the teachings of the Buddha. I was a huge Tina Turner fan, thanks to Mom. She gave me the album Private Dancer for my thirteenth birthday, and I fell instantly in love. I bought all of Tina's albums and saw her perform a concert during my college days. When her biographical movie came out, I saw it in theaters several times. I read up on her experiences with Buddhism and wanted to be one, too, not knowing a shred of what that meant. Hell, I never even read a sutra nor knew they existed.

By the next day, I finished reading the little book. The Dalai Lama referenced several ancient Buddhist texts throughout, and I took note of them, ready to search for them at the bookstore. But these *root texts*, as they are called, weren't translated and marketed as well as the variety of self-help books that people flocked to. So, I settled for another book by His Holiness, took it with me to the little park in the country and dug in.

I danced into Al's office one morning after reading the second book, slaloming cats and my prancing little poodle, with the excitement of Doc Brown explaining something to Marty McFly. "I know what's wrong with me!" I grabbed at his shirt, pulling him away from the computer. "There's something wrong with the way I think!"

"Who let the cat out of the bag?" he laughed.

"Seriously, imagine that you wake up and your heart is beating wildly. You know that that shouldn't happen, and think, 'There's something wrong with my heart.' So, you go see a doctor. Or if you wake up and your hand is twitching uncontrollably..."

"Hey! I take haloperidol for that!" he jokingly quipped about his Tourette's medicine, reaching blindly for his coffee mug while vigorously shaking his hand with comedic exaggeration.

"Sorry but try to get what I mean. You'd say, 'There's something wrong with my hand,' right? How many people actually look at their minds and question, 'Is there something wrong with the way I think?'"

He paused and looked reflective. "That's actually a good question. Wouldn't that be what Descartes meant when he said, *I think, therefore I am*?"

"No, no! Our real issue is *I think, therefore I... am right*!" I started to laugh. "But we're not right! Everything we see is merely an illusion. What does it actually look like outside of this brain?" He stared at me for a few moments, most likely more intrigued by my excitement than what it was that excited me.

"I know you're an atheist, too," I said as I calmed myself and sat on the maroon carpeted floor, corralling Dropspin with my legs, "but do you know anything about Buddhism?"

"He's fat and bald," Al joked. I admit to having the same ignorance, having not seen a real image of the Buddha myself. In fact, that little fat monk seen on display at China Wok in the middle of a water feature full of gold and white koi *was* Buddha to me, and countless ignorant others.

"Have you ever read any of his teachings?" I asked. "Maybe in a college religions course? He sounds like he might have been the first... psychologist."

"Nope," his attention turned back to his work on the computer. "Isn't there a Buddhist temple in Indy?" I didn't know.

Later, when I found a listing for a Zen temple online, I excitedly dialed the number. After introducing myself and stating my interest to learn more about the Dharma, a sleepy baritone voice replied, "Monthly membership is forty dollars..." and then I allowed his voice to trail away as I was completely turned off. *Money, money, money*! I slumped back on the futon, exasperated.

Dropspin jumped on my lap and started her barrage of sloppy, wet kisses. "I wonder what you *actually* look like out there, baby girl.

I think I see you on my lap... but Buddha says I only and always see you in my head."

Over the next few months, my routine enthusiastically made room for as much reading of Buddhist books as I could, keeping a notebook nearby to write down key principles to remember and analyze. The growing list of Sanskrit and Latin terms used by the philosopher translators was aggravating, but so many authors repeated them, and it was apparently a vernacular I needed to learn to benefit from their writings. "*Klesha*," I said aloud, sitting in the warm sunshine, scribbling in my notebook, "means... mental affliction. *Samsara* means cyclic existence. *Dukkha* means suffering." I paused and looked at the long list of terms. "Jesus, the irony of more unnecessary suffering! Why not just translate every word into English?"

Buddhism is divided into what are called the Two Vehicles: Hinayana and Mahayana. These are kind of like denominations in Christianity—with less superstition and no quest for world domination. The Hinayana is said to be a worldview focused on achieving liberation from suffering for oneself alone, while the Mahayana is focused on freeing all beings from suffering. At first blush, it would seem that the Mahayana is superior—Hinayana translates to *Lesser Vehicle* and Mahayana translates to *Greater Vehicle*—but this isn't the case. It's more about capacity than it is about superiority. Imagine that two people attend the same college to earn a degree: the Hinayana student would be earning the degree for their own career, whereas the Mahayana student is an education major, seeking a degree that will allow them the capacity to teach others how to earn a degree too.

Many times, a line would strike me as so profound that I would fall into a trance, examine its simple sophistry, and try to adopt its wisdom. Shantideva, a Buddhist master of the seventh century stated,

> *Unruly beings are as limitless as space;*
> *They cannot possibly all be overcome.*
> *If I overcome my anger alone,*
> *This will suffice in vanquishing all enemies.*

It was such an obvious and overlooked point of view, like a secret that was left out in the open for all to see yet missed by every onlooker. Remove the very concept of enemy and all that remains is a world full of friendships, some yet to be met. Such gentleness was an attitude I thought to be out of my reach, especially since I liked to brag about my red-headed Taurean temper. Memorizing these lines was an initiation into a whole new way of looking at the world, and it contrasted the many pathways that led to dissatisfaction with which I had habituated. And something about this worldview reminded me of John, a modern day Shantideva.

Expounding upon this idea, the Buddha said,

> *He who seeks his own happiness*
> *By inflicting pain on others,*
> *Is never freed from adversaries,*
> *For he begets more enemies.*

My own emotional torment proved the truth of these words, self-diagnosing the vagaries to which DJ and I succumbed. There was a growing anger and hatred in me for someone I once loved more than myself... and I shuddered to think of what emotional changes he experienced with his thoughts about me.

The more I read and memorized, the less frequently I would cry myself to sleep each night. Repeating stanzas like I was memorizing lines from a musical, I would slowly fade, sputter to a close, and subsequently slip into slumber. It seemed to be a good remedy, but the pain was merely numbed, its presence suppressed just below the surface, waiting for any chance to spring up and break me down. This process of replacing my spinning depressed thoughts with the excitement of this new doctrine wasn't dissimilar from a method employed by AA in turning to a higher power. Never having been an alcoholic myself, I did know people who had attended meetings, and in college I learned about the origins of the organization and their methods. I didn't believe in some unseen transcendent agency, as they seemed to promote, but I did seek my answers and comfort in the Three Jewels, nonetheless.

The Three Jewels are the centerpiece of all of Buddhism—the Buddha, the Dharma, and the Sangha. The Buddha is the historical teacher, Shakyamuni—*not* the fat bald guy. His teachings are often referred to as the Dharma, but the Dalai Lama explains that Shakyamuni does not own Dharma, as there have been others before him. And the Sangha, often mistaken in the West to just be a substitute word for *congregation*, is actually the robed monastics and *not* the laity. As His Holiness said, "The laity make offerings to the Three

Jewels, they do not make offerings to the laity."

There was nothing anyone could say that would make me believe in invisible beings offering protection and a better afterlife, but I found the analogy of the Buddha as a doctor, the Dharma as a medicine, and the Sangha as other medical practitioners, like pharmacists and nurses, a better descriptor for me to accept than anything resembling myth. One master named Arya Maitreyanatha said,

> *Just as a disease must be recognized and its cause abandoned,*
> *And just as the state of joy must be attained and the medicine consumed,*
> *So, respectively, are suffering, its cause, liberation, and the path,*
> *To be recognized, abandoned, attained, and realized.*

Getting a glimpse at how vast and detailed the teachings were, I studied assiduously in order to digest this mental medicine, sitting for hours at the park fully absorbed and engaged, reflecting on the Dharma.

Wyatt called one day on my way to a rehearsal and said that he and Jason were moving back to Danville. I was ecstatic. "How do you feel about driving two hours to come work with some of my schools?" I asked.

"Child," he started, "you have no idea how much I would love to do that."

"Indiana schools spend a lot on marching band, so I'm sure you would be paid for your time on the road, too."

Just then, I pulled into a restaurant drive-thru and he jokingly scolded me as I ordered. "Lady, you've got a thirty-inch waist and some nice triceps you can't afford to lose if you're ever going to go husband shopping again!"

As I sat waiting for my order, one of the workers kept coming to the window to check me out. Eventually, he popped his head out and said, eyes flirting, "Hey."

"Hello there," I replied flirtatiously, which caused his milky white cheeks to flush.

"We're just waiting on your fries, but you can wait right here." The aroma of flame broiled meat mixed with a sexy scented cologne—two different but equally delightful smells—wafted into the air as he held the window open.

"I'd love to. Take all the time you need," I said with a big grin.

"They'll be hot and fresh," he said almost stuttering.

"Hot and fresh sounds right up my alley," I flirted.

"What is going on?" Wyatt screamed through the phone, and I nonchalantly clicked the off button and placed it in my lap. This guy was adorable! Big blue eyes, dark hair, pale skin, and full pink lips that gave a vampire vibe. I thanked him, but kept watching him move around inside, turning to look at me again and again.

When he reached out with my sack, he whispered, "Your receipt is attached. You'll want that." He had jotted his name and number on the slip of paper—ANDY.

"I hope it'll come in handy," I said as I pulled away. I called Wyatt back quickly and yelled, "Nothing helps getting over a guy like another guy giving you his digits!"

If only it really was that easy. Thoughts of DJ hammered at me in rehearsal, even with the music playing loudly through the speaker system. After everything that he put me through, I still felt a sense of guilt for not just being flirted with, but actually flirting back. "You're single, Marc," I coached myself that evening driving home. Pulling the receipt from my pocket—*ANDY*—I punched the number into my cell phone. "I need this," I repeated aloud as the phone rang.

Andy pulled into the drive around 10pm and I invited him to the backyard to sit on the deck of the pool with me. I had a couple of beers chilled and some citronella candles keeping the mosquitos away.

"I'm really glad you called," he said shyly, finding it strangely at odds with the boldness he displayed at the drive-thru window.

"Me, too. I haven't had someone give me their number in quite a long time."

He looked puzzled. "Why not? I mean, you're hot."

My eyebrows nearly launched off my face. No one ever referred to me in such a way. Even DJ used words like cute, and handsome. "You should have those eyes checked," I took a swig of beer. "So are you."

"So... what do you do?" the typical question came out slowly.

"I work with marching bands. I'm a color guard choreographer."

"I was in marching band! Alto sax," he interjected. "How um... how old are you? Not that it matters!"

I laughed. "I'm understandably scared to answer that. The dating market only has room for those under 24."

"Whew! I'm 21," he laughed, then quickly feared that he erred. "But age doesn't bother me!"

I readied for a response of shock. "I celebrated my 30th last year—by having a three way."

"Really?" not indicating to which part shocked him more.

"Yup! Me, Ben, and Jerry." He chuckled with relief. "So, thirty doesn't bother you?"

"Why should it? It's just a number. Besides, you don't look it at all."

I did look younger than my age and teachers regularly asked for my hall pass while walking to the band rooms at my various schools.

"I can't believe you haven't been snatched up by anyone yet," I reached over and rubbed the back of his hand.

"Well, I've just gotten out of a relationship," he turned his hand over and started playing with mine. "It's a long story."

"So have I," I said. "And it's pretty long, as well."

For a moment, I felt a little less alone in the world of break-up depression after hearing him talk about how he was still trying to recover, too. After a couple of hours, I walked him to his car and after a clumsy attempt at making a first move, kissed him goodnight and agreed to call him the next day. He jokingly thanked our exes for breaking the ice for an evening of exploratory conversation, and as his taillights rounded the corner my smile faded, doused by his parting reminder. Once again, DJ snatched what little bit of joy the night created. I fell asleep in a puddle of tears.

Though I didn't surrender any of my morning studies, I fit time with Andy into my late nights after rehearsals. He'd engage with me in conversation about the topics on which I had read in my morning by the Reservoir. His intellectual appeal was different than my experiences with other boyfriends, most being superficially absorbed and mentally vapid. In their defense, I wasn't much in the way of intellectual depth for them, either. I hadn't yet fallen in love with my mind... and the average cocktail-holding piece of eye candy on the dance floor wasn't easily turned on with Voltaire or Hugo. Andy was my first boyfriend to arouse me in such a way.

Another night while we were sitting at a restaurant, I tested his intelligence with a fascinating thought I'd found in my readings. "Where do you see this, Andy?" I asked, holding up my cell phone.

"In your hand?" he chuckled a little sheepishly.

"Nope," I said, with the confidence of a fine magician. "You only see it in your head! The way the phone exists in my hand is something we can never really see!"

"What?" he was just as gobsmacked as I had been. "That's freaky!" He took my phone and examined it, his wheels spinning away. "That's amazing, and really profound."

"The really screwed up part," I continued, "is that we're only seeing a mental image, and that mental image of the phone, or whatever, is superimposed with our past experiences."

"So, we don't really know what's out there," he said with a hint of childlike awe. "We're really only seeing our own mind, in a way. Man, western psychology is really in its infancy." The power of such a simple truth cannot be overstated. I went home that night and threw Laura's book, my notes, and lists into the garbage.

Over the course of about six months, I read nearly fifty books, captivated by the scientific nature in which Buddhism explained the causes for the vicissitudes of life. Science served me well in debunking Christianity in my twenties—which eliminated my shame for being gay. Actually, I often joked that being gay eliminated my need for religion. Trying to make sense of my sexual orientation—that I didn't choose—in a world that said I was doomed for hellfire was a journey straight people don't have to experience mostly because those are their parameters—against people like me. Studying the sources of that worldview to prove that I wasn't a loveless monster was liberating. As Isaac Asimov said, "*Properly read, the Bible is the most potent force for atheism ever conceived.*"

It was refreshing to discover that Buddhism has always embraced skepticism, and with spirituality I had much of which I was skeptic. Besides having my mind thoroughly blown with what I called the *intellectual weapon of mass destruction*—which Andy agreed was an accurate label—I found in that first book, a key factor that kept me reading and analyzing was the confidence by which Shakyamuni Buddha invited his disciples to analyze his own teachings. Christianity discouraged any notion of doubt, hence the derogation *Doubting Thomas*. Buddha's entreaty was worth memorizing:

> O bhikshus and wise men, just as a goldsmith would test his gold by burning, cutting, and rubbing it, so you must examine my words and accept them, but not merely out of reverence for me.

The Dalai Lama often remarked on the foundational necessity of logic and reasoning in Buddhism, which is the first thing the young monks study—they're called *tsenyipa* in Tibetan, and it means "one who studies definitions." He described the ancient Indian tradition of debate used by the monks in the monastic courtyards and I found plenty of videos online of Tibetan monks paired up and engaged in the practice. One monk would sit and calmly respond to his attacker who would clap and stomp loudly as he delivered his arguments, theatrically pulling his rosary up his arm for traditional symbolism that represented lifting all beings out of suffering states. It sent me into daydreams, seeing myself dressed in a maroon and saffron robe—though with a full head of hair—yelling and stomping logical syllogisms at a debate partner.

I frequently opened my college texts trying to remember the Latin terms into which some of the Buddhist translators tried to equate the Sanskrit. Many authors chose to create an endless list of Sanskrit terms, and it continued to rub me the wrong way, since most of the authors supposedly received their education from Tibetan masters. It just seemed like a slap in the face to them. Wouldn't translating these terms into English—as the Indian masters helped the Tibetans to translate them into Tibetan—facilitate conveying the wisdom of the teachings, I again wondered? Reading about the *Five Skandhas* in one book as I sat in the park, my frustration erupted, "You translated *five* but not *skandha*?"

Impermanence is a ubiquitous topic in Tibetan Buddhism. A brilliantly colorful picture book of Tibet illustrated it woven into the culture, art, architecture, and ceremonies of the Tibetan people—the most famous of which was the sand mandala. Monks spend days painstakingly placing vibrantly colored sand in deliciously detailed designs within a circular frame. Specks of silicate synergistically render an image like a three-dimensional George Surat. Then after a ceremony around which the mandala is featured, a master ritualistically dismantles it and monks sweep the sand into a vessel to be emptied into a nearby body of water. The destruction of something so detailed and beautiful is reminiscent of the death and impermanence of every individual living creature.

This resonated within me deeply, as my career in the marching arts was much like building a sand mandala—all the work, planning, instructing, and designing that goes into a performance that lasts about six and a half minutes, a brief moment in time, that then disappears into the past. "I've been teaching impermanence and didn't even realize it!" I shouted aloud one morning by the reservoir.

Various masters throughout Tibetan and Indian history completed their meditations on death and impermanence in cremation grounds, something a bit morbid for my American brain. It boggled me that something as such could be part of a path that leads to the freedom of suffering and to lasting happiness. A cemetery is hardly a place for a party, I thought.

And meditation—I had no idea what this animal was. Every book mentioned it, but I hadn't found any that explained precisely how to do it. Guided meditations I found on the internet and on a few CDs I purchased were too weird with their ASMR style voices that tried to hypnotize me. They just made me giggle. The image of someone sitting cross-legged while holding that stereotypical Hindu gesture with their hands turned me off but seeing an image of His Holiness sitting in meditation with his hands in his lap intrigued me. What was going on in his mind, what was he thinking, I wondered?

The Dalai Lama listed six preliminaries to meditation: clean the room and set up a shrine, make offerings, sit in the *Seven Point Posture of Vairochana*, visualize being surrounded by all the masters of the lineage throughout history, recite what is known as a seven-limb prayer, and request holy beings to teach and guide you—I chose to omit the last two parts.

The *Seven Point Posture of Vairochana* was explained in *Stages of Meditation*, by Master Kamalashila:

> *Then, they should seat themselves on a comfortable seat, either in the full lotus posture of Vairochana or the half-lotus posture. Their eyes should not be open too wide, nor too tightly closed, but focused on the tip of the nose. Their body should not be bent forward or backward, but kept straight, and their attention turned inwards. Their shoulders should rest evenly, and the head should not be tilted back or forward or to either side. The nose should be in line with the navel. The teeth and lips should rest in their natural state, and the tongue should touch the upper palate. Inhalation and exhalation should be just barely discernable, gentle, soft and natural, without undue noise, effort or agitation.*

I bought a statue of the Buddha—a candle stand, actually—from Walmart and set up a sacred place on my étagère. A Buddhist altar should have an image of the Buddha, something called a stupa—a reliquary representing the enlightened mind—and sacred texts beside it. Lighting a candle as an offering—not on the statue where it was designed to hold one, but in front of the Buddha—I placed several books beside it on the shelf, a small photograph of the Mahabodhi Stupa in Bodhgaya, and sat cross-legged for the first time, motionless, listening to the silence.

At first it was nice to just let go. But after a while, my mind started to feel like it was swatting at invisible bees, racing all over the place and wouldn't stop... thinking. I listened to my breath, but the voices wouldn't abate. I thought about DJ and the last day together, a rehearsal from earlier in the week, grocery store items that I forgot to get, and a song one of my marching bands was playing in their show. It was louder in my brain than it was in my room! Am I doing something wrong, I wondered? I opened my eyes and looked at my watch. To my amazement it had been less than five minutes. Discouraged, I stood up, blew out the candle, and went to the backyard to stare at the stars.

With Wyatt back in Illinois and driving over to work with me four times a week, I had greater enthusiasm to go to rehearsals since he would be there. However, I was coming to realize that I was just going through the motions with Andy and couldn't shake DJ. Coming out of the emotional abuse had a cost: realizing the truth about all the good memories that constituted the value of my loss—the recognition of the deception behind each snapshot in my mental photo album. *Things appear differently than they actually are.* I didn't just lose a partner and best friend; I lost any joy in reminiscence.

Surprisingly, I didn't make any assumptions about Andy's life away from mine, though, sadly he was a rebound to whom I couldn't fully commit. He was a terrific guy, and to be honest one of the best I ever dated. But our timing was off. No matter how I sliced him—his looks, his mind, his heart—he ranked high among my list of past lovers. However, whenever we talked about the future, he had little vision, few dreams. "I don't have a lot of hope of doing much better than the BK," he said to me once during his lunch break. "Maybe save enough money and open a club one day... maybe."

Andy came from a small Indiana town, like me. An opportunity like any I was blessed with, like touring the country or going to college hadn't tumbled into his life. After a few months, I ended it with him, amicably I thought. The shame of infecting him with my break-up germs made me sicker. Comparing anyone to what I thought I once had with DJ was a diagnosis for failure—and it was just unfair. He wasn't DJ, and that was that.

Breaking up with Andy wasn't easy, but it gave me more time for my Dharma addiction. I was feasting through books in the morning and needed another quick inoculation before bedtime. The masters of Buddhist history were my doctors, and their words and activities indicated a prescription I needed. Without a guru of my own, I went about seeking *over-the-counter Dharma*—I jokingly referred to my independent spiritual studies, haphazardly pulling random Buddhist books from the bookstore shelves like cough syrup from the drug store without a doctor's prescription. The growing presence of Buddhist teachings on the internet presented a feast for my curiosity. I learned not just about Buddhism, but the history of the Dalai Lama, the Chinese invasion, the beautiful stories of the Tibetan people, and a wealth of instruction videos on meditation.

"There are three types of meditation for a beginner," a young Tibetan teacher explained in one video "*Shar-gom, che-gom, juk-gom.* Shar-gom means review meditation, or memorization. Memorize what you're going to meditate on. *Che-gom* is analytical, this means sitting completely still and silently thinking about your meditation topic without the distractions of bodily movements. And *juk-gom* is like familiarizing yourself with unshakeable concentration."

A voice off-camera asked, "Which is best?"

"Analytical meditation is best for making transformation, so *che-gom* should be your focus. Analyze the teachings. Perhaps, spend as much time on Death and Impermanence as you can, maybe for months or even years. You need to have a deep realization, not just from casually reading about these things in a book. If you analyze it deeply, and reflect on it often, you will have amazingly freeing transformation."

The young teacher also cleared up another misconception that I frequently encountered. Many of the meditation CDs placed an emphasis on mindfulness and each soft-spoken voice said to be mindful of the sounds and sensations while sitting peacefully, breathing deeply, and having an open heart and mind. The problem with this approach, according to the monk—who I assumed would have far more authentic and authoritative training than the teachers on the CDs—was that meditation is an inner mental discipline and no matter how peacefully you sit while listening to birds chirping outside, all one is accomplishing is listening practice.

I started going to my grandmother's grave at least once a week to contemplate death and impermanence, just as Milarepa, Naropa, and other renowned masters meditated near cremation grounds. If they thought it to be important who was I to think I could do without this practice? Looking at her headstone—Mildred Wasson—I felt cold, lost in my memories of her. After a few weeks of regular meditations there, a realization shocked me, like sitting on a live wire. There in Albright Cemetery, looking at that headstone, a voice in my head said, "*You will be here one day.*" I looked at the dates under her name—seventy-two years of walking this earth, creating a family and memories, then passing away. Below me in a long box was a rotting library of her life. And she was surrounded by a village of death settled just six feet below my ass. I would one day be a citizen of this city, and it shook me to the core.

I sprung to my feet in a panic, pacing over her grave wildly. "Forty-one years left until I reach your age!" I shouted aloud. I already lived thirty-one years, a measure I could now use to calculate going forward. "This is terrifying! How is *this* going to help me find happiness?"

Just after plopping back onto the little maroon cushion, a monarch butterfly flitted around my head, landing on the headstone and slowly pulsed its wings up and down. I paused to enjoy its beauty and after a moment, every internal voice silenced, and I fell into a fully absorbed examination of this little marvel. For a moment it seemed as though those tiny little eyes were peering back at me, communicating to a deeper part of Marc Moss. There was no time, no space, no subject, no object. For just a moment, these two souls driving two totally different vehicles of flesh met and vibrated into each other their essence. After its requisite divine offering, the little flecks of orange and black trailed over the sleeping necropolis and gifted me the joy of living, sitting in a sea of death.

This must be what those masters discovered! And the importance of this initial meditation on the Buddhist path is transformative. Knowing I was going to die one day wasn't a secret, that fact was etched in stone around me. But the spouse of death is life. Every single creature with consciousness is born and eventually dies. The awareness that death can come at any time gives immeasurable value to every little moment that life still flows in you—even so simple as enjoying the beauty of a butterfly.

"Have you ever thought about death?" I asked Al the next morning in his office. "Like, about your own death?"

"I try not to," he sat for a moment before turning away from his computer. "There was a cemetery behind our house growing up. It terrified me."

In 1996, I accompanied him to Madison, Wisconsin for his father's interment. He took me by the brown and cream cottage style two-story he once called home. His mother lost her battle with cancer and laid beneath the earth as young Al tried to sleep just meters away. I saw the fear in his eyes as he laid his father to rest by her side but thought it nothing more than a man who was just orphaned.

"In my grandmother's cemetery this morning I had a profound experience thinking about my own death," I said, which prompted a disapproving scowl from the man who had intercepted me from suicidal thoughts. "No, not like that," I reacted. "I've just been reading about the importance of death and impermanence in Buddhist meditation and I think it makes sense now."

"It's scary," he emphasized.

Perhaps, but if we recognize that every one of our precious moments that we create in life could be taken away in a flash it might make us pour ourselves into them more and let go of distractions from full awareness of them. I practiced it in front of him, taking in as many details of my surroundings as I could, wondering if I could draw his fears onto myself. He was unmoved and wanted no more talk about death.

✤ Chapter Six ✤

One morning searching the internet for all things Tibetan Buddhist, I discovered that the Dalai Lama's brother, Jigme Norbu, lived in Bloomington for nearly forty years. He was a high reborn spiritual master of Tibet himself, having the title Takster Rinpoche. Rinpoche means *precious* in Tibetan, and it is the title reserved for those teachers that have been reborn again to help all sentient beings. They are emanations from a highly refined consciousness existing on another plane, according to tradition. I didn't believe that.

He not just made a home there but was a professor at Indiana University, founded the Tibetan Cultural Center, and recently hosted a major Buddhist ceremony, *Kalachakra*, which His Holiness personally conducted. This was only two hours away and I wondered if it could lead me to a guru, the importance of which was written in all the Buddhist books.

I pulled into the parking lot of a large, two-story yellow house marked by a sign in Tibetan language on the side of the road. In English, it read *Dagom Gaden Tensung Ling Buddhist Monastery*. There were prayer flags strung along the eaves of the house and stretching into the trees. It was hard to imagine a world-famous religious icon walking these grounds, followed by thousands of attendants to his ceremony as I had read online. Nonetheless, it fit the description of Tibetan Buddhism.

"Tashi delek," the short monk dressed in maroon and saffron with a noticeable deformity of his ribcage invited at the doorway. I assumed it was a Tibetan greeting.

"Hello," I followed him into a sitting room, glancing around but it was sterile, nothing different from any other American room. The fragrance in the room, though was a new smell to me, and yet it felt so familiar and calming.

"My name is Jamyang," he said in a voice that sounded affected by some kind of deep helium.

"I'm new to Buddhism, and I can't get enough!" I laughed through my excitement.

"Good, good," he drew his legs underneath his robes on the sofa. A tall, young monk carried a tea service into the room and placed it on a large ottoman in front of us. "Would you like some tea?"

I wasn't much for tea, hot or iced, but since they went to the trouble, I accepted a cup. "Is it sweetened?" I asked.

"This is chai," the tall monk responded as he poured.

"That's Indian tea, somewhat sweet, with milk," Jamyang explained.

My mouth was accustomed to many Diet Cokes a day, and not much hot stuff. Even my morning coffee needed to be cooled with creamer from the refrigerator. Seeing the steam coming from the cup, I braced my lips for the heat.

"You are both the first Tibetans I've ever met," I said while blowing the steam away.

"Oh, really?" Jamyang said and sipped at his tea unaffected by the temperature. The tall monk didn't introduce himself. After he poured the tea, he quietly retreated behind the door from which he came.

"Yes. I've read many books on Tibetan Buddhism and am embarrassed to say that I really didn't know anything about the Chinese invasion until recently."

"Well, besides teaching Dharma, that's what we are trying to do, let the world know about the killing, the destruction, and the occupation. Don't feel embarrassed, though because so many people still don't know."

"I want to know more," I set my tea down, unable to take a sip. "And about Buddhism. I've read so much already. But I still have no idea what makes one a Buddhist, or what we're supposed to do."

Jamyang laughed, "There are no commandments in Buddhism."

"I guess I didn't mean to imply..." I started to correct myself, "what I mean is, I see these various rituals, and I read about these different methods for self-improvement, but I'm from Kokomo and I don't think there are any other Buddhists there, let alone any teachers. So, I've never participated in any rituals or even know what they are."

"Oh, you're looking for a guru. Yes, yes. A teacher is most important."

"I have never been in a Tibetan temple. Is there a shrine room here?"

Jamyang's feet popped out from under his robe and set on the floor. "Sure, sure. Bring your tea if you like."

I followed him through the door the tall monk exited behind, to another door beside which a sign read: REMOVE SHOES PLEASE. The door was simply a full-length curtain with colorful embroidered designs. Jamyang pulled the curtain aside and swiftly moved into the shrine room and I followed. Stopping just inside the curtain, I stood and watched him go to the large, golden statue of the Buddha and light some incense, the same fragrance that filled the sitting room.

This room was a feast for my eyes. On the walls were beautiful brightly colored paintings called thangkas, all framed in intricate embroidered fabric, topped with a yellow bunting and red ribbons. The images were unfamiliar to me, demon-like beings standing in flames holding strange things in their hands. One was blue with many heads, arms, and legs—*with an erect blue penis*. Jamyang caught me staring. "That's Yamantaka. He is the destroyer of the fear of death."

Three rows of six black cushions sat on larger flat black mats atop a hardwood floor in front of the altar where the large statue of Buddha was central to several other smaller statues I recognized from the picture books. The room was well-shielded from any sound from outside and felt like a kind of vacuum. It was peaceful, not unlike a Catholic sanctuary.

"What made you look into Buddhism," Jamyang asked as he sat behind a short table, just about a foot tall. There was a bell on it, and a couple of long, thin texts.

"I went through a really bad..." I paused. I hadn't the foggiest idea of what Buddhism says about homosexuality, nor the Tibetan people's stance. "Personal situation."

Jamyang nodded slowly. "I see. It's always interesting to me to hear how Americans find the Dharma."

I never considered what the equivalent of a Buddhist missionary would be like for someone. That's pretty much what he was—living in the West in a land where the teachings of his homeland's religion were just being explored and accepted.

"I find it difficult to believe that the Dalai Lama and thousands of people were here just a few years ago. Where did everyone sit?"

Jamyang laughed. "Yes, thousands of people would have to be really small to fill this room. But the Dalai Lama was at the Tibetan Cultural Center, not here. It's on the other side of town. I can write down the directions for you."

I was surprised. I barely heard of anything Tibetan and there were two centers in Bloomington. "Well, if you don't mind, I'd like to hang out here for a while, since I'm already sitting with you and the Buddha."

Jamyang nodded his permission but quickly slipped through the curtain again. "Now just me and the Buddha," I chuckled. Sitting down on one of the cushions, my eyes bounced from one detail of the altar to the next, trying to burn the images into my brain to be enjoyed when I would recall them later. I sat for quite a while alone with brief moments of interruption from my typical torrent of thoughts.

Jamyang finally returned and handed me a piece of paper upon which he wrote directions to the TCC. "Ask for Kunyang," he said. "That's Norbu's wife."

"Would she see me?" I was unsure that the sister-in-law of the Dalai Lama would have time for an unimportant passerby, but I also didn't know anything about Tibetan customs.

"Why wouldn't she?" he laughed.

He led me to the door and just before I stepped out, he asked me to lower my head, and he slipped a long, white silk scarf around my neck.

"This is called a *khatak*," he explained. "It's like a friendship scarf."

I held the ends up and saw symbols faintly woven within the weft and weave. I recognized them from the books as the *Eight Auspicious Symbols*. "Thank you!"

The driveway onto the TCC grounds was similar to the entryway to the Wildcat Creek Reservoir Park. There was a large structure, called a stupa, near the parking lot, and a small two-story white building with angular windows that were wider across the bottoms than the tops was snuggled into the edge of a large woods. I walked up to the door, which was opened just a crack, and knocked. No one came to greet, but I could hear voices speaking loudly within. I opened the door and slipped inside. The same fragrance from the Gaden temple filled the interior and escorted me toward the voices, surely speaking in Tibetan. I stepped into a large room with a long wall of filled bookshelves, colorful murals of different Buddhas and famous historical Tibetan masters grouped in threes on the wall, and a large throne-like seat supporting a giant framed photo of His Holiness with a long blue khatak on it.

"Hello?" I called out, my eyes taking in all the details of the murals.

From behind double doors leading into a kitchen and dining area popped a short, little woman, with dark hair, and features I recognized from the books and the monks at Gaden as Tibetan. She was dressed like any ordinary American woman of her early fifties.

"Who are you?" she said with only a hint of an accent.

"My name is Marc, I'm just visiting and trying to learn about Tibet, Tibetan Buddhism..."

"Yeah, ok." She interrupted. "Come help me with something."

I followed her through the doors. There was a large kitchen on one side of the room, several tables arranged on the other side, and French doors across from where we entered. Two Tibetans stood behind the kitchen island chopping vegetables, talking away in Tibetan. Both paused and smiled at me warmly, "Hello!"

"Hello," I replied, nodding in a way that imitated a short, quick bow.

"Yes, yes, hello, hello. Come this way," the woman hurriedly motioned me to follow her through the French doors.

"My name is Marc, by the way," I repeated and reached out my hand, and she shook it quickly.

"Well, you know who I am, I'm sure. This deck has to be cleaned quickly. Please move the furniture, spray it with the garden hose over there, and pick up all the little pieces of garbage. I'm sorry for the cigarette butts." She turned and walked back into the building.

That was really presumptuous, I thought. The patio deck was a little cluttered and dusty, nothing too bad. But there were a lot of cigarette butts scattered in the surrounding gravel, so I took to them first knowing I would want to handle them less if they were wet. "Dear God, don't tell me this is like a Mr. Miyagi moment from *Karate Kid*," I said aloud.

Just as I finished, Kunyang popped her head out and gave a quick inspection. "Oh, yes, thank you. Very nice. Now come have some mo-mos."

I had no idea what that meant, but I followed her, feeling good that I was an obedient little Daniel-san. There were more Tibetans inside, quickly moving back and forth from the kitchen area to the tables, carrying large pots of dumplings, soups, steamed breads, and noodles while a couple of others set the table where plates of fresh sliced tomatoes, cucumbers, and onions lay on opposite sides. "You can have dinner with us for helping clean up the patio," Kunyang said. "Do you like mo-mos?" She asked.

"Ma'am today is my introduction to anything Tibetan. I'm really a beginner and don't have a teacher."

"That's ok," she said. "Just enjoy yourself. Perfect timing."

One Tibetan woman took small portions of all the dishes and put it on a plate and walked into the large room with many murals. I was gently swept away by everyone following her. She walked over to an altar that resembled the hutch that used to be in our kitchen and laid the plate behind seven bowls of water and a lit candle nestled between the fourth and fifth bowls. The Tibetans began chanting something in unison with their hands folded, and so I pressed my palms together, assuming it was some kind of pre-dinner grace. The whole event was a memorable experience.

Mo-mos are a type of pot-sticker, dumplings filled with beef, onions, garlic, and ginger. The soup was called Tentuk, and it's a pulled noodle stew. The Tibetans were very warm and hospitable but weren't much for conversation as they ate. Kunyang explained that that was their way during meals, and I think it was her way to shut me up from asking so many questions instead of falling behind the apparent race to finish that was underway.

After dinner, the table and kitchen were swiftly cleaned, and everyone went back into the large room and started singing karaoke and dancing in a big circle. Even though I felt completely out of place no one made me feel unwelcome. Two elderly Tibetan women spoke little English, but they still managed to interact with me, smiling through so many wrinkles on their face they looked like light-colored raisins. Two middle-aged Tibetan men sat next to me in the large room, as one Tibetan named Rabten sang loudly through the little karaoke machine, quite off-pitch, to the cheers and laughter of several others making fun of him. He wasn't shaken and sang louder at each taunt.

"Did you enjoy mo-mos? Everyone loves mo-mos," a man named Thubten said.

"I loved them, and I can understand why others do," I answered.

The other Tibetan gentleman didn't introduce himself, and I assumed his English must've been too poor. He simply smiled and gazed at me with the look a father would give his son.

"What did you think of dinner?" a young woman popped between Thubten and me.

I cleared my throat and tried to sound philosophical, "It's a great lesson in impermanence, it would seem."

"Yes, yes!" Thubten started to laugh. "And rebirth is in the toilet tomorrow!" We all erupted in laughter.

Before the night ended, I stood looking at one of the more demonic images hanging by the doorway. It was just like the one I had seen at Gaden. "What is this?"

One of the Tibetan women who remained quiet through the evening and never introduced herself came to where I was standing. "This is a wrathful Buddha."

"I don't understand," I was perplexed. "Aren't Buddhas beyond getting angry?"

She gently placed her hand on my shoulder. "Buddhas are never angry, but they can take on the image, like this, of demonic energy to protect and teach."

"How? I'm still confused."

"Have you noticed how some people who call themselves *spiritual* try to be so polite, and speak so softly as they walk about, almost afraid to be loud." I nodded. "And have you noticed that the Tibetans are not always so quiet?" she smirked. I turned my head away from the painting. "It's ok, saying yes isn't offensive."

I laughed, "Yes. Especially Rabten with a microphone."

"Imagine that you are trying to keep that image that these people have, calm, peaceful, never getting angry, and you're very committed to trying to be like that. If you see someone about to be hit by a car that they cannot see coming, do you keep that peaceful expression?" she squeezed my shoulder softly. "Or do you scream loudly at them to run in order to save their life? Is the scream not compassionate?"

A lightbulb went off, and I got it. "So, these images are a wake-up call, like a compassionate action?"

"Precisely. We call that wrath, a kind of compassion that appears angry."

"How can I understand the difference best?" I asked, needing more clarity.

"One is a tool while the other is an affliction." She patted me one last time and walked away.

I announced my departure and Kunyang pretty much ordered me to return soon. "Volunteers come right after the announcement of Kundun's visit, but disappear after they've had their photo op."

"Kundun?" I asked.

"It's kind of a nickname for His Holiness," she explained. "There's a movie called Kundun. Watch it."

"Well, I'd love to come help whenever I can," I said as I quickly jotted my number on a piece of paper and handed it to her. "Thank you so much for dinner." I smiled out the window of my car as I drove recalling how quickly the evening went and how much of a firecracker Kunyang was. She reminded me of myself with my band and color guard students—no time for bullshit. The night was a memorable first exposure to people whose culture I was falling in love with from my readings.

The next morning, I cried myself awake from a dream about *you know who*. It seemed so real. We were together again going somewhere in his little convertible with the top down, wind blowing through our hair. I looked at him and said, "Please don't let this end. Please! Please!"

"All things come to an end, Jellybean," he said just before I opened my eyes.

I hung my face over the sink and splashed some water on my face, then looked up and stared at my reflection. For a moment, I was like a third party watching my past voices scold me as they had for so many years. "Can't you find real love? What's wrong with you?" It was a strange experience, as though I was divided into two people.

That morning while reading about emptiness in the park, stuck in my car due to the rain, I started to get upset that I couldn't understand this concept. Well, according to all authors I *should* have been struggling with emptiness, as it is considered the most sophisticated topic in all of Buddhism, every school. It was talked about so often, and usually referred to with a few, well regurgitated explanations: *self and phenomena are empty from their own side*; *things lack any self-nature of their own*; or *things lack inherent existence*.

Most of the other teachings seemed relatively easy, and I assumed that that was because of modern education catching the West up to realities anciently discovered during Buddha's time. Having compassion for others, for example leads to more happiness, and that's evident every time we wish someone else to be released from their pains and sorrows. Buddhism doesn't own compassion.

Tibetan Buddhism systematizes the teachings into what's called *Lamrim*, which means *stages on the path*. Through my readings I began to get a clearer outline of Buddhist study and practice. It starts with *Death and Impermanence* and moves on to *Karma*. Understanding *karma*, which simply means action—another Sanskrit word that could've easily been translated into English—requires an understanding of *Dependent Origination*—also known as *cause and effect*.

One teacher explained the network of dependence linking all sentient life on the planet that we all take for granted. After reading the explanation, I considered it in my own life. As a color guard designer, I teach marching band students choreography for a show that Al designed after being hired by a band director; I order costumes and flag designs, and someone manufactures those costumes from fabrics that they purchased from a company who shipped them to them through a courier; The materials of the fabric, like cotton, were raised and picked by a farmer who had equipment he bought from salesmen;

The salesmen sold the equipment for the manufacturers, and each part had a long history involving many, many people.

"It's never-ending," I explained to Wyatt in a little Greek restaurant after rehearsal one night.

"Lady," he said as he took the bill from the waitress, "I think it's good that you're thinking like that. Now, consider how *your* money that you'll use to pay for dinner pays the cooks, the bussers, the electricity, the rent." He chuckled and handed me the bill. "And don't forget to add some of that dependent origination to tip the waitress."

Something like interdependence wasn't too difficult for me to grasp. It was just something that hadn't been pointed out to me before. Once it had been, its simplicity was beautiful and illuminating—and vast. Every little step throughout my life led me to southern Indiana and how the absence of any of those steps could've prevented me from meeting DJ.

My mind buzzed on and on, considering dependent origination through the memories of my childhood. It was a perfect cocktail of Mom's projections intermixing with my own and creating all the difficulties we had with one another. Through the lens of dependent origination, it was becoming obvious that there was more than meets the eye in the blame game.

His Holiness talked about the liberating power of emptiness, and that made me as curious as when I had gone to Craig's church and watched his father jump over pews reacting to the spirit of the Lord. I wanted to experience whatever that was, and similarly, I wanted to know about this freedom emptiness could create. Even if they weren't to become my teacher, I needed someone, to explain it to me. One of the Zen books I bought was written by an American priestess who lived in Michigan. Her contact information was on the back of the book, making it relatively easy to find her phone number online. I anxiously called her hoping she could bring me out of confusion. After a short introduction, a quick-paced volley back and forth about emptiness ensued:

"What is emptiness?" I asked.
"Don't ask that," she commanded.
"Why not?"
"We can't talk about it."
"Then why bring it up?"
"I didn't. You did."

"No, I mean at all. In Zen writings."
"Because all things are empty."
"See? What does that mean?"
"You can't ask that."
"I absolutely can, and I did."
"It's like the finger pointing at the moon."
"I don't understand."
"Is the finger the moon?"
"That's a silly question. Whoever throughout history made such a mistake that that question should be asked?"
"No, no. It means that we can't replace the experience of something with mere words."
"But don't words help point to an experience?"
She sighed. "There was once a student who asked many questions of the master who was pouring them both tea. With each question, the master poured tea into the student's cup. Finally, the student asked so many questions that the tea overflowed and onto the table."
"Why laud such a discouraging teacher? I'd have picked the cup up and poured it on the masters head!"
"I'm not sure how we got here."
"If you could sit with the Buddha would you serve him tea like that?"
"Well, no but..."
"Aren't there over a thousand sutras?"
"Yes, there are, but..."
"And you just told me a story about talking too much?
Click! I decided to avoid Zen Buddhism thereafter.

The Dalai Lama's books regularly referred to the works of a second century Indian Buddhist scholar named Nagarjuna, usually called the Second Buddha, which I found odd because they also say that Buddha Shakyamuni was the fourth Buddha to enter the world. Nothing new in these books, though, was compelling me to adopt these mystical and mythical aspects of the ancient East. I stopped believing that there were any invisible beings conducting the orchestra of life long ago.

I've always been the kind of person who, when faced with a confusing topic, becomes obsessed with figuring out the solution—if that wasn't already clear. His Holiness quoted Nagarjuna in one of his books,

> *For him to whom emptiness is tenable,*
> *Everything becomes tenable.*

> *For him to whom emptiness is not tenable,*
> *Nothing becomes tenable.*

Knowing that I was the latter and wanting to be the former, I looked for every bit of information regarding the topic I could find. I finally found a book that explained and translated one of the most revered texts in the Tibetan monasteries, *The Foundation of the Middle Way* written by Nagarjuna. Carrying my bag with a blanket, the book, and a couple of sodas to my little spot beyond the field of tall grass at the park, I was ready to put all my energy into unraveling the confusion around emptiness.

> *Neither from self, or other,*
> *Both, or neither,*
> *Does anything anywhere whatsoever arise.*

This opening line made absolutely no sense to me and had me flummoxed. "But there's..." I gestured broadly around me. "*Stuff!*" I read it over and over again, then got up and started pacing, trying extremely hard to understand what it meant. After a while, I broke into an inflated rage. "This is bullshit! I discarded one antiquated worldview years ago and now I'm replacing it with another," I said as I shoved everything back into my bag, then stood up.

"Sit down!" A faint, but distinct woman's voice said.

Huh? I looked all around. Had someone come through the tall grass? Was she talking to her dog? I looked down at my feet. To my amazement was a right-turning conch shell, one of the *Eight Auspicious Symbols* revered by the Tibetans.

Every hair on my neck stood on end as I slowly picked up the shell and sat down in the grass. What just happened? I sat in silence for a long while and eventually opened the book again. Why did this piss me off so much? Everything else I read excited me, opened my eyes. But this introductory line didn't make sense, and I tend to get angry over things I don't understand. I read that book all the way through, ignoring the places where I had the most difficulty, hoping that it would all resolve itself in the end like a good fiction novel. Boy, I was wrong. I was more confused, and far angrier by the time I closed the book. The entire text was written with this style that negated everything, and because there was a *real* me reading a *real* book being held by my *real* hands, I was getting upset, like being told to ignore the facts—not unlike Christianity. But I sat that conch shell on my altar in my bedroom as a constant reminder to just keep plugging away.

A month later, after reading a few other books, I opened *The Foundation of the Middle Way* again and took another stab at it. This time, there was no anger, but there was something percolating under the surface. How do things not exist when I can clearly experience them with my senses. Sure, it's a mental image that I'm processing, but it's a process from something *actually* out there, isn't it? I sat and stared at the tree next to the water, a very real, very *there* tree standing in front of me.

Back to basics: if the tree I think I'm seeing is really a hologram in my mind of a thing that's standing out there, how does the tree itself *not* exist? DJ was a mental construct yet wasn't there an actual DJ? My problems with Mom and Dad were similar, but I had a Mom, Dad, and problems that were out there from which I developed the mental images, right? I turned to the idea of myself. Since the day the sperm and egg of my parents came together, networks upon networks were set in motion that culminate in the me sitting here looking at this tree today. I didn't come from my own *self*, but I *did* come from my parents, I thought. How does that first line make sense?

I was getting frustrated again and put the book aside in mental fatigue.

"Al, I'm going crazy," I said as I walked into his office.

"Going?" he joked without turning away from his computer screen.

"Funny. I can't wrap my mind around this shit," I began explaining what I thought I understood about emptiness, though full of uncertainty. I regularly made my students teach a new lesson to one of the older veterans in the color guard as a way to get them to learn quicker. Trying to explain it to Al was a way to put myself through my own lesson.

But then, something quite peculiar happened. Within just a few minutes of my explanation Al's head drooped forward—chin on his chest—asleep. I tried to bring it up again later in the day, and it happened again! We discussed karma, impermanence, and dependent origination and he was engaged, and even helped me see deeper aspects of the topic. But anytime I started on emptiness he was out like a light within two minutes.

One of my books said that the topic of emptiness is very sacred in Buddhism, and the Tibetans revere it so much that many teachers avoid teaching it out of fear of erring in their explanation. Later, I found within another book the mention of a line in a sutra explaining that those who are not suitable to study emptiness will get angry, ignorantly laugh, or... fall asleep. This can't be real, I thought. "I must be making some kind of miscorrelation," I said aloud. Yet, every time I brought up the topic of emptiness in Al's office, he quickly dozed off!

Wyatt arrived at my house early one morning ready to carpool to a rehearsal. I could hear him talking to me as he walked down the hallway. "I'm starving, Lady. Let's hit the road now so we can grab a bite before we go."

"Wait," I said as he entered the room, holding a book open for him and pointing at a line on a page. "Read this." He read the passage I found about those not yet prepared to study emptiness.

"Yeah, so?"

"Follow me," I said, and dashed down the hallway and into Al's office where he had been awake for a few hours working away at the computer.

Now, you have to understand that Al has a unique discipline from which he never strays during the design season. He will wake up just before the sun rises, grab his coffee, maybe a piece of toast for breakfast, and sit in his office working tirelessly until lunch. He doesn't waiver. He can't. With that many show designs, he must make use of every minute of his time to keep shows from falling behind and, hence, his paychecks. Wyatt and I sat down in the office, and I hoped he would get to witness what I had. "Al, we want your opinion on something."

"Just one more second," he said, finishing up a segment he was working on. "What's up?" He turned around in his office chair and faced us, coffee mug in hand.

"Well, I was trying to explain to Wyatt what emptiness is..." I continued on, and after about a minute Al's eyes began to get noticeably heavier and his head started to tilt, his chin falling nearer and nearer to his chest. The more I spoke the more his eyelids slowly fluttered, until finally he let out an audible snore. I looked at Wyatt; his mouth was agape in surprise. We tiptoed out of the office and through the dining room before Al jolted back awake from the sound of his own snoring. "Oh, I'm sorry guys," he apologized.

"If I didn't know you any better, I would swear that you and he planned this," Wyatt said as he sat on my futon.

"How did that happen?" I was still in denial, no matter how many times I saw it.

"Either that book was right or the truth that you bore the man to death can't be hidden anymore," he said, and I shot him a disapproving glance.

That night, I switched off the lights and stared at my bed. We weren't good friends, my bed and me. I'd cry into my pillow missing my sleeping partner and drift into a world of bad dreams. Why should I want to go to sleep, I wondered? I sat for a little bit before lying down, thinking about how Al was lulled to sleep like magic. It was stated in that sutra thousands of years ago: easily falling asleep, laughing as though one is listening to gibberish, and... getting uncontrollably angry. *Oh no!*—what does that say about me? "Damn it, Marc!" I fell back and stared into the darkness.

Days passed and each morning I said a small prayer to Manjushri, the Bodhisattva of Wisdom, as many Tibetan masters prescribed in a picture book that explained the various Buddhas and Bodhisattvas, their mantras and short practices. I recited Manjushri's mantra hundreds of times: *Om Ah Ra Pa Tsa Na Dhih*. After all, the book said that the young monks in the monastery are often prescribed thousands of repetitions of this mantra when they're struggling in their studies, and they say it always works. Could it work on me, I wondered? "Couldn't hurt to try," I said to myself the first time I clumsily thumbed each bead of my newly purchased mala, a rosary made of seeds from the Bodhi tree under which the Buddha sat and achieved enlightenment.

One clear spring morning close to my 32nd birthday sitting in the reservoir park, I stared at the tree again, and closed my eyes. I'd open them and examine the tree, then close them and repeated Nagarjuna's opening line in the *Mulamadhyamika-karika*. Nothing. I opened my eyes and looked at the tree, then closed them and retreated inward, trying harder to think than I've ever thought.

"Come on, *genius*!" I exclaimed mockingly, scolding myself. "Figure it out! *Om Ah Ra Pa Tsa Na Dhih*!"

Then, a flash went through me from head to toe, and I felt as though I instantly downloaded knowledge from the universe. I opened my eyes, starting to tear up, and looked at the tree in awe—a feeling of wonder and amazement at something so simple and innocuous as a tree—as though I were looking at it for the first time.

"Yes! Yes!" I shouted. "My God, Marc! You never see the same tree twice!"

The tree that I was looking at was a stream of data that stretches backward through time and will stretch forward as well. It was a constantly changing thing, changing millisecond by millisecond. If I were to represent every millisecond with a domino, I would have an infinitely long chain of dominoes that stretched backward and forward in time. The tree I thought I saw was really just a sliver of that stream to which I apply the label *tree*. But if I went backward in time, there would be a span of dominos to which I would apply the label *sapling*. Labels to our sense data are not eternal, but momentary identifiers. And that must apply to me, as well! The me that I am is merely this singular domino now, in this moment, an inner voice exclaimed! It was simple and beautiful, so easily missed, yet everywhere around us. Could this be what Nagarjuna meant by:

> *Whatever is dependently originated,*
> *That is explained to be emptiness,*
> *That emptiness reflects dependent origination,*
> *This indeed is the middle way.*

In my mind, I could see that each domino comes from the one before and was placed there by some energy in the past, our... consciousness—*Oh*! "We are doing this to ourselves! All of us, All of it!"

Every experience I ever had was merely a group of observed dominos that somehow were placed in the chain of my experience somewhere earlier down the chain. The thoughts we think, the words we speak, the actions we take, create future dominos and as we move through time toward them, they accumulate and become the experiences we have and the person we become. It was suddenly and freshly clear that everything I ever went through I created myself, somehow—this body, my problems, my relationships. All of the suffering in the world is created by our own mind. We are the authors of all of our joys... and all of our sorrows.

❖ Chapter Seven ❖

Later that month, I dreamed I was in a kind of alternative version of *The Wizard of Oz*. While everyone was reacting in fear to the Great and Powerful Wizard, Toto slipped to the side and pulled the thick curtain back with her Cairn Terrier teeth to reveal the true conductor of the seemingly real illusion. It was all a projection, a hologram that functioned as if it were real. And it was DJ's face that was the Great Oz, hovering in misty clouds at the end of the runway. Though I knew the mechanics of the pulleys and levers behind the curtain, I couldn't switch off my emotional reactions to them and continued to wince and cower from the frightening specter.

The curtain drawn, the canine growling with the fabric in her teeth, the operator realized he was exposed and looked up—it was me! And the face of the specter hovering at the end of the runway turned into my own! The four heroes standing before *Oz* each had my face!

The symbolism in the dream wasn't difficult to understand, I thought as I wrote down all of the details that I could remember in a small dream notebook I kept on the table beside my futon. This was a habit I started after the otherworldly dream of the gazebo I had lying next to DJ back in Decatur. The details of that dream remained as vivid as if it were a real memory, but the details of the rest of my dreams faded fast upon waking that I took to writing them down as quickly as I could. Dreams seemed, to me, to be a mechanism by which the brain continues to problem-solve after we fall asleep, and not some ghostly messages from the beyond like all these new age ideas asserted.

A young Tibetan man named Tenzin introduced me to the *Wheel of Life*, a Buddhist painting found in the entryway to most Dharma centers, temples, and monasteries. In the painting, a large wheel full of various images are seen in the clutches of a demonic figure, with the Buddha standing on a cloud in space outside of the wheel in the right top corner, pointing at the moon in the top left. "The demon is Yama," Tenzin said, "the Lord of Death."

When I told him about my realization after reading Nagarjuna, he encouraged me to keep contemplating it daily, quoting from a short text called *The Heart Sutra*, "Any son or daughter of the lineage who wishes to practice the profound Perfection of Wisdom should correctly and repeatedly see all things as lacking any inherent nature of their own." Then he directed my attention to the outer ring of the *Wheel* in the painting. "These twelve points, just like on a clock, show how consciousness moves from lifetime to lifetime."

I examined the twelve points, "How?"

"The top represents ignorance of our mind in a given situation. This is the foundation for its activity, which is thought. We call this karma."

"I thought karma was action," I said.

"It is," he affirmed, "but our thoughts are the smallest action we do. The brain is simply an organ for thinking. These thoughts are our own doing, so some scholars translate this link as 'volitional act.' These two create all of our suffering by dictating the kind of physical body we have, our senses, even the way we feel good or bad about the contact we have with things and people in the world around us."

There were so many details in the artwork, and Tenzin allowed me a few moments to try to take it all in, mesmerized by all the little painted vignettes and the stories they represented.

"You should hang a picture like this in your home and contemplate its meaning often," he suggested.

"How does this work with emptiness? How can these two concepts help me deal with everyday situations?"

"They are two sides of the same coin. Because all things are empty, they lack any inflexible, unchangeable substance about them. If you don't like the results you're getting in life, change the causes. Emptiness and Karma are like a married couple. Because things lack any real concrete reality, they are changeable. All of your problems have come because of your ignorant mind. Make your mind more intelligent, more wise, and your thought patterns will improve, and so will your outcomes. These twelve links are the mechanism."

"It's just like the dominos," I said, then explained my realization at the park.

"Yes, yes!" he exclaimed. "That's exactly correct! The Tibetan word for impermanent is *kechigma*, which literally means *to only last for a moment*, just like the falling dominos."

Later at home, I hung a picture of the *Wheel of Life* in my room, which already started to look and smell like a little temple. These images were teachings, and reminders of the lessons I wanted to learn, even the Bodhi seed mala around my left wrist everywhere I went served in training my mind.

I made time to go to the TCC as often as I could. Kunyang called to tell me that they finished the foundation for the temple they were building on the grounds and wanted me to come help her. It's an understatement to say that receiving a phone call from the Dalai Lama's sister-in-law was mind-blowing.

She was quite an assertive presence with lots of corrections to my many American foibles, which was starkly different than the other Tibetans. They were more laidback, and very forgiving when I would display ignorance to their culture, giving me gentle corrections, particularly in pronunciation as I learned the standard greetings. I tried to return the favor in correcting subject-verb agreement in their use of the English language.

The Tibetans are the happiest people I've ever met, claiming compassion for all beings as their strength and identity. They embrace joy in all of its manifestations, even when it's self-deprecating. As Americans, we often become too embarrassed at our mistakes in front of others, and the Tibetans echoed Kathy's lesson in showing me the joy in laughing at myself.

This was first demonstrated through Rabten's reaction to a worrisome crash on his bicycle while doing stunts, clad in a tee shirt and the lower half of a monk's robe. The other Tibetans laughed and jokingly warned about the maroon fabric getting caught in the chain, and howled when the inevitable entangling seized the pedals, sending the novice monk ass-over-appetite across the handlebars. Like a spark, Rabten sprung from the ground, bloodied, and scraped, and joined in the good time at his own expense.

Whenever I would have a blunder in front of them, my face became red with embarrassment. Thubten looked at me once and said, "Don't be upset! You're missing out on a good laugh!"

In Kunyang's presence, many of the other visitors and locals would put on an artifice of reverence, hands folded at their hearts as if she herself were an emissary of the Dalai Lama looking for lost *Chosen Ones*. I fell in line as instructed at first, but shook that off pretty quickly, often talking back to her, which always elicited a faint smirk on that firecracker's face.

"How long have you been in America," I snapped at her once

after she was particularly testy toward one of the other regulars.

"Why does that matter?" she quipped back.

"Surely you've observed by now that being a bitch usually chases volunteers away!"

At first, she scowled, as though all holy hell was about to erupt from her tiny frame, but then melted into a smile of approval. "Bravery in the face of wrath," she patted my shoulder and walked away.

I picked up fallen branches, pulled weeds, vacuumed the inside of the TCC, washed windows, and any other task she had. Dad would've been proud, but Kunyang never lied to me about how short of a time it would take. Upon my arrivals, she would be outside with a list in her hand and say, "Oh, thank you for coming, Marc. I don't know if I could get everything finished this week. Please try to get as much of this done as you can today." She would hand me her list and then quietly disappear.

One day in early July, she stepped out of the TCC and motioned me over from the stupa around which I was pulling weeds. A short monk wearing sunglasses that looked like they came off of Erik Estrada in *CHIPS* was standing next to her.

"This is Geshe Loten," she introduced. We bowed to each other. "He'll be giving teachings here from now on. You call him Geshe-la."

Tibetan language uses honorifics, so the 'la' after a name or title is respectful. Geshe Loten was from Amdo, Tibet. His dialect was noticeably different from the other Tibetans, even to my untrained ears. One Tibetan told me, "Amdo is kind of hillbilly!"

"You've been looking for guru?" Kunyang said. "Geshe Loten can be your guru. So, see? Working around the center made good karma for you."

My introduction to the Geshe didn't have any of the magic that the Tibetan stories I read romanticized, but we were in America, so I kept an open mind. I often joked that if Siddhartha had tried to find his enlightenment here, it wouldn't be long after he sat under a tree and began his meditation that he'd quickly hear a shotgun cocking followed by a hick voice, "Get off my *propertah*!"

In the following weeks, many occasions to have conversations with Geshe Loten presented themselves during afternoon tea in the kitchen and on the patio of the Center. His English was poor, and I had only just begun to speak clumsy Tibetan greetings. Still, I learned a lot about the monastery through him. I discovered that it takes sixteen years of educational training for the monks to achieve the Geshe degree, which is like a Doctor of Divinity—on steroids.

I dreamed of living a life devoted to studying the Dharma and sharing it with others, freeing people of the stupid mistakes we make that hurt one another. After my *flash of lightning* as I came to call it, I had taken to write the root text of the *Mulamadhyamika-karika* by hand into a brown Japanese notebook. Nightly, I popped into the nearby Denny's and sat for a couple of hours, sipping coffee and hypnotically writing on the thin rice paper beautifully bound between bamboo covers. Many Tibetans said to me, "You must develop a relationship with these sacred texts," and this was my new lover.

I discovered that the Dharma moves through us, like the Force, and delivers what is needed at the right time to the right person. Late one night, it flowed from the pages upon which I carefully moved my pen, through me, and into a total stranger. This rough looking man upon whom time began to etch itself around his eyes and the corners of his mouth, with the kind of dirt that was tattooed onto his hands and caulked under his nails from his daily grind, was sitting at an adjacent table, eyes swollen and red, as if he had been crying, staring motionless into his coffee. I approached him on my way out. "Sir," I asked, pulling him from his trance, "are you alright?"

He sat up and looked around the empty restaurant, as if to be sure it was safe to drop his manly façade. "Well, I've... made some mistakes in my past and I can't seem to get a break."

I leaned against the back of the chair across from him. "I've been there, too. Still dealing with mental crap myself, day by day."

"It's tough. I've lost a lot of things and..." he paused, probably because he didn't feel comfortable sharing more, "I'm just pretty lost."

"I went through a break-up that made me think about taking my own life," I shared, which pulled his eyes to reluctantly meet mine, sending him every bit of strength and love I could force from my blue irises. He laboriously raised a corner of his mouth, trying to smile.

"I won't bother you anymore, sir," I said, ready to give him back to his trance, hoping he felt just a little less alone than before I interrupted him from his thoughts. Then, as if someone else took control of me, I reached in the glass of water in front of him and pulled out two ice cubes. "Just one thing, take these."

"And?" his self-pity broke momentarily, taking the ice cubes into his calloused hand.

"Now, if I said, 'Give these back to me tomorrow in the same condition,' what would you say?"

"I'd say you're gonna get water," he was noticeably perplexed.

"Right. Now, can you show me anything in our reality that isn't like those tiny ice cubes? Everything is just melting around us at different speeds."

He paused for a moment to process my words, and then his eyebrows nearly jumped off of his face, and his posture shot straight to the ceiling. The dark, red-eyed scowl was brightening before my eyes. "You have no idea how much I needed to hear that!"

For a few moments, his eyes scattered about in space as the wheels in his head began to turn. It was joyful to see him listening to his inner voices rewrite a storyline that lifted him up. I didn't ask for any explanation, and I didn't want to know his story. I merely delighted in the effect simple Dharma can have on those of us who've never been introduced to its beauty. He stood up and asked to hug me.

It is often the case that we humans wander about this life with pieces of the puzzle for finding happiness missing in our worldview. One small morsel of knowledge can have such an impact that it changes what I've come to call our *calibration of consciousness*. This is the shift in the first link in the *Wheel of Life*.

Every discovery I had in Tibetan Buddhist philosophy was recalibrating my own mind—small adjustments to my erroneous understanding of reality. I became engrossed in these teachings and worked fervently every morning to reshape my brain, to see how my mind works and try to understand reality without the pollution of my delusions. Morning after morning I felt like I was going into a mental laboratory and enjoyed the work there, and when I came out things looked differently than before, and my reactions to things changed.

Daily, I would review lessons from previous mornings and strive to keep them in mind in the hopes that I could stop creating negative karma. Karma simply means "action," and it has four principles: karma is certain—meaning effects resemble their causes; karma increase exponentially; no effects arise from actions that aren't executed; and once a karma is committed the results don't just disappear.

While sitting in a drive-thru one day, the driver in front of me shouted so much fiery anger into the window waiting for his food. I normally would have shared his frustration after such a long wait. But I was drawn to the face of the poor girl who finally handed him his order, her face clearly marked with stress and apology. My heart softened, and I heard myself say, "Thank you for the crap that you have to go through with impatient people," when I was at her window.

She looked at me twice, searching for sarcasm but finding none, melted into relief. As I drove away, my mind played out the interdependence of a harsh word—the customer shouts their dissatisfaction, the server carries that stress on themselves, and takes it home to lash out at family members.

Another time in which my surrounding reminders paid off was during a lunch break from a rehearsal. I took three of the other instructors with me to quickly get food. At an intersection just before the restaurant, a pickup truck was in the left turn lane, but the driver was looking back at me over his right shoulder and decided at the wrong moment to move in front of me. I slammed on the brakes, my friends in the car screamed loudly, and we came to a stop just inches from a collision. The driver got out of the car, face red with embarrassment and noticeable concern for us. I raised my left hand in the air out of the window with my finger pointed to the sky, ready to scream at him. "Sir!" I yelled, then paused as I looked at the Bodhi seed mala encircling my wrist. "You... can't do that!" As I drove away, my passengers broke into laughter.

"*Oooh*! You told him!" They taunted.

Later, one of my friends who was in the car, Brayton, asked me why I didn't get out of the car and yell at the man. I told him a story that I read about a Tibetan lama who had a student witness another student make an embarrassing confession to the old teacher. The lama was tender with him and instructed him on the best means of atonement. After the confessing student left, the other student asked the lama why he didn't give a sharper rebuke. "His red face as he made his confession indicated his sincerity," I explained. "It was the same with the man when he got out of the truck. He was already punishing himself."

Often, as I would transcribe Nagarjuna's words into the Japanese journal late at night at the Denny's, I would pause and think how our reactions to others sometimes make things worse than they really are, and our negativities infect the minds of those around us—karma increases exponentially. From the point of view of the *Wheel of Life*, starting with our active mis-knowing of what's going on, our self-grasping thoughts make us choose hurtful words or actions toward someone we think wronged us. This activates our bodies, our senses, and manifest into a physical situation where we actively try to hurt the other. This is called *Becoming* in the illustration. Once we reach that point, it cannot be unlived. Through this mechanism, we trap ourselves in a consciousness that spirals in a circuitous dance, making decisions founded on our erroneous view of reality.

It was now easy to connect the dots from my days of promiscuity, moving from one lover to the next, and arriving at a perfect reflection of it all in the cheating boyfriend, DJ, who was somehow drawn into my life. Laura's book also pointed out an explanation of the psychological process unfolding in a similar way, and it was the biggest take-away from that book I remembered long after throwing it in the trash. Our early caretakers, whether they be parents or guardians during our first three years, help wire into our brains certain archetypes that become the foundation of who we are, how we respond to stressors, and the foundations for our choices. If those first three years are filled with turmoil and trouble, it will ripple through all the years of our lives.

Whenever I felt discouraged, I recalled how the smile on the Dalai Lama's face was genuine, and the history of Chinese aggression on his people and the deaths of nearly two million countrymen never swayed him from continuing to teach happiness. My problems were inconsequential in comparison, so I was certain the answers were put to text somewhere and I just needed the luck to find them.

One night after rehearsal standing in the parking lot beside our cars, Wyatt told me that he and Jason were breaking up. Jason was cheating, and existing tensions mounted so much between them since Colorado that the transition was, "Like taking out the trash, child."

"It'll save you gas money if you come stay at Al's until you find a place of your own," I invited. Al had a spare room across from mine that we rented out to others before, and I knew Al was fond of Wyatt and would have extended the offer himself.

"I might do that," he pondered.

"Ugh," I grunted. "All this cheating in the world. I'm sorry this is happening to you, too. I just can't understand it. Dad, DJ, Alice, now Jason. It's so freaking selfish. Can't people just be happy that they've found someone?"

"Lady, we've all got our own things," he said wisely, almost unfazed by his breakup. "It's finding that balance between getting what you want and not hurting someone on the way to get it."

"I don't know how you can shake it off so easily. My breakup with DJ almost killed me. Buddhism says that all of our desires come from ignorance and selfishness. Maybe I just had too much selfishness in the relationship that I didn't realize..."

"That's what I'm saying," he interjected. "We look at something and think, 'I want that,' and overestimate how much *mmmph* it's going to bring us. Even though that *mmmph* hurts someone else, we still go after it and underestimate how much damage trying to get it will cause."

"Wow, Wyatt," I reacted, a little amazed at the simple wisdom. "Maybe you should open your own little temple! Start the religion of Wyatt-ism?"

"The Holy Church of Wyatt," he said, pulling my mala from around my neck and wrapping it around his hand as if to pray. "Our mantra is: Wyatt's pretty!"

Wyattism wouldn't be nearly as frustrating as visiting the TCC was becoming. Geshe Loten's teachings were more like a series of book talks, and I wasn't learning about the various meditation techniques the Dalai Lama and other authors mentioned. There was no guru-student relationship being offered there, and that confounded me since the foundation of the Lamrim path is the relationship to the spiritual guide. Hell, Wyatt was a pretty damned good guru himself and we had a great friendship.

One day, my frustrations got the best of me as I stood asking Mary Pattison, a senior student of Norbu's, a barrage of questions. "I've read about these mind training methods and watched videos of rituals, why aren't they offered here?"

"Well, your heart is your practice, Marc," Mary said. Another American Buddhist who frequented the center, Sandy, stood beside her nodding, along with Kimberly, the wife of the center's translator, Tenam.

"Yes, I know," my face growing a little more red. "But what are all these chants, rituals, and hand gestures about? There's a tradition there I want to know."

"I can't speak Tibetan, but you can ask Geshe Loten." Mary said. She was such a sweet woman, working tirelessly for the center under Kunyang's hotheaded personality. Mary was a direct student of the Dalai Lama for over twenty years, and it was difficult to get angry with her.

"There's never a translator around," I said exasperatedly. "No offense, Kimberly. I know you and Tenam have a life outside of the TCC." Mary walked out of the room.

Sandy looked at me. "I understand what you're saying, Marc. I've been wanting more, too."

"Can someone just teach us a damned Tibetan prayer or a daily practice, is that so much?" I raised my voice almost shouting then left the center. I returned to Kokomo and calmed myself by rereading Nagarjuna and added a few more lines of it into the journal. Before bed, lying in silence, I was hopeful that the nighttime cries may finally become a thing of the past as they were becoming less frequent.

The next morning at the park, I had an idea as I walked around the lagoon seeing large, flat limestone slabs. I picked up six small, similar sized stones, carried them to the tree beyond the tall grass and painted the Tibetan mantra of Avalokiteshwara, the Bodhisattva of Compassion, on them, one syllable per stone: *Om Mani Padme Hum*. My Tibetan calligraphy skills were nonexistent, but I eyeballed my best shot and was pleased with how they looked.

Then, I went back to the lagoon and found a sizeable slab with the intent to prop it against the tree and paint on it. It was quite heavy, and I could only manage about ten steps before having to set it down and rest. I moved it in this manner for about a half-mile. Once it was against the tree, I painted the face of the Buddha on it—attempted to, at least—not completely proud of my artistic rendering. I later read that Tibetans would never criticize an image of the Buddha, no matter how terrible the artwork. Criticizing the artist is another story.

My little spot had clear Buddhist personality, topping it all off with Tibetan prayer flags strewn throughout the branches above. Sitting in the morning sun in front of the enamel-painted face of the Buddha, the mantra of compassion, and prayer-blessed wind blowing through the branches, I felt a sense of sacredness on my morning perch.

That night after a rehearsal, I sat at the Denny's, scribbling away in the journal and sipping coffee. I was trying to maintain my state of ease and recalled my sense of wonder from my realization in the park. "Excuse me," a voice called out to me. I looked up and a young man with dark hair and glasses in the booth ahead of mine was gazing sullenly back at me. His eyebrows looked as if his face was wet clay and someone pulled the inner corners upward just before firing him in the kiln. Though sad, he was quite attractive, I thought.

"Do you have a lighter I could borrow, please?" he asked. I reached down and took my lighter from beside my coffee mug, slipped out of the booth and stepped toward him, reaching to hand it over. On the table in front of him was a book, *Jesus and Buddha as Brothers*, it said on the cover.

"Are you a Buddhist?" I asked with excitement, never having met one in Kokomo.

"No, I'm kind of going through a spiritual crisis," he laughed, though I could tell it was something that was truly weighing on him. I sat back in my booth and gave him my attention.

"I've kind of had one myself," I chuckled soothingly.

"Well, I pretty much am in this nihilist mindset lately. Nothing really makes any sense to me anymore."

I was intrigued to know what happened to him to bring him to such a view. Shamelessly, I also watched for any gayisms.

He spent the next hour and a half explaining how lacking religious faith caused tensions between him and his father. His intelligence was apparent, quoting quantum physics and psychology often. "I'm a man of reason," he mentioned several times.

I just sat and listened, taking in each detail of his story, his mouth as it moved, the look in his eyes, all of it. For that hour and a half, nothing else mattered as I poured all of my awareness into our united sphere and tried to feel his struggle.

Time and again, I've watched straight guys wrestle with their emotions. It always amazed me how they will project their masculinity and choose whatever option in any situation seems the most *man*. Nathaniel wasn't like that in the least. He was heterosexual—I was sure to ask. But he was intrigued by his feminine side, and he felt emotions deeply. He cried as he told me a story about another male friend very dear to him who was going through a rough patch.

He also once experimented with psychedelics, to which he said pushed any notion of a concretely existent reality that he had left far away because of how they, as he said—disintegrated the ego. But he still had a spiritual sense and wasn't sure if there was some neurological answer for it that science had yet to find. All in all, he sounded like a straight version of me—without any of the drugs!

As I've mentioned, such healthy skepticism is important in Buddhism and is encouraged. If the spiritual seeker isn't eager to analyze something deeply, they can never find the details that make something true—and they should even split hairs when necessary in their analysis. Every single perception we have occurs due to microscopic bits of biological material, ridiculously tiny webbing in our skulls. The loss of one neuron, one junction of those webs could affect the entire outcome of a perception. So, yes, details are important.

The Lamrim describes the qualities a spiritual teacher should possess, and it also details the ideal student. There is an analogy used to illustrate, *three pots*: the pot that has a lid on it represents the student who is not motivated to learn or is not open-minded; the pot that has dirt inside it has an alternative motivation, or some kind of obstruction to learning with pure intention; and the third type of pot has a crack in it, representing a student with low retention or poor memory. Nathaniel was a pot that was clean, undamaged, and open. His crisis brought him there and he had nowhere else to go.

That quality is what drew me in as we sat in the Denny's well past midnight. Remove all the labels of our individual situations and it was easy to see that we were both seeking answers that could restore us to a better version of ourselves. Although, I'm not so sure that I ever had a better version to begin with.

After Nathaniel, or Than as he preferred, finished I started to share with him what I discovered through my studies. I summarized the key points of the Lamrim, which he was intelligent enough to understand. Through everything, he struggled the most with whether he believed in past or future lives, and I admit that I didn't really accept it myself.

He asked if I had a book he could read, and I asked him to follow me home, since I lived in the housing addition across the street. He pulled in the drive behind me and I ran inside and grabbed a book I thought would be helpful.

"I appreciate this, man," he said as I handed him the book.

"Call me if you ever want to get together and talk about this stuff again," I offered, and he drove away. I figured I would never see him—or the book—again.

Later that week, Wyatt brought little with him when he moved in. He said that Jason auctioned off nearly all of their furniture to pay for a drinking habit, another reason to be rid of him. We often chatted through the night and usually fell asleep in my room with the TV on. I felt safe seeing him nearby whenever I woke in the middle of the night.

I had a closet packed full of designer clothing, and thirty-seven pairs of shoes—I suppose it was compensation for having so little my senior year and years of conditioning from the posturing men at gay bars. Wyatt frequently went to my closet to go *shopping*, as he liked to say, since he didn't have much himself—and it felt good to share.

He sometimes went home to see his parents on the weekends, and I used that time to drive off to Bloomington. Sometimes I would pop in and spend some time with Jamyang at Gaden. His English was excellent, and I was able to ask him about points in my studies that needed clarification. I developed a cherished friendship with him since my first trip to Bloomington.

One day, I noticed that there were lots of photos of different lamas and spiritual masters with whom I gained a little familiarity in their usual places around the shrine room, but there was no photo of the Dalai Lama. Something compelled me to wait until I talked to Kunyang.

"You don't know of the controversy?" she asked from behind the bar of her restaurant near the IU campus.

"There's a controversy?"

"Yes, it's a long story. You really don't need to go to that monastery. They're not following the Dalai Lama's advice, let's say."

"Is this something I should worry about?"

She came around and sat on a barstool next to me. "That depends on how closely you want to believe the Tibetan version of Buddhism. There's a protector practice that they follow that His Holiness has said is not Buddhist."

"This sounds more political. I didn't think the Tibetans would let politics tear them apart."

"Oh, good one!" she laughed. "You've read the pretty version. We've had problems with the Chinese for centuries, besides our own political struggles among the different sects. To an American it may seem minor, but to the Tibetan people their spirituality is their identity. Many see the Dalai Lama as a god. To those who are continuing this practice that he has forbidden, he is fallen."

I looked into my glass of Diet Coke, wondering. On the one hand, Jamyang was so kind to me and I thought of him as a teacher, though not the *Heart Lama* that I was hoping to find. But I could not ignore that the Dalai Lama instigated this journey. It caused me some confusion since His Holiness always spoke about harmony and compassion.

"Would there be any harm in me maintaining my friendship with one of the monks there?" I asked her.

She patted me on the knee and stood up. "Again, that depends on you. You're an American. Maybe... don't let arguments you're not a part of stand between you and beautiful friendships. That's what my Lama, Pari Rinpoche would tell me, so I'm telling you. What kind of Buddhist do you want to be? This side, that side. Decide on your own."

I raised an eyebrow, "Kunyang, you're sounding sweet. Are you losing your edge?"

She laughed, "I'm not a bitch! I'm *wrathful!*"

What kind of Buddhist did I want to be, I wondered? And not just about picking some kind of spiritual or political position. As I drove home, I considered how much of a Buddhist I was already. I hadn't found a teacher nor taken vows, and that's technically a defining factor. Thus far, my studies helped a lot. I was worrying about things less frequently, not falling apart into tears randomly, and aside from the stress of competition, I was more at ease. I still had the DJ Circle, but it was less frequent. I was sure that time was the biggest factor for that.

Nonetheless, the Dharma was a beautiful world. Understanding impermanence and meditating on it for almost a year at my grandmother's grave at least once a week helped me to pay more attention to details and look for the beauty of each moment. *Dependent Origination* gave me a view of causality in two different directions on the timeline. And studying emptiness was chipping away at the seemingly solid realness every thing, person, and situation seemed to have.

"I think you're going through a noticeable change," Wyatt said.

"Thank you," I sighed. "I'm glad someone is noticing. Hearing it from you means a lot."

"I'm your best friend, and I'm supposed to notice."

"You don't have to," I chuckled. "But I think I'd tell you to buy your own damn clothes if you didn't."

He jumped up from the futon and flung open the large closet. "Just for that I'm going shopping!"

I sat and watched him explore my wardrobe. He pulled out a small, blue, short sleeve soccer shirt and held it up against his chest. "Where did you get this? It's too cute!"

"Here's a cute story about that shirt," I said, taking it from him. "When I lived in Chicago, a friend of mine, Joe saw this in my closet one night before we went out to the dance clubs. He thought it must've been some designer brand because it was so adorable, and he was a huge label queen, so he wore it that night. Every time we'd hang out together with our friends, he'd make me the butt of his jokes and try to look superior. So, once he started up I looked at him and said, 'Lighten up or all your label whore friends will find out where your little frock came from."

"Where?" Wyatt asked, intrigued.

"The junior miss section of Target. His reaction was priceless! 'You let me go out in a cheap piece of trash?' He was incredibly and understandably nice to me for the rest of the night."

"That's hilarious." Wyatt pulled a tight green D&G sweater over his head and went into the old master bath to look in my cheval mirror. "People get so hung up on superficialities," he said as he turned side to side, mockingly.

"Ah, yes," I started my best Mr. Miyagi imitation, "there is a disparity between the way things appear and where you actually bought them!"

"Oh, the misery of labels," he bowed to me.

Later, I told him about my conversation with Kunyang, "I'm not sure what kind of Buddhist I should be."

Wyatt turned and looked at me. "What does your heart tell you?"

I thought for a moment. "I don't know. I don't know enough. I really am living my own interpretation of much of it. The books help, the analyzing helps. But I want to know more. And I swear if I can ever cut through the unnecessary intellectual narcissism of these translations, I'm going to make it easier on the next guy."

"Then you should try to know more. You'll know when you know. And if you don't know yet that just means you need to keep learning."

"Not sure if that was wise or wise-ass." I chuckled.

"The problem with religion is that people often think that they have to follow it to the letter. Maybe you should focus on Marc's Buddhism, rather than a book's Buddhism, or even the Dalai Lama's Buddhism. What's your hang up, though?"

"Past life, the invisible world of gods and hells. I believe science. But the Dalai Lama makes really good points about using logic to help with what you can't see. And I just don't know the logic of how a great thinker like him could still hold to the idea of past and future lives if he didn't have a logical reason to."

"There are plenty of things we can't see," Wyatt said as he moved to the closet again. "The back of our heads, microwaves, attraction to someone else." He pulled out a stretchy lycra shirt I hadn't worn in a few years. "And there are plenty of things we need to see... on me! Damn, I love your clothing!"

A few days later, I arranged a new altar assembly to accommodate my growing obsession with Tibetan symbolism. There were resources from a website belonging to one of the Dalai Lama's students that explained how to set up an altar and do a morning offering practice called *yunchap*. I took a plain desk and threw a large maroon cloth over it, then carefully arranged the statue, several Dharma books, a bell, a candle, and seven small glass ramekins to be my water bowls for daily offerings.

I moved the Buddha candle holder to the living room and bought a proper brass statue from a shop near Kunyang's restaurant. Traditionally, Tibetans fill hollow Buddha statues with tightly rolled scrolls of prayers, incense powder, precious and semi-precious stones, then conduct a ceremonial blessing called *rabnay*, which is said to create the conditions for the statue to be the same as having an actual Buddha present with you. I thought it best to leave it hollow until I found my guru... if I ever did.

Sitting on my cushion, admiring the images and the peace they inspire, alone, I remembered what Kunyang asked. What would it be like to be such a beacon of wisdom and compassion, eliminating sadness and suffering from everyone, I wondered?

I didn't have any idea how to be a Buddhist in America, though I read from one author his struggles returning to the States after living as a Theravada monk, trying to live by the traditional monastic code. I imagined an America evolving to include the symbiotic support of monastic teachers who were sustained by the offerings of the public, and not being called *lazy bums* by passersby. It could be beautiful, I thought and entertained myself with visualizations of a better world.

Then, my phone rang, yanking me back from *La-la Land*.

"Hello?"

"Hey, are you home right now? Is this your home phone?" Nathaniel's voice was frantic.

"It's my cell," I answered. "But I'm home. What's up?"

"Can I come see you? I... I just would rather come over there. Something really bizarre might have just happened."

"Absolutely, come on. I'll be here." I hung up and figured he was back to his crisis.

He pulled in the drive, just after dark. As he stepped out of the car, he looked troubled, just as he was the night we met, but more shaken as if he just narrowly escaped an accident before pulling into the drive. I saw that he was carrying the book I gave him.

"So, been reading it?" I asked.

"Actually, Marc I gotta be honest with you, I kinda thought you were a little fanatic-ish and didn't really intend to read it." I maintained my composure and resisted an offended expression.

"Ok... let's go inside," I started toward the door.

"Well, my dad and I got into another fight today and I just wanted to piss him off some more, so I grabbed that book and jumped in my car to go find someplace to read. I needed some more validation for leaving my faith, you know?" The door closed behind him as we moved to the hallway to my bedroom.

"I get that," I said.

"Well, I started driving around the country and found this park out in the middle of nowhere…"

I turned to him and paused; my hand was on the doorknob to my bedroom.

"I drove down this long entryway and got out of my car and just started walking around. And then I'm on this trail going around this… lagoon, what do you call those?"

The hairs on my neck were starting to stand on end. "*Lagoon* works."

"Well, then I'm walking through this field of tall grass and trying to go over by the water. Then as I am getting through it I see this big stone with a face of the Buddha painted on it."

I opened the door and he saw a small bench sitting in front of the altar upon which I painted the six-syllable mantra, just like those I painted on the stones.

"And six stones with *that* on them," he exclaimed and pointed.

We stood staring at each other for a moment. His eyes were full of tears. "Was that you? Did you put those there?"

"How often have you been to that park, Than?"

"Never! Once… *maybe*. I don't know."

We sat together on the futon. "What's the likelihood of this? I mean, the math alone is mind-blowing. Of all the places you could go… throughout all of Howard County… it's just… unreal."

"Does this have anything to do with a past life connection?" he asked.

"I have no idea," I said slowly, shaking my head in disbelief of it all. We spent the rest of the night in each other's company knowing that something defining had happened.

✤ Chapter Eight ✤

Than came to study with me in my room many times throughout the following months. We would sit for hours and I would share with him what I learned from my readings and interactions with the Tibetans. I could see the burdens he had from our first encounter lifting from his shoulders and he always left my room refreshed—and with a new book I knew he would devour in short time.

"You have a glow about you lately," I noted to him once.

"Thank you," he said. "Things are making so much sense and I'm really grateful to be able to spend time with you. It's like shining a light into the dark."

My own negative thinking was changing, diminishing the more I studied and meditated, or what I thought was meditation. I had no formal training but what I developed for myself was having a positive effect. Many authors, including the Dalai Lama often explained how the methods of practice within the Tibetan system were designed to train the mind. I was fascinated, and perhaps a little jealous of anyone who had a lama with whom they could learn. I explored many different methods that I read about—at least my understanding of them—and tried to fashion my own daily practices.

To practice concentration, I painted one side of a penny with red enamel to eliminate the details of Honest Abe. In the mornings, after I made offerings on the altar, I sat it in front of me on the floor, about six feet away, and place my gaze on it to see how long I could hold my attention on that little red spot before my mind would wander away and have to be retrieved.

I continued occasional *Death and Impermanence* meditations in Albright Cemetery, but found a quieter place away from my grandmother's grave. There was an older part of the graveyard where the stones were dated in the 1800s, covered in moss, near the edge of the woods where no one came to lay flowers anymore. Albright was close to a large neighborhood, and though some people took walks throughout the twenty-five acres, they mainly stayed on the roads that led through the cemetery and never came near me.

One author of several books I read quoted Chugyam Trungpa Rinpoche many times, and when I looked into this spiritual teacher, I found a few methods he taught that I tried to adopt. Chugyam was a proponent of something called *Lojong*, which literally means *mind training*. We all live in our own little box of what we believe reality to be. Mind training helps us to expand the box by habituating our minds to more beneficial thought patterns, behaviors, and responses to the world around us. The key to being successful with Lojong practices is to see your mind as moldable clay and not rigid, inflexible stone.

The first method I tried was using slogans throughout the day. It was like a *Tibetan 365*, memorizing and practicing a different Dharma slogan a day, like "drive all blames into one" and contemplating as I went about. This slogan, for example, is meant to remind us to not be so quick to let ourselves off the hook with difficulties. We have to examine our role in situations and recognize our own participation in what makes it so bad, rather than finding someone else upon whom to pin the fault. It shouldn't be a new neurotic self-blaming. Rather, it's like looking at that chain of dominos and recognizing that this moment right now that is bringing about unwanted experiences was laid in a past event by our ignorant thoughts, words, and deeds. To react to it negatively was surely to lay similar dominos in the future that we could doom ourselves to experience again. Looking inward is such an important part of the Buddhist path that the very word Buddhist is *nangpa*—insider—in Tibetan.

"*You're so damned stubborn*," I could hear my mother yelling when I was a teenager, and my response, "*Who do you think I go it from?*" echoed back. If only I learned to not respond with anger, to find respect for her and change my attitudes and behaviors so that she wouldn't have had to say that so often, I thought.

Every day, I would write a new slogan on a dry erase board that hung on my bedroom door and jot that slogan onto a Post-it that I would place inside my car. After a while, my dash was cluttered with them and I eventually gave in to my neat-freak streak. Having a clean and organized environment made for a more conducive atmosphere for learning, I always believed. Once when I worked with John in French Lick, I was cleaning and organizing his band room while waiting for him to finish what he was doing so we could leave for the day. I had a strict expectation in rehearsals that the kids were to place their belongings in an organized fashion on the side of the field before stepping out into formation, and John implemented it. But the band room was often in disarray and I set about straightening it up.

"Marc," he stopped me. "Don't worry about that, it's not important."

"Don't you want the room put back together?"

"When I was student teaching in college, one great band director told me that if you see a band room that's clean the director was probably more concerned with that than teaching."

I raised an eyebrow, "John, I thought you worked with the intelligently gifted?"

"I do," he looked confused.

"Can't you do both?" I asked, and he laughed at how obvious something like that had escaped him.

I enjoyed working with the slogans a lot, and they gave me a large vocabulary of advice I could use to help others, including my students. They were a way for me to organize the landscape of my mind, like the band room or my dashboard. By training my mind through the Lojong practices, I could see how it was possible to develop better mental discipline and take control of my emotions, even though I still found myself in the DJ Circle, too often. Was it possible to stop past dominos from continue their long, uncomfortable cascade, I wondered?

Through Jamyang, I deepened my understanding of a variety of topics with which I found difficulty, and he would give me a little morsel of wisdom through his explanations during my short visits. And Geshe Loten never shied from trying to impart some knowledge, though his English was poor, and his accent was quite thick. He taught me a Tibetan prayer meant to draw energy to develop understanding of emptiness I have recited daily ever since. He also introduced me to one of the most beloved Buddhas of Tibet.

"Who is Tara?" I asked him as he poured chai for the two of us in the kitchen at TCC.

"Tara is Buddha of action," he replied. "Very powerful."

"What does she do? Why do Tibetans love her so much?"

"Tara very powerful, always helping, always protecting." He sat and quickly chanted an offering prayer before we drank the tea he prepared. The Tibetans offer their food and drink to the Buddhas so that they can accumulate merit, positive energy that are the causes of goodness in their lives. Unlike thanking God for giving them their food, the Tibetans are keenly aware of who the hell actually did the cooking.

Geshe Loten removed his mala. "You say Tara mantra every day. *Om Tare Tuttare Ture Soha,*" he started slowly, and I took my mala and mimicked him. Then he moved the beads under his thumb faster, his recitation matching pace. We made it around the 108 beads of our malas together and stopped. "Yes! Yes! Do this every day."

Through his challenge with English, he managed to give me just a little more on my journey and I was grateful. I didn't consider him my guru, though. I didn't have the overwhelming feelings about him that the guru-disciple stories highlighted. Nonetheless, I saw him as an important teacher in my life and would have done anything to keep that relationship. One situation arose in which I had the opportunity to put my money where my mouth was.

After one of Geshe Loten's teachings, which typically ended with a dedication prayer followed by everyone rising from their seats with hands folded in reverence as he would leave the room, the short monk began to weep. He started talking again in his native language and we all sat anticipating the translation from Tenam. This was irregular. As Tenam translated, Geshe Loten wiped his eyes. Tenam explained that Geshe Loten was told that he would receive three hundred dollars a month for teaching and he expected to send that money home to his family in Amdo. As we listened to the translator, any air of pride one could have detected in the gentle monk was exhausted like the air in a balloon.

I was moved to tears that this man, who in his homeland would be treated reverently was begging for help in my country. It was embarrassing for me, so I ran to my car, drove to the closest ATM, withdrew four hundred dollars, and returned within a short while.

"Please take this, sir," I extended the money. He smiled warmly and softly pulled the bills from my hand.

"*Thukje che,*" he thanked me in his own language, and I was pleased that I could put some of that amazing smile back together.

Back home in my room, I thought of Geshe Loten as I recited the prayer he taught me and visualized money flowing to him as the Tara mantra sped out of my mouth, thumbing the beads of my mala. I didn't believe there was a green goddess waiting for me to reach a special number in repetitions of her name to make her spring into action, but it made me feel less helpless and focus my mind. In all the amazing things about these wonderful people, they didn't like argument or confrontation. It must've been quite difficult for him to make such a request publicly.

Kunyang called me and asked me to come down and see her. "I'll buy your lunch." That sweetened the two-hour drive. Sitting at the bar in her restaurant, I explained what happened the previous weekend, expecting to be ambushed with a scolding as I dipped into the hummus.

"We've had a lot of problems," she said softly. "I sometimes feel like I'm wading through so many bills, so many things that need done but no one to do them, it's exhausting."

"I'm sure it doesn't help not having enough regular volunteers."

"It doesn't. I'm telling you this because you're the only person that will listen to me bitch without folding your hands and bowing your head at me as I do." I watched countless visitors to the center bow at the statutes, the murals, the building itself, Kunyang, each other, squirrels, the pine trees. It was comical and they didn't realize it. "Why are Americans like that?"

I laughed. "Ignorance. Many who left Christianity are looking for a replacement, some want to be a part of something mysterious like playing Dungeons and Dragons. And a lot of straight guys I know just have an Asian fetish."

"Maybe," she chuckled. She stared at me for a few minutes as I chewed my pita. "Why don't you move down here and help me around the center? You can have a room upstairs."

I almost choked, "Kunyang, I'm not going to get wrapped up in this world more than I already am. I have too many schools that I work with and can't start interrupting my rhythm of what I do for them... or you. My schedule is finally balancing time for both. Besides, I think the world of you, but you like your arguments."

She pulled me away from the bar. "I want to show you something."

I followed her into her little office. It was a tiny little room with just enough space for a desk, cluttered with stacks of papers. She pointed with an open hand to a thangka that was hanging above her desk. "This is my protector. She's female, and she's wrathful. I have to be like this in a world where men push us aside and think they can always do better."

I looked at the image and its symbols common to the other wrathful Buddhas I studied—flames, skulls, blood, weapons. "I think even she would know when to use honey to get the worker bees to do what you need."

She cocked her head. "What do you mean?"

"We have a saying in America, I'm sure you've heard; you can gather more bees with honey..."

"Than with vinegar," she finished my sentence.

"Don't use vinegar with Americans that come to the center. They're all looking for honey."

She patted me on the shoulder. "You're turning into a little Rinpoche, aren't you!"

Not long after that, I woke up at home from another bad dream. Clumsily reaching for the dream notebook, it fell to the floor and I left it there. Sitting up and slapping my head, I scolded myself, "Here we are again!" After my shower, the jeans I tried to pull on were tighter than usual, adding to my already soured mood. My workout routines were neglected for my morning studies. Driving to seven rehearsals a week put me in a rush most of the time and I was eating fast food more often out of convenience. Yanking the jeans from my legs and throwing them across the room, I let out an angry, defeated, and loud groan.

Wyatt came into my room, finding me on the edge of my bed in shorts and my head in my hands. "What's wrong, Lady?"

"I've seriously got to start working out again. I can't button my pants."

He started laughing and came over, giving me a little punch in the arm. "It's not that big of a deal, darlin'. Don't let it get to you."

I looked up at him. "Wyatt, you're as thin as a rail. And you know that having a gut in the gay community is like garlic to vampires."

"So is being over 30," he laughed, hoping it'd get me to crack a smile. It didn't. "Come on. Let's go sit outside. It's a lovely day. A little sunshine'll do us both good."

Sitting in the lawn chair by the pool, my mood didn't improve. I was feeling sorry for myself and upset that I was still dreaming about—things I didn't want to dream about.

"You're not fat, if that's what you're thinking," he tried to comfort.

"Tell that to the button on my jeans," I sulked.

"So, what!? Just put your books down and go for a long walk from time to time or go jogging. You used to love jogging."

"I didn't love it, I just had to do it."

"Had to? Why'd you have to?" he asked.

"So that my jeans wouldn't do what they're doing now!" I said on the verge of breaking down.

He tried not to chuckle, knowing I was starting to spiral out of control, then channeled his father's calming skills, doing his best to get me to land safely. He asked, "What would Buddhism tell you, darlin'?"

"Well, it would tell me to have a teacher, for starters. Which I don't have. And I don't have a boyfriend. I don't have a house of my own. I could keep going. Add all of that to the fact that I've never thought I was that attractive to begin with and now I'm gaining weight. And I'm over 30. What's the point in a jog?"

"You're not unattractive," Wyatt said firmly.

"You're supposed to tell me that. You're my best friend."

"I *am* your best friend, but I don't *have* to be. I *choose* to be. That first day you opened the door when we met, I thought you were so fine. You're more attractive than you give yourself credit for."

"Then why did he leave me, Wyatt?" I shot back, almost directing my anger at him "Sixty times he left me! Sixty times I wasn't attractive enough to keep him from looking around!" I banged on the arm of the lawn chair with my fist.

"That's not why and you know it," he said, putting his hand on my knee. "He was just starved, like you've said before."

"Why wasn't I enough? Why wasn't *I* his banquet? I feel like my whole life I've been looking to be loved and I'm just never enough for anyone. My own mother forgot my sixteenth birthday, the most important damned birthday as a kid. Every guy I've ever dated looked for somebody better. Then... DJ came along and made me feel... different, like it wasn't just about the sex *bullshit*. But everything he wasn't that made him special to me... he *was* to over sixty damned men! He promised me we'd stay together, but it was a lie, all of it. Everyone lies!"

Wyatt stood up, grabbed his lawn chair, and threw it across the yard. "You need to get it through your head that some oversexed son of a bitch doesn't get to tell you who you are or how to feel about yourself! I'm your best friend, and I love you, but you better start seeing what I'm saying!" He pounded his feet as he stormed around the side of the house. A short moment later I heard his car start and drive away.

Somehow, things that had still been simmering inside of me finally boiled over and spilled out in front of Wyatt. I had never seen that side of him and was certain that all the fears I just told him about finally manifested between us, too.

But if there was anyone that could handle my outbursts, it was him. He came back less than an hour later and held me on my futon letting me cry like I had when it all happened, when he was in Colorado and I needed his embrace. And he didn't try to convince me anymore, he just did what his father always did for his mother—he was a sponge and absorbed all the pain onto himself until there wasn't any left.

"Darlin'," he soothed, "I love you and I'll never stop. You're my best friend in the world and I see you hurting, and I see you working so hard on yourself. But you don't need a relationship with someone who did those things to you. You need a relationship with that guy looking back in the mirror. He's worth it, trust me. I love him. And if you don't learn to like him, you're looking at a lifetime of bad company, because he's not going away." He gently rocked me back and forth. "And though I'm not going anywhere, darlin', he'll be with you even on the toilet—I just won't go there with you."

I chuckled through my tears and runny nose. "Thank you, Wyatt. I wish I would've known you a lot sooner. Probably would've saved my ass from a lot of heartache."

"I'm sure I would have, Lady. And you would've saved me, too. Now," he lifted me from his chest and looked me in the eye, "let's get you something to blow your nose with; you're getting snot all over my clothes."

"But it's *my* sweatshirt!"

Nathaniel came by a few days later to tell me that he registered to return to college.

"The Ohio State University in Columbus, Ohio," he said. "Majoring in literature."

Trying to look happy for him, I smiled though I knew I would miss him. "Well, I really hope you get good grades, have a good time, and miss the shit out of me!"

He laughed and gave me a warm hug. "Aw, I think I'm going to miss you the most, Marc."

I held him a little longer, then let go before he might get too uncomfortable. "I've enjoyed you coming over here and spending time studying with me, Than. I've deepened my understanding of Dharma just getting to talk to another human about it, especially one as intelligent as you."

"It's been great," he took a step back, looking like he was about to tear up. "And this isn't over, you know."

I knew he felt some kind of connection from our coincidence as much as I did. "Not at all! Besides, we have to figure out how to make a gay clone of you for me!"

He laughed and I led him outside to his car where he gave me one last hug, and this time the tears had started. As he drove away mine, too, began to run down my cheeks.

On my way into the house, I got a call from Kimberly, which

surprised me since we only spoke a few times at the TCC. "Hey!" I greeted. "It's nice to actually get a call from you instead of our obligatory once-a-weeks. What's up?"

"Aww, thank you. Listen, I know you're getting frustrated at the center and it's such a long drive. But there's going to be a teaching this weekend with a Geshe in Indianapolis. Tenam's translating. I thought you'd really enjoy."

"I don't know, Kimberly," I hesitated. "I think I'm getting burned out. Two-hour drives for a book talk and chores around the grounds isn't what I read about that inspired me to go in the first place. I'm not sure I'm willing to give another group a try, either."

"I understand, believe me," she agreed. "But this teacher is different. I think you'll love him. We're really trying to fill up this venue to welcome him. Please come."

I sat quietly, thinking. "A break might be good, though."

"Please come, just the first one and see for yourself. It's in Indy and that's half the drive you're used to—and I'll be there, so you can sit by me." She paused waiting for a response. "If I don't see you there, I'll drive up to Kokomo and throw you in the car myself. Promise me you'll come?"

"Ok," I relented. "Since you asked so nicely." We laughed and hung up.

I arrived about fifteen minutes late. The teaching was being given in a yoga studio belonging to one of the founders of a new group calling themselves the Indiana Buddhist Center. I found the name odd since they had no real headquarters but was glad that another Buddhist presence was dawning in Indiana, nonetheless. There were freshly printed pamphlets on a stand next to the stairway, and I grabbed a few.

The downstairs had several rooms and an office, and from the smell of patchouli and lavender I could tell the owner was into new age spirituality. The sign on the office door also confirmed this. They offered massage, singing bowl therapy, and reiki, of which I had no interest, but who doesn't like a good massage? "Eighty dollars a session?" I read aloud from the sign on the door. "Cheaper to just rub myself."

I kicked my sneakers onto the mass of shoes at the foot of the stairs and followed the voices of a sizable group of people chanting in English up to the second floor. They concluded just as I stepped into the room with about thirty people seated on cushions on the floor and in chairs that lined the back of the room. There was a monk sitting behind a puja table, the short tables Tibetans sit behind cross-legged and upon which they prop their recitation liturgy. Behind him was a card table covered in a Tibetan brocade altar cloth with a picture of an older monk and a large photo of the Dalai Lama, which quickly set me at ease.

I took a seat on a cushion in the back of the small room. Tenam sat beside the monk and gave me a nod recognizing me, then dropped his focus onto his notebook as he quickly scribbled his translation notes.

The monk was Geshe Jinpa Sonam, I read on the pamphlet. He was from Drepung Gomang monastery in south India. He had such energy, at times looking angry. Whatever he was saying, it was with a lot of emotion and determination. When the translation came, Tenam's conveyance of that was a contrasting monotone.

Tenam had always been kind to me whenever I would see him in Bloomington, but I really didn't know much about this man who had been the voice for Geshe Loten. Still, it was a familiar face in the room, along with his wife.

Half-way through the teaching, my hands wouldn't stop shaking. I squeezed them, then released them to no avail. They trembled as if I was shivering from the cold. But it was quite warm in the room, and a brilliant sunny day outside. My attention left the Geshe's teaching and reviewed everything I ate or drank since waking, wondering if I overdid it with the caffeine.

During the question-and-answer portion that followed the teaching, I remembered something that intrigued me from a reading of Nagarjuna's *Seventy Stanzas* and an article in a science journal about filmmaking and perception. I was the first to raise a hand.

"In Nagarjuna's *Seventy Stanzas* he says that there are 65 moments of mind in the time it takes to snap your fingers. Science has also found that in cinematography, the human mind can't perceive much past 60 frames a second. The first part of my question is how do you see science and Buddhism working together, and second, through what methods did Nagarjuna reach such an accurate assessment?"

The room buzzed with chatter from the crowd. People turned side to side talking to one another after my question. I sank into myself trying not to be seen—I'm *that* guy, I thought.

As Tenam translated, my attention was still on my twitching hands and I didn't fully comprehend the response from Geshe-la. I nodded with gratitude when he finished and tightened my fists to abate the trembling.

The next question came from a short, round sphere of a woman with white hair and almost no recognizable neck. "How do you use the mala beads to count prayers?" she asked with a very Hoosier voice.

Her question was quite elementary, and I immediately knew the audience. This was a group of beginners, and I suddenly felt out of place. After the teaching, I darted down the stairs, put my shoes on and ran out to my car. Two women stepped outside and shouted to me, "Hey! Who's your guru?"

"Don't have one yet," I said as I backed out and drove away.

On the phone with Kimberly that evening, I explained feeling like an asshole know-it-all. She laughed. "It's going to feel like that until we get more people with knowledge and commitment to start coming. You'll be there next week?"

I thought for a moment, "Sure," I said. "Why not?"

I arrived early enough to take a seat on a cushion in the front row. After a short wait, Geshe-la entered and we all stood with hands folded at our heart. The crowd was smaller, about fifteen people who fit more comfortably in the room than last week's crowd. Geshe-la sat and we began to chant in Tibetan transliterated in the prayer books, then in English afterward. As he began to speak in his native language, I looked around at the simplicity of the room, and thought about how it was a great contrast to the bling of the monastery and the TCC.

The tremble in my hands started up again from the week before, and I wondered if the large Diet Coke I drank was somehow giving me the shakes. Though I was not diabetic, I started to worry that I might be having a blood sugar problem.

The teaching concluded, and embarrassingly didn't register with my memory much. He was teaching the basics, and I had read several books on the topic: *The Three Principal Paths*. It's an introductory Lamrim text, only fourteen lines. It explains the importance of renunciation, the altruistic heart, and having a correct understanding of emptiness. Actually, I had snuck into a teaching in Gaden and heard a monk teach this brief text already.

Renunciation is the recognition that since everything in this world is changing and impermanent it is unreasonable to chase after acquisitions in the hopes of gaining the lasting happiness that all beings innately seek. The altruistic heart, known as Bodhicitta is a compassionate attitude that wishes to achieve highest enlightenment ourselves so that we can be better equipped to guide all other sentient life out of the cycle of rebirth and to the same state of freedom. And finally, the correct view is a wisdom that recognizes the illusory way things and beings exist and works to see them in an ultimate way—empty.

My taste with renunciation started when I began to realize the origin of my shopping addiction to clothing, born in my tiny wardrobe my senior year in high school. The obsession with clothing hadn't solved the problem from the embarrassment of those days. And I wasn't happier with almost four closets of clothing. From my readings and studies, I realized that my obsession wasn't solving anything, so I started buying designer clothing less and tried to be satisfied with what I already had.

Another experience with this concept came to me in a gym one night as I was working out. A thought arose—everyone in the gym, including me, was working very diligently to abate the aging process, though we all walked out of the gym an hour or so older. I laughed aloud, cut my exercise short and went home. My new attitude about working out in pursuit of eternal youth caused me to frequent the gym less and less—and my pants grew tighter because of it.

My taste of what I imagine could be Bodhicitta was very brief, but it happened at a dance club one night while I was out with Wyatt. While on the dance floor, I scanned the sea of well-manicured and groomed men bouncing up and down to the music. The cycle of suffering that all of these guys put themselves through, weekend after weekend—getting all dressed up, doing their hair, moisturizing their skin, putting on expensive clothing, and going out hoping to look impressive enough to find themselves someone to be with, someone to numb their pain of loneliness, was an inescapable observation. I remembered the fear Joe had with the Target soccer shirt, and I looked at Wyatt dancing next to me, wearing a DKNY sweater from my closet. I felt an overwhelming sadness and a wish to remove all the fears of loneliness from everyone in my sight.

"Can we go now, Wyatt?" I asked, trying to fight back my emotions, feeling helpless.

"Seriously?" he was shocked. "It's early! What's wrong?"

"I know, I'm sorry. I just can't be here much longer. I'm having a *thing*." He didn't know what I meant but took my hand and led me out of the club and to his car.

He seemed a little peeved on the ride home, which was understandable. "I don't know what to tell you, darlin'. You've got to find a way to stop letting thoughts about DJ surface and ruin you."

"This wasn't about DJ, not entirely. I just saw a whole lot of suffering in the bar everywhere I looked. It just hurt my heart."

"Are you sure you didn't see them trying to stop? Aren't we all trying to stop our suffering?" he asked.

"If we're really trying to stop, why do we do it every weekend?"

And finally, my experience in the park was a miniscule taste of the topic of emptiness. This was my naïve thought that I had a grasp on the *Three Principal Paths*. But merely tasting something isn't the same as consumption and digestion.

At the third of Geshe-la's teaching that I attended, there were only five students. I felt bad for this monk who not only received his sixteen-year training as Geshe-Loten did, but he went for several *more* years, achieving the highest degree in the monastery—Lharampa Geshe—and then was sent to America by the Dalai Lama himself! Such a waste of a brain on us heathens, I thought.

Again, my hands started trembling. On top of that, there was the feeling of butterflies in my stomach and my knees were shaking a little, too. I looked up at Geshe-la, who seemed to speak every word with such fire *at* me—like he was speaking to me directly! Staring at his stern expressions, I realized that my shaking only happened in his presence and nowhere else.

After the class, I jumped in my car and drove straight to Bloomington, whipped into the lot at Gaden, and quickly found Jamyang. He listened with a gentle smile as I frantically told him about my trembling experiences in front of Geshe Jinpa Sonam.

"It's ok," Jamyang tried to calm me down. "It's probably a karmic connection with him."

"What do you mean? Like it's from a past life?"

"Yes."

"How would I know?" I asked, entertaining the concept for a bit. "How do I know that it's not something bad about him?"

Jamyang chuckled. "I know him. He's a good man. We went to the same monastery."

"But," I paused. I had never let on to Jamyang that I was aware of the split in the Gelukpa order—the Dalai Lama's sect of Buddhism—nor that I chose to not participate on his side of the schism. "So, are you telling me that I should give this guy a chance because we might have some connection from a past life."

"Maybe," Jamyang said as we walked around a large circular flower bed encircling a flagpole that flew a banner full of prayers and mantras written on it.

As I drove back toward Indy, I called Kimberly and asked for Geshe-la's address. She said that the IBC was putting him up at some apartment in Greenwood and he'd most likely welcome new company. Before arriving at his apartment, I downed a bottle of water and a sandwich to get rid of any possible food related jitters—just to be sure.

Could this be my guru? I asked myself. Could this monk who teaches while seated in front of a card table used as an altar be the spiritual guide I've been seeking? I got out and walked up to the door but paused and thought about going back to my car and snapping out of this guru worship fantasy. Then the door suddenly opened, and Geshe-la was standing there with a smile. "Hello! Come in." I paused and looked around. Slowly, I stepped into the apartment and he shut the door behind us.

He was dressed in a yellow tank top undershirt and a deep saffron skirt, called a *chupa*. There was little furniture in the studio apartment: a simple bed next to the door, a dining table with no chairs, a puja table beside the wall and under the window, and a large hutch acting as an altar like the one in the mural room at the TCC. He walked to the little kitchenette and started boiling water.

"I've enjoyed your teachings, sir," I said, not really knowing how to start a conversation with him.

"Oh, thank you," he said. "You study Buddhism long?"

"A few years, actually. But I haven't had a guru. I've had a few teachers help me, though, from time to time."

He stood at the stove for a while, then poured some loose-leaf black tea into the water and stared at the pot intently monitoring his concoction.

"Do those robes signify anything?" I asked, having never seen such attire. I sat on the floor near his puja table, facing the altar and the adjacent door to the kitchen.

"Oh, yes! Laundry! This... little bit... monk underwear." He laughed in a high pitch, and it was nearly impossible for me not to chuckle with him. His English was quite broken, and his speech pattern reminded me of Yoda.

"Have you been in America long?"

"Since 1999. Dalai Lama asked me here come."

Once again, I was just one handshake away from His Holiness. "Where have you taught if you've been here almost three years?"

"Last, just come from Independence, Kentucky," he said. He went to the refrigerator and pulled out a gallon of milk.

"Did you like Kentucky?"

"Kentucky quite nice. Good people." He poured the milk and continued staring into the pot.

There was a care package from India on a chair next to the stove, and the label was large enough to read from where I was sitting. He reached in the box and pulled out a large container that looked like butter. Could butter have survived a trip like that, I wondered?

"Is that butter?" I asked.

"Yes, I make butter tea."

"Is it yak butter?" I thought that was a reasonable question since it was in the box.

"Oh! You drink yak milk?" he laughed.

"I've never tried it before, but I enjoy trying new things."

His laugh raised in pitch. "I take you zoo! They have yak. You milk yak."

I didn't understand why he would suggest such a thing. "Will they let people do that?"

"No," he grabbed a hand mixer from inside the box, "yak maybe not like."

My confusion wasn't getting any better. "Yaks don't like getting milked?"

His laughter was getting quite loud, even over the hand mixer that he was using to blend the contents of the pot. He finally stopped blending, continued chuckling, poured some of the concoction into two mugs, and carried them with him out of the kitchen.

"Yak male," he said, offering me a cup, "female called *dree*."

"Oh!" I exclaimed as I took the mug he offered. I started to laugh as he sat on the floor behind his puja table. "Wait, that butter and mixer didn't come from India?"

"No, just using box as table."

I looked down at the steam rising from my mug. It was far too hot for me to taste it yet.

"What did you say this is?" I asked politely.

"Butter tea, very tasty," he took another sip. "You like?"

"I've never tried it before."

"Drink," he said, motioning me to take a sip.

"It's really hot. I have a wimpy mouth."

"Wimpy mouth," he repeated, as if to memorize the words I used.

My hands started to tremble again, and I looked at him. He

remained blissfully unaware. When will this stop, I wondered?

His altar had several statues: a central Shakyamuni, an Avalokiteshwara, two Taras, and a Padmasambhava. There were photos of the Dalai Lama and other monastic teachers I didn't recognize. All of them were behind the glass doors of the upper level of the hutch with the interiors lit from above. I put my mug on the floor and stepped toward the altar for closer inspection.

"You know Dalai Lama?" he asked.

I giggled, "You know him better!"

He smiled. "You *like* Dalai Lama?"

I sat back down and picked up my mug. "The Dalai Lama is why I am a Buddhist. I have read many of his books."

"Oh, that good," he said.

I blew at the steam and brought the cup closer to my mouth. It smelled brothy, and I slowly took a sip. It was buttery, salty, and delicious, not tasting anything like what I expected. I only ever had sweetened chai with the Tibetans. "This is amazing!"

"What amazing?" he asked.

"I mean, it's delicious! This is called butter tea?"

"English, yes. *Buh-ja* in Tibetan," he explained.

"Buh-ja," I repeated and took another sip.

"What your name?" he asked. I was instantly embarrassed for forgetting to introduce myself.

"Marc," I said.

"Mahhhhk," his accent couldn't produce the English *r* sound. I chuckled but didn't correct him.

He was different than any of the other monks I had met, and it could just be that I caught him on his laundry day as he said. There wasn't the properness to which I came to notice in the other Tibetans, and his apartment didn't have the order and neatness of the TCC. The top of his puja table was cluttered with books, papers, and ritual implements out of order, and the top of the dining table near the entryway was in disarray with a lot of things, as well. I resisted the urge to get up and organize everything for him. But I delighted just sitting with him, enjoying the tea and meaningless conversation for a while, taken by his radiant charisma.

After a while, I took my leave and he walked out to the parking lot in his monk's underwear to watch me drive away.

✦ Chapter Nine ✦

Carefully coaxing the vortex from my hand mixer around the boiling broth in the large pot, I watched thick swirls of loose black tea dancing in the milky water as my mind entertained the fresh memory of my meeting with Geshe-la.

"What are you making," Al looked over my shoulder after rounding the corner into the kitchen.

"Butter tea... *Buh-ja*," I said.

"Butter and tea? Doesn't sound appealing," he said, then crossed through the kitchen, into the dining room, and to his chair in his office beyond. "Is it good?"

From the years of living with Alice, Al had learned quite often that things that don't sound appealing may be a delicious discovery for the palate. "I love it. Want to try?"

"Sure," he accepted with a hint of uncertainty in his voice.

"That is, if it turns out the way Geshe-la made it," I said.

"Geshe-la," Al repeated. "What does that mean, anyway?"

"Geshe is a monastic degree," I started as I strained the liquid into the large thermos I placed in the sink. "And la is an honorific, like *san* in Japanese."

"I thought only women could be a Geshe," he said, confused.

"That's Gai-*sha*, not *Geshe*. A Geshe is awarded after sixteen years of studying logic and reasoning. He's a master debater."

Al chuckled, "Don't they go blind after a while?"

"Honey," I laughed as I put the lid on the thermos. "I have twenty-twenty vision and I've been master debating for a couple of decades."

I poured a mug of the butter tea and took a taste. Sadly, something was missing from the recipe as the flavor was not at all what had delighted my tongue in the monk's studio. "Might want to have coffee per usual this morning," I called out, then poured the thermos down the drain.

A little later, I walked back into my bedroom, bed made, and floor cleared as I did routinely before making my morning offerings, with a mug of coffee in my right hand and a cup of piping hot black tea, still with a tea bag inside, in my left. "Well, folks," I said to the statues as I placed the tea on the altar, "Was going to bring you a different libation this morning, but I screwed up."

Descending to the cushion behind a puja table I bought recently, I began flipping through my notes of morning prayers and meditation topics I had gathered from my books and the IBC booklet I kept. I began to read aloud the refuge and Bodhicitta prayer, but stopped half-way through the first repetition and thought, what actually *is* Bodhicitta? Why not just say *compassion*?

"It is the altruistic attitude to achieve enlightenment for the benefit of all sentient beings," Tenam translated at the question-and-answer session of Geshe-la's Saturday teaching. He looked around the small crowd in the yoga studio for the next question.

"I've read that," I spoke again, not satisfied with the answer. "I have read that in multiple books. What's the point in coming here when I could just read?" I could feel everyone's eye on me. "Can you ask the Geshe to please put it into different words, from his own understanding?"

Tenam translated to Geshe-la what I asked amid the murmurs from the other attendees, but I ignored them. I was intent on getting an answer I could understand. Geshe-la began answering in Tibetan, looking at us as he spoke as if our ears were accustomed to his language, rising and falling in pitch, like His Holiness' *goat voice*, as he calls it.

"It's a responsibility," Tenam began to interpret. "One feels in every action, every word, and every thought that you want so badly to become a Buddha to help everyone. Once you have true renunciation in your heart, once you see that nothing in Samsara can bring you lasting happiness, you turn your mind with the thought to be freed. Bodhicitta is greater than ordinary compassion because it is motivated with one's own desire to be free, and seeing all other beings also trapped in this suffering world, longs to free them, as well. Then, one commits themselves to achieving Buddhahood to accomplish this wish of freeing others."

"How is that protection?" I continued questioning. Tenam looked surprised. "We say we go to the Three Jewels for refuge, for protection. How does that protect?"

The room remained quiet, and I assumed others must have had the same question in their minds but never asked. Tenam's pen moved quickly, trying to commit as much of Geshe-la's answer to paper as he could.

"If you were to put your hand on a hot stove," Tenam began, "and no one had ever told you that hot stovetops can burn you, then you are without any fault and without any protection. But when you have a teacher who tells you that the stove can burn your hand and you touch it anyway, you are also at fault, having ignored the protection of the teacher. The greatest activity that your teacher can do, the greatest protection that the Buddhas give is in their speech, in their teachings."

Many of the faces of my students over the years popped into my mind, and I was happy to think of myself as a protector to them. With a smile on my face, I nodded to Geshe-la, accepting the answer and decided I would spend time analyzing and reflecting on his words.

In the morning sessions at the park that followed, I looked up everything I could about Bodhicitta. His Holiness explained in one book that two of the practices for developing Bodhicitta were through the *Seven-Point Cause and Effect* method and through *Tonglen*.

The *Seven-Point Cause and Effect* method requires a belief that all beings have been our mothers in past lives, and not being able to accept a continuum of consciousness after death I moved on to the other practice. *Tonglen* means *Taking* and *Giving*, and it is a visualization practice of taking the suffering from someone else upon ourselves and sending them our happiness. The Dalai Lama might have achieved a state of happiness, but I was still far off. Feeling a little exasperated, I closed my books and sat in the morning sunshine next to the water.

Back in Geshe-la's apartment later that week I asked him for more help understanding Bodhicitta. He looked at me with confusion. "Bodhicitta?" I said again, and then learned that the Tibetans didn't use the Sanskrit terms like we did in English. "Great compassion," I tried.

"Oh, yes," he understood. "You do mala of *Chenrezig*, think love and compassion coming fill you from top of head." Chenrezig was the Tibetan name for the Bodhisattva of Compassion, Avalokiteshwara.

He picked up the daily prayer booklet we used on Sundays, found a prayer, and handed it to me. The pages of the prayer booklet had Tibetan script with an English pronunciation guide and translation beneath. The prayer he pointed to said:

> *Chenrezig, figure of white, all Buddhas regard you as a Buddha*
> *For your great compassion. I prostrate to you, Lord Chenrezig.*

Geshe-la chanted the prayer in Tibetan and I followed along. It was so much more soothing and hypnotic than the clumsy English that wouldn't make it into any songbook, to be sure.

"You say this," he explained. "Then, say *Om Mani Peme Hum*, with mala. One bead, once say." He moved his thumb along the beads as he recited the mantra, just as Geshe Loten had demonstrated the Tara mantra.

"Peme?" I asked. "Not *padme?*"

"Oh, Indian say 'Padme.' Tibetan mouth say 'Peme.'"

"Ah," I understood. "How will this help?" I asked.

"Make more compassion, bring more compassion energy in heart."

He recited along with me as I practiced it with my mala in front of him. I brought my attention to the sound of our voices, and I watched the beads twist and pass under my thumb. When we got to the bead with the tassel, he stopped me, "This guru bead, don't cross guru." Then he took his mala and flipped it around so that the last bead of the circuit became the first bead of the next. I did as he instructed and flipped the mala and started on our second time around.

"Thank you, Geshe-la," I said calmly as we put our malas down.

Geshe-la rose from behind his puja table and went to the altar. He retrieved a framed photo and brought it to me. "This Bodhicitta."

The image was gruesome. It looked like an emaciated beard-clad beggar sitting like the Buddha. He was so skinny you could see the veins on his ribcage, and his eye sockets were strikingly deep. Then, I realized that this must be an image of Siddhartha prior to achieving Buddhahood.

"Six years this Bodhicitta mind, great compassion for all beings, then finally make Buddha." Geshe-la spoke slowly and deliberately, trying to find the right words that he knew.

The next morning under the tree at my little spot I imagined having such devotion as Siddhartha sitting under the Bodhi tree. After about a half-hour sitting cross-legged and zipping through my *Mani* repetitions on my mala, my knees started to ache. "Glad the world didn't depend on these knees for Dharma."

Wyatt wasn't interested in Buddhism, but he would let me talk his ear off about my exploration and discovery into the mystical East. Whenever I would talk about something I read, he would often compare it to his Catholic upbringing.

"Well, maybe Bodhicitta is like Jesus dying on the cross for all mankind," he opined from the passenger seat as I drove us to a rehearsal. "Do you have a few minutes to talk about our Lord and savior?"

"Don't talk like that, please. I'm not in the mood to go ring doorbells today."

"You know what I mean," he said through a chuckle. "His intention was for everyone else."

"I suppose," I replied, "I just can't get past that whole *immortal-being-killed-by-mortals* thing. I mean, Jesus would have had to pretend to die, and that's kinda the same as lying, isn't it?"

"Yeah, now that you put it that way, I guess so."

"But I see your point. Still, Jesus hung there for only three hours and Buddha put himself through this for six years, only eating what he could put on a long blade of grass. It's hard to believe that that's true, giving up necessities let alone things you enjoy. Although," I mustered a little pride, "I have mostly succeeded in diminishing some of my own obsessions. Like, I'm staring into these books every morning instead of chasing boys."

"With your past, that's saying a lot," he laughed loudly. "But what boys are up at 6am?"

Later in the week, I pulled into the parking lot of Gaden to spend some time with Jamyang. He was on the back porch of the monastery and called me around.

"Hey, Marc! Good to see you!"

"Tashi delek," I greeted in Tibetan.

"Oh, yes," he was surprised. "Tashi delek. You're studying Tibetan language now?"

"No, no," I shook my head as I sat in a cushioned chair. "I'm just trying to say the greetings and such."

"How is Geshe Jinpa Sonam?" he asked, handing me a cup of chai.

"He's doing well... seems to be. I can't imagine being alone this long in a country with no friends and barely have a grasp on the language."

"He's a very devoted monk. The world is his home," Jamyang assured. "Are you enjoying his classes?"

"The ones I can attend," I said. "Most Saturdays are contests and I have to take my students. If there isn't a contest, there's a rehearsal. I've been able to make a few of his teachings, but not as many as I'd like."

"Well, you go see him when you can, anyway. Maybe you can learn Tibetan from him, and he can learn English from you?"

It was a really good idea, I thought. "Do you have any Tibetan language books here in the monastery I could use? I mean, really basic instruction."

"Actually, I do." Jamyang went into the monastery as I sat drinking the chai. He returned a few minutes later with a small stack of books, and I put them in my shoulder bag.

"Please be sure to tell Geshe-la I said Tashi delek," I sensed that he missed his friend and wondered why anyone would choose to abandon flesh and blood friends and family for an invisible being. It made me a bit ashamed of this controversy about which I knew so little. The situation between Geshe-la and Jamyang reminded me of my Dad and his brother, Bruce and the whole Jehovah's Witness garbage—after Dad accepted draft into the military, the church excommunicated him, and Bruce never spoke to him again thereafter.

The next morning in the park I opened my first Tibetan language book and started trying to learn the alphabet. I got terrific grades my freshman year of high school in my Spanish class, and my junior and senior year in French. I took to the languages well enough that I didn't worry much about the homework, which I tried to do little in our tumultuous house. I did really well in French, in fact, my teacher told me that the only reason she was giving the French academic award to someone else was because he was the valedictorian and he'd use it more than me. He later went and spent a long time—in *Argentina*.

The Tibetan writing was developed from the Devanagari letters by a collaboration of scholars in India with Tibetans. Tenam told me that it really had nothing to do with translating and reading holy texts as so many people believed, but more because the King of Tibet at the time wanted a way to send thank you letters for gifts he would receive. Until then, there was no written language in the Land of Snows.

The letters are quite beautiful, and they remind me of Klingon from Star Trek. Each letter has a flat head, and the variations are drawn out beneath with sharp points and scallops. There are thirty letters and four vowels that, with a little practice, are not that difficult to identify, actually.

However, the pronunciation is a totally different story. There are subtleties in the pronunciation of many letters that sound too familiar for western ears, and the books don't really help with the distinction. After a couple of weeks writing the letters into a notebook, I went to see Geshe-la for help.

We sat together for a couple of hours, and he showed me the correct stroke for each letter. My hand imitated every stroke he demonstrated for each letter. He gingerly corrected me when I erred and patted me on the back when I did well.

Pulling out my voice recorder, I asked for him to pronounce

each letter. Afterward, I tried to repeat him, but the first three letters sounded the same to me. Then he took my hand and held it to his mouth and said them so I could feel his breath move. I then repeated what I had thought was a better attempt and his face lit up! I drove home with my left hand two inches in front of my mouth and my right hand on the wheel, saying *ka—kha—ga* over and over.

Wyatt started spending more time away from the house with a guy he started seeing, and that gave me more time to spend in my studies. The day after Geshe-la had shown me the correct way to write, I carefully recreated each letter just as he had shown me, saying each one aloud. I spent nearly the whole day writing Tibetan letters that by the time I went to bed I had filled an entire notebook.

In order to make room for my language practice, I supplemented reading with audio books, many by the Dalai Lama—disappointingly read by someone else, so I didn't get to hear that charming broken English. By the end of the month, I had one full notebook for each letter of the alphabet—a total of thirty notebooks in all. I could read the Tibetan in the prayer booklet, though my pronunciation wasn't good. I felt a sense of accomplishment I hadn't felt since passing the real estate licensing exam—that I, incidentally, never used.

Every morning I spent about a half-hour reciting mantras that I learned and kept a journal logging the number of recitations of each, as well as adding notes about my morning mood before and after reciting them. Mornings in which I woke from a bad dream I simply marked—*DJ*. After several nightmares in a row, I went to see Geshe-la, concerned that my practice might be failing.

"I don't think my Bodhicitta practice is working," I said, ashamed.

"Why you say?" he asked.

"I've been doing the practice as you told me, but I've had some setbacks. I still have really bad dreams, and I kind of want that person to feel as bad as he should feel after hurting me so much."

He went to the kitchen and came back with a green plastic pitcher full of water and a saltshaker. "This water your mind, whole lifetime bad thinking, bad attitude." Then he took two small pieces of salt in his palm. "This your practice," he said, then dropped them into the water. "Flavor change much?"

I sighed, wondering how stupid I must look to a master such as him. "Thank you, sir." I promised myself to keep practicing—hoping that I could eventually change *my* flavor.

Geshe-la encouraged meditating on Bodhicitta with one of the two techniques the Dalai Lama wrote about. The *Seven-point Cause and Effect Method* starts off with the recognition that all beings have been our mothers. This is called *mar-she* in Tibetan. I suspended my disbelief and imagined that I have had this relationship in the past with everyone I knew. After a while of meditating on this point, I had a realization that made the meditation easier. In order for me to have a perception of someone I know, I have to have neural networks in my brain devoted to all the information I collect about them. In a way, they are a physical part of who I am, and their very presence in my life has sort of created the me who I think I am. Therefore, they really are my mothers, from a certain point of view. That was doable, I thought.

If all beings have been our mothers, they have been kind to us by carrying us in their womb, caring for our needs, feeding us, protecting us, and going without things for themselves. This step in the meditation is to bring to mind these kindnesses—*drin-dren* in Tibetan. Logically, the third step—*drin-so*—is to think of the importance of repaying those kindnesses. We owe our mothers so much, for without them we wouldn't even be alive. One lama said, "Goodness is repaying all kindnesses given to you; Evil is kindness unrepaid."

Love, or *yi-ong-jam-pa*, is the wish that others have happiness, and so the fourth step is to generate great love for our mothers, wish that they have all that makes them happy. Every time I came to this point in the meditation, I found myself smiling as I saw all those around me enjoying their lives and having all that they desire.

Nying-je chen-po means great compassion and is the fifth step, a wish that our mothers be freed from suffering. It's not enough that they have all things that make them happy, but they should have the freedom from suffering and be freed of even the causes of suffering. At this point sitting on my cushion, I imagined everyone with little pieces of black scattered throughout their bodies to represent the sufferings they endured and carried. To me, compassion was a wish to remove those bits from them and fill them with healing light.

The sixth step is called Exceptional Thought, or *lhak-sam nam-dak*, and it's a thought that overcomes us when we wish to remove the suffering from our mothers. When it happens, it pervades your mind and heart, a responsibility to undertake everything to help them yourself. And this is the final rung on the ladder to the seventh step: *jang-sem*, the Tibetan word for Bodhicitta—the wish to achieve highest enlightenment to be of best benefit to all sentient beings. Becoming a Buddha is considered the best way to help because of the omniscient mind one achieves at Buddhahood. With that one can see exactly what another being needs in order to purify their consciousness of negative karma and what activities one should undertake to accumulate the collections of merit and wisdom needed to become a Buddha themselves.

Mom called one morning and invited me to lunch, and we went through a drive-thru, got a bag of food, and took our food to the Reservoir Park to eat at a picnic table.

"How long did you have bad dreams about Dad after the divorce," I asked.

"Oh, Birdy," she looked up at the sky. "They never go away. There're just longer spaces between them as time passes. Still having nightmares?"

"Yeah," I wasn't happy with her answer.

"Well, it's been two years, right?" I answered her with a nod. "Have they gotten less frequent?"

"Yeah, they have, but not enough. They're often about us being together, just the feeling I used to have when we'd be doing something, anything." I stared off briefly, recalling a recent dream. "I wake up and the feeling of loss is so powerful, every damned time. I cry for a while, then try to put my attention on my morning practice."

"Practice?" she asked.

"Buddhism, Mom. The morning prayers and offerings and stuff. They always say, 'practice.'"

"I believe in karma," she said, which surprised me. "Yup, the things we do echo through time and come back to us."

It was comforting to hear her speak in such a way that accorded with my newly adopted worldview. "You mean like keeping Ed and my adoption a secret to me and that coming back to bite us both in the ass?"

"That, too, but I was thinking about how I just couldn't wait to get away from your grandmother, so I married young. I was so scared of her. She was a mean old broad," she referred to strong women as such.

"I'm not sure how you're connecting that to karma. Explain."

"After Ed and I got divorced, which was right after you were born, your grandmother took you away from me. I could only hold my little boy whenever she permitted."

"Why?" I was confused.

"She told me that if I wasn't competent to be a wife, I wasn't competent to be a mother. So, imagine the confirmation she got when she came into the bathroom right as you slipped under the water in the tub while my attention was on something else. She slapped the living hell out of me saying, '*You don't have the sense God gave a goose!*'"

"You tried to drown me?" I joked.

"She pretty much raised you until you were five. But you probably already remember a lot of that. And then I asked Joe to adopt you right after we were married. It wasn't to keep you from Eddy."

"You were keeping me from Nanny," I said slowly as the realization arose. She nodded.

"For a while, I hated her, and I hated that you seemed to love her more than me. You never treated me like your mother, you treated Nanny like your mother. Our relationship was more like a younger brother to his older sister. We never had the kind of relationship the boys and I have had. It's no fault of yours, or mine, actually... it's just the way it happened... being with Nanny, raised those first few years by her... was enough to plant the wrong perceptions. Whatever the vehicle that manifested it, the disrespect I had for my mother came back as having a child disrespecting me."

I reached across and took her hand. "I get it," I said gently. "And honestly, losing her was like losing a mother, but I just assumed everyone felt like that at the loss of a grandma."

"Sometimes, looking at you is like looking into a mirror—my little reflection."

As her eyes started to well up, I moved to her side of the table and put my arms around her, laying my head on her shoulder. "You are right," I said. "That's karma... at least what I know about it."

"I shouldn't be surprised that you are a Buddhist," she said, laying her head against mine. "Considering the memory of your little dream, I'm just surprised you didn't get you there sooner."

I sat up so quickly, we knocked our heads together. "Holy shit, Mom! I *totally* forgot!"

We sat and recounted a dream I had when I was four years old. When Mom and I went to pick Dad up from his weekend with the National Guard, I was lying in the backseat on our way home, slowly falling into a hypnotic trance from the slow rhythm of the streetlights as they passed the window. Just as my eyelids closed, I was suddenly lying in a wooden cart full of hay, my wrists and ankles restrained in black iron shackles, and the streetlights transformed into crucifixes, each with different corpses in various stages of decay. It was so frightening that I shot up from the backseat, crying to Mom and telling her what I had seen. The only explanation that she could come up with was a dark imagination of a dreaming child.

However, while in high school at seventeen years old sitting in World History class, the teacher began to talk about the Appian Way, the long road from Rome to Carthage where the soldiers lined the sides with crucifixes to send a clear message to anyone traveling. As my teacher spoke, my hands began to tremble, and I started to tear up without reason. I asked to be excused and went into a stall in the restroom where I cried uncontrollably. That afternoon, when I started to tell Mom about my peculiar emotional outburst, her face turned white and she recalled the dream I had all those years ago in the backseat of the car.

When I stood there in the kitchen and asked her what it meant, she shook her head and said, "I really have no idea, Birdy."

As we sat at the picnic table in the park she asks, "Do you think it has something to do with a past life?" Considering how my hands had shaken so much when I first met Geshe-la and my strange reaction to hearing about the Appian Way, I simply said, "Maybe... maybe."

When the cold weather set in, I stayed in my room instead of going off to the park. Even though the coincidence with Than made it all the more sacred of a place to me, I couldn't sit outside long when the air would bite at my skin. One morning as I was reciting *Mani* mantras, a thought popped in my head and I sprang from my seat and went across the hall to wake Wyatt to tell him that I wanted to design a Tibetan themed show.

"What time is it?"

"It's 5:30am, you can go back to sleep after I get this out of my head."

"Child, I ought to smack the bejesus out of you!"

"I want to do a show about Bodhicitta! I want to put the *Mani* mantra on the floor, on flags, everywhere!"

He rolled away from me, pulling his covers higher. "Have you thought about how you're going to choreograph a show about a big Buddha concept and get the audience to understand."

Winter guard is an activity where the color guard of the marching band puts together a show on their own. They can use any music they want, or poetry, or spoken word, and with props and sets, in a gymnasium with an artistic floor covering. It's actually more competitive than marching band, mostly because it costs less to fund a guard of no more than thirty than it does bands that have no limit in numbers. I make most of my money designing marching band shows, due to the fact that the nicer weather doesn't hinder the number of groups with whom I can service in person. I've gotten skilled at being able to send videos of my choreography to schools I will never see, and I can do one show in an afternoon. But winter guard takes more time to design and develop. I usually work with fewer groups so that I can drive less during the snowy weather and reduce my chances of accidents.

"This show could be extravagant, like a Tibetan thangka painting come to life! Each of the kids could be different animals: a peacock, a swan, a flamingo, a lion, a cheetah, a panther, a leopard, you get it? With more theatrical make-up than has ever been seen in winter guard!"

I convinced Wyatt to help me design the show with one of our schools. Western had never had a winter guard at their school, but the girls worked so hard and developed dance and equipment skills so quickly in the summer and fall that I wanted them to have a memorable production, especially since their band has been nationally ranked throughout the years.

The kids loved the concept and we worked hard throughout the season. One young freshman, Kathleen, became a model of hard work I would brag about to other schools. In the fall, when the girls were working on their splits, Kathleen was standing up, legs spread wide apart, but nowhere near the ground. "Kathleen, you can go farther than that," I scolded.

"No... I... can't," she said straining.

That winter, during a stretch block at the beginning of one rehearsal, I noticed Kathleen had almost gotten her splits to the ground. "How did you get so limber so quickly?" I asked, astonished.

"You told us to stretch at home every morning," she said with a confused look.

Wyatt and I almost had heart attacks! "A student who listens?" Wyatt exclaimed with joy.

After Christmas, a new girl, Katy, with color guard and dance experience moved to the school. I wanted her in the show, but we had so much momentum with half the design completed, I wasn't sure how to put her in.

Then one night, I had a dream of the Potala Palace in Tibet, where the Dalai Lamas have traditionally lived until the Chinese invasion. Seated in space in front of the Potala was Avalokiteshwara, sitting just like in the paintings. He floated into space and out over a large field of a variety of animals, raining white light down onto them. I woke the next morning and quickly scribbled in the journal next to my bed what role I would give Katy.

"You are going to be the Bodhisattva of Compassion!" I said with excitement.

She half smiled and said, "Ok," not understanding, but excited to get to perform.

"Instead of you having to learn the whole first half of the show, I'm going to build a prop of the Potala Palace where the Dalai Lama used to live in Tibet and you'll sit there in front, wearing a crown and a large cape with this Tibetan mantra appliqued on the back. Then, you'll spring to life and come dance fiercely, making all the animals get along and be happy!"

"Whatever you want me to do," she said, and I felt like I had just danced up a storm in front of my mother again—*ribbit*.

I hoped Geshe-la would find the idea of my show design worthwhile when I tried to explain it to him that week. Sadly, I don't think I was successful at explaining winter guard to him, let alone the idea of a Tibetan thangka come to life with flags, rifles, sabers, and dancing.

"Marc, why you not coming my teaching?" Geshe-la asked as he handed me a cup of butter tea.

I told him about my schedule, my students, my responsibilities, and all the driving. "You see, my students are my Dharma."

"Oh, that true," he said, and sipped his tea. Then, he looked at me, pointed at his cup and asked, "This tea, hot, yes?"

"Yes, very hot," I nodded.

"Remember: *ja dang gaygen tsani gyal*. Say!"

I repeated after him. "What does that mean?"

"Tea and teacher best hot."

Thinking back to my world champion staff, I agreed, and I committed his words in both languages to memory.

I recently made my first mala, using natural stone beads I found and strung them with Tiger Tail jewelry wire. "I've read about the materials for making a mala but wasn't sure if I could use this."

He inspected the rosary, counting the number of beads, then looked at the wire. "Oh, this good."

"So, it's ok to use metal wire?"

"Yes, yes. You smart. Where you get wire?"

"From Walmart," I answered.

"Oh, Little Beijing!" he laughed.

When the competition season finally came, I spent nearly three hours most Saturdays on the students' make-up, personally doing each face exactly the way I wanted. The kids loved performing the show, and really came to life in front of an audience. I sat on the sideline, watching with such pride.

Three weeks before State Finals, I asked Al to come and help. It had been a few years since he worked with a competitive indoor color guard. After a summer and fall of nearly thirty marching band shows, winter was a break for him and a time to put himself in order before the next year's planning meetings, which typically start at the beginning of the second semester. He was excited to get up off the couch and come synchronize some choreography, and he was good at it.

Before our preliminary competition that would qualify us for State Finals, I pulled the guard together for a talk. "This show is about the importance of compassion, you know. Bodhicitta is a kind of compassion that comes from the heartfelt responsibility one takes upon themselves to free others from suffering. Well, your audience is suffering. They have bills, relationship problems, personal crises that they want to be freed from. We, as performers and entertainers can give them just a breath of fresh air."

"How?" one girl asked.

"By our commitment to our performance. Our mindfulness of the techniques in dance, equipment manipulation, and emotion are compassionate activities, not just something we're competing with. Give this show to the audience as a gift, and let the judges decide what your placement should be. Fall in love with compassion."

Wyatt cleared his throat loudly, then said, "And if all else fails, you know exactly what to think to have a great performance. What's the real mantra?"

"Wyatt's pretty," they said and giggled in unison.

He slapped me on the arm and said, "See? You should've had that sewn on to that back of that cape!"

At State Finals, the kids had the performance of their lives. Watching Katy come to life half-way through the show as Avalokiteshwara, spinning in circles on her toes as the cape swung round, reaching a climax and turning her back to raise the cape that read *Om Mani Padme Hum*, while the rifles rotated in the air behind her. It was definitely one of my most favorite performances throughout my career, and I have worked with over 300 programs across the country. The audience loved the show so much, they sold out the photo collages of our group the circuit photographer was selling at his booth.

The secretary of the circuit, Kim, a warm, energetic successful designer and educator devoted to the activity in Indiana told me that day that we had achieved the highest placement in the state's history for a group in their charter season. Third place was a huge accomplishment for those girls, and I watched them work their tails *off* throughout the whole season—and then perform the house down at state finals with tails *on*!

My dear friend, Gina, came and helped out with that show, a brilliant talent at her craft and a lovingly devoted instructor. At finals, after I placed medals around the necks of all my students, the first time I had the opportunity to do that in my career, I turned to Gina and she put one around mine. "Welcome to the medal club, darlin'," she smiled with pride, and hugged me warmly.

I walked over to Al, who was in tears, always happy for the accomplishment of his students. "Thank you so much," I put a medal around his neck. "For more than just getting this show together with me."

I stayed in Indy for the rest of the weekend. But when I got home late Sunday night, Al was asleep on the sofa with his medal still around his neck.

❖ Chapter Ten ❖

I arrived at Geshe-la's apartment to share with him the news of my students' victory. He opened the door, and as I entered, I could see on his puja table a mala that was mostly standing straight into the air. I chuckled to myself, pointed to it and asked, "New project?"

"No," he said disappointingly. "Wrong wire."

"I'll take you to Little Beijing later and show you which one is Tiger Tail."

Geshe-la made tea, as usual, and when he sat to drink with me, I showed him all the pictures from the Finals performance. "That really nice," he said, closely examining the photo of the *Mani* mantra in shiny letters on the back of the fully extended cape.

"I was hoping that Tibetan people would appreciate this for all that I've learned from you."

"I no Tibetan, I from Ladakh!" he corrected, then explained that Ladakh is a Tibetan-like region in northern India. "Tibetan say 'Tashi delek,' Ladakhi say 'Julee.' Both language similar."

"But aren't you speaking in Tibetan when Tenam translates?"

"Yes, only speak Ladakhi with other Ladakhi."

He gave the photos back to me and placed his tea on the puja table beside a book that said *Heart Sutra* on the cover. "May I see it?" I asked.

"Yes, Heart Sutra, very important."

"Will you teach me?" I asked eagerly, hoping to receive a teaching whose oral lineage stretches unbroken from the Buddha to today.

"You memorize Heart Sutra, then I teach." I had a copy of the English translation at home and made a mental note to start memorizing it.

After finishing our tea, I took him to Walmart to show him where the jewelry wire was, and then to a nearby grocery store. He was quite the sight to many who would stare at his attire. From the waist up he wore a tee shirt and ball cap, but he wore the lower robes that looked like a skirt and he carried his monk's shoulder bag, which looked like a type of purse. Once, while he was looking at loaves of bread, a white-haired woman was staring at him uncomfortably long. Catching her eye, and with a kind grin on my face, I facetiously said, "He's a monk, not an out-of-work drag queen, ma'am."

The week that followed, I recited and memorized the Heart Sutra. I had a copy in my car and would have Wyatt test my memory as we drove from school to school. I returned to Geshe-la's apartment the following week and was excited for my first lesson.

"I've memorized the Heart Sutra, Geshe-la," I said, sitting straight up and proud of my accomplishment.

"Oh? Then say."

"Thus, have I heard at one time, the Bhagawan was dwelling in..."

"What you do?" he interrupted.

I paused, quickly wondering if there might be another teaching also called the *Heart Sutra*. "I'm... reciting the *Heart Sutra*," I said, confused.

"No, not English. Tibetan," he replied with a big smile.

"Geshe-la, I don't speak Tibetan."

"I no speak English. I teacher," he laughed, then told me that the monks in the monasteries have to memorize a text before their teachers would explain them. Woven into the written lineage of the teachings is a rich, living energy shared through the oral lineage. I wanted to be a part of that, but I feared it could be a long, long time before I got to receive this teaching.

Geshe-la told me a story to illustrate the importance of memorization to the monks. The night before his logic teacher was to take the Geshe exam, he was reciting many of the texts aloud while sitting up in a tree. A couple of monks came and asked him why he was in the tree. He replied, "It is my alarm clock! If I fall asleep, I will land on the ground and wake up and can continue memorization practice!"

It was a little disheartening that I wouldn't be learning this sutra from him that day. I didn't go home empty-handed, though. He gave me what is called *loong*, which is the oral transmission of the energy of the *Heart Sutra*. I listened as he chanted, imagining that I was receiving the blessings of a long history of masters.

On the drive home, I sat the IBC prayer booklet that had the phonetic pronunciation of the Heart Sutra on the passenger seat and held my mala in one hand. "Let's begin," I said, and read the first four Tibetan syllables—*di-keh dag-gi*—and repeated them around my rosary as I drove. After that, I added the next five syllables—*du-pa du-chik-na*—and continued doing this everywhere I drove, intent on memorizing the two pages of this most beloved text.

At his next weekly teaching, Geshe-la told the story of a master who used a mind-training method that intrigued me. This master used to carry with him three small bags: one with white stones, one with black stones, and an empty one into which he would move stones from either of the other two whenever he had a positive or negative thought, word, or action. At the end of the day, he emptied his bag onto the floor and compare the number of white and black stones that indicated how well he had behaved.

"That's brilliant," I said aloud after Tenam gave us the translation.

I decided to try the trick myself. The only place in Kokomo I could find colored stones without painting them myself was at a local health food store. They also sold a variety of new age wares, and I delighted in the new friendship I made with a tiny elf of a woman with lilac contacts named Joan. She spoke softly with an unwavering smile and was excited to meet someone who knew something about Tibetan Buddhism.

"I have those Tibetan prayer flags hanging all over the store," she pointed out. "They give off such positive energy, I feel."

Normally, I would've rolled my eyes at the thought of humans sensing forcefields and such, and I smiled as I remembered a young, new age guy at a spiritualist gathering who waved a jazz hand over a woman's abdomen and claimed her ailing liver would be healed. "Now those are real spirit fingers," Wyatt whispered to me as we watched the quack. But Joan was so sweet and helpful, I let her have her way.

There was a display case full of smooth stones at the front of the store, and I told her of the technique I was trying. While I counted out my choices, she found little muslin bags that were used for purchasing loose leaf tea, and I put the stones in them and hung them from the vents in my car, intent to overcome my embarrassing road rage.

On my way from one school to the next, I usually only had an hour before the next rehearsal would begin, and just about that much time to travel depending on traffic. I could be quite the hothead behind the wheel, and on many occasions, Wyatt would put both of his hands on the ceiling, bracing himself, while jokingly screaming obscenities.

He once gave me an illuminating math lesson as I sped along I-465. "Marc, you do get what the *per hour* part of a speed limit means, don't you, darlin'?" Realizing the negligible amount of time I would save by driving so fast, I slowed down to a more reasonable speed.

After I put the three bags on my vents, he jiggled one of them and peaked inside. "I'm trying to train myself to stop being such an asshole driver," I explained before he could ask.

"Lord, Jesus, please let it work!" he exclaimed. "Or Buddha... or Krishna... or anyone who will listen if I'm going to be in this car!"

Along with the three bags of stones hanging from the dash, my copy of the *Heart Sutra* always sat on the passenger seat whenever I drove alone and, after a month, I was able to chant the entire two pages. It was a nice feeling of accomplishment, even though I had no idea what the sounds meant. Chanting them with Geshe-la the first time, I wept and trembled. "You ok?" he asked afterward.

"Yes, yes," I said as I blew my nose. "I'm just really happy. Thank you so much!"

Geshe-la started to explain the meaning of the teaching within the sutra, but paused because his English was too poor, but I implored him to try. "I make mistake with broken English, then maybe cause more suffering for you."

"Please, Geshe-la," I begged as I took his hand. "I've suffered so much in life. I really want to learn."

He paused and stared at his table for a few moments, and I was afraid he wasn't going to try. Then, after examining the seriousness in my eyes, he began my first teaching of a Buddhist Sutra. He struggled quite often to explain, as I did to understand. But we spent the afternoon together as master and student, and I wouldn't relent when he would try to end the teaching when he couldn't find the English words he wanted.

The *Heart Sutra* is a short text, the most recited sutra in all of Buddhism. To summarize, it begins with the Buddha and his entourage near a village in northeastern India called Rajgir, at a place called Vulture's Peak. The Buddha is sitting in the background, already in a deep state of meditation when one of his students, the great Bodhisattva named Avalokiteshwara is just beginning an analytical meditation called the *Profound Perfection of Wisdom*. One of the junior students named Shariputra asks Avalokiteshwara how one should practice this meditation. He responds guiding Shariputra through a list of things to analyze, looking for any inherent existence within them, and tells him to correctly and repeatedly see that everything lacks self-nature.

For something to have inherent existence or self-nature, it has to exist from its own side, from its own power, and be independent, whole, and unchanging. Avalokiteshwara says that anything we experience with our senses lacks self-nature. The word used to describe this lacking is emptiness—*Form is empty, emptiness is form*. Whatever we see with our eyes—*forms*—are merely illusion-like and do not exist the way we think they do. They are merely a snapshot in an unending stream of transient networks of causes and conditions, like the string of dominos I often refer to. And this applies to the rest of our senses.

But Avalokiteshwara goes further by explaining that all five layers of who we are—the skandhas—are also lacking any intrinsic, concrete reality of their own: no feeling, no discrimination, no compositional factors, and no consciousness. Geshe-la said, "You know Hindu word 'atman?'" I nodded, understanding this term to be the equivalent of the Judeo-Christian concept of soul, the deepest part of who we think we are, being unchanging and eternal. "This kinda meaning no atman." I nodded a confirmation of my understanding.

"No eye, no ear, no nose, no tongue, no body, no mind?" I asked aloud, then looked at him with confusion.

"You think eye real?" he chuckled. "If this you think, then confusion. But think 'this eye empty.' Then, try find... *un-empty* eye. No find." He laughed louder.

"Oh!" I exclaimed. "When it says, 'no eye,' it means 'no un-empty eye?'"

"Yes!" he burst out, like a good teacher seeing the lightbulb go off over the student's head. "Avalokiteshwara say think this way again and again."

The confusion of this part of the Sutra comes by forgetting that we're looking for concretely real elements of ourselves, parts that are inherently existent. Sure, we have eyes, ears, noses, and so on. Buddhism never denies that, and many who misunderstand that mistake Buddhism to be nihilistic. However, the Buddhist position is that we don't have *un-empty parts*. They are all chains of dominos, and because we cannot see the invisible chains stretching backward and forward through time, we assume the appearance to be true. So, it's easier for me to think of this part of the sutra as "no un-empty eye, no un-empty ear..."

"Thank you, so much, Geshe-la," I folded my hands at my heart and bowed my head. "I will study this deeply. I can't begin to explain how amazing this is to me."

"You understand mantra? Gaté Gaté Paragaté Parasamgaté Bodhi Soha?" he asked, referring to the mantra in the text.

"I know the English—'Gone, gone, gone beyond, gone completely beyond, awakened.'"

"Oh!" he replied. "First Gaté—Gone. This Path of Accumulation."

He pulled out a blue dictionary on Tibetan terms and I found the entry for what he called the Five Paths. Briefly explained, the consciousness moves through various stages of realization over many lifetimes. After developing a strong desire to be liberated from the cyclic continuum of rebirth, it enters a stage called the Path of Accumulation, represented by the first Gaté—Gone—and progresses through deeper understanding of emptiness intellectually onto and through the Path of Preparation, the second Gaté in the mantra.

Then, when one's concentration is clear, stable, intense and focused on emptiness the practitioner enters the Path of Seeing—Paragaté—a direct perception of the ultimate. At this point the individual is now called an Arya, and this is the term that is often translated as *noble* in the Four Noble Truths. So, in actuality, they are the Four Arya Truths, meaning that the four truths are only true to beings who have had a direct perception of emptiness. For ordinary beings, logic and reason are needed to come to the same conclusion. After that, the consciousness has been liberated from negative emotions and can no longer produce them. In fact, Geshe-la said that it is no longer possible to create negative karma.

The subsequent Path of Familiarization, represented by Parasamgaté, is a period in which the consciousness is purifying itself from the subtle impressions from the kind of karma that prevent the omniscient mind—the state of a Buddha, which is the Path of No More Learning, or Bodhi in the mantra. Soha translates to "so be it." These five paths are explained in the oral tradition to be represented by each of the five syllables in the mantra, making it an easy reminder of the full spiritual journey.

He looked lovingly at me. "This very important. You think this every day, analyze, use logic, then negative emotion totally reduce."

A few days after that, I drove through the Burger King to grab something for the daily drive ahead of me. At the pick-up window, I heard a familiar voice yell my name and looked up to see Andy running toward the window. Channeling the Heart Sutra, I said, "No ex-boyfriend, no ex-boyfriend, no ex-boyfriend." Then I put on an appropriate face, just as I had seen my mother do many times when she saw someone she didn't really want to talk to.

"Marc!" he exclaimed. "I've been wanting to find you and thank you!"

"For what?" I asked with surprise.

"I've enrolled in college," he explained as he filled a cup with soda. "I'm taking classes, and it's kind of because of you!"

I was shocked. "What did I do?"

"All of our conversations about the future, you said that we can do, be, or have anything we want, if we just put the right dominos, as you liked to say, in our path. It just kind of finally sunk in."

"Well," I countered, "you had to fill out the applications and do the work yourself. I didn't do anything, really."

"That's not true! You inspired me. Can you come around and talk for a few? I am just about to take a break."

We stood in the parking lot talking for the duration of his time off the clock. "Why don't you come back some time and let's talk some more?"

I agreed to return that evening after my rehearsals. We had such good conversation that, after that night, I would come to BK every few days and sit in the lobby, often past close, talking with him about Dharma, science, politics, you name it. Several of the other workers would come to our table on their breaks and join in. It was a relief to have someone in Kokomo, once again, that had intellectual depth, and he was the only ex I've had with whom I wanted to spend time, even though he was happily coupled with someone new.

As was becoming routine, I wanted to share with Geshe-la all of my weekly experiences I had since my last visit. However, I wasn't sure how he'd respond to my stories of conversations with an ex-boyfriend since I still had uncertainty about how his culture viewed homosexuality and if it would bring an early end to a relationship upon which I was coming to rely. It was time to come out all over again.

I walked into Geshe-la's apartment with my finger inside the Tibetan dictionary I brought from the car, firmly holding the place at the entry for *homosexual*. Noticing my troubled expression, he asked, "What wrong?"

I hesitated. Though I had never felt a sense of shame in the years since coming out to myself and then my family, I wasn't wearing my pride kneeling beside his puja table.

"Geshe-la, I need you to know something about me. I'm worried how it will affect our friendship."

"I no understand," he said, looking confused.

Drawing a deep, bracing breath, I handed him the dictionary. He stared at it for what seemed much longer than the time that actually passed, then, handed it back and said, "Yeah, I know two women in

Bloomington, same. No problem."

After a big sigh of relief, I explained to him that I had given up on the pursuit of a religion when my childhood prayers to be turned straight went unanswered.

"How find Buddhism?"

He sat listening intently, through what English he could understand, about the break-up and seeing the Dalai Lama's interview. "I still have bad dreams from time to time."

"Yeah, you need compassion."

"I've meditated on compassion," I said, and explained that the thought of the suffering of another creature can bring me to tears.

"No," he leaned in, "you need compassion for *him*. Meditate on compassion for *him*."

"What?" This shocked me. "Compassion for one who's causing suffering? So, just let him off the hook and he gets off scot-free?" I asked, a little peeved.

"You make compassion for him. Want more happy? Make more compassion, even for enemy."

He smiled at me as though it was such an obvious solution and handed me a piece of paper from his puja table. The top read *Eight Verses for Mind Training* by Langri Thangpa.

"Memorize," he gently ordered.

I looked at the paper, one line jumping out at me:

> *Even when someone I have helped,*
> *Or in whom I have placed great hopes*
> *Mistreats me very unjustly,*
> *I will view that person as a true spiritual teacher.*

"Patience, forgiveness, tolerance, love, compassion, these things very powerful quality," he said. "You want these, without other sentient being, how get?"

It made sense, I thought, remembering the stubbornness I shared with my mother. How different things would have turned out if we had both just practiced some patience with one another, I pondered.

"Great compassion having, then totally change mind—also body."

"How do you mean?" I asked.

He pointed to a green book on his table. "This teach meditation really nice."

I grabbed it, and Geshe-la directed me to a page that claimed that at a certain point in developing consciousness through compassion, the body no longer requires coarse food or drink, but relies on subtle sustenance, like air. I smiled and closed the book.

"I don't believe that, sir," I said. "If that happened scientists would have pounced on it already."

"Oh, you trust science," he said.

"I'm sorry, but yes. Buddhism is amazing, but science still has details and proof, more than anything I've yet seen."

"*Yet!*" Geshe-la repeated emphatically. "Read book. Then understand meditation."

I left his apartment, not particularly thrilled with my new practice orders, but I was determined to add it to my morning ritual. I paced by the water of the reservoir the next morning, reciting and trying to put to memory the eight verses, one repetition per bead on my mala, 108 in all:

> *By thinking of all sentient beings*
> *As more precious than a wish-fulfilling jewel*
> *For accomplishing the highest aim,*
> *I will always hold them dear.*
>
> *Whenever I'm in the company of others,*
> *I will regard myself as the lowest among all,*
> *And from the depths of my heart*
> *Cherish others as supreme.*
>
> *In my every action, I will watch my mind,*
> *And the moment destructive emotions arise,*
> *I will confront them strongly and avert them,*
> *Since they will hurt both me and others.*
>
> *Whenever I see ill-natured beings,*
> *Or those overwhelmed by heavy misdeeds or suffering,*
> *I will cherish them as something rare,*
> *As though I'd found a priceless treasure.*
>
> *Whenever someone out of envy*
> *Does me wrong by attacking or belittling me,*

I will take defeat upon myself,
And give the victory to others.

Even when someone I have helped,
Or in whom I have placed great hopes
Mistreats me very unjustly,
I will view that person as a true spiritual teacher.

In brief, directly or indirectly,
I will offer help and happiness to all my mothers,
And secretly take upon myself
All their hurt and suffering.

I will learn to keep all these practices
Untainted by thoughts of the eight worldly concerns.
May I recognize all things as like illusions,
And, without attachment, gain freedom from bondage.

These eight verses spoke deeper and deeper into my being the more I recited them. It wasn't difficult to understand why the Tibetans revered this short text and its ability to tame the heart. After a few weeks of contemplating them, I wrote about my growing understanding in my journal:

> *The highest aim means to achieve final enlightenment. If I want to evolve, I have to see my interaction with other beings as the vehicle for getting there. Whatever I have learned it has been because of what others have taught me, and my emotional responses to them have been ingredients in creating my personality. I, therefore, owe them gratitude for the things about myself that I value, and for any amount of patience I've gained, for any sympathy and empathy I feel from watching them and feeling with them. I recognize that people who test me can show me just how far along the development of patience I really am, how long my fuse is. May I grow to love them. May I grow to have compassion for them. May they even have my happiness and give me their suffering.*

The book he gave me, *Calm Abiding and Special Insight* was written by a meditation expert, Geshe Gedun Lodro, one of the best in hundreds of years who had recently passed away. It was a detailed explanation on the discipline and gave me so much more ammunition to take to the cushion. Far from the erroneous mindfulness teachers in the CDs I bought in my early days of exploration, this author had clearly explained the training of concentration, its benefits, and its rewards. There are nine mental states through which the practitioner progresses in relation to a mental object. The first two states develop the stability to hold the mind over time on the mental object, the next four mental states develop clarity of the mental object, and the seventh and eight levels develop intensity. The ninth mental state is a fully mature and effortless concentration that is stable, clear, and intense. It's also quite rare.

Apparently, when the practitioner is able to make emptiness the mental object—not nothingness, but the absence of an inherently existent self or essence—the consciousness slips out of this realm, the Desire Realm full of hell beings, wandering spirits, animals, humans, demi-gods, and gods, and into what is called the Form Realm. Though these other dimensions were still mythical to me, the fact that Buddhism had such a refined understanding of concentration was captivating and it made me wonder if the claims in the book of the seemingly magical expansion of consciousness at the higher levels had any veracity. Nonetheless, it gave me far more confidence on my cushion thereafter.

Over time, the dreams became less and less frequent, and I never missed a day of visualizing DJ's suffering—though I didn't know what it could be—in the form of dark soot leaving him and entering my heart where I would destroy it and send him loving light. For a while it felt very fake, and it was.

Throughout those months I would also spend time at the Burger King with Andy, though it was uncharacteristic for me to enjoy being with an ex. We both looked forward to sitting in one of the booths and talking, and I tried to not get annoyed whenever he had to spring up and handle rush times and angry customers.

"Why don't we get together sometime outside of work," I suggested. "Maybe sometime and somewhere without distractions?"

"Well, honestly," he looked down, looking a little ashamed, "I'm kind of taking you for granted. My boyfriend, Rob, isn't fond of how much I talk about you, so there's that. And I like to spend a couple of hours with him and my friends after work, then I wake up late in the morning and have to get my homework done before classes that last until just before I have to go to work, so there's no time to fit you in. I just kind of expect to see you whenever you show up."

I wasn't upset at all—I understood—and I was pleased to be able to get time together however we could find it. "Then let's just keep it that way," I said, relieving him.

One day as I was meditating on compassion for DJ, I had the thought that the selfishness that led him to cheat on me was an illness, and I started seeing that illness in my Dad, in Wyatt's ex-boyfriend, in Alice, and everyone else I knew who had cheated in a relationship. If they had cancer, I wouldn't get angry at the various noticeable symptoms, would I, I wondered?

Then, I saw my own various selfish thoughts as an illness with which I had yet to be diagnosed. Every decision I made that was merely for my own interests was like little bits of black polluting my bloodstream and my muscles.

But then, a devastating realization that brought all my previous revelations together in one—all the selfishness throughout my past—I had been projecting that outward and into my mother, my father, my brothers, my best friends, the relationships, the breakups, the losses, and my depression. I recognized the penmanship from the author of my sorrows, and it wasn't just one book—it was volumes. That soot coated my insides, every organ, every muscle, every cell.

Geshe-la's compassion meditation revealed its purpose, and I cried. I wanted to take back any negativity I had ever given to anyone, and I didn't want them to have to pay me back for anything that they had done to me—not even DJ.

I found an explanation of the Refuge Vows with an accompanying affirmation that spoke to my heart, and I adopted reciting it in the morning:

> *My life's purpose is to free every creature from every suffering and to lead them to the highest joys, especially the sublime happiness of full enlightenment—Buddhahood. All my enjoyments and every past, present, and future happiness—including enlightenment—are dependent on others,*

and their happiness depends on me. If I actively love all of them, then they will receive no harm from me and have peace instead. Therefore, I am also responsible for their peace and happiness. I must become a servant to serve all without discriminating between friend and enemy, whatever they do. To succeed, I must become a Buddha. Therefore, I am going to create virtue through all the actions of my body, speech, and mind so that I can be of the greatest benefit to everyone, which means to achieve enlightenment as quickly as possible. May my actions not cause the even the slightest harm but benefit all so that they, too, may as quickly as possible, achieve enlightenment.

The Vows are to not harm or kill, to not lie, to not steal, to not take intoxicants to the point of heedlessness, and to not commit sexual misconduct. I contemplated these, and admittedly was stuck on the meaning of sexual misconduct and what that entailed. Nonetheless, I thought I could at least hold the other four and, without having taken the vows formally, I went about trying to live them. I became more careful with my steps as I would walk, aware that my large body could kill anything I stepped on. Though I still had a fear of spiders, I would force myself to stare into webs and observe these scary little things. "I promise I'll *try* not to kill you or your cousins," I said to a particularly industrious arachnid whose web stretched the full length of the top of a shrub outside my window.

I quit drinking any alcohol, though I hadn't been drinking too much in the last couple of years, and I didn't steal. Lying was an interesting vow because in my rehearsals I was called out once by one of my girls. It's common in dance and color guard to tell the performers "one more time" before every repetition, even if it isn't really one more time. A student named Allison jokingly called me out on the lie,"I thought you were only supposed to tell the truth, Mr. Buddhist!"

After living with the vows for a while, I decided to request to take them formally from Geshe-la, so I went to his apartment to ask him. To my surprise, the Indiana Buddhist Center was having a vow ceremony at the end of May, during the Tibetan holy month of Sakadawa. It was also the day of Geshe-la's birthday, and the observance of the birth, enlightenment, and passing into Paranirvana of Lord Buddha, all of which happened on the same day. What a perfect opportunity!

The day of the vow ceremony, a small number of people arrived at Tenam's home around 5am and slowly, sleepily, entered, greeted with butter tea and light edibles. We moved in single file up the staircase and into a little room in which Geshe-la was already seated behind his puja table. The room was dimly lit and being a smaller room than where we held the teachings, the incense was much stronger, but quite pleasant.

I sat on a cushion and looked around at everyone, pleased that the others had come to the same conclusion to follow the path of Dharma enough to commit to it officially. We began chanting and I felt a sort of safety a child feels in the presence of their loving parent.

But then, Tenam translated the part of the recitation that says *from now until this time tomorrow*, and I realized we weren't taking the lifetime commitments. These were the one-day precepts, the same as the Refuge Vows with three other expectations to be kept for twenty-four hours. The ceremony concluded, and I was a little disappointed.

We descended into the kitchen and dining room to where Kimberly had some breakfast food ready for us. While everyone was eating and socializing, I couldn't help but stare sadly into my bowl of cereal. Geshe-la noticed and came and asked me what was wrong.

"I'm sorry, Geshe-la," I barely lifted my head to speak, "but I thought I was taking the lifetime vows."

He examined my face. "Oh." He patted me on the shoulder and walked away.

The other members of IBC slowly departed, one by one, most heading straight out from there to start their workday. Tenam intercepted me before I walked through the door and said, "Geshe-la would like to see you upstairs."

When I walked back into the room in which we took the precepts, Geshe-la was sitting there again, this time looking stern with his arms folded across his chest. Nervously, I entered behind Tenam who quickly dropped onto his cushion beside the monk.

Geshe-la spoke quickly, as I stood in the doorway waiting for Tenam to translate.

"From today onward," he started, "our relationship changes. Are you ready for that?"

Realizing that he was about to give me the vows, I nodded very quickly and dropped to one knee.

Geshe-la instructed for me to say my name when indicated in the ceremony, and to say *leg-so*, which means *excellent* in Tibetan, at the appropriate times. I stayed on my right knee with my hands folded at my heart and repeated as I was instructed.

When Geshe-la concluded, he took a pair of scissors and cut a small lock of my hair. He then told me my Refuge Name would be *Sonam Tsering*, which Tenam wrote on the back of a business card for me, also writing its meaning—*Lucky Long Life*.

Before we rose to leave the room, I said, "This is such an important day for me, and I thank you so much. The Dharma has become such a major part of my life, and I have seen so many beautiful things happen in such a short time. I want to be able to learn more and help others stop suffering."

I began to cry. Tenam handed me a tissue as Geshe-la responded, then translated, "Never take the Dharma lightly. Respect it with everything in your heart." I nodded.

On the drive home, I thought about how I came into the world and was slapped with the name of a man who left my mother, then forced to take the name of a man who raised me as a favor. I now had the name of a man who chose to nurture my spiritual well-being for the rest of this lifetime. He was now my guru, my spiritual father.

Whether it was simply the psychology of highlighting in my mind the ceremony with Geshe-la and Tenam, or the true living energy of the blessings of the lineage, the fact that the following month brought with it no nightmares was enough for me. Mornings were far fuller of hope than ever, and I would go about the day saying my refuge name to myself—*Sonam Tsering*—trying to identify myself with it and a fresh new beginning.

Not long after that, the little yoga studio was abuzz about a visiting Rinpoche we were to host and his touring entourage of monks who were coming to raise funds to repair their old, decrepit monastery in Bhutan. There was a flyer on every cushion when I entered, and an old Bhutanese man with a large, embroidered, funny shaped hat peered back from the glossy page in my hand. Dorje Loppun Rinpoche Ngawang Tenzin was his name, and he was the second oldest reincarnate lama in the country.

This holy soul sat in solitary retreat in a mountain cave for eight years meditating on compassion for every single creature, and he would be in Indianapolis, of all places. Somehow, I had the karma to meet someone the likes of which I'd never find in the States, and I quickly checked my finances knowing that I would inevitably part with quite a bit of money to offer.

In the weeks leading up to Rinpoche's teachings, my concern for winning and competing chipped away, like old paint and revealed a more timeless and endearing attitude with my students. This teacher—me—was still hot, like good tea, but had developed a better motivation. Teaching Dharma values wrapped in marching band—community harmony, compassion for the audience, joyfully applying effort to achieve long term goals, and sharing wisdom—when I could do so without sounding preachy—became my new calling. Geshe-la was my role model, and I wanted to be just like him... with better English... and a full head of hair.

Having read that the Buddha said, *Giving up the householder's way of life is completing half the Dharma*, I started giving away my possessions, little by little. I wanted to simplify my life and, realizing that everything is impermanent, they didn't make much sense in my quest for something lasting. Besides, it's America—if I want them again in the future, I'll just buy new ones, I thought. Wyatt took a large portion of my wardrobe, and who would blame him. There were a lot of nice frocks in that closet that wouldn't be seen in a dance club on me anymore as I found no entertainment going out on the weekends like I used to.

Geshe-la taught me many new things after receiving my vows: the proper way to make the morning water bowl offerings—*yunchap*—and how to take them down at the end of the day, how to make the thirty-seven-heap mandala—for which I bought a decent quality offering set, how to prostrate, how to sew covers for prayer texts, and much more.

Eventually, I had committed all the Tibetan prayers for my morning practice to memory, though I was simply repeating phonetic transliterations I had written into a small, black leather-bound notebook. On the cover, I painted the Tibetan word for *mantras*, and carried it in my monk's shoulder bag like the one carried by Geshe-la. At every water break we had during rehearsals, I would pull the little book out and memorize the daily chants and mantras, often surrounded by students enjoying a repose with their water, marveling at the sounds as they flowed out of my mouth and into their hearts—where I hoped a lasting impression on their consciousness would germinate.

Rinpoche's first teaching was in another little yoga studio just north of downtown Indianapolis. I sat as close to the front as I could, holding my hands at my heart out of reverence when appropriate, and trying to impress his words into my notebook as he spoke. Geshe-la sat to one side with the other monks, and Tenam sat beside Rinpoche, transferring the wise man's words into understandable, though monotone, English.

Afterward, the monks, Geshe-la, and Rinpoche scurried into a van outside and were whisked away by the board President—a tall and muscular, soft-spoken man. His wife, the vice president, held court afterward and feigned her fatigue with all of the responsibilities of attending to the arrival and accommodations for the entourage. I took mental note to offer help at the next teaching.

There were activities planned throughout the week, making as much use of the visit of a high lama as possible. Rinpoche was to give three empowerments, which are permission to engage in secret practices of the lineage, called tantra. A public talk at a Unitarian church, and all the monks performing a religious dance at St. Luke's were also scheduled.

Rinpoche's empowerments and the teachings were held in our little yoga studio, where he sat off the ground on a makeshift throne we had put together and laid his texts on two stacked puja tables Geshe-la arranged. He spoke with a gentle, loving voice that remarkably didn't need amplification, just translation.

After the first session of the weekend-long empowerment, the vice-president once again sat in the center of a huddled group of attendants and talked about how demanding her week had been, taxiing monks, preparing literature, making phone calls, and other preparations.

"I have nothing on my schedule this week if you need a hand," I offered.

Almost looking down her nose at me, she said, "You can help by just setting up the chairs and putting them away at the end of these sessions." I nodded my acceptance to her assignment, and she went back to her somewhat mild but conspicuous histrionics.

The yoga studio belonged to her. And she was more new-agey and into crystals, reiki, and other things for which I had little regard, than she was Buddhism. She treated Geshe-la as though he were her own private monk with whom the rest of us could share a weekly enjoyment, even having him babysit for her and mow her yard.

At the lunch break of the Saturday session, I dashed out, had a quick lunch, and returned to my cushion in the front row to clarify my notes. After a few minutes, I heard the downstairs door open and the voices of Rinpoche and his main attendant, Lama Karma starting up the stairs. I quickly rose to my feet and held my joined hands at my chest as he entered, with complete reverence for such a holy being so devoted to the world's souls.

He came up to me and patted me on the shoulder and said something in Bhutanese. "What are you doing, young man?" he asked through Lama Karma's translation. He looked down at my breakfast tray that I used for a desk and retrieved the black leather-bound book with the Tibetan word—*ngak*—on the cover.

After I explained that I wrote my prayers inside for memorization, Rinpoche opened the book, but there was nothing recognizable for him since it was merely a pronunciation guide. He pointed to one of the pages, and I started to chant the prayer I wrote on it. His eyes lit up and he gave out a deep, bellowing laugh.

"Oh, no," I looked at Lama Karma, "am I butchering it?"

He uttered something to Lama Karma, and then quickly pointed to another prayer. This time, as I chanted, he joined me, his voice just under my own as if he were a lifeguard teaching me to swim with his hands gently under my trunk while I kicked.

"His Eminence is impressed," Lama Karma said encouragingly. We continued on for several minutes as he flipped the pages and pointed to prayer after prayer. Finally, he handed me the book, patted me approvingly on the shoulder, and motioned for me to return to my studies. I remained standing, as was the custom of his people, until he had taken his seat in the corner.

As I was just getting back into writing, Lama Karma came and stood in front of me, just a few steps away from where his own seat was. "Rinpoche would like to see you," he quietly announced, and though I found it humorous that he could have just said so from less than fifteen feet away, I stood up, took my few steps toward him, and knelt in front of the puja tables.

His Eminence spoke for a few minutes and then allowed Lama Karma to translate. "Rinpoche hasn't met another American layperson so devoted to memorizing their prayers like you," he started to say.

I interrupted with a laugh. "Is this your first stop on tour?"

"Oh, no," Lama Karma corrected, his face was quite serious, "this is one of the last. Rinpoche would like you to have this picture." Dorje Loppun handed me an 8x10 glossy picture of himself, like the photo in the flyer. I took it gently and held it as if it were a precious newborn.

Rinpoche spoke again, and Lama Karma looked rather surprised. The seventy-year-old master then handed me a piece of paper from his shoulder bag. Tibetan texts are written in loose-leaf books in a format called pecha, in which the pages are written in a style mimicking the original banana-leaf writings of the ancient Buddhists. On the page Rinpoche handed me were two pecha blocks of Tibetan writing.

"He wants you to have this," Lama Karma began. "This is a prayer he wrote while in solitary retreat."

"Thank you so much," I made a short prostrating nod, and placed the paper gently on the photo.

"He hasn't given that to anyone on our tour," Lama Karma said slowly speaking for himself, not translating something from Rinpoche.

My jaw dropped and a great sense of gratitude and humility filled my heart, staring into Rinpoche's loving gaze fixed on me. As I rose to take these treasures downstairs to my car, I noticed the vice-president standing in the doorway, having softly ascended the stairs and witnessed me kneeling before the master.

She met me downstairs at the doorway as I came back into the building. "Marc," she whispered. "I could really use your help today. Rinpoche gets really exhausted being around our negative American energies. It would really be good if you could help me keep people away from him and honor his need for distance."

Her true intent wasn't well hidden in her words, and I quipped back, "Number one, it's thirty feet from wall to wall with twenty people, there's going to be crowding issues. Number two, you need to do more studying because enlightened masters don't tire from negative energies, otherwise Shakyamuni Buddha would never have been able to keep his enlightenment around ancient barbarians. But lastly and most importantly, he asked me to come kneel in front of him. So just for the record I'm calling your bullshit and your need to be the most important. It's pretty negative karma to distance other students from their teacher—he's not just yours."

A small, well-timed group of students returning from the lunch break interrupted any chance of rebuttal from the shocked masseuse.

Just before the session reconvened, Rinpoche started to speak to Geshe-la and it was clear from his repeated glances at me that I was the subject of their conversation. Geshe-la took his seat and smiled approvingly at me.

After the empowerment had concluded, Geshe-la asked me in a shouted whisper, "You take me and Rinpoche my apartment?" I was excited but confused as to why he asked.

"Sure," I said, and dashed out to my car to ready it for holy guests, quickly spritzing air-freshener and transferring things to the trunk. Back at the door, Geshe-la was guiding the old holy master down the stairway. Suddenly, the president shouted down, "I'm almost ready!" Which made Geshe-la respectfully hurry the master faster.

"No problem," he shouted back, "Marc taking. You stay."

They swiftly entered my car and away we went on the most memorable mile that little black Cavalier ever drove. From the opposite side of the world, seated in my passenger seat was this reincarnate lama! Few people in his own country get to be this close to him, and I wouldn't let such an opportunity go underappreciated.

"Want to go to McDonald's?" I asked as Geshe-la laughed in my rearview mirror, but emphatically declined the offer.

Like a perfect gentleman on a date, I ran around and opened the door for Rinpoche. As he climbed out of the car, he patted me on my head as I lowered it in reverence. Geshe-la's hand reached out after Rinpoche had stepped aside, and I felt him squeeze with appreciation. I didn't follow them to the door, feeling that I had been given enough of a blessing, and they disappeared into the little apartment as I stood watching, full of gratitude of such a short but blessed moment.

Incidentally, I drove that car until it reached around 444,000 miles before I retired it, and it was still in great working order. It's hard to believe, and I am certain the old lama had blessed it with more than just his presence.

After the final session of empowerments, the next day, through Lama Karma's translation, Rinpoche invited me to a lunch at the home of his Bhutanese host family. I didn't hesitate with my acceptance. The two rode with me for the half-hour drive. Rinpoche asked about my career, and as I maneuvered through the traffic of I465, his eyes gazed at me lovingly and approvingly hearing me speak of my students.

Sitting at the table, I watched Rinpoche eating a plate of rice and curries with his hands, to which I put my fork on the table and mimicked him. He smiled as he squeezed the rice into a ball, popping it in his mouth and waiting for his little white, redheaded new friend to imitate him.

After dinner, there was no conversation. I bathed in the blessings of having such an opportunity to simply be in his presence. And I thanked Geshe-la, in my mind, for presenting such an auspicious encounter.

The monks performed an ancient ritual dance in the sanctuary of St. Luke's, dressed in colorful brocades, frightening masks, and long black wigs to the clashing sounds of cymbals, and loud unmelodic honking of long double-reed instruments called *gyalings*. I sat close to Geshe-la and Rinpoche—close enough to feel a part of their sphere and to have the vice-president's crosshairs locked on me, but far enough to be respectful of their space.

Rinpoche and Geshe-la stepped outside, and I followed. There were wooden seats in the courtyard by the old church, and as we began to sit down, I remembered that I had my color guard equipment in my car and dashed away to get them. I returned with my flag and rifle and began to dance and spin for my holy audience. Both were dazzled by my performance.

Rinpoche asked to see my rifle, a wooden mock replica of a working gun, modified for students to throw into the air and dance without danger. He spoke to Geshe-la as he twisted the rifle back and forth, never attempting to let it into the air as he had seen me do. "Rinpoche say thing of war made into thing of beauty."

"Yes, I agree!" I shouted.

"He ask, 'You teach children this?'" Geshe-la translated.

"Yes, I do. It's so much better than drugs and problems they would find on the streets."

Geshe-la gave Rinpoche his best translation of what I had said. Rinpoche spoke again through my master, "This Bodhisattva action, change thing of war into peace."

I paused, feeling a wave of humility wash across me, thinking about the marching arts in a way I had yet to view them.

Days before Rinpoche and his entourage were to leave, I had committed his prayer to memory so that I could offer a recitation to him before his departure.

At the final ceremony at a local Unitarian church, I found one last moment to have an audience with His Eminence after he had been in front of a camera and a news reporter covering our event. He motioned me to sit beside him, and I began chanting to his quickly brightening face, soon chanting along with me. Afterward, sitting there in front of a window beaming with sunlight, we smiled as my friend snapped several photos.

I framed the photo Rinpoche had given me and sat it slightly behind and to the side of my central picture of Geshe-la. Geshe Loten's photo was on the other side, and my little pantheon of spiritual teachers was blossoming.

A few days later at the photo shop, I was struck by a delightful detail in a picture of Rinpoche and me in front of the window. The guru bead of my mala was clear crystal and was glowing from the sunshine behind us, and Rinpoche's bald head also reflected the sun! With the guru and the guru bead both illuminated, I accepted it as a shining sign of divine approval.

PART III
NIRODHA: THE NOBLE TRUTH OF THE CESSATION OF SUFFERING

What is the Noble Truth of the cessation of suffering? It is the total abandonment, renunciation, purification, and exhaustion of the craving which produces rebirth, and which is accompanied by passionate desire, and which is total delight in this and that. It is the complete freedom from, cessation of, pacification of, and termination of desire.
—Buddha Shakyamuni

If we remove the causes for unpleasant and unwanted results, they simply cannot arise. On a grand scale, Nirvana is a state that is free of emotional afflictions. But we can experience little cessations in our ordinary, everyday lives without being divinely recognized like that of a holy being exalted in scriptures, sculptures, or paintings. If we stop drinking, the problems associated with alcohol also stop. My grandfather smoked cigarettes for over four decades, but a few years after he quit a doctor examined him and thought that he hadn't smoked a day in his life!

Ending our suffering is the reason why we sit with a therapist and reflect on earlier years throughout our lives, to find the causes that are responsible for the pain and sorrows we wish to eliminate. Once we recognize them and actively re-contextualize them with wisdom, they cease to produce the unwanted effects from which we desperately wish to be liberated.

*Liberation is the exhaustion of karma and the afflictions.
The perpetuation of proliferating elaborations
Coming from karma, the afflictions, and mental concepts,
Ceases by the realization of Emptiness.*

—*Nagarjuna*

❖ Chapter Eleven ❖

Not long after Rinpoche and the monks had left, I decided to do a week-long retreat, and found a place online in the mountains of Colorado. With a cabin reserved and my things packed, ready for the long drive through four states, I planned a short detour to see DJ, thinking enough time had passed and I could receive some final closure. Surprisingly, he agreed, and we met in the parking lot of a truck stop diner. After an awkward salutation—and seeing that our cars were the same make, model, and year—I gifted him a khatak and a mala.

"What are these?" he asked, and I explained as my hands trembled nervously in the living presence of a character from my dreams and memories. I handed him the mala, and he twirled it around on his index finger.

"A Tibetan friendship scarf and a Buddhist rosary," I replied, wanting to ask him to show some respect to my gift.

"Well, do you want to go in and have something to eat?" he invited. I placed the khatak around his neck, and just afterward, the cigarette in his hand ruined the offering with a small round singe. In that very instant, my nerves calmed, my breathing relaxed, and I felt a release from the years of being under his spell. It was like magic, and I had a sudden desire to leave very quickly. All the power his eyes once had on me ceased. Seeing the hole burnt into the white silk sickened me, and I felt uncomfortable being near him.

We spoke for a little while longer, though admittedly I don't recall a word he said. He didn't matter anymore, and I knew that this was more than a closure, it was a slamming door. I spent the twenty-hour drive marveling at how other-worldly our rendezvous was. For years, I had been under some kind of hypnosis, a dark depression that was slowly lifting but intermittently returning in my dreams. Somehow that small negligent act with his cigarette reached a part of my consciousness and his hold released its final grip.

As I looked out the window, staring into the eternally stretching snow-spotted Kansas fields, I thought of Geshe-la's meditation assignment, focused on developing compassion for someone who hurt me so deeply. I wept as I drove, tears of joy, and relief, but mostly of genuine love and hope for the happiness of the ex-boyfriend I left behind.

In one of his teachings, the Dalai Lama said that if one was a Tibetan Buddhist but not a Tibetan themselves, they owed the Chinese soldiers a debt of gratitude for bringing the Dharma to them. In the 1988 Spring edition of the Snow Lion Newsletter he stated, "Perhaps the only good thing that has come from our tragedy is the spread of the teaching and practice of Tibetan Buddhism." Such an enlightened thought after nearly two million deaths of his own countrymen and the destruction of so many temples and monasteries was beyond my capacity of understanding. But as I considered this closure, I realize that for the joy of finding the Dharma it took DJ to push me into that quest, and for the first time I *could* see him as a holy spiritual teacher.

"I swear, Wyatt, I've been trying to muster any negative emotion thinking about him." I laughed into the phone. "It's just utterly amazing! I've visualized him with other guys, tried to get myself jealous and I just can't."

"That was a few too many years in the making," Wyatt said, and I could hear relief in his voice. "So, does this mean you're done with Buddhism?"

"Absolutely not!" I replied, but aware of the reason of his question. "This is now a way of life and not a destination. I think when I started on this journey with that self-help psychology book, I had a real desire to get him back. Now, I'm just in awe of how much my mind has changed practicing and studying the Dharma. I'm going to continue to enjoy this way of life."

Finally, I had complete freedom from the DJ Circle! And over time, the thought of even dating anyone else became a thing of the past, having lost all interest in romance—not that my sex drive had disappeared, mind you. But the thought of being single was far better than getting into a relationship with anyone who wasn't willing to join me on my spiritual path, and I was hard-pressed to find any other gay men who had spiritual inclinations. There were gay Buddhist groups I found online, but they were all in other states and the gamble of giving up being near Geshe-la for a *hope* of finding a partner was too high-stakes. I reminded myself that even relationships are impermanent and, as a deterrent, visualized myself in another break-up before striking up a conversation with a new would-be date.

Back at the yoga studio in Indy a few months after my retreat, an American woman who was a nun in the Tibetan Buddhist tradition came for a weekend as a guest teacher, instructing a program that was designed to give Americans an education modeled on the monastic tradition. It was a seven-year program of which all the materials were free for download on the internet.

If this program was like going from kindergarten to graduation, all of my previous years of reading and study bounced around from grade to grade. A renewed excitement grew in me to fill in as many gaps in my studies as I could.

After her weekend of teachings, I downloaded all fifteen programs and put them in individual binders, making a new shelf for them in my room, feasting every morning on the Tibetan words and definitions, memorizing as much as I could. There were hour long teachings in each chapter of the lessons that I burned onto CDs and listened to wherever I drove.

Devoting all of my morning hours—and as much as I could at night when I returned home from rehearsals—to this wealth of organized knowledge, I went through the seven-year program in a year and a half. Geshe-la helped me during my weekly visits to understand points where I had difficulty. To memorize all of the terms and definitions in both Tibetan and English I made flashcards and had Wyatt and other friends quiz me whenever I could. Geshe-la never said anything, but I could sense his approval of my progress.

There were three final courses in this program, each had to be done in person. The inaugural weekend with the American nun was one of them, and when I heard of a teacher's training program offered at their headquarters in Arizona, I scheduled a semester to attend and take the final two requisite classes as well.

Before attending that fall, I spent the summer on tour with a drum and bugle corps for the first time in fourteen years—The Blue Stars, from Lacrosse, Wisconsin. After a hasty change of staff, I was asked to fill the role of Program Coordinator, and I accepted. We traveled all around the Midwest and East Coast that summer, earning the bronze medal in our division at the world championships in Massachusetts.

After that season, I shared with Geshe-la many stories of my students and showed him photos of them in action, and he was quite delighted. Knowing that I sacrificed a lot of work to tour for the summer, he asked, "Now what you do?"

"I would like your blessings to go to Arizona for a teacher's training course I've enrolled in," I said.

"Oh, that good. Good idea," he approved, and I was out the door and on the road in a couple of weeks. I drove twenty-four hours from Kokomo to Bowie, Arizona with barely a word to another soul, except for gas station attendants and fast-food workers. As I pulled into a gas station at one end of Bowie, a sheriff walked out of the little shack of a shop and saw my license plate. "I'm from Indiana, born and raised," he said.

"Oh, really? Whereabouts?"

"Little place called Noblesville, heard of it?" he said.

"Heard of it?" I asked with a big grin. "My mom hatched me out there on her way home back in 1970."

He stood and talked to me for a good while, telling me about his move to Arizona and how he bought this gas station, and after comparing notes about our childhood, we concluded that it was quite possible that his mother, who was a nurse, might have been on duty in the very hospital in which I was born! I saw this as an interesting welcome from my new place of spiritual study.

Just ten miles north of Bowie was a plot of land where the courses were to be held. There were a couple of houses, a temple under construction, a kitchen yurt into which we placed all our food and ate communally, and several outdoor shower stalls near a large, gravel parking lot.

In the hot Arizona sun, I set up my tent that first afternoon and after dinner stood in the open shower stall looking at the Chiricahua mountains that embraced the little encampment. Looking out at the sun beginning to set behind the soft mountaintops, I tried to imagine Geronimo being chased and captured, then held in Fort Bowie nearby. The landscape was completely foreign to my Hoosier eyes and I looked forward to taking hikes and seeing the historical sites scattered near the temple grounds.

On my way back across the dry riverbed, just after sundown, about twenty feet in front of my tent—the granddaddy of all fears crawled slowly toward me on the trail. Every chemical in my fight-or-flight mechanism coursed through my blood and froze me in my tracks. It stopped moving—the first wild, uncaged, free-range, hairy, black and orange, terrible tarantula I'd ever seen! Nothing stood between me and this hairy-legged terror, and I dashed back to my car to sleep inside until the sun returned the next morning.

This became a nightly ritual, and the horror of possibly waking in the middle of the night to a windshield covered in tarantulas, giggling in their little spider voices that surely sounded like Vincent Price on helium, was cause enough for tension and agita. Off the temple grounds, I found a nearby store from where I purchased a large umbrella that I used as a walking stick for climbing the steep path to a large white house where one of my classes was held. It remained ever at the ready to be opened as a large target between me and any acrobatic spiders or diving rattlesnakes that might jump onto the trails in front of me. When the sun rose, all beasts were sent into dark recesses where they hid away from the hot sun, and I could relax. This was my relief and time to get serious about my studies before classes. I would drive off the temple grounds as there was a code of silence from 10 p.m. to 10 a.m., and go sit at the trailhead to the Fort Bowie ruins for a few hours to study alone, where I would have a chocolate milk and donuts that I picked up from the Sheriff's gas station before making my way to the little picnic table.

One morning, a woman from Spain who attended the semester with me, a thin, laughter-filled soul named Maria came with me to my study spot and introduced me to the Law of Attraction. She handed me a book by Charles F. Haanel called *The Master Key System*. Its premise is simple: everything is created by our mind and we can learn how to deliberately use it to change our lives.

"It sounds like fantasy and psychology mixed together to create customers for this book," I said slowly skimming the pages.

"You know what tantra is, right," Maria said, pulling the book down to meet my eyes. Her long, curly dark hair cascaded over her shoulder as she tilted her head with a devilish smile. "Just think about it."

For a moment, I paused to appreciate the smell of sandalwood oil from her skin, and the early morning sun kissing her tan cheeks that illuminated a radiant and honest countenance.

"How is this like tantra? Getting worldly things and being trapped in desire after desire isn't very... Dharma."

"No, no," she sat up straight and took the book, "the Desire Realm is about wanting, yes. Your mind creates a seed from a desire, and it grows over time. That energy is the same that you use in tantra to create your future enlightenment. They're the same thing. This just makes it easier... like *Buddhism Light*."

"Hmm, probably more like *I Can't Believe It's Not Buddhism*." I joked.

"How is it not Buddhism," she said as she tilted her head with a glint in her eye. "The first line of the Dhammapada, Buddha's own words, says, 'All things are created by mind,' right?"

Admittedly, it sounded plausible with Buddhist philosophy. However, in regard to real-world application, I was quite skeptical. These Buddhist deities were symbolic, I believed, and not to be taken as actual entities. They and the practices associated with them serve a neurological function that we just haven't discovered, I had long believed. So, the practice of tantra must be a mental crutch to aid the practitioner in growth, very much like the visual motor rehearsal visualizations I used with color guard kids before a contest; I had them visualize their performance, sitting still while listening to the show music, to help put their body and mind in union just before bringing their show to life in front of an audience.

"I have studied this and Buddhist tantra for years now," she tried to convince me, "and it's almost one hundred percent the same."

"Give me proof," I said. "Show me something to prove it."

"You make your proof. Visualize something that you want to happen that you can imagine happening and believe it to be real, like it has already occurred. Make that visualization fifteen minutes every morning and depending on how clear it is and without contradicting the mental image with poo-pooing thoughts, it will happen. And *feel* it, really feel it with honest emotion as though it has already happened."

"We'll see," I said, and snatched the book back from her. "I'll use this for a while, thank you."

The sun was soon to set, and I could feel fear brewing in my bowels. Maybe I could use this Law of Attraction to find some courage with my eight-legged neighbors, I thought.

Finally, after several days, I stepped into the kitchen yurt and sat at the table, intent on asking one of the other students, Julia, to help me overcome this embarrassment. As I spoke, she put both hands on my cheeks and held my face in her gaze. I thought it was an endearing gesture. But after I told her that I wanted to touch a tarantula since I saw so many others do it on television and I knew it had to be possible there in the desert, she told me the reason she had held my face to hers:

"Barry just came in and took one from the shelves as it was crawling behind you."

I dashed outside to find Barry, an attractive, long-haired, ever shirtless groundskeeper, just up the trail away from the yurt, kneeling down.

I came up behind him and saw the creature moving its eight legs slowly onto the ground in front of him having just crawled off his hand.

"You don't have to do this," Julia said, having followed curiously behind.

"Yes, I do," I knelt beside Barry.

"Move slowly, and be gentle," he instructed. "They don't move fast and won't bite you."

My body was tense, and I felt the flood of chemicals trying to call me back, but I persisted. Slowly, I reached my finger down and made the gentlest contact with the spider's back.

Instantly, I felt a rush of emotion flash through me, releasing every bit of ancient fear that gripped me and I saw it as a small gentle creature. A little sentient being to whom I vowed not to harm. He freed me and saved every one of his future creepy-crawly brethren from accidentally falling victim to my fearful reactions.

With the same diligence and enthusiasm for my studies as in the reservoir park, I enjoyed every moment of my classes and delighted in my homework. Each morning I would sit under a little pavilion next to the trailhead that led to the old fort ruins and memorize my class materials, complete my homework assignments, and enjoy the silence with the occasional interruptions of a screaming falcon flying overhead.

During my Teacher's Training class, the Lama explained the importance of being a living example of Dharma for our students. "A qualified teacher should have spotless morality," he said, and I hung my head thinking about my years of promiscuity before trying to have a monogamous relationship with DJ.

"Why do you look like you are about to cry, Sonam?" Lama Marut asked in front of all the other students.

"I am not particularly proud of my past before coming to know the Dharma, sir," I responded, a little embarrassed.

"This isn't about you, Sonam," he said, firmly but with a gentle intent to heal. "This is about the Dharma. It transformed you, it can transform others. You will find the Angulimala Sutra and read it. Angulimala was a murderer that the Buddha tamed and led to enlightenment. If he can do it, I'm sure whatever it is that has you feeling shame isn't so bad to keep you from enlightenment, too."

"Thank you, Lama," I said, wiped my tears, and promised myself that my past wouldn't bring me an ounce of shame and guilt again.

One day, several weeks into the semester, I pulled up to my usual spot feeling quite sleepy. I left the car running and reclined my seat with the intent of having a short nap. Just before falling asleep, not quite awake, I heard a woman's voice, just like the one at my little spot near the Wildcat Creek Reservoir, say, "Consider the hearts of species, it is noble to draw the diamond."

With a gasp of surprise, I shot straight up, thinking that someone just spoken to me, but my window was closed, and I was alone inside the car. There was no one else around, no cars parked nearby, and when I got out and circumambulated the vehicle, I could find no footprints or indication that anyone was nearby. Throughout the previous weeks, I had only seen a handful of cars, and only spoke with the local ranger when he made his rare stop. No one was there, but I felt that voice shake my chest and rattle my eardrums. It was clearer than a dream, and yet I hadn't fallen asleep.

It was one of those strangely spiritual events in my life that I knew I would remember forever, like the dream of the gazebo and the talking white animals with red ribbons around their necks. I often hoped for that dream to repeat itself or to have another just like it. If ever there was something that made me feel like I was receiving messages from the beyond, that dream—and now this voice—fit the description.

That evening I found Maria and told her about my experience. "Who do you think it was?" she asked.

"I have no idea," I said. "I don't even know if it was a 'who.'"

She laughed. "These grounds have been dedicated to Vajrayogini, and it's quite possible she spoke to you. And that message was for you alone. Kind of like a Japanese koan, perhaps."

I knew nothing about this being of whom she spoke. But I definitely felt something in the car, and I was pretty shaken by the experience.

"I don't really believe in past lives, or invisible beings, or becoming a future Buddha. I have to admit that. Sure, Buddhism has given me a lot, but it's been psychological-spiritual not heaven-spiritual, you know?"

She had a glint in her eye and said, "Let's prove it together then, ok?"

She kneeled on the ground and grabbed a bunch of rocks. "Look at this rock," she handed me one. "Is that a changing thing or an unchanging thing?"

"It's changing, although imperceptibly to our senses."

"Right," she said, and laid five stones in a line. "These represent five milliseconds of that rock. Each millisecond is a brand-new rock, even though it looks the same."

"Okay," I said, staring at the five stones. I explained to her my choice of description as the chains of dominos.

"That's exactly right! Now, your perception is simply a mechanism to get the information out here in the world in there to your brain. Right? So, when your eyeball sees the rock it is a direct perceiver, making direct contact with the light that has bounced off the rock. Then, that is turned into vibrations that go through your eye, onto a nerve that goes back to your brain. Then, it becomes a mental image. Your brain must find out what kind of image it is, in this case it fits into the category of *rock-ness*, and then you come up with the defining label—*that* rock, Maria's rock, or something specific. Got it?"

"Right, that's pretty much science. That doesn't prove past lives, though."

"Just wait. Each of these five moments we've pointed out all require awareness energy, in the organ, in the nerve, in the cells of the brain. Awareness energy is fundamental in all tissue. Pay attention to that energy, that awareness throughout all of these moments I'm showing you."

"Yeah, yeah," I said, still not impressed with anything new.

"If I took a stack of five pieces of paper and placed them on a target and shot them with a gun, would the bullet pass through all five at once, or individually one at a time—no matter how quickly?"

"Each individually," I answered. "Anyone can see that on slow-motion camera."

"Exactly. Now, keep in mind that processes in our brains and minds are even faster than that. So, look here again at the rocks representing contact with a sense object. Moment number five is about moment number one. You're a little bit behind time."

"Whoa!" I was shocked. "That's... that's right, actually. I've never thought about that."

"The rock continues to be something new in each successive moment as you perpetually try to catch up."

"Keep going," I said, sensing something bigger coming.

"For every awareness, there will be those five moments. Trace your physical body back through time, like the domino chain you told me about. The moment that sperm and egg come together in conception, which we would say is the very beginning of your physical life, you have moments in the chain prior to that. Your body is part of a long stream of data that branches off into other streams and so on. Conception is the meeting of two of those streams—mom and dad."

"Ok, the physical data makes sense, like Carl Sagan saying we're all dinosaur poop or star stuff." I scratched my head. "I learned this long ago after reading a text by Nagarjuna. Where's the big *WOW* Maria?"

"Is your mind made up of parts—not the brain, but the immaterial mind."

"It's made up of earlier moments, earlier dominos in the chain. Sure, makes sense."

"Trace those back, just like the five rocks," she said taking the fifth rock and making it the first, and repeated this as she continued, "and when you come to the moment of conception at the same time as the physical stream, is there a preceding moment? A domino before that moment?"

I thought as I stared at the five rocks, and then like a flash, sprang up and screamed, "Holy shit! There has to be four earlier moments for that one to exist!"

"Bingo!" she said. I fell on my knees and started to cry and laugh, just like I had done at the reservoir park.

"It's real! Our consciousness never ends! Damn you, Maria! Damn you!"

"Why?" she laughed, taking my hands and kneeling in front of me.

"I'm gay! I never thought that I could ever have a *real* spiritual journey!"

At the end of the semester, I called Geshe-la excited to share my grades with him. Though I did not do well in high school and improved in college, I had a near perfect score in my teacher's training courses and was delightfully proud.

"I almost had a perfect score, Geshe-la," I said into the phone.

"Oh? Almost?" he asked.

"Yeah, I just missed it with a ninety-seven in one class, and a ninety-eight in another!"

"Better next time, maybe," he said, then burst into laughter.

The day after I returned home from Arizona, I pulled out the book Maria gave me and started to follow its weekly training. I looked for the topic on the internet and it was vast, to say the least. How could something so easy as was described in that book not be given attention in the mainstream world, I wondered? Did it work?

One teacher of Law of Attraction I found on the internet explained how powerful vision boards were for making things manifest into our lives, so I made a small one to look at as a visual aid. I didn't tell anyone about my new fascination to see if I could make anything happen with mere mental suggestion.

At first, I told myself that I wanted to win the lottery, but I didn't buy tickets. Nonetheless, I tried visualization, but nothing every came of it. Then I realized that I probably should visualize getting a ticket from someone. And for more than a week, nothing happened. Then, Wyatt and I stopped at a gas station and he ran in to get us something to drink. When he came out, he handed me a cold soda... and a lottery ticket.

"What the hell is this?" I asked in astonishment.

"I just felt like buying a ticket for us, something to do. You can keep whatever you win," he laughed then started the car.

After I quickly summarized the Law of Attraction and what I had been visualizing, he said, "Can't hurt to scratch it off, can it," and handed me a penny.

Excitedly, I quickly scratched the gray latex from the card and blew it clean. Nothing. For a moment I was discouraged, but the fact that he bought me a lottery ticket for the first time since I met him still fascinated me.

As the weeks progressed, more little things started to manifest—finding a lost friend I hadn't seen in over ten years, getting my lunch for free, attracting new work, and much more—I became a believer.

"*Consider the hearts of species; it is noble to draw the diamond.*" From the time I heard these words in my car, I pondered them often. If this was a message for me, what did it mean? And why did the voice use the word *species*? Was this a dream and my own brain was the creator of this phrase, or was this really some message from a spirit guide—like Vajrayogini?

Looking for new reads at the local bookstore, searching for other authors that were said to be teachers of the Law of Attraction, I found a title that jumped out at me: *Evolve Your Brain*, by Joe Dispenza. The introduction indicated that it was a detailed summary of how the brain works and how we can learn to deliberately control our emotional landscape. The author had a remarkable history of his own with self-healing and transformation that was inspiring and seemingly miraculous, to say the least. I purchased the book and took it to the bank by the reservoir, under the tree—my mental lab.

Suffice it to say, all the things I was learning in Buddhism could be summed up in a series of amazing realizations I experienced guided by this phenomenal author. He explained that our emotions are merely chemicals, part of the fight-or-flight response in our brain. In one simple statement, my understanding of my own reactions to the world around me were exposed and would never again be the same: "*If you cannot stop an emotion from happening while it's happening, you're addicted to the chemical.*" Within just a couple of days after reading this and understanding it, long lasting negative emotions and reactions were—gone! Whenever I would feel anger starting to rise, I would tell myself that it was just a chemical and it would slowly vanish. Had there been a Joe Dispenza statue for sale, I would have bought one and placed it on the altar with the rest of the gang!

If the realizations that I had reading Nagarjuna were a homerun, this statement alone knocked it out of the ballpark, across town, and into another ball diamond, altogether! "Thank you, Maria!" I shouted, full of gratitude for being introduced to this world that, I believed, partnered with the teachings of the Buddha like a fine wine with the most delicate of culinary masterpieces. After memorizing that simple statement, whenever a negative emotion arose in my mind, I quickly told myself, "It's just a chemical, Marc," and it faded effortlessly. Master Langri Thangpa would be proud that I could finally practice his revered line,

> *In my every action, I will watch my mind,*
> *And the moment destructive emotions arise,*
> *I will confront them strongly and avert them...*

A smile from ear to ear adorned my face, almost incessantly for days. In fact, it was from that moment onward that my beaming countenance became my calling card. Since then, many friends and students frequently commented on how often I was seen smiling. Geshe Loten noticed during one of his meditation classes I popped in to attend during a short visit to the TCC. "You used to be so sad, always frowning and depressed," he said in front of a room full of attendees who turned to look at me. "Now, every time I see you your smile gets bigger and bigger."

The following spring, Wyatt's parents moved to Florida and I wondered how long it would be before he followed them. He'd moved to Indianapolis the previous year, taking up a job outside of his color guard rehearsals. He did quite well, and I eventually moved out of Al's and in with him after returning from Arizona. It put me just a half-hour away from Geshe-la, and I looked forward to being able to spend more time with him.

Tenam gave me a few Tibetan language lessons, not much more than what I already learned from the books. Realizing that I was ready for more, the next step was to spend time with someone and learn conversation, parts of sentence structures that the books didn't explain. Tenam was patient and gave me good advice. I used flashcards to memorize over a thousand words, and he helped me with my pronunciation, which was still problematic.

"Whenever you are with Geshe-la, you should try to use Tibetan words as often as you can, even if the rest of the sentence is in English, you will build your vocabulary quickly. Geshe-la will help you."

Geshe-la actually wasn't much help, probably because he was too busy learning English. And for some reason, I shied away from trying to speak Tibetan with him. The IBC signed him up for evening classes and when I came for my weekly visits, we'd sit and read Dr. Seuss instead of improving my Tibetan or answering any philosophy questions. I didn't complain. Just being with him was as much a part of my spiritual journey as everything else, and I can't put into words how delightful it was listening to my Yoda read *One Fish, Two Fish, Red Fish, Blue Fish*.

One day in May, my friend Jon handed me a magazine in which he had highlighted an article, "I thought of you and thought you would want to see this."

There was a story about a young Nepali boy who was studying in a Tibetan Sakya monastery and left to go meditate in the jungle. He sat immovably for ten months without anything to eat or drink—no sustenance at all—and yet he was still alive and in deep meditation, under the same species of tree as Shakyamuni had sat 2600 years ago.

A team of scientists visited the site and filmed ninety-six hours of this remarkable boy not moving a muscle. "This is humanly impossible," one scientist said and then explained what happens to the body after just a few days without food or water. He showed no indications of any health problems, and the night-vision camera showed no signs that anyone snuck him food. When I told Geshe-la about it, he didn't share the same wondrous excitement as I had.

"Yeah, this happen many times. Many great Bodhisattva do this thing."

"How?" I asked.

"You say you trust science. Then what science say?" he was grinning, throwing my words back at me.

"They don't know."

"Yeah, science kinda behind Buddhism. You eat words now?" he laughed loudly while trying to hand me a saltshaker. "Maybe sprinkle some of this on words."

"He'd have to be beyond the ninth mental state to do this, wouldn't he?" I asked. Geshe-la just shrugged. I stared at the picture of the dingy, white-robed boy nestled in front of the Indian Fig, imagining what was going on in his mind to give him such abilities.

"His name is Palden Dorje," I told Andy as we sat in a booth at the BK that evening, and he remained transfixed reading the article. "I wish I could see him and ask him so many things."

"I'm a little bit jealous of you," he said, laying the magazine down. "You have all this time to study Dharma and you have a Buddhist master." I was keeping up my regular nightly visits to see him at work, giving him a regular dose of Dharma when I could.

"Don't be jealous," I soothed. "You can come meet Geshe-la sometime. Just get some free time and I'll take you."

"Well, I'd love to," he started, "but Rob is kind of jealous of you. I talk about our visits all the time." He picked the magazine up again, staring at the article. "I wonder what he'll think about this."

"Invite him along!" I exclaimed. "And also let him know that I wouldn't be much of a Buddhist practitioner if I got you to cheat on him with me. That's kind of bad karma, right?"

A few months passed and I got swamped in design preparations and rehearsals. I hadn't attended a weekly teaching in a long time, which happened quite often over the years. Geshe-la never asked, and I never thought I needed to say anything. But I went quite a while without a weekly visit, which also was not unexpected that time of the year. I replaced too many visits with occasional chats on the phone with the master as a quick fix.

When I showed up at his apartment that fall, I was surprised to see his belongings in boxes. "What's going on?" I asked with a note of fear.

"IBC kinda make rebirth," he laughed. "We find house. Now move making." The Indiana Buddhist Center was finally getting an actual headquarters, a place of their own, and it was even closer of a drive for me.

"That's wonderful!" I exclaimed.

"Small house, but big room in back. Kinda same as studio." He went to his altar and removed a silk covering from the statue I had given him to bless. "Here, rabnay finish."

When I got home, I joyfully placed the statue—which had remained hollow until my own spiritual teacher had filled it with the appropriate blessings—back on its central perch. "Welcome home, sir."

Wanting to repay Geshe-la's kindness to me and to celebrate the new center, I took up the task of creating a useful offering for him and the IBC. Making new prayer booklets for the center became my new obsession. I spent hundreds of hours of free time creating a pecha style book that resembled the Tibetan holy texts. It was difficult because I didn't have the proper font on my computer, but I found a way to enter English letters into a translation tool from a university and copy the Tibetan script that followed. After a few months, I took the books to the new property where Geshe-la and one of the other members of the IBC were living together. He was incredibly happy with my gift and put them to use at the next teaching, and every one that followed thereafter.

In keeping with my on-going downsizing of my possessions, I gave the IBC several pieces of furniture that I hoped would make Geshe-la's new home a little cozier. My own room was more spacious—even though I felt I still had more stuff than I needed—and I had far fewer things in storage that had been there since the move back to Indiana from Decatur.

Mom called me one night before bed and asked if we could have breakfast together the next day. I tucked a little statue of Tara into my bag so I could remember to give it to her when I met her at the Bob Evans.

"How are your dreams now?" she asked.

"They're gone," I said, sighing with relief. "I feel normal, or whatever it is I've imagined normal to feel like. And whenever I start to have a negative emotion, I just remind myself that it's a chemical, and it almost magically dissipates."

"Let me have a little of that, would you? I've never been normal. And I've never been lucky enough to have normal husbands."

Mom remarried again almost two years after she and Elton finally divorced, which was just a year after Kent and I moved her out. My stepfather's name was Ron, and I only met him twice.

"Troubles with Ron?" I asked.

"Not troubles, just not much of anything. He refurbishes antiques, and that gets most of his time. We just keep each other company, like roommates."

"I don't understand why you've always felt you have to have a husband," I said, not knowing what else to say.

"Marc, a woman is nothing without a man. That's the way it's always been."

"I don't believe that. There are many great women throughout history and even more today that are quite happy, quite successful, and quite powerful without a husband."

"Well, that's not how I see it. I'll be fine."

"Will you?" I asked, pressing for more while blindly searching for the statue of Tara in my bag, thinking it was a good time to introduce her to a powerful female icon.

She looked off toward the other side of the restaurant, lost in her thoughts. Then turned to me and said, "Ron and I have never consummated the marriage."

"What?" I was shocked and stopped searching my bag. "How? Well, I know *how*... I mean *why not*?"

"He's just not interested." And she wouldn't talk about it any further. Of course, my homocentric thoughts immediately assumed Ron was in the closet. After all, he was into antiques and not interested in my mother's large breasts, and that just added up to a gay man in my experience. "He probably shouldn't be your step-father," she continued. "And you know... Eddy Lyon shouldn't have been your father."

"I don't understand," I said, confused.

"My first and only real love, David, should have been your father." She went on to tell me about him, and how my grandmother chased him away. "He was a *yahoo*, your grandmother said. She didn't like him—he wasn't good enough for me. But I loved him anyway." She looked down into her coffee mug, lost in her memories for a moment. "He was killed in a motorcycle accident not long after we were forced to break up. She didn't show a bit of concern and simply said, 'See, you could've been on that bike with him.'"

"Funny," I gave a short chuckle.

"What?"

"The love of my life was *also* a guy named David, I met in college. And his parents yanked him out of Ball State because they were Christians and thought I was the Devil."

"But... DJ?" she looked as confused as I had just moments prior.

"DJ wasn't the love of my life," I said. "Believe it or not. He was the *longest* love of my life, but he wasn't *the* love of my life. I just got hung up—really hung up—on the shit he did to me. No, not the love of my life at all."

The waiter came and settled the bill at our table. "Alright," Mom said, grabbing her purse. "Walk me to my car." Just the way she said it, it reminded me of all the times she asked Craig's father, Floyd, to walk her home... and it made me remember a question I had never asked her.

"No, wait. Let's finish our coffee. I have a question for you I might need to stay seated for: did anything ever happen between you and Floyd?"

She was stunned. "No! Goodness, Marc, no! He was just a friend."

"You both always seemed so close, maybe too close. Greentown wasn't an unsafe place, but you always had him walk you home late at night after playing cards. Or you'd sit out on the front porch and talk for hours, just laughing away."

"He was like a brother to me, really. Maybe more than a brother—but not a lover."

I examined her face. "With the secrets you've been able to hold..."

"I have nothing to hide anymore. I'd tell you if something happened—but I never cheated on any of my husbands. Floyd's just a good-hearted man and was a good friend. That's all."

"Well, I know you started going to church with Shirley recently, so I guess you know the dangers of lying." I laughed.

She looked at my face for a moment, studying. "You're not afraid of going to hell for being a Buddhist?"

I nearly spit my coffee out. "We've both been through hell already, Mom. But no, I have no concerns about it. I gave up on that a long time ago, you know that."

"Do you think you'll be reincarnated?" she asked.

"I didn't until recently, but now, though it's still hard to imagine I can see that it's totally a possibility."

She smiled at me, lovingly. "I'm sure we do continue on... somehow."

"I've seen the logic and it makes sense," I said, "now, I would just like some *real* proof, you know?"

"What kind of proof? Watch someone die and see if you can see their soul leave?"

I laughed. "Probably not going to go around asking to look at dead bodies."

"Well, when it's my time to go, just know that I don't want you to see *my* body," she said, and lifted the coffee to her mouth.

"What?" I was almost insulted. "Why not? I better be able to say my last goodbye!"

"Nope," she insisted. "When my brother James was dying of

cancer, Shirley and I went to see him so often, we watched that disease eat him away. That withering man's form replaced every beautiful memory I had of him. I don't remember what he used to look like before cancer. I've tried so hard, Birdy. Shirley said the same thing. We both agreed that we wouldn't come to see the other when it was our turn. We don't want to lose the precious memories we share. We've already said our goodbyes, and I know she loves me. So, I'm telling you the same thing now: don't come see my body."

I couldn't accept it but figured she wouldn't be able to stop me when the day inevitably came—she'd be dead, after all. Reaching back into my bag, I pulled out the little statue of Tara and handed it to her. "Please, at a minimum, just put this above your bed for me, a little way that we can sort of be together from now on."

She smiled and examined the little gift she held, listening intently as I explained the benefits of the Tara practice. She even recited the mantra with me after I taught it to her! "Thank you, Bird." Pulling out a clean handkerchief, she wrapped the little statue and place it in her purse. "Anything else you'd like to know before we leave?"

"Now that you mention it, who the hell was Hilda Bauer?"

She cackled, explaining how she saw the label on a bed in a store long ago and thought it sounded like an old witch's name. "It was the name of a mattress company!"

That spring I gained more weight and was feeling physically weak, which was out of the ordinary for me since I hadn't had a cold or flu in about four years. Geshe-la suggested I see a Tibetan doctor who had a practice in Bloomington. Though Tibetan medicine is quite ancient and all-natural, it was being looked at seriously by the Indiana University School of Medicine. Surprisingly, they had been having Tibetan doctors as guest professors for years.

The young doctor's hand examined my wrist, and he felt three separate pulses simultaneously—indicating blood, bile, and phlegm—something I didn't know was even possible, then instructed me to reduce the number of cold beverages that I consumed a day and try to drink more hot liquids. I left his office with a small bag of little round Tibetan pills with instructions to take three in the morning crushed and stirred into a small glass of hot, boiled water.

"Look like rabbit shit," Geshe-la joked, making tea in his new kitchen where I found him on the way home to share with him what the doctor said. As he poured two mugs for us to drink, I remembered the Tibetan word for *ice* I saw in the Tibetan dictionary and remembered Tenam's instructions to use more Tibetan words.

"Geshe-la, may I please have a small piece of *gyak-pa* for my tea," I asked, almost proudly.

Geshe-la looked at me carefully, handed me the cup of tea and said, "I monk, no harming." I was certain he was trying to insist on the doctor's orders of hot beverages, and so I simply blew on it until it was cool enough for my lips.

A week later, I returned to the center, and as Geshe-la poured tea for us, I again asked for a piece of *gyak-pa*. "I monk, I have vow. No killing!" Wondering whether the temperature would make a difference to my health or not, I gently blew the steam away. Geshe-la explained no further, and so I tried to take cautious sips.

On my third visit after seeing the Tibetan doctor, my familiar stubbornness kicked in and I walked past Geshe-la to the freezer to get a piece of ice myself.

"Marc," he looked almost angry, "What you do?"

"Geshe-la the tea is too hot for my mouth," I said, almost defiantly, "a piece of ice won't change the temperature much."

Then his eyes lit up. "Oh! You want ice?"

"Isn't that what I've been telling you?"

"You say *khyak-pa*," he said, emphasizing the aspiration of the initial consonant and I heard the difference.

Then, remembering how his response had been about harming or killing, I asked, "What's *gyak-pa*?"

"Shit!" he laughed so hard he actually fell to the floor, rolled onto his back, and kicked his feet in the air.

"Are you kidding me?" I howled. "Of all the words in the language?"

We both laughed uncontrollably, and it was such a perfect moment. "Tenam said, 'Geshe-la will help you.'" I said mockingly. "That was a lie!"

At the end of winter guard season, Wyatt decided to follow his parents and moved to Florida. My partner in crime, and company on my drives, would be gone and I had to figure out how to fill the vacancy he left in my life. A retreat to reclaim my balance was in order, I thought.

My friend and former student Jessica offered her home for such a getaway. I mentioned at a staff meeting we both attended that I wanted to go off grid for a while but said I didn't have the extra funds to make any trips or book any cabins. She and her husband had a two-story home for just the two of them and said that I could have total privacy with the upstairs to myself. I accepted.

Jessica and Jarrett both worked throughout the day, leaving me alone to do my recitations and my meditation. I ate breakfast and lunch alone and skipped dinner to avoid them in the evening. One night, I had a dream of DJ from which I didn't awake sad or depressed, I actually awoke jealous and angry at myself.

In the dream, I was back in our house with him in Decatur, Illinois. There were several people walking about, workers that were busy doing renovations and painting. I looked at DJ with confusion and asked, "What are we doing here?"

He was talking to a carpenter-looking guy and dismissed him to answer me, but instead looked over my shoulder. "Who's that woman behind you? She's giving off such beautiful energy!"

I turned and looked, only to see a bright, brilliant light with no face. Quickly, I turned back to DJ and said, "I don't know, but why are you talking all new-agey?"

Every detail remained vibrantly clear when I woke. The DJ in the dream spoke like a lot of the spiritual hippies I kept at arms-length that, all-to-often, flocked to Dharma centers, reeking of marijuana. I was jealous that DJ might be on that side of the spiritual fence with some new granola-eating boyfriend, and it pissed me off that after all the time that passed since my last dream of him, here I was again.

Before Jessica left, I walked down the stairs. She was surprised to see me, since I burrowed away from all nearby life. "Good morning, darlin'!"

I told her about the dream, "I just needed to tell someone, to just talk about it. You know?"

"Do you have any idea what it means?" she asked curiously, having a growing interest into the paranormal since the passing of her father.

"No," I turned toward the stairs, "Other than I still apparently have a long way to go. I'm pretty upset that I have a resurfaced feeling of jealousy."

I laid in bed for pretty much the rest of the day, almost punishing myself. No matter how much I reminded myself that my emotions were just chemicals, I couldn't get myself to snap out of the feelings the dream created. After taking a long, hot shower to see if it would help, I retired just after dinner and slept without interruption for twelve hours.

The next morning, I awoke refreshed and recharged. After Jessica and Jarrett left for work, I had some breakfast and went for a walk through their neighborhood. When I returned, the phone was ringing as I walked into the kitchen to grab a banana. The answering machine on the counter picked up after a couple of rings, and the voice of another one of my former students with whom Jessica had attended school was urgently asking her to help find me.

"Hey, Mackenzie." I said into the phone before she hung up.

"I figured you took her up on that offer," Mackenzie sighed with relief. "Call Al."

I chuckled. "Mackenzie, He can wait until I finish my retreat. It is never something important with him."

"Trust me, Marc," she implored. "It is this time. It's really important."

I could hear her desperation and, out of curiosity, promised her I'd call.

Certain that it would be something unimportant, as he his calls were often just a means to keep tabs on where I was and what I was doing, I took my time finishing the banana and a bottle of water before picking up the phone.

"What could it possibly be that you can't wait two more days to tell me?" I asked when he answered.

"Call your brother, Chris," he said, which made me stop pacing through the kitchen. I hadn't talked to Chris in years.

"Why do I need to call him?"

"Just do it. Call your brother. That's all I can say."

"Tell me, Al. Tell me now."

There was a long pause. "Your mother has passed away," he said, sending a shockwave through my body that made me fall onto my knees.

"I'll call you back," I hung up and began to cry, every moment I cherished with her began flashing in my mind. "No, no, no," I said as I gasped for air. "Not yet, Mommie, please!"

Standing up and shaking my head in disbelief, barely able to breathe, I ran the sleeve of my sweatshirt across my nose and dialed Geshe-la.

"Geshe-la, help. What do I do? My mother has just passed away," I said slowly, trying to be as clear as I could be so he could understand me over the phone.

"Oh, no! I'm sorry! She need you happy now, you say mantra, I do puja, just stay happy," his voice was stern and gentle, but sounded critical.

A few minutes later, Chris's stuttering, gentle voice confirmed that it was true. She had passed in her sleep two nights earlier and was cremated as quickly as she had wanted. The phone slipped from my hand and landed on the floor as I walked to the back door to step outside to breathe. It was unseasonably warm that early spring, but the past few days had ushered in an unexpected cold-snap, and all the flowering trees were slowly sprinkling their colorful blooms to the ground. I drew a long, deep, cold breath standing on the patio, and with a complete loss of control began to wail loudly and fell to my knees once again.

After about a half-hour, I went back into the house and called Jessica to see if she could come home early from work and see me out. She left work and returned quickly, walked me outside, and held me as I cried next to my car. I pulled away, just about to get in, when she said, "Hey, maybe that woman in your dream was her?"

"Oh my God," I gasped, imagining that Mom somehow created my dream to distract me so she could have her wish to keep me from seeing her body. "Maybe it was."

As if she were physically there with me, sitting in the passenger seat, I spoke to her as I drove. "Did you know that I thought you were a good mother? Did I ever tell you? Did you know?" Guilt and fear raged through my blood and I tried to remember pictures we had taken together, but I couldn't remember a single photo of her and her three sons in the same picture. Ashamed, I cried aloud, "Did my damned stubbornness rob you of that?"

When I got to my brother's house north of Kokomo, Chris and I held one another for a few minutes, and I'm sure that it was the longest we ever embraced. He was the first to learn about her death, and since he had more time to come to terms with it, he allowed me to cry in his arms as long as I needed.

Mom was already rendered to ashes, in a plain brown little wooden box he handed me. "How, Chris?" I asked.

"She just went to sleep... and didn't wake up."

The urn vibrated in my trembling hands. "Do you mind if I just go sit outside with her?" He opened the door to the backyard, and I slowly walked out into the brisk air.

Sitting on the ground under a tree in his back yard, rocking her back and forth in my arms for about an hour, I held her tightly against my chest, thinking about the good times I cherished—gone. "No eye... no ear... no nose... no tongue... no body..." I said quietly to myself. "Even no mind? Do you still have a mind, Mommie?"

Then, the faint scent of her favorite perfume, *White Shoulders*, was in the air and I believed it was her—I knew it was her. She stood close by, letting me know that there is something after this life when we finally close our eyes—or as she would have said in her own unique sense of humor, when the oven timer goes off.

Chris and I agreed that Evan, who had been living for the past ten years in Tennessee with Dad, should have the ashes. "It's what she'd want," I sniffled. "She'd want to keep an eye on him. He'll probably set her up on a shelf above his bed, surrounded by his Freddy Krueger paraphernalia."

Chris gave a short laugh. "Nowhere else she'd rather be. She loved horror movies, too." He pointed to a box on the cocktail table in his living room. "I brought some of her things back from Ron's today. Take whatever you want, Marc."

"I don't really need anything, Chris," I said as I walked over to the table. Then, surprised, I noticed at the top of the stack of all the books and photos in the box was a picture of the four of us my freshman year of high school on vacation. The memory came back to me in a flash, Dad behind the camera, and the four of us standing in front of a mountain view in Kentucky. Pulling it out of the box and holding it gently, I felt as though she answered my question, calmed my worries. Then, as I sat down on the sofa to spend a little time staring at the photo, a small golden sparkle turned my head to see what was just out of view behind the box—the small statue of Tara, shiny and clean.

The next morning, I set out for Greentown to break the news to Floyd and Geneva. Mom moved away so long ago that I wasn't sure if they stayed in contact, or if they had any mutual friends that would have told them.

When I arrived, there were a lot of cars in the drive and out on the street. Floyd and Geneva had a large family from Tennessee, and they had them up several times a year. I figured I had shown up on just such an occasion. As I got out of my car, Geneva was walking out the front door, dressed to the nines, like she had just gotten back from church.

"Sorry to catch you at a bad time, Geneva," I started. "Family reunion?"

"No, Marc," she said, holding a cell phone to her ear. "Everyone's up for Floyd's funeral and I'm heading down to Tennessee for a while."

"What?" I asked in astonishment, almost shouting. "When did he die?"

"The other day."

"Exactly when, Geneva, it's important!"

"April 10, why?"

"How did he die?"

"We don't know. He just died in his sleep."

My jaw fell agape, and I started the strangest emotion I have ever felt, laughing in amazement while crying in abject loss. "Geneva, I'm here to tell you that Mom passed away, in her sleep on April 10."

"You're a damned liar!" Geneva shot back, in disbelief.

"Geneva, I'm a thirty-six-year-old man. I don't need to lie for attention anymore."

We stood staring at each other for a moment with two totally different expressions. "Did you hear that?" she said into the phone, then handed it to me and I knew it was Craig on the other end.

"You're not making this up, are you?" the familiar voice spoke to me for the first time in nearly sixteen years.

"My God, Craig, she asked him..." then he joined me in saying, "to walk her home."

✦ Chapter Twelve ✦

I drove hastily through the countryside, needing to see Shirley and share with her the message I was certain Mom left me in her passing. "Gaté Gaté Paragaté Parasamgaté Bodhi Soha," I repeated through my tears. To any onlooker I would have appeared a complete psycho, bouncing back and forth from exuberant laughter to irrepressible tears and wailing.

"Shirley! Shirley!" I tore open the back door and ran to into the house. She stood up, threw her arms around me, and joined me in tears.

"Oh, Marc," she started, "Where were you?"

"It's a long story, but you will never believe what happened!" I told her of my visit with Geneva, and Shirley sat back into her chair, listening intently, her countenance bursting with brilliance as she came to the same conclusion that I came to—life continues.

"You know, Marc," she said after a long pause, seeming to stare into her own memories. "When your uncle James had cancer, your mother and I drove back and forth from Lafayette to see him. He just withered away."

"Yes, Mom told me. It's quite sad."

"On the night he died, your mother and I were driving home after our last visit, long after sundown, so it was dark. A large, white owl flew in front of our car so closely I thought we were going to hit it. When we got home, we received the phone call he had... slipped away."

She stood up and walked across the room and grabbed a framed photograph of Mom, staring at the face behind the glass as she carefully carried it to me. For years longer than I can remember that picture had sat in the same spot, and I had barely given it more than a glance. Now, I examined every detail as though it were fresh and new.

"The other night when your mother died, I had been helping your cousin, Tami, with some redecorating in her house and left pretty late. On the way home, almost exactly as the night your uncle died, I'll be damned if... another white owl didn't fly right toward my car. I didn't think that much about it... and then I found out about your mother the next morning."

My thoughts were swirling trying to make sense of everything. "This is all... kind of amazing."

Shirley reached out and gently tugged at the mala around my neck." Do you know about the jade Buddha?" She asked, sparking my curiosity then explained that during the divorce with Ed, Mom had only requested his jade Buddha statue in their settlement. This was the first time I ever heard that my mother knew anything about Buddha before me. Sadly, Shirley didn't know if Mom ever got the statue. The grandfather clock in the hallway ticked through a long pause of silent wonder.

"So," Shirley finally began to speak again, "have you called him?"

"I have to, don't I?" I took the tissue she handed me to wipe my eyes and blow my nose.

"You really should. He's still your Dad. How long has it been?"

"*Legally* my Dad..." I was suddenly overcome with shame and lowered my head. "About... fifteen years. I don't know if he'll even talk to me. He might hang up the phone."

"Well, you need to try, Marcus Wellaby. It's the right thing to do."

Several days passed and I spent time calling other friends and family to tell them the story of Mom and Floyd. Each time I heard it come out of my mouth, I was just as full of disbelief as my listener, and it filled me awe, as if I were hearing it for the first time. It was a magically impossible coincidence that not only amazed everyone who heard it but took a little bit of my fear of death with each recounting until I believed that I was ready to depart this life, like someone about to leave the country for the first time, eagerly awaiting the driver to arrive and take them to the airport, off to exotic lands of which they only read in storybooks.

After I called everyone on my list, I stared at the phone, putting it down then back up again, hesitating my deliberate request to hear a voice that brought so much fear and anger as a child. I rehearsed a variety of things I would say, if needed, and finally found just enough courage to dial the number, counting the rings in hopes that he might not pick up.

Without any kind of greeting—apparently having seen my name on the caller ID—that familiar voice began to speak, and every muscle in my body tensed. "Before either of us say anything," he spoke softly, "we don't need to discuss anything about the why, the how, or the what concerning the years that have passed. Just know that there are three sides to every story: yours, mine, and the truth."

My body flushed every fear, just as it had with the tarantula, realizing they were unnecessary. The wisdom of his words revealed a man who had also replayed his past, wishing things went a different route, but resigned that it, nonetheless, arrived at a place of transcendence. A warm feeling of love and appreciation I never felt for this man slowly replaced years of anger and I sat with the phone to my ear with a little shame for not having come to this new emotional landscape years before my mother's final sleep.

He listened to me tell the story like he never listened before. "No, shit!?" he exclaimed. "There are no words, Marc, none to explain what that tells my soul."

When I finished, our wonder slowly faded to the awkwardness of two strangers not knowing what further to say to one another. A few minutes of small talk, and I was ready to hang up, satisfied that I had done my filial duty.

Then his wisdom returned, "I want you to know, Marc, that when your mother asked me to adopt you, I went to my dad... you never think that your own parent will give you bad advice, and I pretty much worshipped him back then—I asked him how I was going to raise someone else's son. He looked me in the eye and told me to turn you over my knee and make sure you knew who was going to be boss in that house." He paused, drew a breath, then said, "I wish I would never have listened to him."

In that instant, every neuron in my brain busily rewrote decades of information, voices in my head solving many childhood mysteries. Compassion filled me as I realized he had been handed a torch from his father, who most certainly got it from his father, and so on. I could no longer blame Dad for faithfully following his father's advice. Then, he told me that he had wanted to tell me since the day I found out about the adoption and tried to find a perfect time to bring it up—his eyes behind the wheel of the car after he dropped me off at my friend's house on graduation day came to mind. After a moment of silence between us, my sniffles indicating to him that his words hit their mark, I thanked him, hung up the phone, and cried... with Mom close by, I'm sure.

About a month after Mom's death, I woke with a pain on the back of my left calf, like someone had hit me with a ball-peen hammer, and I was having a hard time breathing. At first, I thought that I must have strained a muscle during some forgotten activity. I had no clue as to what could be happening. As for the breathing, I assumed I was coming down with a cold or flu.

A trip to the emergency room and a chest x-ray later, I was sent home with medication for bronchitis. After a few days, my condition worsened, feeling like I was breathing through a straw, and I found myself in the parking lot of the emergency room crawling on my hands and knees on the asphalt. Several nurses ran to my aid, put me in a wheelchair and whisked me to safety.

After I regained enough energy to breath easily, I called Geshe-la, "I'm in the hospital and I don't have insurance. I'm a little worried, so any prayers, mantras, or pujas you could do would be appreciated."

"Don't worry, stay happy," he tried to convince me, but I was already calm and quite peaceful.

The next morning, an African American doctor entered my room. "Oh, good!" he said, checking the IV in my arm. "You're still alive!"

I was puzzled. "Was there any concern I might not be?"

"We put TPA through your body and it can cause fatal internal bleeding."

"*Can a bitch get a memo?*" I almost shouted. "Maybe I should have known about the dangers so I could make some phone calls last night, don't you think?"

"Well, you're still here and that's all that matters. You had hundreds of clots in your lungs. You'll be in here for about a week. Just rest." He turned and walked out before I could ask anything further.

I called Shirley and told her what happened. She arrived in just a couple of hours with my oldest cousin, Tami, who was close to the same age as my mother.

"How are you doing, Marcus Wellaby?" Shirley said, bringing a big smile to my face.

"Emotionally, I've never been better. That hasn't changed at all in the past month. Physically, they say that I'll be on blood thinners for the rest of my life."

Tami stepped forward and stared curiously, examining my face. "You sure look like Linda, you know that?"

Mom once showed me a picture of her as a young girl, with two big buns on the side of her head. "Who does that look like, Birdy?" I shrugged as I looked at the little black and white Polaroid. She then placed her thumbnails over the buns and asked, "See it now?" I jerked away with sudden surprise, seeing myself looking back at me—in drag!

"Yeah, I know," I replied to Tami, still looking at me as if I was her only means to recall the face of my mother. "It's strange not having gotten a chance to see her body, to pay my respects, you know?"

"Yes, Marcus, I do," my aunt said as she sat in the chair next to my bed. "It doesn't feel real. It's like she's snuck off into the world somewhere and just hasn't come back yet."

"Well, you know Mom," I started to chuckle, "If she could talk to us now, the first thing she'd want to tell us about is how long it took to burn her boobs in the oven."

My aunt howled, and Tami slapped my leg, but couldn't help laughing herself. They knew her humor, and it truly would be something she would say if she could.

Tami sighed then put her hand on my leg, an endearing touch I never would have expected from her. "Do you remember a conversation you had with her on... I think it was your thirtieth birthday?"

"Very well," I answered.

"She called me after that phone call with you, just crying into the phone. I couldn't understand a word she was saying. I said, 'Linda, what's wrong?' and she pulled herself together enough to say, 'He told me that I was a good mother.'"

I drew the most refreshing breath of my life, exhaled all the worry that I carried in my chest, and thanked Tami for jogging my memory—the greatest gift she could have given me. "Thank you for telling me that. I couldn't remember if she ever heard me say it."

"Marcus Wellaby, you're going to be alright," Shirley said. "Just take every dose of the medicine they prescribe. And don't be stubborn like your mother and stop taking it."

"*Stubborn*," I said slowly, remembering how we always seemed to compete to *out-stubborn* each other. "Holy shit, Shirley! She won!"

"Won what? Who?"

"Mom!" I sat straight up. "She told me she didn't want me to see her body. She won."

"Stubborn till the day she died," Tami chuckled.

"And beyond," I said.

The Tibetan texts say that it takes forty-nine days for the consciousness to move from the death of one life to the rebirth of the next life and that there are in-between levels, called *bardos*, in which the consciousness passes. Just after Mom died, I could sense her presence near me, most likely a psychological phenomenon of wishful thinking. But there were times that the smell of her perfume, the feeling of her touching my cheek, the distant sound of her cackling laughter made me feel as though it was real. If it truly were her, she would slowly move on to the next life over the course of the seven weeks as the Buddhists described.

But after two months, I was still experiencing a presence near me. My friend, Cheryl, was a reiki master and suggested that I lay on her table with five of her students present for their training in order to help restore my health. I agreed—though I didn't believe in the laying of hands—and a woman in her early twenties was instructed to stand at the head of the table with her crown touching mine, visualizing loving light going from her heart and into my central channel. The whole experience was pleasant, though I would have preferred to have all those hands massaging my muscles rather than pretending to manipulate unseen fields of energy by merely touching me.

After the session, I sat in a chair drinking a bottle of water outside Cheryl's room while she talked to the students about my health and fielded their questions. The young lady who had held her crown to mine through the session asked, "Do you know if his mother has passed away?" I nearly spit out a mouthful of water. "I sensed a presence that hovered over him saying, 'I love you, I'm here! It's real, it's real!'"

Instantly, I could see an image of my mother in my mind, waving her hands in front of my face, herself amazed that she was standing in front of me, but that I couldn't see her. Somehow, perhaps, this young lady was attuned to a spiritual frequency that could hear my mother's words of wonder as she tried to reach me from the other side.

The next day, I sat in Geshe-la's as he stood at the stove making tea and asked him if the forty-nine-day period was asserted to be an absolute. "How your mother die?" he asked, and I suddenly felt embarrassed that I called him when she passed but never told him how she died.

"We're not sure," I said, watching him stir the pot. "She died in her sleep."

"Oh!" Geshe-la said as though he had a realization of something he didn't previously know. He turned off the stove, walked to the table, and sat down in front of me. "Now things little bit different."

Through the labor of his broken English, he explained that when someone dies in their sleep it is possible to achieve liberation since the gross mind is shut down and has no attachment to the physical body.

"Are you saying that it's possible she... that my mother could have..."

In my mind, it made sense. Somehow, she attained liberation, and maybe she helped Floyd achieve it, too. Whether any of it has real truth or not, it was my truth and it was the story that helped me see my mother as a real holy being whose mission to guide me to the Dharma had succeeded.

Back home in my room, just off to the side of my three lamas, I placed a small, framed photo of my mother on my shrine, believing that she had revealed to me that she was more than a parent or a teacher. She was some kind of spiritual guide that gave me just enough lessons in this lifetime and, after successfully untangling myself from them, left me with a reward—one last message, like a popcorn trail, leading from this life to wherever she went in the hereafter.

Smiling at her picture with the wonder of it all, gently whispered, "Are you on the other side of some kind of heavenly two-way mirror?" I placed a kiss in my hand and touched the glass of her picture. "I'm sure you can see me... though I can't see you."

Next to Mom's photo was a small, framed picture of Palden Dorje after he had come out of meditation briefly and made a public statement. He was in a solid maroon robe, and his hair was quite long, covering his eyes. Keeping up to date with his image, I replaced the picture of him on my altar with a new one from his public darshan where thousands of people lined up for twelve days to receive his blessings—and I printed a smaller photo for a key chain fob to carry around with me. Everyday, I checked the internet in hopes of finding new information about this phenomenon happening in Nepal. News online traveled at the speed of light, but getting information from the jungle was slow... if there was anything going on at all.

In the backyard around two dying sycamore trees, I planted a flower garden full of maroon and saffron flowers—lilies and marigolds. After finding a statue of the Buddha as a center piece for the garden, I painted its skin with 18ct gold leaf, using colored enamels for the details of the eyes, lips, the black hair, and the crowning topknot, but paused before painting the robes. Images I found online of Shakyamuni's robes were detailed beyond my artistic abilities. After deciding to just paint the statue's robes solid white, I placed the Buddha on a white and yellow ceramic plinth in the center of the circular rows of lilies.

Two weeks later, I saw online that Palden Dorje made a new

public appearance—in white robes! A large stupa was built in his honor, such an accomplishment for a master so young and still living. Near the stupa, so that this holy being would not have to sit directly on the ground, the local farmers made a raised seat for him, a kind of throne made of cement that had been painted simply... white and yellow. The photo of him sitting on the platform looked strikingly similar to the centerpiece of my garden, and I marveled every time I considered the coincidence, wondering if there could possibly be any connection between this powerful Nepali meditator and me—a gay color guard choreographer from Indiana.

On my birthday the following year, Nathaniel called, having never missed one since we met. When I told him about Mom, he had the same stunned wonder as everyone else who heard the story that I never tired of telling.

"You must be going on some kind of intense Dharma trip," he laughed.

"It's been pretty amazing," I said.

"I've read that when once you start on the path of Dharma it's pretty usual to experience a lot of déjà vu and unexplainable coincidences."

I chuckled, "Confirmed!" Then I told him about Palden Dorje and the statue, and he was pensively silent for a few moments.

"You know, Marc," he said quietly, almost cautiously speaking, "every time I call you, I hang up a completely different person. It's just unreal the things that I know you've gone through, the things we've experienced together. I cherish these calls, I really do."

There was a moment, not too unlike parental pride, listening to him talk about his graduation and his upcoming plans to teach English in Taiwan. Even through the distance and the years, Than was very close to my heart.

One day in May, I received a message from someone in the Palden Dorje Google Group to which I subscribed. The sender was also Buddhist and was concerned with the new age members dismissing the phenomenon as something not related to Buddhism, that Palden Dorje represented a new religion entirely.

I set out to write many essays explaining Buddhist philosophy and Buddhist science as I came to understand them after years of study. Each essay was met with comments from other members of the Google Group dismissing my words, none with a shred of Buddhist training or knowledge. I was determined to bring people out of the darkness of ignorance that Geshe-la did with me over the years.

Many people expressed their appreciation for the essays, but there were still some, a core group of strong personalities that dominated every thread that was insistent that this phenomenon was beyond Buddhism. "Palden Dorje said that he's doing his meditation for all beings, not just Buddhists," one commenter submitted.

"Every Buddhist on the Mahayana path makes that same dedication daily," I responded.

"Labels, it's all labels and they don't mean anything. Words have no meaning," another commentator stated.

"You just used an awful lot of words to tell me that words don't matter," I replied. "And Shakyamuni Buddha left over a thousand teachings. That's a lot of words."

So many people quoted Alan Watts, Deepak Chopra, Eckhart Tolle, and other new age thinkers to help them prove that Palden Dorje was not a Buddhist, but none quoted any Buddhist teachings, nor the fact that Palden Dorje was raised in a Tibetan Buddhist monastery, that he spoke fluent Tibetan, or that he made the decision to do this austere and devoted meditation after being inspired in Bodhgaya, at the site where Shakyamuni achieved enlightenment.

Often, I logged off the site and was determined to stay off. But, after a few weeks, curiosity called me back to the same confusing arguments on every thread. I worked hard to create clarity in my essays, and it seemed they had little impact on many readers.

There were several regular commenters that remained active, insisting on their position, never considering the history of the monastic analysis of the Dharma. There were no experts, no one who even completed a class, and no one with awareness that this religion, unlike so many others around the world, was much more than a pamphlet and a series of haiku statements.

One commentator told me that spirituality and science are polar opposites. To which I replied that the Dalai Lama has held annual conferences with some of the greatest scientific minds of our time. He has called for the major monasteries of his tradition, exiled in India, to initiate a modern science curriculum to be added to the nearly two-decades long training toward the Geshe degree.

One commenter said that my posts seemed angry and that Buddhists were supposed to be calm and peaceful. "Ever see Tibetan monks debate?" I asked.

Even though I received heated personal emails from several of the core commenters, I refused to let these online spats consume too much of my time and resolved that it should be no more than an occasional curiosity with which I would briefly engage.

When I went to see the doctor for a follow-up, he told me that I had hypothyroidism. "You'll be on Synthroid for the rest of your life," his words disturbed me deeply. I didn't want to already be starting a lifetime of medication. Along with my blood thinners I would now have to take thyroid medicine—and I wasn't that old, I thought!

"Tibetan medicine cure thyroid," Geshe-la told me when I went to see him.

"Cure?" I asked.

"Totally cure," he reassured. "You go India, see Yeshe Dhunden, Dalai Lama's doctor, he give medicine, maybe eight months, finish."

India was on the other side of the planet and not a simple two-hour drive away. It wasn't the answer I needed, but it was an answer I needed to consider. "If I can make enough money someday, I'll go."

"You want happy body? Happy mind? Then find enough money," he poked my shoulder as he spoke.

"Ok, Geshe-la, I'll try."

"No! *Try* kinda lazy word. Make happen!" he seemed emphatic. "Khen Rinpoche here coming. He monk. No money. He find."

"Who's coming?"

"My teacher, Khen Rinpoche. He coming here!"

My teacher's teacher was going to come to our new property for a blessing, all the way from South India. As was the case with most of my Buddhist experiences, I had few people with whom to share my excitement. I explained to Wyatt over the phone, "This is my Yoda's Yoda!" Andy laughed when I repeated my line sitting at the BK.

"Maybe you can get a day off and come with me?" I suggested. "He's going to be giving a teaching throughout the weekend."

"I really can't, Marc," Andy thought he was disappointing me again, but I assured him I understood. After all the conversations we had sitting in that booth while he worked, I wanted him to have a chance to join me, to get started really exploring Dharma like me—with me.

Khen Rinpoche arrived with his small entourage, and Geshe-la was like a little boy again in the company of his childhood teacher. He dashed around throughout the small three-bedroom house, straightening things as he went along, making gallons of tea for all the IBC members who came to hear the old soft-spoken monk teach the Three Principal Paths.

This would be the third time I've received this teaching but was eager to hear it from someone who hadn't any experience in the West.

At one point during Rinpoche's teaching, he explained the importance of having healthy faculties and being born with no defects if one was to achieve enlightenment in one lifetime. My little bit of self-doubt started to resurface for the first time in quite a while, and I wondered if being born gay was something that would be a hindrance to me. It really started to bother me, so I got up from my cushion and made my way out of the tiny, crowded room and went to sit in the kitchen.

A few minutes later, Geshe-la entered and sat beside me. "You ok?"

Concerned that what Khen Rinpoche explained would prevent me from further spiritual growth, I told him that I believed that my sexuality was something biological, something of which I had no choice and was worried. He took my hand and gently squeezed it, saying, "This no problem. This I tell you before, I no lie. You come, listen teaching." It was a reassurance that soothed me deeply.

Not long after Khen Rinpoche and the monks left, the Board of Directors for IBC discovered that there were mistakes made on Geshe-la's visa. He was to go back to India until the corrections could be made. I went into a panic, fearing I may never see him again.

"You no worry," he told me, sitting in the passenger seat as I drove him to the going away party that was being thrown for him. "You just drink less Diet Coke!" He lifted my large beverage cup from the holder and shook it back and forth.

"Geshe-la, I promise I won't drink another Diet Coke until you've returned." And I didn't. He was gone for nearly eight months and I cut soda entirely out of my diet.

The day of his departure, many of the IBC members offered khataks to him and wished him a safe journey. In her overly dramatic fashion, the vice-president of the board of directors wept as Geshe-la was driven away, then announced, "He's like a father to me. If he can't return to America, I'll move to India to stay near to him."

Each morning I awoke and looked at my emails first thing, seeing if any news from the IBC had come that Geshe-la returned. Without my regular drives to see him, I poured myself into my rehearsals and my studies, making the eight months pass by in a flash. When I went to see Geshe-la after he returned, I opened a bottle of my first Diet Coke since he left—oh, that sweet burn on the back of the throat!

Interestingly, around the time of Geshe-la's return, the president and vice-president got divorced and moved to the opposite sides of the country. Remembering my warning about the karma of separating other students from a shared lama, I wasn't surprised, but sort of relieved. Geshe-la told me that neither of them would answer his phone calls. "They embarrassed, I think," he told me.

During Geshe-la's first teaching—and a welcome back party in one—a woman I met in Bloomington at the Tibetan Cultural Center attended and told me that she would be hosting a weekend Vajrayogini empowerment with Druppon Rinchen Dorje Rinpoche and asked if I would like to attend. Her name was Barbara, and she had as fierce of a personality as I imagined Vajrayogini to have—center of attention, intelligent, quick to correct someone, loving and compassionate, and quite nonconventional. I was drawn to her and told her about the voice I heard in Arizona.

"Species?" she said excitedly as we sat in a breakfast nook of her large home. "That's a beautifully succinct and delicious word she used to sum up 'all sentient beings', don't you think?" She raised an eyebrow mischievously as she stared at me, holding her coffee mug to her mouth, speaking with certainty that Vajrayogini had, indeed, given me a message.

"I've come to that conclusion myself," I said, studying each little move of her varied expressions. "But what does 'it is noble to draw the diamond' mean?"

"It's quite obvious, my dear. You are familiar with the Mani mantra, and its meaning?"

"Yes," I replied. "The Jewel in the Lotus. Inside every being—which are like flowers, lotuses growing from the mud of Samsara—is a radiant, multifaceted gem—like a shard of the great divine. But what does that have to do with what I heard?"

"She said the Mani mantra to you in English, silly," she said as though I was a child missing the most obvious answer. "It is an exalted—or *noble*—mind that sees all creatures as lovely, diverse, ever-growing beauties. And each one of them has this core of perfection—flawlessness—that you need to recognize again and again... *draw* it out of them, have compassion for them."

I stared at her with my mouth agape, stunned at how smoothly and eloquently she answered me, and how her explanation made sense. Barbara placed her hand under my chin and lifted upward. "Don't be a mouth-breather, darling. It's not attractive."

I took the Vajrayogini empowerment at her home that weekend, and as the vows made during the ceremony are secret, I never discussed them in detail with anyone else, not even Geshe-la. Suffice it to say that if this being was my spirit guide, I made a commitment to her and looked eagerly to what influences on my path she may lead... or continue to lead.

Around Christmas, Than made his reliable holiday call and I listened as he told me that he left his Taiwan trip early, concerned that the kids he was teaching were more concerned with abandoning their culture and adopting American attitudes and behaviors. He was overcome with guilt to be participating in it, returned to America, and jumped deep into the corporate world. "It doesn't get any more American than that," I chuckled.

"Assimilating another culture is arguably more American," he laughed defensively.

Throughout the winter, thoughts of traveling to India became more frequent, and I started investigating what the reality of such an endeavor would entail. I had never left the country and didn't know the first thing about passports, visas, airfare, booking accommodations, and so on, but Geshe-la pointed out how easily the Drepung monks had come to America, and the IBC sent Geshe-la to India and back again with such ease that I started to gain confidence that I would be able to make this dream happen. The teachers of the Law of Attraction I listened to from time to time said to never worry about the *how*, only focus on the *what*. My *what* was a trip to India. So, it was time to put the Law of Attraction to the test again.

This time, I hung a vision board on my wall with a large map of India in the center, around which I placed a variety of things I wanted to try to make happen in my life that year: a picture of a healthy thyroid in one corner with images of healthy people—hoping to attract better health, a picture of Geshe-la laughing—hoping to attract more positive people, several images of trophies and money—hoping to attract more success in the marching arts and more work to pay for this trip. I spent about fifteen minutes each morning visualizing that these things were already in my life, trying to manifest all of it into my reality.

My 39th birthday came around quickly, and sure enough, Than called. After the birthday greeting to which I welcomely anticipated, he told me that he had vacation time he wanted to use and said that he wanted to go on a retreat.

"Do you have Refuge Vows?" I asked, wondering if he would have taken them without sharing the event with me.

"No, no, I haven't taken them yet." He replied.

"Hmm, I don't know what to tell you then, because most of the retreats that are offered around the country require that one have those vows at a minimum."

"Well," he said after a short pause, "I was hoping I could go on a retreat with you."

It surprised me. "You know I'm not a lama, right?"

He laughed, "Yes, I know. But I've learned a lot from you, and we haven't gotten to spend any time together in a long while. You book a cabin and I'll pay for it."

Immediately after the call, I booked a cabin at the TCC and looked through all of my resources around which I could build a retreat schedule.

May 25th came, Than picked me up and we headed to Bloomington. We stopped at a grocery store just before arriving at our cabin and purchased enough food to get us through five days without having to leave. As we were unpacking, I explained to him that we would be switching off our phones, closing the curtains, and strictly following the instructions of the retreat.

Just before I started the ritual prayers to bless the retreat site, my phone rang. I didn't recognize the number and thought it could be a new band director wanting to hire me. I sheepishly looked at Than and asked him to excuse me as I took the call.

"Oh, hey! It's Andy," the voice said.

"What number are you calling me from? I don't recognize it."

"It's my new cell number. You probably don't recognize it because I always call you from BK's phone."

"That makes sense. What's up? You know I'm getting ready to go on a retreat, right?"

"Yeah," he said. "I actually thought I would get your voicemail and wish you well on your retreat. I was also going to ask you not to make any plans on Saturday after your retreat so that we can get together. Rob and I talked, and I really want to spend some time with you outside of work."

"Wonderful!" I exclaimed. "But you could have waited until after the retreat to call me. I had no plans."

"Well, I wanted to catch you before you had a chance to make any with anyone you're on retreat with."

"Oh," I hadn't told him this wasn't a formal retreat, "it's just me and a friend."

"That's cool," he paused. "Who's your friend?"

For a moment, I could've sworn he might be a little jealous. "His name's Nathaniel."

"Nathaniel who?" he pressed a little like a nosey mother. It seemed like an odd question since we didn't share many mutual friends.

"Nathaniel Jude."

"You know Nathaniel Jude?" he asked excitedly.

Holding the phone to my chest, I turned to Nathaniel and asked, "Do you know a guy named Andy Turley?"

Nathaniel sat up, laughing, and his eyes immediately began to tear. "No freaking way!" he exclaimed as I handed him the phone.

They talked for a few minutes, and I could tell that there was a history between them by the way Nathaniel was talking. The tears running down his cheeks, the look of awe in his eyes made me anxious to know how they knew each other. Nathaniel finally hung up the phone, laid it on the table and stepped out onto the deck behind the cabin, overlooking a long hill into the woods that surrounded the TCC property. I followed and sat beside him.

"Who the hell are you?" he asked as he looked at me, laughing through his tears.

"What just happened? How do you know Andy?"

"We grew up together, we were best friends."

"I'm confused—Andy's from Sharpsville and you're from Ohio."

"No, I go to school in Ohio," he corrected. "When you met me, I had just withdrawn from school and went back after we went through the summer together. But I grew up not far from where you did."

"Wow, I didn't realize..." I started, but he continued.

"Andy was my best friend until he tried to come out to me our freshman year. I was straight, and I wasn't ready for it. I've always regretted letting our friendship fade. We grew apart. But my senior year, Andy reached over in one of our classes and wrote on my notebook cover, *'If I have consciousness now, then I must necessarily have consciousness in the future in order to be aware of my consciousness in the present.'* And I couldn't disprove it. I wracked my brain for months... years. That's what led me to nihilism—searching for anything. It's what led me to the Denny's that night, sitting right there in front of you. Andy is quite literally the first domino in the chain that led me to you."

Stunned and amazed, we sat quietly in the experience, letting it fill our hearts.

For the next three days we followed the retreat guidelines perfectly. We would discuss a topic of the Lamrim for about fifteen minutes and then meditate on it for forty-five, breaking for lunch for an hour, and continuing that schedule until a dinner break, and finishing the evening around 9 p.m.

On Wednesday, Than broke into tears during the morning session, saying how much he wanted to take the Refuge Vows, and that the phone call with Andy was a sign to him that his commitment to Dharma should be sealed. I didn't know what to do, as Refuge Vows can only be given by a fully ordained monk. Then I remembered that Arjia Rinpoche was still on the property and told Than to excuse me while I left the cabin.

I went to Rinpoche's house at the front of the property and asked to speak with him. He permitted, and I told him of the coincidences that Than and I shared, and that he wanted to take the Refuge Vows.

"Please," I begged, "can you give him the Vows?"

Rinpoche looked at his little planner, "You come here tomorrow at 10 a.m. and I'll give him the Vows, ok?"

"Thank you!" I darted out of the house and back to the cabin. Than was ecstatic and began to weep again.

The next morning, I stood witness for the first time to someone I love dearly taking Refuge in the Buddha, Dharma, and Sangha. It was a beautiful moment to me, and I took in every detail, Rinpoche's voice, the words of the ceremony, the sunlight shining through the window, and all of the books and little statues neatly arranged on the shelves. Than rose at the end of the ceremony and Rinpoche gave him his Refuge name—*Dawa Dorje*.

We invited Rinpoche to come eat with us, and I prepared dinner that evening, like a servant, and stayed out of the way for Than and Rinpoche to sit and enjoy each other's company, a student with his new master. They sat and talked for a couple of hours. After Rinpoche left, Than stepped out onto the deck, and I followed.

"I have no way to express my gratitude for you, man," he put his arm around me as we stood against the rail looking out into the woods.

Sitting in his room at the center, Geshe-la listened intently as I recalled the events. "Yes," he said approvingly. "Dharma do many thing just this way."

"What does it all mean? The park, my mother, Andy and Nathaniel? Is this all some kind of past life stuff?"

"I no Buddha. I don't know," he said.

It was a big riddle and I needed to find the answer. "I want to go to India," I blurted.

He nodded. "You go India, many teacher there staying."

"Will you help me?"

"You get passport, then we talk."

That week, I went to the post office and filled out the application for a passport. I expected it to take nearly a month, but it arrived in just five days. I went to see Geshe-la.

"I have my passport," I handed it to him. He smiled and handed it back rather quickly.

"You get visa, then we talk."

That night, I looked online and found that the Indian Consulate in Chicago did same day visa processing. I asked Matt, one of the other members of IBC to accompany me, and we left early one morning, dropping my passport off as soon as they opened, and returned right before close to retrieve it. The stamp was lovely, and this trip felt a little closer and a little more *real*. Matt was about as excited for me to go as I was, recalling many stories of Buddhist masters who traveled to Tibet. "I'm not an emissary for the Dharma, Matt," I chuckled. "I'm going for my own curiosity."

Geshe-la held my passport again in his hands, looking at the page with the Indian visa. He handed it back. "You get plane ticket, then I help." I sighed.

Later at home, I scrolled through the internet, looking at everything I could about Dharamsala, the exiled home of the Dalai Lama. There were mountains, beautiful vistas, and a large Tibetan community. Fantasies of living in a Tibetan community, learning to speak their language and developing endearing friendships closed my nights and guided me gently into slumber.

I decided that I would go for the entire traditional U.S. academic year, leaving at the end of September and returning a week before my 40th birthday. It was a little frightening, but the excitement was more intoxicating, and I finally ordered my tickets after finding a decent price.

Geshe-la opened the door with a warm smile and said, "You land India September 28 at midnight!" I have never figured out how he knew that. "My brother, Sherab Choepel meet you at airport, you stay him apartment one week, then go Dharamsala. My sister, Rinchen Pel take you find room." Apparently, he had been planning things for me all along.

I asked Al if he would take care of Dropspin during my trip. "Of course," he assured. "This is her home." Neither of us saw our pets as property and he felt that since she had lived in his home for nearly eight years, it was her home and she would be welcome there, with his four cats until her natural death.

All the plans were laid, and I finished the summer rehearsals, making sure my designs were complete and moved all of my belongings into storage. I asked Geshe-la to watch after my statues and altar objects, which he put in his bedroom closet at the center.

"You be sure to take gifts," Kunyang instructed when I went to Bloomington to share with her the news of my coming adventures. She suggested taking lots of little American hat pins, or the spoons that say Indiana on them that you can buy at large truck stops to give to the different people I would meet. She also urged me to see her lama, Pari Rinpoche, and take a nice pen that had his name engraved on it. "Tell him I sent you."

I gave her a hug, "Thanks for everything all these years, Kunyang. You've been a wonderful teacher."

"I'm no teacher, pssh. What have you learned from me?" she chuckled.

I struck a pose like the image in a Vajrapani thangka and said, "Wrath!"

The night before my flight, Geshe-la and I sat in the IBC and repacked my suitcases for the trip. Several Tibetans in Indianapolis heard that I was going to India and brought packages for me to take to relatives in Delhi. "You kinda, little bit Tibetan FedEx," he joked.

Before we closed my bags and put the locks on them, Geshe-la dropped little orange grains of barley in all of them, and put some in my wallet, as well. "These Nechung channay," he said. "These blessed by Nechung oracle, give protection."

Nechung is the oracle of Tibet, and His Holiness consults him regularly and has said that Nechung has never been wrong throughout the years. I wasn't sure what the grains could do, but I learned to suspend my disbelief and just trust Geshe-la.

"Now, you no worry," he said as he put the little bag of grains on the table next to the big white sectional.

"I won't worry if those little grains can help me speak Hindi in the next 48 hours."

"Oh, many Indian speak English. Also, very smart, I tell you this one story," he said, and looked at me like a little kid with a secret. Three of his friends were in Nepal in the early nineties and one of them had a penchant for exaggeration, telling the other two that he could speak Nepali for the three of them wherever they would go. He would pull out a Nepali dictionary and do his best to talk to the locals, but usually with fail. When they went to the train station to buy tickets to go to Dharamsala in Northern India to attend a teaching by His Holiness, he reached in his pocket for the dictionary, but it wasn't there. The other two looked surprised and were afraid that they wouldn't be able to get the tickets. The monk told the other two not to worry and walked up to the counter confidently, then said, "Dalai Lama! *Chugga-chugga choo-choo*!" And they got their tickets!

The next morning Geshe-la and Tenam drove me to the airport and walked with me to the concourse. Geshe-la pulled out a long white silk khatak from his shoulder bag and put it around my neck. I looked at them with excitement, but also with a bit of fear. "Fear no benefit," Geshe-la said, sensing my worry. "Now, go enjoy. Study hard and take many picture."

I turned and walked away, heading toward uncertainty, excited for the new path I would be on for the months to come.

PART IV
MARGHA: THE TRUTH OF THE PATH TO THE CESSATION OF SUFFERING

> *What is the path that leads to the cessation of suffering? It is the Noble Eightfold Path, which consists of right view, right thought, right speech, right action, right livelihood, right effort, right mindfulness, and right contemplation.*
> —*The Buddha*

The various practices and methods of Buddhist philosophy lead us to the elimination of the emotional obscurations, to Nirvana. Eventually, with even more diligence it is said that we can remove subtle obscurations on the mindstream that prevent omniscience. These practices are the religious-like patterns adopted by Buddhist practitioners in their quest to attain liberation from rebirth and the final state of the evolution of consciousness—the state of a completely perfected Buddha.

We are all on a spiritual journey of our own, and the Dharma is the guidance for the evolution of our consciousness. There are five paths that all beings traverse to reach Buddhahood: accumulation, preparation, seeing, familiarization, and no more learning. Practitioners on each of these paths have different energies and intuitions as their consciousness becomes aware of the ultimate nature of itself and reality.

First, we gather the right energies, called merit, in order to understand the ultimate. Then, we prepare to have a direct experience with it by refining our intellectual capacity. With a pristine and clear understanding, we enter into a deep state of meditation where our mind directly perceives emptiness, the lack of any concretely real existence. After seeing emptiness directly, we familiarize ourselves with the understanding we gained until the consciousness is completely free from the various obstacles that lead us to the fully enlightened state of a Buddha, where there is nothing more to learn.

Every creature with a mind is destined to reach this highest state of consciousness. The Buddha was just another being like the rest of us, but he made diligent strides to achieve enlightenment for himself and to be of the highest benefit for all other sentient beings. His life serves as an example and his teachings illustrate the methods and trainings for us to liberate from this cyclic existence. The various masters that we meet demonstrate different levels of spiritual progress that speak to our hearts and minds and draw us to them. They are role models to whom we aspire to emulate, and they can appear in our lives just when we need them, demonstrating the path to liberation. They are the embodiment of the path.

✤ Chapter Thirteen ✤

The little boy inside of me delighted as I pressed my face against the window, watching the world shrink smaller and smaller, the houses becoming little pixels in the road-lined landscape far below. I marveled at the sights, interrupted only by the few rogue clouds in the sky. The vast expanse of ocean's blue lulled me to sleep, and I woke in Germany.

After a four-hour layover, I switched planes and boarded the surreal world of an Indian airline. Though I was sleepy, I lost my breath in wonder at all the saris, turbans, and smells of sandalwood perfumed oils and thus sat in my seat sculpting every shape and color of this new experience into my memory. I must have looked like a deranged fool, smiling incessantly, practicing my Namaste to anyone who'd meet their eyes with mine—and there were many.

While midflight, whenever I excused myself past several people in the aisle, each would bob their head side to side—not up or down—and I had no idea if it meant that I offended them or if it was some gesture of indifference. A kind stewardess giggled when I asked her about it out of earshot.

"That totally depends on the question or the situation," she explained, and I smiled realizing I had eight months of this glorious accent ahead of me. "If the person being queried is indifferent to the question, they will lower their eyebrows and bob their head slowly side to side. But if they are in high agreement, they will raise their eyebrows and bob quite vigorously!"

Comically, and as though rehearsed, two stewardesses bobbed their heads side to side quickly with their eyebrows raised as I exited the plane. I gathered my two suitcases from the carousel in Indira Gandhi International and put them on a cart, pulling it behind me as my sleep-deprived but excited body moved about the complex, anticipating the new world outside. Would Geshe-la's brother be holding a sign with my American or Tibetan name, I wondered? I didn't have much of a clue of what he looked like, but hadn't a care in the world, trusting that my master had seen to every detail of his student's arrival into this country.

Two armed military guards stood on either side of the vestibule as I pulled my cart down a long corridor of people and carefully examined the sea of signs the drivers held, looking for one with my name being held by Sherab Choepel. When I got to the final doors I cautiously stepped outside and into a smaller crowd in the sweetly scented, humid Indian night. The realization that no one was there to greet me emptied all excitement from my body, and I went into a little meltdown.

"Do you need a phone?" a well-dressed salesman summoned me toward his kiosk, but I just shook my head and walked to a vacant fissure near the vestibule. A panic began to grow in me, realizing I knew so little about what I had gotten into.

The salesman approached me again, "Do you need to call someone? I have phones, very good prices."

"I'm sorry," I said timidly, "I haven't exchanged any money."

"No problem, you can make an exchange with me, best rate," he had one eyebrow raised and his head bobbed side to side at an intermediate speed.

"Oh, come on!" I shouted. "What does *that* mean?"

"Excuse me, sir?" he asked confusedly.

My panic was reaching the red line, and I responded through gritted teeth, "Please... I don't know how much anything costs here." He stepped away obligingly.

I felt so many eyes on me, and their faces began to bleed together like someone just poured water onto a freshly painted canvas. My heart was racing, and I was afraid to step outside, fearing I wouldn't be allowed back into the airport.

Drawing a deep breath, a voice within me scolded such behavior. "*Those are human beings! You're a Buddhist!*" I calmed myself and summoned the courage to go through the automatic double-doors. "It's just a chemical, it's just a chemical," I repeated my mantra quietly under my heavy breathing until I was calm.

An older gentleman with a long gray beard and moustache, dressed in a sharp dark blue business suit and tie with a matching turban approached me, "Would you like to use my cell phone, sir?"

"I'm sorry," I started to decline, "I don't know any numbers here and I haven't even met the people who are supposed to pick me up."

"You can call America," he encouraged again, as though he were offering a nut to a squirrel. "I lived in Washington D.C. for twenty years. I understand your fright."

I thanked him, drew a deep, cleansing breath, took the phone, and called Geshe-la.

"You in Delhi now?" he was surprised. "Oh, I make wrong day. You no worry. I call Sherab Choepel. You no worry."

I hung up, knowing that the Geshe would be frantically ringing his brother's phone, worrying for us both. "Thank you," I returned the phone to its distinguished looking owner. "He got the dates mixed up."

"I had a similar experience on my first trip to the States," he said. "I was quite confused and frightened myself."

Never having met a Sikh, I looked at his turban and said, "I'm sorry, I really don't know anything about the Sikh religion. Would you mind if I asked about it?"

"Please, do. You're going to meet a lot of Sikhs here," he laughed. "Have a healthy appetite on Wednesdays. Sikhs have big festivals on that day and all the food is free!"

"Ah, you did spend time in America," I started. "You learned the language of the fat American male!"

We stood and talked for a long while, and within about ten minutes, I found myself surrounded by twelve turbaned men, all joining in our discussion. They taught me so much about the Sikh religion, their commitment to compassion and helping others—and the free food! And I got more details on the variations of the head bob.

Eventually, I was left to sit on a curb and wait for my host. I felt ashamed for my panic attack, and simultaneously grateful for such a warm, welcoming conversation.

The taxi arrived and Sherab Choepel gave a rushed introduction to his accompanying nephew, Lobsang, and a handshake, then threw my suitcases on the top of the car and nearly pushed me into the backseat. I lurched back as the driver tore away from the curb and onto the long road away from the airport.

My two Ladakhi hosts had little resemblance to Geshe-la, nor one another for that matter. Choepel was short and both were mustachioed. Lobsang's English was far better, though his accent was more British sounding than the Sikhs with whom I conversed.

The car zipped along, slaloming slower vehicles like we were in a race. I braced myself, holding the back of the front seat. "Please," I begged, "My bags on the roof aren't strapped down! It's all I have for the next eight months!"

"Bags fine, no worry," Sherab Choepel exclaimed, then started speaking to the Indian driver in Hindi.

"This is your first time in India?" Lobsang asked calmly, jostling back and forth without care. I nodded, watching the traffic through which our driver maneuvered.

"I've never left America," I said. "Can we stop somewhere so I can use the restroom?"

In just seconds after my request, the taxi came to a stop beside the road. "Pee here!" Sherab Choepel motioned to the bushes just beyond the curb.

"What?" I asked.

"This India, pee anywhere!" he laughed. "Look," he said, turning my attention to several men in our headlights facing the bushes with their backs to us.

"Baby steps," I chuckled. "I think I need baby steps. I'll hold it."

When we got to their apartment, Lobsang pointed out the bathroom and I went quickly inside. There was no toilet, just a porcelain hole in the floor. Finding no tissue, I called out to Lobsang, a little embarrassed. When I asked him how I was to finish up, he pointed to a small hose under the sink. Without missing a beat, I asked, "What's that like in December?"

The next morning, Sherab Choepel placed an omelet and a mug of butter tea on the table next to the sofa where I was laying. "Geshe-la say you like butter tea."

I stretched as I sat up. "I love it!"

A red wall hanging in Tibetan caught my eye, and I stared at it trying to translate it as I sipped my tea. *May you have the happiness of gods, may your health be solid as a rock, and may you swiftly accomplish all your wishes.*

Lobsang came and sat next to me. "Uncle Geshe says that you should stay in Delhi for a week before going to Dharamsala so that your body can rest and acclimate. There's plenty of time to make arrangements for your travel."

"Are you free to show me around Delhi?" I asked, as I began to eat. Sherab Choepel came from the kitchen of the small apartment with a stack of chapati and placed one on my plate.

Choepel noticed my inspection of the chapati and said, "Chapati like Indian tortillas." I smiled and took one.

"Sure," Lobsang said. "After you shower and make yourself fresh, I can take you to Majnu-ka-tila and see the Tibetan settlement."

"This isn't the Tibetan settlement?" I asked, confused.

"No, no. We are in Rohini, quite a distance from MKT. This is the Tibetan Youth Hostel where many students who are attending schools stay."

After my breakfast, I asked Lobsang to take me outside for a walk to see my first glimpse of India in the daylight. There was a large park across the road from the hostel, and it was filled with people exercising, doing yoga, and sitting in groups for meditation. One man nearby was practicing some kind of laughing yoga and bellowed out the loudest and most fake sounding guffaw. It was a strange sight to see everyone dressed as normal, many working out in what looked like their daily attire. "No one get the memo about gym clothes?" I joked.

"You must be sure to have yogurt with every meal for your first week here," Lobsang instructed as we walked through the park. I was being stared at by every Indian I could see.

"Why is that?"

"It will prevent you from getting Delhi belly," he patted his abdomen as he spoke.

"My Mom would've said *the shits*," I smiled.

" Oh, *the shits*, yes." Lobsang laughed.

After I had a shower, and just before we left the TYH complex, one of Lobsang's friends ran up to us, eager to meet his American guest. Lobsang introduced me to Tenzin Gyalpo, a young man who looked a lot like the Japanese antagonist in the Karate Kid sequel. "Oh, you're fat!" he said.

"Ah, yes. There's that Tibetan brutal honesty," I said with a smile as I shook his hand.

Lobsang led me down the street toward the Metro station, and I listened to him tell me about his home in Ladakh, but my eyes were darting around at all of the garbage in the streets. Empty bags and wrappers littered the gutters and lined the grassy edge of all the buildings. I said nothing.

Lobsang continued talking as I followed him through the turn-style, up the long stairs, and to the platform. *Please mind the gap*—the female voice warned through the speakers as the train doors opened. We stepped inside, swallowed by the mass of transiters pressed window to window.

I watched in horror the passing polluted landscape through the window as we zipped through Delhi, and my stomach began to sour. "Oh my god," I finally said. "This is unbelievable." Everywhere I looked there was garbage, piles of it on the sides of roads, blowing about the feet of people as they walked. At one point, Lobsang pointed to trucks in the distance driving up a large hill and told me that it was a mountain of garbage, and I lost my mind like I had in the airport.

"I'm sorry, Lobsang," I said, grabbing both overhead rails with my hands. "I need to go back to Sherab Choepel's and pull myself together."

He was taken aback, "Go back? But we haven't been gone long."

"This is drastically different than America! I didn't know! How can the people accept this? Don't they deserve a cleaner home, a healthier environment? I'm going to be here for eight months! Oh, my god. Please take me back."

Two hours later, Lobsang gently nudged me awake from a nap under the wind of the ceiling fan. "*Marse*, are you alright?"

I laughed. "The c is pronounced like a k," I corrected as I rolled over.

"Excuse me?"

"It's Marc," I explained. "That's a new one, though."

"Sherab Choepel is at work and I need to go do some errands. If you get hungry please enjoy the Cantina downstairs." He left and I rolled onto my side to stare out the window.

"Remember, Marc," I coached myself quietly, "you're here for the people, not the trash."

The hostel compound was immaculately kept, spotlessly contrasting what I saw beyond the gate of the compound. There were hand-painted signs encouraging it: *Cleanliness is next to godliness*, and *Think globally, act locally*.

Of the four buildings that made up the youth hostel, the Cantina was attached to one of the back buildings and had an open-air layout, with marble topped tables and concrete benches. Large black crows flew in to clean the tables and floors of the scraps the students carelessly dropped. I giggled to myself, hearing their caws—*Marc*! *Marc*!—thinking they were giving a better pronunciation of my name than what Lobsang first attempted. I slowly walked inside and up to the counter and ordered a plate of mo-mos and some chow mien from a young Tibetan girl, who promptly greeted me in perfectly clear English.

"The students like to eat here instead of the cafeteria food, sometimes," a white-haired Tibetan man looking of his mid-sixties said to me from behind the cash drawer just down from us, under the watchful eye of a large, framed photo of His Holiness on the wall behind him.

"Are you a headmaster?" I asked, biting into a hot dumpling, dripping with flavorful juices, though they did not have the familiar flavor of beef.

"No, no," he said, wiping the counter with a washcloth. "I just take care of the Cantina." He watched me look curiously inside one of the mo-mos. "Oh, yes! Those are made with deer meat, not beef. You are probably used to beef."

"Oh, ok," I said, laughing to myself that after all the years of living in Indiana and having the acquaintance of many hunters, I got my first taste of venison in India.

"What is your name, may I ask?"

"Well, my American name is Marc, but my Tibetan name is Sonam Tsering."

His eyes lit up. "You are Buddhist! Wonderful! You can call me Pa-la, it means father, but it is our custom to call older members of our society mother and father instead of mister or missus."

As I finished my food and approached the counter with my empty plate, an older Tibetan woman entered from the back door and began talking to the old man. I assumed the two were married by the way they carried on. She looked at me several times, and I smiled back as warmly as I could, knowing that I quickly became the new subject between them.

"Ama-la would like to invite you to her apartment for tea," Pa-la said.

"Please tell your wife I would enjoy that," I replied.

He quickly laughed and said something to her. "She is not my wife. She used to run the Cantina and is kind of like my boss. Come through here and follow her," he motioned me around the counter and to the back door.

Stepping outside, Ama-la gently took my hand, examining my smiling face as we walked toward a rear corner of the complex. The Indian sun was brutally hot, but she didn't show even a glimmer of sweat anywhere on her skin. Her hair was pulled back, jet black, and apparently dyed as little flecks of silver roots peaked from underneath. As I examined her face, knowing what atrocities her country faced that led to her living in exile in India, I wondered how many of the thin lines around her eyes and mouth and on her forehead were etched there by things too unspeakable to imagine.

Through my poor Tibetan, I was able to tell her that I didn't speak the language well, and she tried to use Tibetan words that a young child could understand.

"No worries. Let's have tea," she said, pulling the embroidered door curtain aside and guiding me into her apartment after I removed my shoes.

It was a simple room with plain furniture except for the ornate, handcrafted altar that resembled the hutch from my childhood. She motioned for me to sit on one of the sofas that was merely a flat platform with a mattress and pillows, doubling as a bed. There was a large, framed photo of the Dalai Lama with a small shelf, just below, holding offerings of a few pieces of fruit, a package of cookies, and an electrically lit butter lamp.

"May I look at your altar?" I asked in broken Tibetan. She nodded and slipped into her kitchen.

It was a modest display of a Buddha statue behind two glass doors, several Tibetan books, and other small ritual implements. The daily water bowls were filled, and the lamp had already flickered out. The room smelled of incense, just like the kind I used in my room and if I closed my eyes, I couldn't tell that I wasn't at home. On the walls beside the altar were plastic wrapped thangkas, yellowed with age and incense resin. Hanging beside a thangka of Tara were photos of her family, I assumed. She had a husband, a daughter, and a son.

She quietly came and stood behind me, then pointed at several framed photos of her family on the wall. "My son, Kalsang Dorje, my daughter Tenzin Drolkar." Then she pulled on my sleeve and pulled me to a photo of a young girl. "Granddaughter Tenzin Yegah."

"Sonam Tsering," I said as I placed my hand on my chest.

"Sonam Drolma," she repeated my introductory gesture.

"We're both Sonams!" I exclaimed.

We sat drinking butter tea for nearly a half-hour when the door curtain pulled aside, and a beautiful thin Tibetan woman of her late twenties stepped in, already jabbering away quite loudly to Sonam Drolma, and I assumed this was her daughter.

"Oh, hello," she turned to me. "Who are you?"

"My name is Sonam Tsering," I extended my hand. "Are you Tenzin Drolkar?"

She looked surprised, "Yes, I am." Then she started speaking to her mother again, and I could make out that she was asking how I came to be sitting in their apartment. Sonam Drolma told her of our meeting and everything she learned from our discussion.

"Oh, so your teacher is Sherab Choepel's brother?" she asked.

"Yes, Geshe Jinpa Sonam," I pulled my wallet from my pocket and showed her a photo I had of us together.

She took the wallet, every movement like a caramel-colored marble statue come to life. I thought it a shame that someone with such a glamorous air should live in a tiny apartment such as this. Ama-la took the wallet when Drolkar offered it and smiled, looked at the photo, touched it to the top of her head, which is a Tibetan gesture of reverence, then returned it to me.

"So many Tibetans are named Tenzin," I mentioned.

"They are named by His Holiness," she answered before I asked. "Tibetan parents usually take one child or more to receive their name from him. His name is Tenzin Gyatso, so we receive his first name and a second name of his choosing."

As we sat and talked, Drolkar would effortlessly switch back and forth between Tibetan and English. One of the Indian groundskeepers popped their head in briefly and Drolkar spoke Hindi to him. Astonished, I queried about her fluency and she explained that most of the younger Tibetans spoke all three languages, and some many more.

"We speak Tibetan to communicate with one another, Hindi to communicate with the Indians, and English to communicate with the world. Others learn the language of their new country if they immigrate."

After a little while, I explained that I had plans with Lobsang and thanked them for a memorable visit. They invited me to return for dinner, and I took my leave to find Geshe-la's nephew.

Majnu-ka-tila was a system of alleys full of Tibetan shops and restaurants, and my wallet itched to buy things that would be four to five times more expensive online or at home. I spent the afternoon with Lobsang, ignoring the garbage in the streets and reminding myself that I was on the other side of the planet, and that brought a greater sense of love and wonder to me with every new face I met.

A woman carrying an infant on her hip grabbed my arm and pulled back and forth to get my attention. Looking to me like a starving image right out of a National Geographic photo, she gestured to the baby's mouth and then at her own, begging for food. Their filthy bodies and the deeply sad expression on the mother's face nearly broke my heart, and I pulled out my wallet, until Lobsang explained that there are professional beggars just like this woman everywhere, and that many women like her rent babies for the day. "Look again," he said. "That baby is fat. Does he look starved?"

Though the Tibetans maintain their homes and shops with great care for order and cleanliness, the alleyways of MKT were a little muddy since the shopkeepers often threw water onto the steps and the road in front of their store to reduce the dust being blown about. Inside every shop was a feast for the eyes. Tibetan artwork is brightly colorful and full of detail. A thangka shop swallowed me in to flip through rows of paintings, and I walked away with two at a nice price, according to Lobsang.

Across the street from there was a bookstore that had many Tibetan style scriptures, and I ran out of time before Lobsang suggested other sights.

He showed me how to exchange my money and my Traveler's Cheques and how to find the best rates, how to talk down a rickshaw driver's price, and many other things I would need to know in India. We bought a little prepaid red cell phone—ridiculously cheap—and Lobsang was shocked when I told him the cost of the same phone in America.

I loved walking through the crowded alleys, and everywhere I looked the image of the Dalai Lama smiled back, and somehow, I had the sense that I was... home.

On our way back to Rohini, he took me to the Qutub Minar, an Indo-Islamic minaret made entirely of brick built around 1200AD. Unlike historical sites in America, I was able to place my hand on the smooth, shiny marble surface of the tower, and my fingers traced the laser precise etchings in the stone, almost unaffected by the millennium of time and weather.

Lobsang took many photos of me, and I took some of him for Geshe-la. As we were standing trying to take a photo together, two kind older women came up to us and offered to help. They found the best angles for us, with interesting and incredible scenes behind us. As I took my camera and thanked them, one of them said, "You should show her how grateful you are of her talents," and realized they had done it under the prospect of monetary reward and not plain old good heartedness. I gave them a fair amount, though they hid any sign of satisfaction.

We popped into a little restaurant, which looked more like a garage with the door pulled back, and we sat at a picnic table inside. "Remember, you should eat curd with this meal. It is good for the digestion," Lobsang instructed. As I tasted each dish, I felt a child-like greed to taste more and more, everything was delicious beyond my expectations.

Returning to the hostel, we parted ways so I could have dinner with Ama-la and her family. Practically running to the back of the hostel, I eagerly removed my shoes as I called into the apartment. "Yes, Sonam, come in," Tenzin Drolkar called back. "Ama-la is almost ready for dinner."

Inside, an older Tibetan gentleman sat on the couch, reading a Tibetan prayer book. He wore a tank top undershirt, due to the heat of the day. I walked across the room to shake his hand, and his eyes, soft and loving, met mine welcomingly. "Tashi delek, Pa-la," I greeted.

He closed the book and took my hand, pulling invitingly for me to sit beside him. Gently squeezing his hand, I told him that my Tibetan was poor, and he patted me on the leg approving of what skills I demonstrated.

Drolkar emerged from another room, her hair was long and wet from a recent bath. "Ama-la didn't make dinner for us tonight," she began an apology, "so we are eating from the Cantina. But Ama-la said that you should come here in the morning for a home cooked breakfast."

Her five-year-old daughter, Tenzin Yegah, came from the room and sat beside Drolkar and stared at me curiously as her mother ran a brush through her dark, shiny hair. We all sat around the coffee table where Ama-la placed our food in front of us, and as she was pouring tea, I folded my hands and began a Tibetan prayer recited before meals, hoping to impress my hosts. They joined in just after I started chanting, as if we were all in the monastery and I was the leading chant master. Afterward, Ama-la said something to Drolkar, staring at me with such a delightful expression.

"Ama-la is impressed with you," Drolkar said.

"I have all of my prayers and mantras memorized," I said, picking up a pair of chopsticks. "My conversational skills in the language are quite poor, though."

"They will improve," Drolkar encouraged. "Just try to learn at least one new word a day, and by the end of the year you will have 365 words!"

Ama-la sat beside me, pulling a notebook from my shoulder bag that was at my feet. I nodded that it would be ok to look inside, and she gasped with amazement when she saw my Tibetan handwriting, her voice was suddenly high pitched, speaking quickly to Drolkar.

"Ama-la wants to know if you wrote this."

"Yes, I've practiced for many years."

Ama-la continued to speak with excitement, too quickly for me to even recognize a single word. As the notebook circled around the table, they each joined her, all talking over one another. Then Ama-la took the notebook, tapping her finger on one of the pages, said my name and then something I didn't understand. I looked to Drolkar for a translation.

"Ama-la said that your handwriting is better than that of most Tibetans, and she is quite impressed with your skill. So am I! It's true!"

"That means the world to me, and after the change my life has gone through because of what your culture has given me, I feel it is the very least that I can do to help preserve it."

After dinner, I sat and told them the story of my mother and how she passed away, and that Tibetan Buddhism helped me to overcome so many traumas in my life. It was an emotional moment, as I was both filled with joy and sadness, but more so with appreciation to be in India with this beautiful family, sharing something dear to my heart.

Ama-la and Pa-la told me how they followed the Dalai Lama into exile, and how Pa-la joined the Indian military. Ama-la used to work making beautifully detailed and colorful Tibetan rugs. They were from Shigartse, Tibet, and lived in India since the mid-sixties. They never spoke an ill word about the Chinese, and I knew that came from their admiration for His Holiness and their aspirations to be as compassionate and loving as his teachings. Each member of the family was the most exemplary of hosts for my first night in India, and I fell asleep on Sherab Choepel's sofa that night, bathing in the fragrant Night Jasmine in the air, excited for breakfast the next morning.

I arrived before the food was on the table, but Pa-la was already away for the day. Ama-la came from the kitchen with a pitcher of water and motioned me to join her at the altar to offer yunchap—water bowl offerings. To my surprise, she handed me the pitcher and indicated that she wanted me to make the offerings by saying "*bul, bul!*" I poured the water into each bowl exactly as Geshe-la had taught me and arranged them in front of her statue. When I was finished, she smiled and, in English said, "Good."

As we ate our breakfast of chapati with peanut butter and honey, omelets, and fresh fruit, Drolkar and I made plans for the family to visit a newly constructed Hindu temple—the Swaminarayan Akshardham—that Ama-la had been wanting to see. There are so many historical sights to take in and my stay in Delhi would end within the week. Before I left, Ama-la gave me a hug, then patted my belly and said, "Sonam! No more than two butter tea per day," and I laughed, understanding her Tibetan clearly.

Lobsang offered to guide me around after breakfast. I hung my head out the side of the rickshaw, feeling the wind cooling the sweat from my face. The number of people walking on the sides of the road was incalculably huge, comparable only to New York City during rush hour, and just about every one of them were watching the smiling white guy putt-putt past them. At traffic stops, motorcycles, bicycles, and street vendors would fill the spaces between cars, and I felt the looks of many rubbernecking out of their tuk-tuk to catch a look at me.

And then there were the cows. They are free to roam wherever they please, and one popped her head inside our little lawnmower-like taxi and gave me an Indian bovine sloppy kiss.

In just my first couple of days, I felt as though I stepped into a magical world, and I had. The food, the people, the temples, the smells—good and bad—fascinated and pleased my senses, and I was sad that Wyatt couldn't be with me.

Lobsang and I spent the rest of the week touring Delhi, and I took nearly five hundred photos of the most toured locations, including Gandhi's home and the Eternal Flame where he was cremated, the Lotus Temple, the Red Fort, and many Hindu mandir. But no matter where I went, it was nothing like walking up and down the alleyways of Majnu-ka-tila and being surrounded by the Dalai Lama's countrymen.

Whenever I entered an Indian shop, I was bombarded with "My friend, my friend! I make you special price!" But the Tibetans were laidback with business, and I was free to look around whether I was wanting to make a purchase or not. I tried to explain to one Indian shop owner that Americans don't like being sharked when shopping. He explained that he would not be a good businessman if he didn't push for a sale.

The prices in India were ridiculously cheap, and I could easily have filled all my baggage with statues, paintings, and everything that delighted my eye in just that first week. Instead, I restrained myself and bought only a few items. I did, however, bring gifts to Ama-la and Drolkar. Before I was to leave for Dharamsala I bought two lovely handbags and filled them with jewelry, scarves, and skincare products. They received them with sincere and glowing appreciation.

Lobsang helped me book my short flight to Dharamsala where

Geshe-la's sister, Rinchen Pel, a nun, was to meet me and take me to my room she had booked with Kirti monastery. I had breakfast every day with Ama-la, and on the morning of my flight she placed a khatak around my neck and gave me her blessing.

Drolkar sat beside me, translating Ama-la's words. "She said, 'Your mother has passed away, and that is most unfortunate, but the story she left you is remarkably beautiful and filled with hope. Nonetheless, you have no mother in this world now, and I want you to see me as your new mother, as I look at you as though you are my child I have just found again.'"

Her words were as dear to me as Geshe-la's when he gave me a part of his name as my own the morning I took my Refuge Vows. Ama-la tenderly welcomed me into her family, and I have never since seen her less of a mother than my own dear Mom.

The flight from Delhi was quite short, and the Kangra Airport was surprisingly small, much like the Howard County airport near Kokomo. The Dalai Lama frequented this place and I imagined that I received a blessing simply by landing there.

Two nuns with beaming smiles greeted me at the carousel holding khataks. The shorter of the two wore rose gold framed glasses with tinted lenses resting halfway down her nose, and she looked at me from over them, "Hello, Marc! I'm Rinchen Pel, and this is my friend Norzom." They placed the long white scarves around my neck, and I saw Rinchen Pel had a noticeable lazy eye. It was a charming imperfection on such a warm, glowing face. After brief introductions, we hopped in the taxi and rode along winding roads through a breathtaking landscape.

"We are going there," said Rinchen Pel, pointing to a thick green mountain that was dwarfed by gray giant snowcapped peaks beyond. Clusters of buildings and houses spiraled around through tall evergreens, leading to the town of crowded structures at the top.

"Are those the Himalayas?" I asked, soaking every detail of the marvelous vista I could with my feasting eyes.

"The gray rocky mountains with snow are called the Dhauladhar mountain range, a part of the Himalayas, yes."

"My God, I'm going to be living in a painting for the next five months," I said, with my head poking through the rear window.

Throughout the forty-five-minute drive to McLeod Ganj—an old British military installation turned exiled home for many Tibetans and His Holiness—I watched the mountains grow closer and closer, and marveled at the sights I could never see back in the endless flat cornfields of Indiana. Cows roamed the streets freely and shepherds herded flocks of goats and sheep through town roads, blocking off traffic until they passed. There was a smell that settled every nerve in my body, a mixture of burning incense in every nearby home and shop and the moisture from the earth.

As we made our way up the green mountain, a large troop of macaques slowed our tight one-way traffic. "Wow!" I said, having never seen monkeys outside of cages or free of glass barriers.

Rinchen Pel turned around in the front passenger seat and looked sternly at me, "Don't look them in the eye and don't smile at them!" She exclaimed. "They are very dangerous, and you must be careful."

"Why can't I smile at them?" I asked. "As a Buddhist, isn't it good karma to smile at everyone?" Rinchen Pel smiled widely, baring her teeth as Norzom laughed. She then leaned toward me, playfully trying to bite my arm. "OK, I get it," I said as I lifted my shoulder bag as a shield from her. "The monkeys aren't Buddhist."

"No!" she exclaimed as she settled back into her seat. "They have no compassion at all! They're not even Hindu! Just watch out. They're very mischievous and can be dangerous."

I nodded, and watched the monkeys moving about, noticing the reactions of the local pedestrians throwing rocks to chase them away. "Maybe they're Jehovah's Witnesses," I whispered to Norzom.

Our taxi arrived at Kirti monastery and I was quickly escorted by a short, fat monk who waddled in front of us jingling a handful of keys, to my tiny cell with a private bathroom. "A western toilet!" I was thankful I wouldn't have to squat.

The bed was hard, like a doctor's examining table, and there was a flimsy armoire in which I could place my belongings. Though the room was simple and plain, the balcony overlooked the entire Kangra valley, a view that held me captive and motionless for a half-hour after I unpacked.

Looking down as I leaned against the rails, a paved road slithered down the mountain through thickets of pine trees like a long, gray snake. A few little shops and tiny tea stalls—called chai wala—were spaced out along the side of the road, and I chuckled as I thought that it seemed that the Indians couldn't go twenty steps without needing a tea break.

The road disappeared into the compact cement village in the valley, which was called Lower Dharamsala. McLeod Ganj and Upper

Dharamsala blended together, and I don't know which was which as there were no demarcations or signs and all of the shops pressed against one another except for an occasional narrow alley here and there. A winding river separated the mountain upon which Kirti was built and another mountain just like it, thick with pine trees and only but a few houses.

From my position I could see the other side of Dharamsala and the newly built soccer stadium with its red roof ringed around the complex. And far into the distance, the sunshine danced on the water of a large lake.

But the most amazing part of the view was just off to the right, past Kirti monastery and on the other side of another narrow valley in which the road to Lower Dharamsala was carved was the Dalai Lama's complex. Just behind it, nestled among a curtain of green fir trees, I could get a glimpse of his residence. I was now a temporary neighbor to the holy man who started me on this journey!

That evening, before the sun set, I took off to walk the circuit around the Dalai Lama's complex. The Tibetans called this route the Lingkhor, and there were many prayer wheels and cairns full of rocks with prayers and mantras painted on them all along the way. The older generation of Tibetans made the circuit every morning and evening, spinning their own handmade prayer wheel in their right hand and counting their *Mani* mantras on their mala held in their left.

At one wooded place along the path, a troop of monkeys sat, grooming themselves. I had a package of cookies in my pocket and threw some to them, one by one. A male sitting close by grabbed a cookie and began to eat when he noticed my gawking stare and ear to ear smile. He made a short-lived charge at me, and threateningly bared his teeth. I remembered Rinchen Pel's instructions and quickly lowered my head apologetically. "Shit, shit, shit! Sorry, sorry, sorry!" I laughed, a little frightened. The monkey returned to his sweet treat and I walked slowly away. Though I was startled by the monkey's aggressive advance, I was fully entertained by the experience.

The more than a mile long Lingkhor ended at the gates to the Tsuglhakhang, the main temple complex in which His Holiness gave regular teachings. After passing through large iron gates, there was a small book shop and a museum at the end of a long walkway—seeing the gruesome photos of what the Chinese had done to the Tibetans, too unconscionable to imagine, I left the museum with tears in my eyes.

A long ramp led to a secured entrance with two armed Indian

guards and a Tibetan gentleman dressed in a suit and tie who patted down each entrant as a Tibetan woman checked bags and took any prohibited items to be stored until later. I expressed gratitude to them for protecting the Dalai Lama and everyone who visited, and they kindly responded with smiles. Once past the metal detector, I stepped into an aromatic atmosphere where wisps of Tibetan incense danced in the air. The large lower concourse was covered by a vast canvas overhead, and many people inside were doing a circumambulation, called khorra, around the downstairs walls of the temple—while monkeys sat watching in the rafters and ran along the rails of the surrounding fences.

On the upper level outside the throne room where the Dalai Lama would sit and give public teaching were about twenty long planks of laminated wood, upon many of which older Tibetans were showing their devotion by prostrating, sliding their bodies prone upon the wooden platforms. I stood and watched one old Tibetan woman who appeared to be in her eighties chanting continuously as she brought her folded hands to her crown, throat, and heart then quickly and fully prostrated, springing back up like a nimble child to repeat the process.

Affixed to the exterior walls of the main shrine room were rows of prayer wheels, the size of beer kegs, that devotees would turn and make prayers as they passed by. After doing one circuit and turning the wheels myself, I stopped at the front of the throne room doors and looked out above the lower level. Just beyond the walls of the complex was the most awe-inspiring view of the snowcapped mountain range, and it took my breath away.

The first week in McLeod, I took over five hundred photos and walked what felt like a thousand miles, doing daily khorra, exploring the streets, shops, temples, and restaurants. There was a small village nearby, called Bhagsu, that had a beautiful waterfall, beside which stairs led to the top where a rustic little restaurant served chai and omelets.

Another village, called Dharamkot, was home to the world headquarters of the Fellowship of the Preservation of the Mahayana Tradition—FPMT—called Tushita. I sat on the back steps of the temple there and got to see a world-famous teacher, Lama Zopa Rinpoche, wave to me from the window of his quarters.

Temple Road gently sloped down the mountain from the main square in McLeod to the Tsuglhakhang, the Dalai Lama's temple. Tightly lined on the shoulder of the road were tables full of merchandise, little individual makeshift shops where Tibetans made their livings selling khataks, statues, malas, ritual items, and clothing to tourists. I sat from time to time and had tea with several different Tibetan merchants, learning their names and hearing their stories of escape from Tibet... and not one of them ever pushed a sale on me.

I signed up for classes in the Tibetan Library of Works and Archives where I could take intermediate language classes and study Shantideva. There were so many ancient texts translated into English, and I found several that I would take to my room and copy word for word into my laptop.

One day, as I sat having morning coffee outside a shop close to the Dalai Lama's temple, the streets began to get crowded, and I heard someone say that His Holiness was returning from one of his many trips. All the Tibetans lined the streets holding burning incense and a khatak in their hands. The westerners stood empty-handed, falling in line to the side of the road. I ran to a shop and bought as many khataks as I could and several boxes of incense and started handing them out to as many westerners as would take them.

Two older Tibetan women sitting on the steps outside a shop, turning their prayer wheels in their hands, smiled and gave me a thumbs-up. "This is my karma!" I laughed with them. "Now I am offering forty khataks to Kundun!"

The entourage of black SUVs and police cars sped through the clouds of incense, and I snapped a photo of the Dalai Lama waving from the backseat of his vehicle. I showed it to the two Tibetan women, and we sat and talked over chai.

To almost everyone I met, I was Sonam Tsering, and Marc Moss was a name by which I tried not to identify for the months I stayed in McLeod Ganj. A smile was immovably painted on my face, surrounded with so many joyful reasons to be constantly elated, and I massaged my sore cheeks each night lying in bed.

One morning outside of the library, a young Tibetan woman introduced herself as Gang Lhamo. She had spent three years in a Chinese prison and was a woman's rights activist in the Tibetan community. She looked at my fat belly and said, "You come to my home and I will teach you some yoga and special breathing exercises."

"I appreciate that," I started, "but I'm afraid my body isn't this way from laziness. I have a thyroid condition."

"Yes, yes," she said in her deep alto voice, "I used to have thyroid issues. You learn these exercises and then see Doctor Yeshe Dhunden, and your thyroid will be cured."

I went to her home the next morning as instructed and she showed me several Yogic asanas that were easy enough. Then she demonstrated the proper breathing exercises as preparation to meditation. She placed one finger on her nose, closing one nostril as she breathed in, then closed the other as she exhaled. After three repetitions, she reversed it. Finally, she inhaled quite forcefully through both nostrils and held her breath for a long time, exhaling slowly until she was curled forward and empty. Then, with great force, she drew a deep breath and repeated the process.

She gestured for me to join her and I imitated her demonstrations as best I could. Afterward, we sat in meditation for an hour and, to my surprise it was the clearest my mind had ever been during any meditation sessions I had done at home. She got up to boil some milk and honey for us to drink while I continued to sit for a few moments in peaceful stillness.

"Now, you need to make an appointment with Yeshe Dhunden, soon," She instructed. "You will need to take the first pee of the morning with you for your appointment."

"And you're certain he can cure my thyroid?" I asked.

"He cured mine, and I wouldn't lie about that."

As Gang Lhamo instructed, I made my appointment to meet with the doctor early before sunrise. The day before my scheduled time, I found an apartment to rent as Kirti only allowed guests a two week stay. An older Indian gentleman owned a small complex next to the monastery that descended down the mountain side, and though I was on the first floor, I had to take three flights of stairs from the roof down to my apartment. It had a bedroom with two beds, a kitchen area with no appliances, a dining space, a large bathroom with a seated toilet, and a long balcony with nearly the same view as the one at Kirti since it was just a little further around the path.

There was a little tea stall just outside the entryway where I stopped to have a chai whenever I would leave my apartment and just as I would arrive. Inside, Sundeep, an Indian local around nineteen years old, made the tea and watched a small television. His English was poor, but I enjoyed sitting and trying to have conversation as I sipped the piping hot beverage, served in a little juice glass.

"What show are you watching," I asked Sundeep as he laughed at the comedy on the television.

"It is called... *Mother and Wife*," he said after some trouble trying to find the English words. I sat and watched with him, though I couldn't understand Hindi and there were no subtitles. But there was enough slapstick that I found parts at which I could join Sundeep's laughter.

On another occasion, I popped in for some chai just before going to my room after a long day of walking around McLeod. Sundeep was staring intently at the television, watching what I assumed was a drama or some kind of Indian soap opera. "What is this show," I asked.

"It is called *Father and Husband*," he said, eyes never leaving the screen.

I chuckled. "The originality of these titles is brilliant," I said, wishing Wyatt were with me to appreciate the humor of the moment.

On the morning I was to meet the doctor, I left my apartment before dawn with my urine in a plastic apple juice container zip locked inside a plastic bag. I stood in a long line of people in a dark alley to Yeshe Dhunden's office, amazed at how many were awake so early. After more than an hour of waiting, I was called into a room where the old doctor in monk's robes sat with a translator. He took my wrist and gently pressed his fingers down, feeling my three pulses, then shook the container of urine, examining it closely. He then began to speak, and I watched his old lips move, listening carefully for any Tibetan words I recognized.

"You have hypothyroidism, that's true," the translator said. "It is relatively easy to cure."

"Will I be taking this medicine for the rest of my life?" I asked.

Yeshe Dhunden's face expressed confusion, "If it's cured, why would you need medicine?" he asked through the translator. I smiled with satisfaction.

"If it's easy to cure, why won't American doctors cure it?" I asked.

"Your country profits from sickness," the translator spoke intermittently as he relayed the doctor's words, "nearly twenty percent of America's GDP last year was from treating illnesses."

He wrote on his prescription pad, tore off a page, handed it to me and said, "You take this medicine for about eight months. Your right kidney is also weak, so I'm including medicine for that."

I thanked him and went into the adjoining room where three women stood behind a counter filling small plastic bags with a variety of round Tibetan pills that they procured from nearly one hundred large jars on rows of shelves behind them. They took my prescription, and moments later they gave me four bags of medicine to last eight months. It cost me less than thirty USD.

I was given three different types of pills to be taken with each meal and pills that were individually wrapped in silk, called Precious Pills—rinchen rilbu—that are photosensitive and must be prepared and taken in dim lighting.

On my way back to my room, I stopped at the nearby pharmacist—in India, they're called chemists—and asked if they had any medication for hypothyroidism, just to check a rumor I heard about medicine prices outside of the US. The Indian pharmacist asked, "Synthroid or Thyroxin?"

"Synthroid," I answered, and he turned away and went to bring me a bottle. "How much?"

"One hundred and sixty rupees per bottle, one-month supply," he said.

"That's like just over two dollars!" I shouted."It costs me eighty-eight a month in America!" The man nodded emotionlessly. I bought the bottle and put it in my bag and walked back to my room feeling the first bit of real anger since my plane landed in India.

✦ Chapter Fourteen ✦

Sitting in a crowd of Tibetans in front of the main throne room in the Tsuglhakhang, I was full of excitement to attend my first live teaching from His Holiness. Gang Lhamo walked past as the crowds settled into their seats.

"Do you have a coffee mug?" she asked.

"No," I responded, confused. "Why?"

"No worries. The monks will give you a cup when they bring tea around."

Shortly after the Dalai Lama entered and took his throne, the entire complex began a long hypnotic murmur of the traditional prayers and recitations prior to a teaching. An old Tibetan man sitting next to me patted me on the back with approval, hearing me chant the prayers from memory. "My name is Sonam Tsering," I said to him when we concluded. He simply smiled and nodded.

After about fifteen minutes into the teaching, I noticed monks walking throughout the crowd, some with big silver pots of tea, with long spouts and others walking around with big wicker baskets full of Amdo bread, a type of Tibetan bread that is very much like a large English muffin. When I received my bread, I pulled out a handkerchief from my bag and laid it on my lap and began to imagine the monks working in the monastery kitchens making thousands of these round loaves. Then, the monk with the tea arrived and pulled me from my brief daydream, handing me a small Dixie cup for my tea. As he poured, the old Tibetan man beside me pulled out a large stein and I was amazed that the monk poured tea into it all the way to the brim.

"You need one of these for the teachings, Sonam-la," he smiled. During the lunch break, I made a quick trek to the closest shop and bought a travel mug with a lid that fit easily into my bag.

For the next two months, I made friends with many international Buddhist students that met for lunch and dinner on the rooftop of a restaurant called Carpe Diem that had the most spectacular view of the Dhauladhar mountains. There, we would inform one another of the various classes, teachings, and empowerments all around the mountain and in places throughout the Kangra Valley.

One lovely and classy woman from Australia, Vicky, took me with her to meet Karmapa, the head of the Kagyu lineage. We waited in a long line down the middle of his monastery to offer a khatak, and when I stood before him, he was not only frowning but looked shocked to see my ear-to-ear grin. It puzzled me, and I mentioned it to Vicky as we sat awaiting our individual private audiences she had scheduled.

"Can you imagine being revered as this holy being and being gawked at by people always coming to you with pitiful reverence?" she asked.

"The dreams of every color guard designer I know," I joked, but she hadn't a clue of what I was talking about.

I was escorted into the room where Karmapa was standing and waiting. Just as the door shut behind me, he gestured and said, "Wait! Please do not prostrate. Just come here and have a seat."

I hadn't taken a step when the door flew back open and a young Tibetan man stepped in and yelled a traditional entreaty, "*Karmapa Khyen-no!*" Karmapa shook his head as the two Indian guards pulled the devotee away and closed the door.

"I'm guessing that's why?" I asked.

"I know they mean well, but it does gets old," Karmapa said, relieving me of any need for synthetic reverence, and I plopped down on the sofa next to him,

He flipped through the notes I showed him that I had put together on comparing Dharma and the Law of Attraction. This was an opportunity for me to validate my research, and he nodded as I pointed and explained the various images and charts that I sketched.

"This is true," he confirmed, "but you should use this information for enlightenment and not worldly acquisitions."

"Oh, of course," I responded. "May I ask you why you reacted the way you did when I reached you in line?"

"You were the only one smiling. Every person in that line, as they always do, had their head bowed and hands held at the heart, looking at me as if I can save them from all of their problems. It was out of the ordinary seeing you smiling, and I'm sorry for my surprise."

We took a photo together, standing side by side, and I thanked him for the audience. When I went back into the waiting room, Vicky was seated waiting for me in a daze from her own audience with Karmapa, and a few Tibetans were in their chairs weeping reverently.

For the entire taxi ride back to McLeod, Vicky talked on and on about how a psychedelic trip on ayahuasca in the Brazilian jungles gave her a vision with the Great Grandmother of the aboriginal tribes of Australia, telling her that her path would lead her to India to meet holy men who would heal her body and spirit. The more she talked about this ayahuasca the more I became intrigued with psychedelics.

She was far from the stereotypical drug-loving hippies that frequented the Dalai Lama's hometown, and she and I often joked about how they used spirituality as an excuse to just be high all the time. It was almost embarrassing as a westerner to see nearly half of the tourists from America with dreadlocks, dirty clothes, and filthy fingernails wandering around like they had grabbed some Rastafarian pamphlets that had printed the wrong country for their travel adventures. The Indian people were far from dirty and unkempt, even in the less touristy areas the locals maintained a better hygiene than many of these tourists, and I often wondered what they thought when they watched them walk down the street in their big, baggie genie pants and backpacks.

McLeod is a bustling tourist attraction, not at all the peaceful utopia most people would assume for the residence of His Holiness, the Dalai Lama. Taxis incessantly honk, not out of anger but as an Indian habit behind the wheel to announce their presence—seemingly every ten feet of driving. Sitting in a cab watching the driver repeatedly press on the horn as he returned Vicky and I to the front of the main temple, my patience wearing thin, I asked about the absurd overuse of the horn. "Because it is on the car!" he shot back.

Looking out the window at the brilliant, cloudless sky of the lovely sunny day, I quickly asked, "Then why aren't your wipers on? Those are on the car!" He quickly became puzzled and lost in the logical dilemma he created.

At night, the taxis retreated into the Kangra Valley and the sound of horns were replaced by the unbelievable number of stray dogs barking until the sun returned. The first nights in McLeod, I thought I'd never get to sleep, but eventually they disappeared into the background as I became used to it.

Vicky and I took a walk with several of her friends from Canada to a quiet retreat site far up the mountain from the tourist areas. There were several handmade mud huts that monks and nuns used for personal retreat, scattered around the stupa that was erected in honor of

His Holiness' tutor, Trijang Rinpoche. Around the stupa, there were walls of prayer flags strung between the trees, bright colored squares of white, red, green, blue, and yellow with Tibetan prayers printed on them in various degrees of fade from age. It was the quietest place I found in my short travels in India and returned there alone many times over the duration of my stay.

Near Trijang Rinpoche's stupa was a smaller one erected for a man named Yeshe Tobgyal, who in 1989 achieved *Rainbow Body*. This is a remarkable phenomenon in Tibetan culture in which a highly advanced meditator is able, at the time of death, to dissolve his body into rainbow light. Many times, I stood in silence reading and rereading the placard on this stupa, marveling that the Dalai Lama himself recognized this event and validated it.

As November approached, many of my friends said their goodbyes and parted. The tourist season was winding down, and many Tibetans prepared to head south for warmer weather—off to Goa, an Indian state that seemed a lot like Florida, from what I heard.

My apartment became a study nook for many monks to come and practice conversational English, and non-Buddhists to come and learn about the Dharma. For westerners, I would give my best little three-hour presentation of what I confirmed through Karmapa to anyone who would come sit on my balcony and listen.

Even on the other side of the planet I played counselor and confidant to friends back home. One of my favorite band students of all time, John—a drummer—often messaged me online needing advice about a girl in whom he was interested. John was good looking and just needed a boost to his self-esteem. We had many discussions about the Law of Attraction, and before long he let me know that he asked the girl out—and she said "yes!"

"So, Dharma is a lot like this new thing called the Law of Attraction," Ronan, a young man from Ireland asked me, feet propped up on the iron rail as we sat in the Indian sunshine on my balcony.

"Pretty much," I responded, "the mind creates our reality, and we just have to learn how to make the right mental images for them to manifest."

"I could find the perfect girlfriend?" he asked, prompting me to chuckle to myself that so many straight guys would always ask the same damned question.

"I believe so wholeheartedly," I replied. "You just have to see it in your mind and hold it with emotion as though it's already happened.

There is one line from the Bible, Mark 11:24, that sums it up perfectly, the only line in that book that I believe. All of tantra is pretty much based on the same principle as is in this statement: 'Whatsoever you desire, ask for it in prayer as though you have already received it and it shall be yours.'"

"Then why are you still single?" he asked without hesitation.

"I've finally come to a point where I'm quite happy being alone. Besides, most gay men I've met aren't that spiritual and are very superficial."

"Can't you visualize one who is spiritual?" his rapid and simple response was so perfect—the overlooked obvious answer.

"I honestly cannot believe I let that one slip by me," I laughed.

Many friends over the years sent me messages telling me how the Law of Attraction was working for them. I considered Ronan's simple and succinct question and realized that I had never attempted using it to attract romance into my own life. That evening, after Ronan left, I sat and wrote a list of all the things I would want to find in a perfect partner. I wrote a full page of qualities and characteristics that Mr. Right should possess and lit it on fire in a small container on the balcony, envisioning the smoke as an offering to the universe in the hopes it would return blessings by fulfilling my written desires.

Three days later, standing outside a bookshop waiting for the owner to return from lunch, I saw the most attractive blond man walking down the middle of Jogiwara Road, coming right toward me—staring right at me. Butterflies in my stomach started to flutter and I looked around behind me to see if I happened to be erroneously between him and someone else. He walked right up to me. "Hello," he said without a smile, but laser-locked eye contact.

"Do you know me?" I asked, somewhat dumbfounded to be greeted by such a good-looking stranger.

"No," he smiled, pulling his backpack from his shoulders, "you just look friendly and approachable, and I'm looking for anyone who could help me around."

His accent was Russian, but his English was impeccable, and I told him so. He laughed and told me that he used to be a translator for the Russian army as he pulled out a tourism guidebook, called *Lonely Planet*, from his backpack and started flipping through the pages. "Why don't you put that away and let's look at it over lunch?" I invited. "My name is Marc."

"I'm Yuri," he said, shaking my hand.

We sat atop Carpe Diem, lounging on Moroccan cushions around the tables, flipping through his copy of *Lonely Planet*, slowly picking at the lunch Ramu, the Nepali waiter brought us. I was in heaven—eating delicious food cooked by Nepali chefs, sitting on the rooftop of an amazing view of the Himalayas, and soaking in the eye candy of this marvelous manifestation of my smoke offering.

"So, what brings you to India?" I asked as he continued staring at the pages, seeming to memorize all the local scenes he wanted to go to.

"I divorced my wife last year and needed to get as far away from St. Petersburg as possible," he said. Why did he get divorced, I wondered?

"You're soul searching?" I asked, curious to know more while sneaking the occasional lustful glance.

"Yeah, I suppose so. I'm following these spiritual ideas, they speak to me. I don't know why, but I have a curiosity to these kinds of things. So, I'm backpacking through India for a month and then New Zealand, Australia, and then I'll go to Thailand on through other parts of Asia."

"On foot?" I asked, trying to imagine such an adventure.

"Yes, it's easier to meet people. And who knows, maybe I'll find a new wife," he laughed, shattering every bit of my magical moment in a flash. I looked away, thinking about how he had pretty much checked off everything on my list: he was extremely attractive, intelligent, mysterious, kind, spiritual, and available. I started to laugh to myself as I realized the one thing I hadn't written on the list.

"Something funny?" he asked, closing his book.

"Nothing, really," I said, "just something particularly important I forgot until just now."

Yuri didn't smile much, and whenever I said something that tickled his funny bone, he'd quickly recompose himself after a short laugh. When I pointed out his overly masculine guard, he blamed it on years in the Russian army.

We spent the rest of the afternoon wandering about McLeod, popping in and out of shops, sitting on a ledge overlooking the valley and talking, and doing a circumambulation of the inside of the Dalai Lama's temple. I invited him back to my apartment, and we sat on the balcony talking about Dharma and Law of Attraction well past dark.

"This Law of Attraction sounds like it's correct if it's as you describe. How can I use it?"

"Practice visualizing what you're wanting. I say this all the time to everyone I teach this to, just remember these words from the Bible..."

and I quoted the passage from Mark to him.

"I will try this when my travels are over," he said. "Maybe I can find my soulmate."

"Why wait?" I asked. "The sooner you get to practicing these mental images the sooner they become habit and accumulate. If you have to pick up a penny a day, why would you wait when there are already pennies on the road immediately before you?"

He nodded, accepting my logic. "You're right. I'll begin in the morning. So, I should go back to my room," he said, "It's late."

"Go back tomorrow," I said. "There are two beds here, and it's not so late that we can't just keep talking." He accepted my invitation, and we laid in our respective beds, facing each other, talking until we both dozed off.

Yuri was traveling with a small amount of money, so it didn't take much convincing for him to accept my offer at breakfast to stay in my apartment for the month in Dharamsala he allotted. Everything he had for his trip was in his backpack, and he often joked with me about my two suitcases.

"If you think that's bad, take a look at the kitchen," I said. "Every appliance in there I bought for my five-month stay."

"That's wasteful, don't you think?"

"Not really," I said, showing him my cookware, "I like to cook for myself and don't want to hit the restaurants all the time. That's wasteful. Besides, I'll give everything to the nunnery when I leave."

A few evenings after he moved into the apartment, I told him about Palden Dorje and my plan to go see him at the end of November when he was supposed to give a public darshan again, according to a woman from the Google Groups who had already been to the jungle and received a blessing. He was skeptical but interested in knowing what I could share with him about it. "I don't know about this," he said, "Someone must be smuggling food to him when no one is looking."

"Yuri, he's a teenage boy. Besides not being off playing grab-ass with the other youth, he's sitting still every minute of the day. Can you sit that long?"

"So, you are going to go see this boy?" he asked. "Maybe I should make a trip to Nepal, too."

"Well, with the tourist visa I can only stay in India for six months at a time. Then, I'll hop over to Nepal for this darshan and be back when it's over, getting my new visa stamp in the process. Most everyone else just goes shopping for a couple of days and returns to get re-stamped. I'm planning on at least two weeks."

"Why that long?" he asked.

"Last year, when Palden Dorje gave public darshan four hundred thousand people lined up for twelve days to receive a blessing."

We began a nightly ritual in my apartment after all the shops closed; we would bring back snacks like Pringles—a kind local grocer was able to procure some simple delights I missed from home—and Yuri discovered a new favorite in the sour cream and chive flavor. He found DVDs of bootleg movies to watch on my laptop before going to bed. I didn't know anything about these illegally pirated movies. We both burst into fits of laughter when we saw the silhouette on screen of someone getting up to leave the theater. "See!" he pointed at the laptop. "Someone filmed this with their video camera sitting in the cinema!"

Often, when we were lying on ours beds on our bellies watching movies on the laptop situated on a small wicker ottoman, my eyes would focus on his reflection on the screen and entertain fantasies of this blond haired perfection—my magically manifested Adonis. Several times, I could swear he was looking back, staring into my eyes and setting off swarms of butterflies in my stomach. Our nightly ritual was a welcome end of each day, I felt, looking forward to studying his handsome reflection on the laptop screen. I would often pretend to fall asleep first just to look over at him in his bed, wishing he would have possessed the omitted key detail on my list.

With Yuri as a constant companion, I traveled around to more of the local points of interest that I otherwise wouldn't have seen. We decided to hike the rest of the way up the mountain upon which McLeod was settled to a peak called Triund. It was the last stop before trekking onward for most hikers into the Dhauladhar mountains—where the green mountains turn into the big, gray stony ones with snowcaps.

It took us five hours to walk up the winding roads to Triund. There were several tea stalls on the way, and we took many pictures of the breathtaking view of the valley. Several hang gliders circled around in the air, slowly descending to a landing site in Lower Dharamsala. "We should do that!" Yuri said, as he removed his shirt to beat the heat, and I sighed to myself as I went unnoticed staring at his naked torso, a breathtaking view that wasn't on the *Lonely Planet* map.

After a couple of hours on the peak, the sun set, and darkness was approaching when I started to feel sick.

"It must be from the altitude," he explained. "We'll get a tent and stay the night here. You need to drink lots of water and rest."

I woke in the middle of the night and couldn't figure out how I had gotten into a sleeping bag. When I poked my head out, Yuri was lying next to me without a sleeping bag of his own, only his jacket that had been in his backpack. I wasn't sure if he was asleep, and I paused to stare at him as I often did in the apartment, but this time it was with deep appreciation for his tender care.

A few days later, we heard of another point of interest just an hour away by taxi—Tatapani—a thousand-year-old temple built on hot springs that a local taxi driver, Hari, told me would make for an interesting visit. Hari spoke perfect English and became a trusted resource and a friend. He was also one of the rare Indians that I met who spoke fluent Tibetan. He drove us up frighteningly narrow roads in the mountains, on dirt paths through amber and green fields, taking abrupt detours avoiding flocks of sheep that flooded roads like rivers of puffy wool, and stopped behind the home of a remote farmhouse where the temple stood. "Now, go have a good soak," Hari said as we all got out of the short taxi-van.

Yuri and I walked around and inspected the pink painted cement structures—temple chambers that supposedly were constructed a millennium ago. There were many different smaller rooms away from the main temple, each with statues of various Hindu gods and goddesses covered in kumkum, a red-vermillion shaded powder made from turmeric mixed with lime. The acid in the lime causes the orange turmeric powder to turn a rich red when mixed and dried. The sweet smell of the springs and the sounds of it splashing into a large bathing pool drew us to the heart of the compound, and Yuri reached his hand in the water. "It's really warm," he said.

"I hope so," Hari laughed. "Tatapani means *hot water*. If you want to bathe you can." He turned and walked into one of the small temples where a statue of his family goddess was housed.

"Where can we change clothes?" I asked Yuri as I took a few steps looking around.

"Are all Americans so shy this far from public?" Yuri chuckled and started to remove his jacket, then slowly pulled his shirt off, and I stared a little too long at the light brown swirls of hair around his navel. I grabbed my towel and wrapped it around my waist under which I could remove my pants modestly. Yuri yanked his trousers off and stood up, nude, with a big grin on his face. I didn't budge an inch while my eyes rapidly scanned my Russian dreamboat's exposed beauty, and he showed no signs of embarrassment or disapproval of my gawking. After slowly pulling up a pair of bathing trunks, like a reverse strip tease, he starting toward the pool and asked, "Will you come?"

"Eventually... definitely... for sure" I said, and I heard him let out a short chuckle as he started to climb into the water. "You go ahead. I'll be there... in just a second."

A few days later back in McLeod, while he was away exploring on his own and I was having study time at my dining table, the upstairs neighbor came down to tell me about an empowerment the Dalai Lama was giving at the end of November. He was a Canadian named Rory who had become a monk in the Tibetan tradition and was studying to be a translator. When we first met, he introduced himself with his Tibetan name, Khedrup—which I thought he said *ketchup*, and it became my nickname for him.

"It's highest yoga tantra," Ketchup explained. "You'll need to receive the initiation some time, and who better to give it to you than His Holiness?"

"Darn it!" I exclaimed. "I'm planning on going to Nepal. I'll have to take the initiation at another time. I've been wanting to go to see this boy for almost four years. Besides, I'm not ready to visualize sexual union with a consort."

As the month continued, I neglected to make any arrangements to leave the country as I had originally planned. Something in my gut said that I shouldn't go. I told Yuri at dinner in the apartment, and he smiled and said, "You must be enjoying your time with me too much!"

While it was true that I enjoyed every minute with him, it was something else, something that just didn't feel like the timing was right. Yuri asked about the empowerment and considered taking the Refuge Vows during the ceremony. I encouraged him and handed him a short text explaining the commitments.

"Are you going to stay for the empowerment?" he asked.

"Yes, but I most likely won't take the initiation."

"Why not? Isn't this important in your religion?"

I shrugged. "Asking it that way feels like the obligatory shit I thought I got away from a long time ago. But to answer your question, this practice is part of tantra, yes."

"You've explained that, so what's wrong? You practice tantra, right?" he pressed.

"Yes, I do. But this practice involves visualizing myself in sexual union with a female consort, and I just don't think that will work for me on a daily basis, if at all."

He laughed. "Petty! What's wrong with visualizing that?"

"Sure, you can say that. But imagine the shoe on the other foot. Could you see yourself in sexual union with a guy? Careful of your answer, Yuri Medvedev, I can turn that bedding down like lightning."

He let out a loud guffaw. "Okay, I see your point. Don't take the initiation then. Stay in Samsara with your boys and your Pringles."

"But I'd love to sit with you as you take your vows," I said, and placed my hand gently on his shoulder. "Movie time?" I asked as we took to the bedroom. "There's still plenty of time for me to turn down the bed, by the way!"

We made it into the temple early and found a close spot to lay our cushions. There were Tibetans on one side of us and a large crowd of Russians, so Yuri turned and talked to his countrymen quite often. The Russian Buddhists commissioned the event, and they distributed flyers and booklets filled with explanations of the ceremony in Russian and in English.

Ketchup waved to me as he passed looking for a nearby seat in a sea of cross-legged Tibetans while Yuri was lost in conversation with the other Russians near our perch. Earlier, Ketchup also joked with me the day before about the visualization that I refused to do.

The initiation was for Thirteen-Deity Yamantaka, who stood in an aura of flames in sexual union with his consort. Yamantaka is a manifestation of Manjushri, the Bodhisattva of wisdom in wrathful form, destroying the fear of death. Yuri gently pushed the photo into my face, joking, "You don't know what you're missing out on, man."

"American humor is not becoming for you, comrade," I chuckled, shoving the photo away.

The Dalai Lama gave a teaching in three sessions that day to prepare the initiates for the next day's empowerment ceremony. At the end, just before nightfall, he made an announcement: "I know that the Russian Buddhists have gone to great lengths to provide the proper materials and have come a long way from home for tomorrow's event. But I have been meditating and thinking about this initiation and have decided to give the Solitary Hero form of Yamantaka instead of the Thirteen Deities."

I turned my head to Yuri in a snap, "I'm taking it!" Ketchup was sitting nearby, and I glanced at him from time to time throughout the teaching. When I looked over at him after the announcement, he pointed at me, grinning widely, and mouthed the words "you can take the initiation now!"

His Holiness instructed everyone to get a red blindfold and some kusha grass from the monks on our way out of the temple. I told Yuri to sit still and wait as the Dalai Lama exited. Then, we watched the crowd become unruly and nearly violent trying to get the necessary items from the monks.

"These are Buddhists?" Yuri asked loudly in amazement over the shouting of the crowd.

"I know, crazy," I said as I watched behaviors His Holiness would certainly strongly admonish.

We finally got our items and went back to the apartment. "What do we do with this grass again?" Yuri asked.

"Place a small piece under your pillow and the rest under your mattress, then try to remember your dreams in the morning. Look for certain signs that indicate whether you should take the empowerment or not. Simple enough."

That night, I dreamed that I was back at my high school during a basketball game and everyone was talking about the half-time entertainment—Cher—who was busy warming up her vocals in the cafeteria. I ran in to watch her prancing around with a microphone, dressed quite unlike the entertaining diva I adored. She was wearing pastel pink slacks, high heels, and an angora turtleneck sweater. When she came to the end of "Jesse James," she walked up to me and I thrust a pen and paper at her, "Can I have your autograph?"

"Sure thing, darlin'," she said as she took them to sign her name. But then, she looked up over my shoulder with a look of absolute terror on her face. When I turned around, there was my mother in her housecoat and rollers in her hair.

"Get your ass out of bed, you're going to be late!"

I then woke up to Mom gently rocking me to the sound of Cher's "Jesse James" on the radio, the alarm on my dresser beeping loudly. "Wake up Birdy," she said and kissed me on the forehead.

"You're never going to believe the dream I just had, Mom," I started as she stepped across the room to turn off the alarm. "It seemed so real."

Suddenly, she turned around and it wasn't Mom, it was—Cher!

"*Just like Jesse James!*"

I laughed myself awake around 3am, and it woke Yuri, as well. "Did you just wake up laughing?" he asked.

"Yes," I stretched, still giggling. "It was so funny—a dream within a dream!" I reached for the notebook next to my bed, having continued to log my dreams while in India.

"What are you writing about?" he asked as I scribbled away.

"Ever since I had the most vivid dream of my life, I've tried to write down as many details of every dream I have." I told him about the dream of the gazebo near the cliffs overlooking the beautiful sea, with fields of flowers and talking white animals.

"So, is laughing yourself awake a good sign for taking the initiation?" he asked.

"I don't think it gets better than that," I said and told him about the dream as I put the notebook back on the stand beside the bed. "And before you even ask, no I don't always dream about Cher because I'm gay. That was the first time."

"What does Yamantaka Solitary Hero look like, by the way?" he asked, sitting up in his bed.

"A lot like the image on the front of the booklet they gave us," I reached for my copy from my bed stand and tossed it to him. "Without the woman—and he has a big fat blue erection."

"Bullshit!" he said as he looked for any hints that I was pulling his leg.

"Show you in the morning," I said, and rolled back to sleep.

As the crowds filled Temple Road on the way to the gates of the Tsuglhakhang, I pulled Yuri into a thangka shop and pointed out an image of Solitary Hero. When no one was looking, I pointed to a part of the painting, "See? A big, blue penis!"

Yuri started to laugh, "I have to imagine this in a daily practice?"

"Welcome to the other... blue... burgeoning... foot," I laughed as I smacked him on the arm.

A few days after the initiation, he was ready to leave Dharamsala for the remainder of his trip, though I wasn't ready to watch my new, dear friend depart. "This has been an amazing month with you here," I said to him at the bus before he boarded.

"You've made me feel different, very happy wherever we went together," he looked like he was fighting back tears, and it made mine start to swell. "I'm going to..."

"Miss me?" I asked hopefully, to which he nodded. "Well, you better not show any emotion," I sniffled as I joked. "The Russian army wouldn't be pleased."

He gave me a long goodbye hug, then I placed a khatak around his neck and watched him climb into the bus. After a few minutes, the taillights disappeared around the corner and I walked back to my apartment alone.

Two weeks later, he called me from New Zealand, almost shouting into the phone with excitement. He explained that he was doing visualizations each morning since I explained the Law of Attraction, and he met a girl in Christchurch while couch surfing. "Really, Marc, she's almost everything I envisioned."

"Any plans to keep this going between you two?" I asked, trying to suppress any jealousy.

"No, no," he said, his excited tone returning to Earth. "She's going her way and I'm going mine. But it really makes me believe, you know?"

Three weeks later, he again called, this time screaming in Russian until he calmed down. He had left New Zealand, spent some time in Australia and had just landed in Bangkok. Hopping in a taxi to get to the closest cybercafé to check his email, a young woman's voice from another cubical shouted, "Yuri?" It was his travel partner he met in Christchurch, there in the flesh! He called me as soon as he could pull away from the wonder of the manifestation of his deliberate daydreams.

The winter came and it got a bit colder, so I purchased a couple of space heaters for my drafty apartment. It remained toasty warm inside, and each monk that came to study with me said that it was too hot. Ketchup and I started having tea together after our morning practices were finished. I admitted my consternation for having a big crush on my former straight Russian roommate, but with Ketchup's humorous deflection about his own attraction to Jolene Blalock, the actress who played the Vulcan science officer on *Star Trek: Enterprise*, I wasn't too embarrassed.

As the end of February approached, I knew that I needed to make plans to go to Nepal for a couple of weeks to reenter India and renew my visa. I received an email from the woman from the Google Groups who had alerted me about the darshan to which I decided to not go. She explained that it was wise that I chose to stay in India in November for two reasons; the Indian government changed their visa laws and if I had left the country, I would have had to stay away for two months. This would have caused a problem with my apartment and my belongings. Also, for some reason, Palden Dorje did not come out of his six-year meditation as he had the previous year, and no one received blessings, nor was there a public speech.

She went on to say that Palden Dorje stated in a small private meeting that he achieved his "inner goal," as he called it. I sat and read that part of the email several times, excited that this boy could be a Buddha in my lifetime. It made me weep imagining what that could mean to the world. Could it be that there has arrived a being who has achieved freedom from this suffering reality, who could teach us all to make the Earth a paradise, I wondered?

Then, I realized that if the visa laws changed, I wouldn't be able to cross the border for a reentry and renewal. My return flight was already scheduled for April 15, so I had to try to get that changed as soon as possible.

The travel agency told me that they could not reschedule my flight, per the agreement I made when I first booked my trip. I called the airline directly to try to exchange my ticket, but it wasn't possible. My funds were low, and I feared that I would not be able to stay any longer and needed to use what I had to fly back to America before the six-month deadline and swallow the loss of the return flight in April.

I sent an email to my friend from the Google Groups and told her my situation. "Do you have any idea what I could do?"

She responded early the next morning, "Perhaps pray to Palden Dorje. If he has achieved great spiritual power, he may hear your prayer and send you some kind of help."

I shook my head in defeat. I was not going to pray to a boy sitting in a jungle somewhere as a solution to a very real problem. Logging off the computer, I went to Carpe Diem for breakfast, walking past Ramu as I ascended the stairs to the roof with only enough words for him to make my usual. With my elbows resting on the table and my face in my hands, I silently prayed, "If you are enlightened, then you can hear this prayer. Help me fix this problem with my ticketing as soon as possible, such that it's obvious that you've answered my prayer and I'll know what to do."

Raju, the owner of the restaurant, came up just as I lifted my head. "Why you not smiling like you usually do?"

"Raju, I've just got some issues trying to keep from losing the money I spent on my return flight."

"When is your flight to America?" he asked.

"April 15," I answered.

"What time of day?"

"It's late, around 10 p.m.", I said, staring into space.

"Go to Nepal." he said.

"I can't afford the trip back to America if I go to Nepal, and I can't reenter for two months once I leave the country."

"Go to Nepal like you had planned, you still have enough for a flight. Stay for a couple of months, go to that jungle, and see Palden Dorje, fly back in the afternoon on April 15, then stay inside the airport until your flight. It's an international airport so you don't have to have a current visa to be there. You just can't go outside."

And like that, within five minutes of making the prayer, an answer had come!

I sprang from my chair. "Thank you, Raju! You've just saved me!"

"Where are you going?" he shouted down as I quickly descended the stairs.

"To book a ticket onto the path that leads to the end of suffering, I think!"

The woman from the Google Groups sent me contact information of someone in Kathmandu she trusted for a place to stay for two months. He owned a homestay and was a devoted Buddhist practitioner and avidly interested in Palden Dorje. Dawa-jojo, as they called him, picked me up from the Kathmandu airport and brought me into his home.

It was a large, two-story home and very western in style. I was relieved to see that I would avoid squatting again for the two-month duration when I examined the bathroom attached to my bedroom.

Dawa and his family called me Brother Sonam, and it did have a Branch Davidian cult vibe I wasn't used to in other Buddhist venues. But they were so kind and welcoming that I didn't care much.

Dawa means Monday in Tibetan, and though he was a Nepali, his family closely followed the Tibetan traditions. Dawa was born on a Monday, and his parents named him that, of which he was quick to tell new friends.

Dawa-jojo also ran an orphanage, and the stories he shared with westerners were meant to pull at your heartstrings to open your wallet. All I could do was deflect the conversation from any talk of money whenever I could, otherwise my funds would dry up and I'd need to start telling sad stories to get *me* money.

I took to the street and headed to Boudha Stupa at my first opportunity. It was another new world, and this one I had seen in countless picture books and a movie with Keanu Reeves. I turned the prayer wheels around the stupa as I walked, chanting the *Mani* mantra and gawking at all the Nepali architecture—fang-filled snarling dragon heads reached out on each of the four corners on many roofs, and the *Eyes of the Buddha* were painted on walls, at the top of stupas and on tee shirts hanging in shop windows. There was a sizeable Tibetan community, and their eyes always lit up when they heard me start talking to them in their language.

The first night, Dawa and I sat on the roof of his home, under a million stars. "I've read your essays, brother," he said, "and I am thankful that you took so much time to try to explain what is happening in Halikoriya."

Dawa was nearly my age, with a thicker, better build. He was a father of three and had an adorable wife who seemed to never stop smiling. Her mother lived with them and remained permanently stationed on a sofa in front of the television.

"I'm glad someone liked them," I said, sipping the chai he brought up for us. "There were just too many people on that site that refuse to give any recognition to Buddhism. Guru-ji's name is even a Buddhist name. It's kind of maddening."

"Yes," Dawa said softly, then took a sip. "I want you to know that we knew you were coming and I'm waiting for a call from someone near the meditation site."

I was taken aback. "We? Who's we?"

"Mr. Waiba takes care of the jungle and speaks directly to Guru-ji. I let him know that the person who wrote those essays was going to be staying in my house. He will call us in a few days."

"Lovely," I said. "I'll be glad to talk to him. I hope I didn't make too many mistakes in my writing."

"Oh, no, no, no. Your writings were very good, very scholarly. Mr. Waiba was also impressed."

"Then I look forward to talking to him. You can never have too many friends, right?"

After a few days of sight-seeing around the Kathmandu Valley, Dawa called me into his office space in the house. "Brother Sonam, Mr. Waiba will be here to visit tomorrow."

"Oh? I thought he was going to call on the phone."

"He did, but you were out, and he said he would be in Kathmandu soon anyway, so he wanted to make sure that you would be here. He may stay for dinner."

The next morning, I assured Dawa that I would be back after lunch and await Mr. Waiba's arrival at the homestay. There were so many amazing places in Kathmandu that I just didn't want to sit still for any longer than I had to. I walked into Boudha and had breakfast in a nearby restaurant.

After I gave the waiter my order, I pulled my Tibetan pills from my bag and crushed them, swallowing them down with a drink of hot water. An older Tibetan monk at another table watched me with great interest, staring at me uncomfortably long after I took my medicine. He smiled whenever I looked up and met eyes with him. It seemed odd, knowing that he must have seen westerners before as Kathmandu is quite a touristy place.

"Excuse me," he finally spoke as he approached my table while I was eating. "I see your mala around your neck, so I assume you are in Kathmandu for Buddhism?"

"Please, have a seat," I politely stood and offered. "I'm a Buddhist, yes. But if you're going to ask me for money, I need to tell you that not all touring Americans are loaded."

He laughed. "No, I'm not interested in money. I'm a monk. I am also Tibetan. Have you ever been asked for money by a Tibetan?"

I thought for a moment and realized I hadn't. "No, never, actually. I have been hit up by beggars all over India, but none of them were Tibetan."

"Yes, yes, they are almost professionals, aren't they?"

When I asked him what it was that he wanted with me, he told me that he saw me taking Tibetan medication and wanted to know from whom I had received my prescription. When I mentioned Yeshe Dhunden's name, he lit up with Tibetan pride.

"Oh, the Dalai Lama's former personal physician, yes. That is wonderful. How is it working for you?"

"Well, actually—exactly as he said it would." He listened to me explain that before meeting with the old doctor I felt full as soon as I woke up and couldn't eat much at meals. Hypothyroidism seems so illogical—the less you eat, the more you gain. Just a few months into taking the medicine my appetite returned and the pounds were shedding quickly from all of the walking. He smiled when I told him that after the first full meal that I was able to finish since starting the medicine I wept, and that it was more out of sadness that my own country was neglecting actually healing people in lieu of profit.

"May I suggest that while you are here you seek Aama Bumpo for a blessing, as well?"

"Who is that?"

"She is a recognized shaman. Her powers have been acknowledged by His Holiness. It will help you; I promise."

I laid my fork down, "Is there a kickback for you? I pay this Aama Bumpo and she gives you commission for finding a sick westerner?"

He laughed. "Certainly, you know us monks have a vow of poverty, so truly money is in no way my motivation. You have a warm face, and a delightful smile, so surely you have a good heart, and I wanted to give you good advice for your healing."

"Well, thank you, sir," I wiped my mouth with my napkin and placed it on my plate. "I will look into this shaman and tell her you sent me. Your name?"

"Dakpa Sangye," he reached out to shake my hand.

"I'm Sonam Tsering."

We sat and talked for about a half an hour, and I shared with him the story of my mother's death. He listened with such interest, it almost seemed as though he knew me.

"That is a beautiful story, Sonam-la," he said. "All our lives are intertwined in such a way we cannot see the connections. You know, consciousness is like a mirror: it reflects everything it sees, and all that it sees is merely consciousness."

I stood up as he excused himself and left, then sat back down for a few minutes, reflecting with appreciation on what he said. "Simple and brilliant!" I shouted, and quickly paid my bill, dashed outside looking everywhere for the old monk, but he was nowhere to be found.

A thought popped in my head and I ducked into a cybercafé to do a quick search on the internet about reflections and physics, hoping for any morsel of knowledge I could add to my understanding of Dharma. The old monk had set a new thought in my mind ablaze, and I scanned through webpages, wondering if I had just had some kind of holy encounter and tried to find the proverbial popcorn kernels he possibly dropped for me. The Law of Reflection caught my attention, and though I stared at the definition for a long time, I couldn't make sense of what Dakpa Sangye might have meant if he were some emanation intent on giving me spiritual wisdom.

Late that afternoon, Dawa-jojo came and knocked on my door.

"Mr. Waiba has arrived."

Dawa led me to meet the guest seated in the living room, who quickly stood, took my hand and shook it vigorously. He was a short man with salt and pepper hair, dressed no differently than a farmer from Indiana, in fact. "It's very nice to meet you, Brother Sonam," the short, gray haired man said behind thick black framed glasses. "I've read all of your posts and I truly appreciate the amount of information you have offered."

"Thank you, sir," I said as we both sat on the sofa. Dawa crossed the room and sat in a chair, listening quietly. "I'm glad that what I wrote had some benefit to anyone. There have been so many incorrect assumptions by the various members of that website, it's sad that there are no scholars helping to spread the knowledge of this remarkable phenomenon."

"Yes, it is sad that too many people refuse to see what is happening is part of a history of similar occurrences," he said.

Mr. Waiba spoke for almost an hour, telling me about his professional life that took him to the UK and the Netherlands, and his early retirement to return to Nepal and serve Guru-ji. "Sometimes when we need to talk to him, we go to his meditation spot, but he is not there. So, we wait for a while and he just—appears."

"Like from the bushes?" I asked.

"No, just out of... nothing," he said. His face was stone cold, and I believed that he believed what he was saying.

I looked at Dawa, and he lowered his head and started chanting something to himself.

"I have shared your essays with Guru-ji, and he was quite pleased with your writings," he shocked me.

"Like directly to him?" I asked in amazement.

"Yes. I will talk to him when I return tomorrow and ask for permission for you to come see him."

"Will there be any vacant hotels that I can stay in while I'm waiting?" I asked.

"Why wouldn't they be vacant?"

"Surely I'll need accommodations with so many people there for darshan," I said.

"There is no darshan," he stood and began to button his jacket. "This will be a private audience."

I was stunned. He shook my hand and Dawa-jojo walked him

out the door.

A few days later, Dawa called me into his room as he was taking down the offerings from the altar for the evening. "I just received a call from Mr. Waiba, and you will be taking a taxi in a few days to see Guru-ji."

"This is crazy, I just can't believe it's happening," I took the pitcher of water and held it as he emptied the bowls into it. "Dawa-jojo, have you been to see Guru-ji yet? What's it like?"

"No, brother, I haven't had the blessings for that yet. I've been too busy here and with the orphanage."

"Would you come with me? Certainly, Mr. Waiba would be ok with that."

"This trip is for you, brother," he said slowly, but apparently considering the offer.

"It would mean the world to me if you came along," I said. "I insist, Dawa. You've shown me such kindness, and you have so much devotion to Guru-ji. Please come with me."

He agreed, and before he went to bed, I could hear him making prayers to Guru-ji, thanking him for the blessings to join me.

The next afternoon, Dawa told me that he posted the great news on the Google Groups site and that many of the regular commenters put their money together to send one of them to join us. "Brother Lyndon will arrive at the airport tomorrow and join us when we leave in a few days."

I wasn't happy about this, feeling that they didn't trust me to give an accurate account of my experiences when I would later write about them. But I didn't want to create any negative karma in the situation, so I told Dawa I was eager to meet him.

Lyndon arrived and took up the room next to mine in the homestay. He was a bit dopey, tall and thick, reminding me of Baby Huey. Before dinner, he told me about all the religions he had converted to, and he believed that all the holy icons throughout history were taking turns coming to earth to teach. I struggled to remain a silent participant during his rants and chose only to speak to correct his mistakes concerning Dharma. It happened so often that I realized he had no training in Buddhism at all.

When we arrived on the other side of Kathmandu to meet the taxi service that would take us over the mountain range and to the jungle, three people were waiting for us. "Mr. Waiba asked if we would bring these people with us," Dawa said. There were two Malaysian men and one Indian woman. The shorter of the two men asked to be called "Danny Boy," and the taller man was married to the Indian woman who seemed to look down her nose at everyone. Their last name was Robin, but I missed their first names when they introduced themselves. Still, I saw no harm, and my private audience was now up to six people. It was still an amazing opportunity and I was happy to have others come along.

We packed ourselves into the red Jeep and started toward the mountains. Looking back at Kathmandu, a dome of amber smog covered it, though I hadn't noticed anything unusual when walking about in the days before. "Is it usually that dusty?" I asked.

"Oh, sometimes even worse," Dawa said.

"When will you be going back to America?" Mr. Robin asked.

"My flight is from Delhi on April 15," I said, staring out the window at the most spectacular view of the circular valley around Kathmandu.

"Oh, you leave just five days after Guru-ji's birthday," Dawa said.

"That's too bad," I said mindlessly. But then, I did a quick calculation. "Wait... what?" I shouted with surprise. "When is his birthday?"

"April 10, brother," he replied.

"Stop the Jeep, please!" I shouted.

The vehicle came to a stop on the side of the road, and I stepped out and walked toward the side of the mountain among some trees. Dawa hopped out and walked slowly toward me, seeing that I was noticeably moved in a way of which he was unsure.

"Are you ok, brother?" he asked.

"Dawa, do you remember the story of my mother's passing I told you on the roof?" He nodded. "She died on April 10, so did my best friend's father. Everything seems so connected and I just can't figure out why."

Dawa knelt beside me as I sat on the ground hugging my knees to my chest. He said nothing for a moment, rubbing my left shoulder as I rocked back and forth, offering me comfort and support.

"Brother, I do not know the answers, but maybe Guru-ji will know. It is truly a holy and beautiful thing that continues to reveal itself to you. You must use this to develop your faith. Something amazing and beyond us is happening in this world, and it's happening to everyone who comes to believe that this is a holy moment in our history. One mute girl was gifted a voice after a blessing from Guru-ji, but she was not a vegetarian and lost her voice as soon as she took meat again. When she received a second blessing and her voice returned, she swore she would never eat meat from that day onward."

"Is that true?" I asked, looking him in the eye.

"Yes, brother," he said. "It is fact. And you have your own miracles now that don't make any sense. Perhaps, if you think about it all with a mind as simple as mine, you won't need anything else to be proven. Just accept the wonder as it unfolds for you."

I stared out over the valley through a thin veil of tears starting to swell, but then wiped them away and stood up. "Alright then, let's go see some more magic."

✦ Chapter Fifteen ✦

It was another four hours to Simara, and despite the beauty of the Nepali landscape—thousands of farms etched in stair-steps patterns along the mountainsides—I was ready to be out of the Jeep and away from its occupants—except for Dawa. He delighted in pointing out sights along the way, and I could tell he had great pride in his country. "Those are cabbages, brother," he said, pointing at the rows of little green balls on a long field cut into the side of a hill in which several women knelt and tended.

"Your culture doesn't understand how to respect holy teachers," Mrs. Robin criticized repeatedly on the trip, though I didn't rebut. I couldn't. The Western world didn't have respectable holy teachers, I thought. Besides, I wasn't ready for another argument as the last one with Lyndon left me drained.

From the day he landed in Kathmandu airport, Lyndon made statements that contradicted things that were written clearly about the Dharma in sutras and commentaries, causing Dawa to raise an eyebrow and for me to correct him—and I cited sources, teachers, and texts to demonstrate that it wasn't my personal opinion. Killing, for example, even in self-defense is still killing. He argued against it, and I'm sure that came from his years in the military and the brainwashing that one must undergo to take the life of another so easily, quickly, and without knowing the full story behind the bullet you fire. In the Jeep, it finally came to a head with him, "You're a damned know-it-all; I just want to hear you say that you don't know everything."

"The topic isn't *everything*, Brother Lyndon, it's about a specific fact concerning Buddhist philosophy. Have you gone through even one class with a master? Do you know for fact that what you say is supported by a lineage of scholars and masters? Mention them, say their name, tell me what they've written, and I'll consider it. If you've taken the Bodhisattva Vow, then you must be aware that it is our duty according to the Secondary Downfalls to correct mistakes about the Dharma."

I paused and looked back to see him scowling at me—and Mrs.

Robin was listening intently, smiling almost mischievously like an old biddy soaking up some gossip in church. "Remember," I quipped, "this isn't like American Christianity where any jerk with a book and a building can start their own spinoff religion."

He started to respond, but I insisted on finishing with, "You're on your way into the jungle to meet someone you believe to be an omniscient being, and it doesn't get any more *know-it-all* than that, does it?"

We arrived in Simara and were taken to our hotel. As soon as I put my things away, Dawa stopped me at my door to thank me for my words with Lyndon. "If we don't correct mistakes wherever we can, it's like letting litter collect across the land. We'll have to pick it all up someday," he said.

"Correcting mistakes in other Dharma practitioners is part of the Bodhisattva Vow, just as I said in the Jeep." I explained, to which he patted me on the shoulder approvingly and walked with me down the hallway and out of the hotel.

Taking an exploratory stroll into the village, we were met with smiles by everyone we saw. The people of this small village in Bara District were as hospitable as they were intrigued with the smiling Caucasian walking through their streets. Children ran up to have their picture taken with me, instantly reviving me from my fatigue from the drive, hearing their adorable Nepali voices yell, *Cheese*! as I instructed before Dawa snapped many photos.

Our little group had a quiet dinner that evening with the owner of the hotel, and I retired early to be fully rested for our trip into the jungle the next morning. I sat my keys on the bedside table with the picture of Palden Dorje in its plastic frame sitting so it would greet me as I rolled out of bed.

As I sat staring at the photo before turning off the lights, I thought about all that led me to the other side of the planet, ready to see for myself the Buddha Boy, as the various media called him. "If this is real, give me a sign tomorrow," I said to the photo. "Make it unmistakable, and I'll know to keep on my path."

The next morning, we climbed into the red Jeep and the taxi driver tore away rather quickly. Dawa spoke to him in Nepali with a look of concern on his face. They continued for quite a while, and then I noticed two cars following behind us.

"Dawa," I tried to interrupt, "what's going on?"

But they kept talking, and the driver picked up speed, turning onto a thin unpaved road, kicking dirt into the air behind us. Mrs. Robin started to complain, and everyone was asking Dawa to translate to us what the driver told him.

"There's a taxi strike today," Dawa finally started, "and he's not supposed to be driving. The other drivers are coming to stop him."

"Call Waiba," I shouted. "Make the driver stop and have Waiba come get us."

"Mr. Waiba doesn't have a car," Dawa replied. "Just hold on. I told him to at least get us to Waiba's home and we'll figure the rest out ourselves."

The cars kept up the chase, almost rear-ending us a few times, pulling up beside us imitating every cinematic chase scene, only much slower. We may have been moving quite fast by Nepali standards, but I chuckled to myself because our speeds weren't much more than an unimpressive 30 mph.

Mr. Waiba met us outside and immediately began yelling at all the drivers in the fastest Nepali that I found it hard to believe that there was an intelligible language coming out of his mouth. Dawa instructed us to remove our things from the Jeep and I grabbed his bag while he stood still watching Waiba.

The drivers lowered their heads and spoke softly, but it was clear that they weren't going to give up on the strike. All three vehicles left us with Mr. Waiba, and I worried that we had no means to finish the journey nor return to the hotel afterward.

"Ok, nobody worry," Mr. Waiba commanded. "Let us have some food before we leave."

"Leave?" I was confused but we followed him around the back of his house, a charming little farm that didn't look much different than those in the Indiana countryside of my childhood. A large gray barn nearby housed a tractor, lots of hay, a few cows, and a weathered wooden fence that encircled the property.

"This looks quite lovely," Dawa said as we stepped onto Waiba's patio where many dishes of food were arranged on a serving table.

"Please, help yourselves," Waiba said and took a seat.

I never saw any of the dishes before and didn't know what I was putting on my plate. A bright red gravy with what appeared to be stewed tomatoes and little bits of onions caught my eye, and I took a spoon of it to my lips. I closed my eyes with pleasure as the flavors delighted my tongue, and I put several heaps on my plate, then found a chair by Waiba.

"Brother Sonam likes the achar?" he asked laughing.

"This?" I pointed to the tasty tomato concoction.

"That's a condiment, brother," Dawa joined Waiba's laughter. "Nepali catsup!"

I took a big spoonful and held it to my mouth, "I would most certainly smother a hotdog with this, sir!"

"Waiba-ji," Dawa asked, "How will we travel to Halikoriya?"

"We will just have to take my tractor. I will put lots of hay inside to make it softer for your behinds."

After we finished eating, we climbed into the hay-filled cart and Waiba took us through town, reminding me of a 4H parade float. Children came running down the street yelling and waving to us, and I was disappointed to not have candy to throw. As the others were waving and cheering at our growing following, I noticed that Lyndon was sitting with his head down, hands folded in prayer in what appeared to be fabricated piety, quietly ignoring the scene. I said nothing but shook my head.

Waiba pulled us for nearly an hour on the paved roads, through other villages. Dawa pointed at large brown disks that were affixed on the outside walls of many houses and asked, "Do you know what those are, brother?" I had no clue. "That is cow dung. Families use it for fuel."

"Seems pretty shitty to me, my friend," I said, and Dawa's eyes turned into thin slits on his face as he laughed.

Mr. Waiba brought the tractor to a stop beside a bridge, pointed to the dry riverbed below and said, "Hold on! We're going down there!"

After bouncing us down the hill, he drove along the shoreline of the waterless river and to the edge of large forest where there were several monks and nuns waving to us. A tall monk wrapped in a maroon shawl came to Waiba and spoke to him in Nepali. He then turned to us and said, "Welcome, I am Rakesh, Guru-ji's attendant. We have tea waiting for you. Please, follow me."

I joyfully jumped up and grabbed my bag, excited to finally be at the location of this boy of whom I had read so much, and thankful to give my knees a much-needed stretch. Our little entourage followed Rakesh, and I noticed that Lyndon was still silent and holding his folded hands to his chest with his head bowed.

"Lyndon," I said, "don't you think we should enjoy every detail of this experience?"

He shook his hands at me, "I'm being respectful."

"Probably less arrogant to follow the lead of our hosts," I pointed out. "And they're not doing that." He looked up at Waiba and Rakesh and lowered his hands and began to look around.

We walked into the jungle and into a small encampment around which several large buildings had recently begun construction. A few foundations were laid and cement pillars with long shafts of rebar reaching for the sky poked out of the top. Two nuns greeted us then led us to a small shack and quickly brought out trays of tea and cookies. Sitting in the windowsill was a small jade Buddha statue, and as soon as I saw it, I gasped, thinking that maybe Mom was near, sending me a sign of her presence.

Mr. Waiba introduced us to a few other young Nepali men and said that they were relatives and friends of Palden Dorje and would join us the rest of the way. Guru-ji's younger brother, whose name I missed, looked amazingly like him in the face, and I found myself staring at his smile.

"Guru-ji is just a ten-minute walk from here," Rakesh said.

"There is a stupa built in his honor nearby, isn't there?" Dawa asked.

"I've read that there is a chamber beneath the stupa," Mr. Robin interjected, "so he can use it if the weather gets bad."

"Yes, yes," Rakesh affirmed to both questions. "You will see the stupa just before you see the Guru."

We finished our tea, thanked the nuns, and followed Rakesh as he started down a dirt trail that led deeper into the jungle. "This is the Path that Leads to the Cessation of Suffering," I whispered to Dawa, jokingly. He smiled, though he was full of reverence, looking straight ahead.

My cheeks felt as sore as they did my first week in Dharamsala, aching from the smile that hadn't left my face all morning. My eyes darted around, trying to take everything in and commit it to memory, thankful to my friend Jon for giving me the article in the magazine years earlier. "Be mindful, Marc," I repeated to myself. "Pay attention."

After about ten minutes of following Rakesh, he turned solemnly around and said, "Please remove your shoes. You are now on holy ground."

Mrs. Robin complained a little, but we all did as instructed and left our shoes to start down a smaller dirt path. The only sounds were our footsteps and the birds chirping and flying about. It was a perfect environment for meditating, I thought. After a few minutes, I saw the stupa ahead through the trees. Something in the air changed, and it felt ancient even as it was fresh and new. To the side of the stupa was a Bodhi tree, and through the many trunks that came together as one, I saw the back of a figure in a white robe, and my smile tried to expand past its limits.

Each of us rounded the stupa in a clockwise direction, and one by one prostrated in front of it. There was a doorway at the base, and I could see inside and make out the trap door that led to an underground chamber that Mr. Robin mentioned. I stood up after prostrating and reached in my bag for the khatak I would offer, draped it over my hands pressed together and rounded the stupa into a clearing in front of the large white and yellow concrete platform that was built for him by the locals, reminding me of the statue I had placed in the flower garden around the sycamore tree.

The site of him took my breath away and made my heart race. To anyone else, there was nothing spectacular to see. A young Nepali man with long black tangled hair, a dirty white robe, sitting on a large oval cement platform shaped to look like the base of a Buddha statue—painted white with yellow trimming and lotus petals molded into the bottom perimeter. But to me, this was a being whose compassion fulfilled him, sustaining him without any food or water, and he was intent on finishing the evolution of his consciousness on this planet. I was humbled, and overcome with awe, gratitude, and hope. I fell to my knees and performed the most heartfelt prostration I've ever done, and offered my long, white silk scarf. After he placed it around my neck, I stepped back to watch the rest of my travel companions.

I watched him with full, wondrous awareness as he sat motionless, eyes watching those in front of him prostrate and offer their khatak to which he draped quickly around their necks and returned to his pose. One by one, each stepped back with me into a semi-circle around the throne, waiting for the last of us to join.

Rakesh took a place beside the young meditator, eyes and body fixed toward his master. Mr. Waiba approached Palden Dorje and exchanged words, then motioned us to come forward. Dawa knelt and took a handful of dirt and rubbed it on his bald head, a sign of reverence in his culture—the soil was holier than himself—and tears streaming down his face. We sat in front of the cement platform and waited for Guru-ji to speak, his eyes moving lovingly from one person to another as his body remained immovable like marble.

As he spoke in Nepali, I fixed my gaze on him, trying to memorize every detail of his image; his hair was unkempt and tangled, the result of the wind and weather blowing about him as he sat unwavering through his austere meditation, white robes dinged with dust and dirt, but they did not diminish the regal radiance of his presence. There was a great feeling of love and compassion filling the atmosphere, the likes of which I only felt in the gazebo dream from which DJ awakened me.

Mr. Waiba cleared his throat and began his translation, "Whatever you are wanting, have trust, and it will happen."

I gasped. In that single sentence a fulfillment of confidence, wonder, and appreciation satisfied my soul, and my eyes began to well with tears. He essentially said what I was saying to so many others—the Mark 11:24 quote I used to sum up the Law of Attraction! I looked at Dawa, but he only stared at the ground in front of the throne, head lowered in reverence and tears streaming down his caramel cheeks, unaware of my amazement.

Mr. Waiba looked at me and said, "If there is anything you wish to ask, now is the time."

I rose to one knee, and with gratitude whispered, "What he just said answers all my questions, and I wish to thank him for that. My mother passed away on his birthday and I would just like to say her name here so that his ears may hear it—Linda Wasson."

Guru-ji said something to Mr. Waiba, his eyes lovingly staring into mine as he spoke.

"She is well," the translation came, and I sat back onto the earth, feeling like I crossed some kind of spiritual finish line, like something had come to completion. Every muscle in my body relaxed and my mind became as clear as crystal.

Mr. Waiba looked at me, waiting to see if I would say anything more. There was a long silence, all of us transfixed at the beauty of the audience we were granted. In that moment, I knew that I was in the presence of a Bodhisattva, and possibly a fully enlightened Buddha, and held my awareness on each little detail that I observed.

Guru-ji began to speak and, after a few sentences, Waiba quickly said to us, "This is just kind of like business talk now."

As they spoke back and forth, Lyndon suddenly started blurting out, "Hey, does he know this guy?" I didn't move, keeping my eyes on Guru-ji. "Hey, ask him if he knows this guy," he would say at every little break between the two Nepali voices.

I turned slowly to look at Lyndon, who was holding a framed 8"x11" picture of Jesus in a meditation pose. "Where did you..."

I began to ask, wondering how that photo fit in his bag. Catching myself before uttering a hasty rebuke, I drew a breath, hoping that there wasn't a hell I would go to for a snap of anger in the presence of such an exalted consciousness.

"Brother Lyndon," I said with the calmest voice I could muster, "don't you think that it would be respectful to enjoy this moment with our Buddhist hosts?"

He quickly snapped his head at me and barked, "My friends and I want to know if he knows Jesus. This would answer a lot of our questions."

Rakesh turned his gaze away from Palden Dorje for the first time and looked with shock at the framed photo, to which he closed his eyes and drew a deep breath to collect himself, shook his head, and then took a few steps toward Lyndon. In a gentle voice, as not to interrupt the conversation between his master and Waiba, he said, "Please put the photo away."

"Will you just ask him, please," Lyndon insisted. "We really want to know."

"That is for your own heart to decide," Rakesh said. "Now put the photo away."

My top teeth dug into my bottom lip, and I was relieved to watch the framed picture of a being I believed to be a fictional creation of humans disappear into Lyndon's shoulder bag.

Mr. Waiba asked us to gather around the throne for a group photo. I walked over to Dawa, "Brother, are you ok?" I asked, putting my hand on his shoulder.

"I've never been happier," his teary eyes met mine.

As we were gathering around, Mrs. Robin started a small commotion, pushing her way to stand right at the side of the throne. She leaned in to get closer to the Guru with her hands pressed together, her purse hanging from the crook in her elbow, which she then rested on the cement surface beside him. Turning to look at him again and again, she cackled with laughter as though she couldn't believe what she was looking at, and then abruptly looked somber, bouncing back and forth between the two extreme personalities. She leaned in quite close to Guru-ji, almost touching her elbow to his knee. For a moment, I was embarrassed for her.

"Be mindful, Marc," I said to myself, folded my hands and waited for the photographer, Panit-ji, to finish taking pictures of us.

Afterward, I turned toward the Guru and retrieved my keychain photo from my pocket and held it toward him. Mrs. Robin sneered at me as she watched. As I was asking Mr. Waiba to translate to him that I carried his photo with me everywhere, the Guru's hand reached down quickly and touched it, a response that he must have given to thousands of devotees who had lunged personal items at him to be blessed.

"No, no," I laughed. "Please tell him that I wasn't asking for a blessing, just wanted to show him." Mr. Waiba began to laugh, and Palden Dorje also chuckled.

Then something in the atmosphere turned. Mrs. Robin started to rip through her purse, pulling random items out and shoving them in front of Guru-ji for him to touch. She pulled out her cellphone, keys, photos, giddy with laughter all the while like she was a child amazed at a pet's trick. Panit-ji captured the absurdity in a series of photos.

Almost pushing her aside, Lyndon came forward with a book to be blessed, then walked back to where his bag lay on the ground. He rummaged through the contents, looking for other items to take before the Guru. I watched in disgust and stepped slowly backward to the perimeter where we initially waited after our prostrations.

When the last of the contents of her purse had been touched by Palden Dorje, she pressed her hands together and wildly laughed and stared almost mockingly at him, like he was an oddity on display. Then, Lyndon returned with another item from his bag and, again, moved her out of the way for another blessing. There appeared to be a competition underway between the two of them, and it was the antithesis of Mrs. Robin's criticisms in the Jeep.

Dawa came over to where I was, apparently watching with the same embarrassment. "This is not good, brother," he said slowly, shaking his head.

"We've overstayed our welcome," I said. "We need to leave him to his meditation."

Guru-ji's brother, Ganga Jeet, walked up to me and offered to take me away on his motorcycle. I followed him out of the clearing and down the path. I stopped for one last photo with Dawa and then continued to follow Ganga Jeet back to the small shack where the nuns had tea waiting for us again. The rest of the ensemble arrived about five minutes later. I wanted to talk to Rakesh and ask questions that arose in my mind after the event, but Lyndon blocked my every question with his own, none of which seemed as pressing as the manner in which he would interrupt me. Palden Dorje's first words to us echoed in my mind and I told myself to be satisfied with that.

"Jojo," I addressed Dawa quietly. "I'm going to go with Ganga Jeet. My knees can't take that trailer anymore... and I really don't want to be around... them." I pointed inconspicuously at Mrs. Robin and Lyndon, and Dawa nodded.

Ganga Jeet took me away on his bike to the location of the original tree under which Palden Dorje first sat for ten months, catching the world's attention. He disappeared for a short time to find a more peaceful location away from the thousands of devotees who came to make daily offerings. I immediately recognized the tree from the first photos I saw of him. The site was encircled by three fences, each extending farther away than the last. Ganga Jeet told me that he built them himself to keep onlookers at a safe distance, but the larger the crowds grew, the farther they needed to be kept away.

There was a placard placed where Palden Dorje had sat, the Tibetan holy syllable HRIH, a recognition of the holiness of this spot. Just about a hundred feet away was another Indian fig with a similar placard at its base. "This is where he first started his meditation," Ganga Jeet told me. I was unaware of there being a different initial location than the one from the photos.

"How long was he here?" I asked, walking over to look at the placard.

"He sat for ten days. I would come to see him, and he would change colors." I looked at him, confused. "He would turn red, then blue, then green. He was surrounded in these auras of color."

I found it difficult to believe, but not his conviction. It was clear that he believed what he said had occurred. Like the other Nepalis I met on this adventure, there was no indication of lying or deceit.

I looked up at the tops of the trees, then gasped. "They're growing into one another!"

Ganga Jeet looked up and saw what amazed me and he also drew a loud, deep breath. The two trees, the locations of the beginning of his six-year meditation, were leaning toward one another, creating an arch of branches that appeared as if they were trying to embrace. "I haven't noticed this until now!" he exclaimed.

As we stood there, the rest of the entourage arrived on the trailer behind Waiba's tractor. Lyndon and Mrs. Robin appeared to be unashamed of their antics, and most likely unaware. Mr. Waiba came up to Ganga Jeet and me, and I pointed upward. Ganga Jeet spoke in his native tongue, telling Waiba of my observation. He looked up in amazement, "Beautiful! I've come here hundreds of times and have never noticed this!"

The rest of the group started to walk to where we were standing, and Ganga Jeet caught and understood my glance, then led me to his motorcycle to leave the scene. We zipped along, bouncing over rocks and bumps on the trails to the small village in which Guru-ji had been raised. His parents were waiting on the front steps, and his mother rose and took me on a short tour of their little home. Palden Dorje's bedroom was kept neat and clean, and the altar in his room had fresh offerings that his family made each morning.

Just outside the house, his mother showed me where she gave birth to him. She apparently sat down on the ground against an outside wall and couldn't ignore the labor pains any further—on April 10, 1989 he entered the world.

There were four women next door, stomping barefoot in unison on a large pile of green leaves, flattening them on a wire screen underneath. They smiled and waved and, when I gestured my confusion as to what they were doing, one of the larger women pointed to a large field of marijuana growing behind Palden Dorje's house. Even though I loathe the smell of weed and have never smoked it, I took a few pictures, knowing some friends at home would be excited to see such a sight behind the birthplace of this holy being.

As we started to pull away from the little village, Ganga Jeet said that he needed to stop and put some gas in the bike, and I offered to pay. "No, no, you are our guest!" He refused any money, and I realized at that moment that I hadn't spent anything on this journey. Even the hotel accommodations were provided.

Ganga Jeet left me at Waiba's long before the rest of the group returned, and I walked hypnotically into the field of tall grass beside the farm to reflect on all that I experienced.

I didn't speak a word for the next day and a half—not at the hotel, not in the Jeep on the way back to Kathmandu, and I certainly did not say anything to the Robins when we parted ways. Lyndon and Danny Boy stayed in Simara and would be back a day later than the rest of us, and I wondered what machinations of the mind Lyndon would bring back with him.

"Are you alright brother Sonam?" Dawa asked standing in the doorway of my room.

"Oh, Dawa," I sat on the edge of my bed, "it was embarrassing, don't you think? Watching the two of them almost mocking him. She became the very thing she criticized in the Jeep. And Lyndon? Well, I could go on for far too long about the ignorance he's displayed since he landed here, not just the comedy that we witnessed. It infuriates me that my opportunity to see the living proof of the path of Dharma was marred with a framed image of what I believe to be mankind's greatest fiction."

"Yes, brother, I agree. It is most sad to see these things happen in the presence of such a holy being."

"I guess everyone's karma ripens differently," I said shrugging, remembering the way the crowds fought and pushed each other to get their blindfolds and Kusha grass once His Holiness left the temple during the Yamantaka initiation.

Just a little while after Dawa left my room, he called me to his office space where he sat in front of his computer, shaking his head. "Brother Lyndon has posted something very disturbing."

"What? How?" I looked at the Google Groups page on the computer screen.

"There is a cybercafé in Simara. He must've written this there."

Lyndon posted a short message that Palden Dorje said that he wasn't a Buddhist. "When did he say that?" I shouted.

"He didn't. He never said it when we were there. We will have to ask Lyndon when and where he heard this when he returns."

"This is why the people on that site pitched in to send him here, to shoot down anything I might have to say about this phenomenon. It's like they're discriminating against Buddhism. Forgive me, Dawa-jojo, but I want nothing to do with those people anymore."

"This is so troubling," Dawa shook his head, "if Guru-ji said that he isn't a Buddhist I don't think I can follow him."

"I'm sure this is something that Lyndon made up," I said. "And I would stop following Guru-ji if he did say it, as well. To me, it would be nothing more than a hijacking of Buddhism just to degrade it."

"I understand, brother. Will you sit with me when I speak to Lyndon?"

I wouldn't miss that conversation for the world, I thought and agreed to join his confrontation.

The next day, Lyndon didn't even have time to unpack when Dawa called him into the living room. "Brother Lyndon," he started, holding his hands behind his back while the dopey American walked into the room and sat on the sofa. Dawa looked at him like a father about to gently scold his own child. "Why did you post on Google

Groups that Guru-ji said he isn't a Buddhist?"

Lyndon sat up like a belligerent child yelling back at his father, "That's what he said! 'I am not a Buddhist!'"

"When did he say that? I was there listening to every word spoken, English and Nepali, brother. Brother Sonam heard nothing, himself. So where are you getting this idea? This is a very serious concern."

"Mr. Waiba told us... after everyone left," Lyndon replied.

"Of course, he did," I said sarcastically under my breath.

Dawa wasted no time going to the phone and calling Waiba. They spoke briefly, and only in Nepali, and Dawa hung up and returned in just a matter of minutes.

"Brother Lyndon," he started, "Guru-ji said, 'I am not *only* a Buddhist,' and that has a far greater meaning than what you wrote on the internet."

Lyndon stared at Dawa, mouth agape. He made a few sounds, trying to put something into words, but said nothing intelligible. Dawa turned to me, "It would be good if he would take back those words—publicly—on the website, don't you agree, Brother Sonam?" I nodded and stood up, satisfied and ready to leave the room.

"Why are you so quiet? You've got nothing to say for once?" Lyndon snipped.

"Oh, I do," I turned around and took a few steps toward him. "Since you and the Google Groups members have the unbelievable audacity to think you can tell people in this culture what one of their own is *actually* saying, allow me to explain this in *your* language as to cause no confusion—get up off your ass, Bucko, and go write that recant! How dare you fly over here with some offensive agenda rather than listening to these people who were blessed to have this being born into *their* world—and kind enough to invite us here to experience it!" I stared at him for a moment, looking for any sign that what I had said registered. "We are merely guests."

Lyndon's face was red, and he looked like he might stand up and take a swing. I crossed my arms defiantly, leaned forward and said, "Get to writing," then turned and left the room.

That night I had a dream that Palden Dorje showed me a beautiful gold and silver mandala hovering in the sky. At its base were seeds, black and white, that supported a second tier full of grass. The third tier had fruits and flowers in full bloom, and a multifaceted brilliant jewel sat atop, glowing in every direction. Light from the facets delivered more seeds to the base and nourished them. I told a thangka painter in Boudha about this dream and asked him to paint it for me. "I will make one for you and one for me!" he said after listening with wonder. The finished product was stunning and colorful, and he detailed it with 18 carat gold-leaf. There are only two in the world of this Nepali work of art.

After a couple of weeks, I left Dawa-jojo's and spent the rest of my time in a hotel in Boudha. I distanced myself from all things Palden Dorje and, even though I had nothing but admiration for Mr. Waiba, Dawa, and his family, I wanted to protect my experience and memory of the event from any threat of tarnish. My admiration and praise of this remarkable being who I believe is finishing his own spiritual journey here in this world has not waivered, but his presence is attracting many with whom I am not yet spiritually strong enough to understand.

"Well, Lady," Wyatt said looking back at me on the computer screen as I sat in a cybercafé in Boudha. "Do you feel like you met some kind of holy Buddha, or whatever?"

I paused and reflected momentarily on the events that I experienced. "I have a new and different understanding of that word—holy."

"And what's that?" he asked, and I gazed at my best friend's eyes looking back through the screen, briefly marveling at the technological ability for him to be seated in his Florida home while I sat on the other side of the world in a shop in the Kathmandu Valley.

"Before this event, before all of this, I thought of *holy* as being a divine privilege, kind of like being born into the right family. But now, I see it like I'm in kindergarten looking at seniors in college... professors, actually. We're all in this great big school into which we didn't even know we were enrolled, learning about the multidimensionality of our being. We humans just can't think outside of the confines of our three-dimensional existence—up, down, side to side—that's all." I paused, looking for better words.

Wyatt stared back at me, and I suddenly became aware of all of our history together, all of our stories and love for one another being transmitted between us, beyond the technology of the computers and the satellite link. It was something beyond words and time, I thought. "There's a whole lot more to who we are than what we're attached to thinking that we are. I believe that Palden Dorje is holy, but so are you... and me... and every creature, even spiders. Everything is holy. Guru-ji is merely a visitor letting us know that we need to get on with getting out of here."

"So, what is heaven? What's next after this life? Where is your mother?"

Lowering my head and closing my eyes, the image of her face came to mind, and sitting there in that little cybercafé, a faint scent of *White Shoulders* surrounded me. "She's in the next room," I said then looked up with tears beginning to fill my eyes. "When we die, we just go through a doorway into a new room... one that matches our new vibration—*if* it's new. We're traveling, looking for our destination—home."

"Is that heaven?" Wyatt asked.

"No," I started to cry. "The truth is we never left home—and we're not really going anywhere. We really are just asleep, but we can get a glimpse of the truth, like opening your eyes in the middle of the night and falling quickly back to slumber. It's enough to break it all down, destroy the chains that bind us in these never-ending circles, eventually waking up—dreams over. Then . . . *that's* heaven." Sniffling, I grabbed a tissue from my bag, then remembering Geshe-la's explanation of the Heart Sutra, began to slowly chant, "Gone... gone... gone beyond, gone completely beyond... awakened."

Wyatt cocked his head, confused, and asked, "What are you saying?"

"Something Geshe-la told me that I think I might understand now. I don't really—really—exist. No eye. It isn't me. No ear, that's not me, either. No nose, no tongue, no body... none of this is me! And no mind, it's always changing and changing. Maybe one day, if I put the right... stuff... into it I'll be a Palden Dorje myself, sitting in a jungle on a meditative mission of love and compassion to lead others who are ready... into the next room."

He sat quietly looking at me pensively, and the expression on his face as the realization began to dawn on him was beautiful to me. "I think you just summed it all up... everything since you started down this path," Wyatt said smiling back, and he wiped away a tear that trailed down his cheek, born from his own understanding.

Eventually, Aama Bumpo saw me and gave me a ritual blessing as Dakpa Sangye suggested I receive. In the waiting room in her house, there was a plaque of recognition for her abilities by His Holiness, the Dalai Lama. It set me at ease to see that the old monk told me the truth, and I was open to experience the blessings of this Nepali shaman. Though I didn't experience any physical unexplainable energies, each of the photos that my friend took of the event are quite peculiar. Whenever Aama Bumpo was performing the ritual, she was always out of phase for the camera, blurry like she was vibrating tremendously fast. The few photos of her after the ritual turned out crystal clear.

Due to the haste in my booking the trip to Nepal, I was able to reenter India a few days early and took my flight back to Delhi—on April 10th. Ama-la was surprised to see me enter the apartment days before she expected me. She immediately noticed that I had lost weight. "I guess I can have three butter teas now, yes?" I said, causing her to let out a good belly laugh, and she was pleased that I said it to her in Tibetan.

During my preparations to return, I called Geshe-la, missing him dearly, to share with him my trip in the jungle. He listened carefully and I told him I would not disbelieve him again, which caused him to laugh. "We will see!"

Than quickly responded to an email I sent him, asking if he could pick me up from the airport when I returned. My excitement to see him and share all that I learned was off the scales. We decided a reunion was in order, and bought tickets for him, Andy, and me to meet at the teaching the Dalai Lama was to give in Indianapolis in May.

My Tibetan family and I spent my last day together, disappointingly without Pa-la, walking the park at India Gate, and later at a little festival where Yegah and I rode a few rides and ate cotton candy. It felt like I belonged to this family, as if they were my blood, though there was little resemblance between us.

Walking around the pool in the Central Vista lawn, the reflection of the four pillars of the India Gate Canopy on the water was so breathtakingly beautiful, and I made sure to get a photo of the four of us in its foreground. I was certain Mom was watching and sending her approval through the four large, white birds that flew close enough for us to feel the wind from their wings. It made us all shriek with high pitched laughter, and I watched a young Indian boy playfully skip a rock across the pool, causing the reflection to dance through the rippling waves.

"Do you know anything about dreams?" I asked Ama-la and Drolkar as we walked.

"What about them?"

"What does it mean to laugh yourself awake?" I asked, and Drolkar translated my question.

Ama-la took my hand and spoke. "It means your Dharma practice is succeeding," Drolkar translated. "Keep on your journey and reflect on the Dharma until it becomes your every thought, word, and deed."

The night of my departure, she dropped grains of Nechung

channay in my bags before I zipped and locked them, ready for the flight home to share this amazing journey with anyone who would listen. Her soft, white silk khatak she placed around my neck tugged at my stubble as I turned to admire my reflection in the windows down the concourse of Indira Gandhi. The dark night outside transformed every window into a mirror, and there I was each time—wearing a big, fulfilled smile looking back—like a new friend with whom I was excited to get to know, without a trace of the years of childhood opprobrium to which I had been accustomed. Wyatt would be proud of the good company I finally found in that reflection, I thought.

My journey through the Dharma in this lifetime untangled so many webs of knots in my heart and I boarded the plane with gratitude as I reflected on the long road behind me and wondered what lies ahead. An attractive pair of eyes and a smile gazed back at me from the window beside my seat on the plane and I turned my head to offer a grateful and direct smile to a handsome American man who had been staring at me. His reflection, my reflection... Yuri's reflection... the reflection in the India Gate pool, the airport windows, the bathroom back home in Greentown as a child... all these reflections now seemed like messages from the beyond, and I let my mind open to all the possibilities as we started down the runway.

The Law of Reflection states that the angle of incidence is equal to the angle of reflection—three points: the object, the mirror, and the observer. But Dakpa Sangye's explanation that consciousness is like a mirror, reflecting that which is placed before it—the soul is both mirror and observer—and there are only two points: the object and the ever-present watcher. Everything that consciousness sees is, therefore, some version of itself. And it has many variations, each person a different kind of looking glass.

There are those who see objects appear closer than they actually are, some who see distorted images like those in a funhouse hall of mirrors, and sometimes we meet those who create an image of a never-ending corridor simply by reflecting our own mirror with theirs, face to face.

Mirrors don't get to choose whether to reflect or not, that is their nature. Thus, it is also the nature of mind to behold the likeness of another until it moves away. There is great liberation in the realization that the mirror is never stained by the reflection—good or bad—for so much suffering comes from staring too long into the looking glass of the mind, wishing to redo, or undo, things it once gazed upon.

Geshe-la helped me to see the reality through the illusion, something Mom had done first during Christmases of my teen years. I had resented her for that, but reflecting on all the bumps in the road, I'm convinced that it was she who placed them there in some heavenly, calculated plan to guide me to a transformation of my soul.

I am sure I will thank her one day, when I finally see her again... sitting under a golden glowing gazebo, sipping butter tea, surrounded by white animals wearing red bows, near a cliff overlooking a beautiful, peaceful, and reflective blue ocean.

Epilogue

"Your coffee's gonna get cold," I said, watching Brock scribble away in his notebook as we sat in a little coffeeshop about a half-mile from the Indiana Buddhist Center. A former student of mine—a drum major from one of my marching bands—Brock recently came out of the closet and had a growing interest in Buddhism. We agreed to meet and spend some time together so I could answer the many questions he had about my path and practice.

"I know," he put his pen down and grabbed his mug. "Your story is really amazing. I'm just trying to write down as many details as I can. Have you thought about teaching this stuff? You were such a good instructor for our band—very strict."

"Ja dang gaygen tsani gyal," I echoed Geshe-la's words he once told me. Brock stared at me, clearly waiting for me to translate. "It means, 'The teacher and tea are best when hot.'"

He smiled and grabbed his pen. "How do you spell that?"

Brock was eager to learn about Dharma and his joy for each new concept he encountered reminded me of myself, so many years ago reading *The Four Noble Truths*. Many of my former marching band students turned to me to learn about Buddhism. Often, I was their go-to guy to help them through their religious studies courses and papers they had to write about the topic in college. It should come as no surprise that the young, gay men who turned to the Dharma as an alternative spiritual tradition to the world of Christianity—from which their small closed-minded communities had spit them out—found a soft spot in my heart. It was comforting knowing that I could present a possible shortcut through all of the confusion that a beginner usually faced, and to also be an example of pride in being one's authentic self, as well.

"I teach introductory Buddhist philosophy at our center," I answered. "My job is to get all of the newbies up to snuff with terminology, concepts, practices, and so on so that they can attend Geshe-la's teachings, which are understandably a bit more advanced."

"Why don't you start your own place?" he asked, then waved at the waiter to come top off our mugs.

"There's no need," I chuckled. "Geshe-la is more than enough for me, and I don't need to get wrapped up in the world of arrogant white guys culturally appropriating the traditions of the Dalai Lama's people in order to gather followers and fame. After you've studied Buddhism for a while, you might see it as embarrassing as I do. I'm not saying that there aren't westerners who should be teaching, but on average there are too many that haven't even had any actual realizations from the Dharma. Besides, the Tibetan people continue to produce amazing teachers. I am nobody... just a marching band designer from Indiana who's been blessed to learn and grow from the remarkable offerings Tibet has given to the world. Serving Geshe Jinpa Sonam is my way to help promote and preserve their culture."

Brock looked at me for a moment. "And before you say anything," I continued. "I'm an American practicing Tibetan Buddhism—I'm not a Tibetan."

The waiter came to our table and started refilling our coffee. "I like your necklace," he said, looking at the Tiger's Eye mala around my neck.

"It's a Buddhist rosary," I said, taking it off and handing it to him as I often did for admirers who asked about it. "I got this in northern India."

He stood and inspected it for a few moments, then handed it back. "I'm really interested in Buddhism. Maybe you could come back here sometime and let me ask you some questions when I'm not working?"

"Certainly," I chuckled. "That's what I'm doing here now." I reached in my bag and pulled out a business card for the IBC, quickly wrote my name and number on the back, and handed it to him. "I'm Marc—secretary and senior student to the Indiana Buddhist Center and Geshe Jinpa Sonam, our spiritual director."

Brock smiled, watching the attractive young man return to his rounds attending the other customers in the store. "He's cute. You think he's gay?"

I laughed, laying my mala on the table. "He's also probably thirty years younger than me! What would it matter if he's on our side of the fence?"

"Oh, I'm sorry," he apologized. "You probably have vows of celibacy."

"Hardly!" I exclaimed. It never ceased to amaze me how many people think that spiritual people can't be sexual. "Lay vow-holders don't have to be celibate. In fact, Buddhism isn't about commandments.

Dharma is mostly about studying and understanding cause and effect. If you're not interested in worrying about your liberation or your future lives, then don't. But once you start down the rabbit hole of examining the obvious, hidden, and deeply hidden layers of reality, you might be inclined to make better decisions that influence your future."

"So, you still have sex?" he asked, seemingly looking for confirmation that he wouldn't have to abandon the calls of his libido.

"Well, not really," I chuckled. "But it's not because of my vows. It's because I just don't look for it anymore." He smiled, and as he raised his mug to his mouth his eyes glanced across the room at the young waiter. "But I'm not a twenty-one-year-old man trying to deal with desire racing through his blood, like you. You don't have to be celibate. Just find a balance. Don't let it control you."

I tapped on his notebook to bring his attention back to our table and he quickly looked back at me, cheeks beginning to flush as though he had been caught doing something he shouldn't. "I'm sorry," he said.

"Don't be," I laughed. "You had other questions?"

"It's really hard to believe that your mother and your friend's father died in their sleep on the same night. Did that move your friend on a spiritual level like it did you?" Brock asked.

"It's sad that it had an opposite effect on Craig," I answered, remembering one of the only conversations he and I had about their deaths nearly five years after it happened. Craig was so afraid that it was God's punishment for a shameful secret between us from our youth that he took to studying the book of Revelation in the Bible on a near daily basis. Yet for me, I saw a beautiful message about spirituality—not religion—that I deeply wished he could see.

"So, you're not afraid of your years of promiscuity being some kind of obstacle to your enlightenment?" he said, grabbing his pen and preparing to record my answer.

"Buddha lived in a brothel before seeking enlightenment," I responded, to which he snapped his head up to look at me, dumbfounded. "I'd be more afraid to think that after all I've learned I would still somehow be caught up in thinking those temporary pleasures are the way to lasting happiness."

"I guess it also depends on how quickly you want to reach enlightenment," he said.

"Yes, yes," I responded. "Remember, enlightenment is an English word which too many people use to describe their granola-eating, vegan yoga teacher who mispronounces Namaste. But what that word is supposed to represent is called *moksha* in Sanskrit. In Tibetan it is *jang-chub*, and it literally means 'to finish learning.' This refers to a Buddha. They are said to be on The Path of No More Learning."

He quickly wrote something in his notebook, then said, "That's very helpful, thanks." Setting his pen down and trying to hide his eyes wandering across the room, asked, "So, you said that you can use the Law of Attraction to find the perfect partner? Like your friend Nathaniel did?"

"Than. He likes to go by Than instead of Nathaniel. But yes. He called me while I was in Dharamsala and told me that he was having mind-blowing success with his practice of the Law of Attraction and that he wanted to use it to find his soulmate. And it worked. His wife, Julia, is the perfect match for him. She's an angel... or dakini, as they're called in Sanskrit. Hell, if I weren't gay, I would want a woman just like her."

"So why are you single? Why haven't you attracted the perfect soulmate into your life?"

I turned my head to look out the window and into my memories. "I thought I did once."

"Yuri?" he asked.

"Yuri," I sighed. "Maybe not a soulmate, but partner—I hoped. But he's straight. And now he's married to a wonderful Malaysian, woman and they have a child together. And I... I just can't get fascinated at the idea of being in a relationship anymore. It just seems so ephemeral, so unnecessary. No matter how close of a relationship I ever have with someone, the death experience is solitary. We came into this world alone and we leave alone. It's better to have as few emotional attachments as possible, I think."

"What about DJ?" he asked, bringing my attention back to the table. "You said that he wasn't the love of your life, but did he ever go through some kind of karmic payback for what he did to you?"

"My goodness, I hope not!" I exclaimed. "DJ is the reason I turned to the Dharma in the first place. I owe him now, not the other way around! Think about our journey of multiple lifetimes that lead to our liberation. One lifetime doesn't make that much of a difference when compared to beginningless time. A good guide would be more concerned with getting someone out of Samsara than making that lifetime comfortable. It's like staying in a hotel and spending thousands of dollars to redecorate it, just for that one night, then waking up the next morning and returning to your long journey home only to have to stop at another hotel again. The guide hands us a map that shows a shorter road that leads home. I'm trying my best to follow it."

Brock was noticeably confused and stared at his notebook not knowing what to write. "Doesn't it suck that he just gets away with doing all that stuff to you?"

I tapped the table to get him to look up at me and emphasizing my words. "We're not supposed to be here," I said, which made him quickly look around. "No, not this coffeeshop. Here, in Samsara. We're not supposed to be here. This," I gestured broadly at everything around us, "isn't where we're supposed to be. That's what I mean by the hotel rooms. We're supposed to be home, liberated and fully enlightened. Our negative emotions keep us in this cycle. Even having a desire of schadenfreude for DJ's negative actions with me are shackles preventing freedom—and that's also basic psychology for this lifetime. He's married now to a nice guy, and they have adopted a child together. I wish them well. And I truly hope that he never experiences any of the pain I went through."

A smile slowly stretched across his face as my words reached his heart. "That's lovely," he said, then took to his notebook again. He flipped the pages back to read the notes he took from my story and asked, "Why did you leave Dawa-jojo's and spend the rest of your trip in Nepal elsewhere?"

I slowly sipped at my coffee to take a moment to gather my thoughts. "There appears to be a lot of people bringing controversies to that little area in the jungle, and I saw it coming. Palden Dorje goes by Dharma Sangha now—a name he says was given to him by Maitreya Buddha, the next Buddha to come into the world after Shakyamuni. I don't have a hard time seeing this person—this being—as a Bodhisattva who's finishing his spiritual journey on Earth. But I do have a hard time with the countless number of people, mostly westerners, who continue to create problems in his presence. One woman has accused him of..." I gestured quotes with my fingers, "'sexual assault.'"

"You don't believe her?" Brock asked.

"I believe that her accusations should be investigated," I replied. "But she and I messaged one another before my first trip to India and she wasn't playing with a full deck. Her bio on her Facebook profile was the same as Palden Dorje's, verbatim—except that she changed his name to hers. And when she went to see him, she constantly invaded his meditation space, refused to leave even when he asked her to, and she went around telling everyone that he was the return of Jesus. So, I'm skeptical that these controversies belong to a guy who had so much love and compassion that he no longer required sustenance and could meditate for six years but was selfish enough to commit sexual assault. It doesn't pass the sniff test. A thorough investigation is necessary and I'm sure he would welcome the truth to be brought forth. Seriously, though, so many people get a little cuckoo around holy teachers."

"Why do you think that is?"

"I really have no idea," I started. "You're going to see it at Dharma centers, too. There's so much competition to get closer to the Lama than anyone else. That competition is karmically quite bad. And I've seen it tear groups apart. I'm thankful that Geshe-la picks up on it pretty quickly and puts the kibosh on it right away."

Brock reached over, took my mala, and held it closely to examine the beads. It reminded me of a gift I placed in my bag for him, an onyx mala, which I pulled out and handed to him. "For me?" he asked.

"Yes," I replied. "I have given so many malas to former band students over the years it's crazy. I used to make them and give them away. But that got too costly. I can spend less to have a bulk of them sent from a friend in Delhi."

His fingers clumsily flipped from bead to bead, and I smiled as I remembered my first time around a Buddhist rosary.

"Do you think Geshe-la will like me?" he asked as he carefully watched his fingers moving each bead.

"I can't think of anyone Geshe-la doesn't like," I chuckled. "Why wouldn't he like you?"

"I don't know," he stopped messing with the beads. "I'm just a little nervous about meeting him."

"People usually are, and I can't quite understand that. Sure, it might be intimidating if you were going to go try to debate him. But he's a monk who has dedicated his life to compassion and wisdom. I can't imagine why people aren't sprinting to see someone like that."

Checking his watch, Brock asked, "When did you say we were going to go see him?"

"His daily practice isn't over until about noon," I answered, looking at my own watch. "We've got about twenty more minutes. That's not a question for the paper your writing, is it?"

He laughed. "Of course, not." Then he asked me to tell him more about my time in Nepal after returning from meeting Palden Dorje.

Later in the week after Lyndon recanted his claim to the Google Groups, Waiba and a couple of Nepali boys who were in the jungle during our trip came to Dawa's for dinner. After eating, we went to Dawa's roof to discuss plans Guru-ji and Waiba had for building a temple.

"We need someone to design blueprints," Waiba said. "We're wanting a nice, western style building with a large hall for teachings and group meditations."

"I could make the blueprints," Lyndon said quickly with excitement.

"Do you know how to draw blueprints, Lyndon?" I asked with surprise, wondering if his military training may have included such knowledge.

"No," he responded, still staring at Waiba with hope that he would approve. "But I'm a fast learner."

Waiba continued telling us about the various undertakings for building the temple. With each new task, Lyndon quickly volunteered himself for the job. Of course, I followed each time by asking Lyndon if he had any experience that would make him a suitable candidate, and I could tell it was getting on his nerves. After Waiba mentioned that he knew a donor from Vietnam who wanted to pay for a high-quality sound system for the temple, Lyndon volunteered to install it.

"Do you have any audio-visual experience, Lyndon?" I asked, which set him into a fit of anger.

"What's your problem with me, man?" he asked loudly. "Why are you picking on me every time I volunteer for something?"

"Every time, Lyndon," I said, crossing my arms. "That's the problem. It is every single time Waiba mentions a task, you jump for it without any expertise! Don't you think these people—Palden Dorje—deserve qualified and competent artists and skilled builders?"

"What are you going to do?" he asked. "Are you going to volunteer to do anything?"

Mr. Waiba looked at me and said, "I was hoping that you would be a kind of international spokesperson and fundraiser."

I laughed. "I have no experience in any of that, sir. If you want an opening ceremony for the temple with brightly colored flags twirling around and musicians moving about in entertaining formations, I'm your guy. Why not seek out people that are qualified for what you need?"

"I might not have expertise," Lyndon started, "but I'm willing to help."

"Then, help," I shot back. "Lift things, move things, do the things that you are trained to do, and do them well. But Lyndon, seriously, if Waiba had told us about a job that required a woman I'm almost certain you'd have stuffed your shirt and said, 'point me where to go!'"

"You didn't say that, did you?" Brock laughed.

"I sure as hell did! Forgive me if I'm not the stereotypical pacifist so many think Buddhists should be. I shoot from the hip. Geshe-la does the same thing. If something's not right, beating around the bush about it just gives it time to fester."

"So, you didn't help with the temple?" Brock asked.

"No. In fact, after I returned to the States, I decided to maintain a distanced interest from the events in Nepal. I haven't been back since."

"But you've been back to India?"

"Four trips in total," I said almost proudly. "I went back a year after my first trip. Pa-la passed away and I went to be with Ama-la and the family. While I was there in Delhi, I tried to help one of Geshe-la's students, Namgyal, get his visa to come to America. He didn't get it. But he finally did a few years ago and he lives with Geshe-la at our center. So, now we have two monks!"

"Should I be prepared to make an offering to them both when I meet them?" he asked as he pulled out his wallet.

"Not directly. Geshe-la doesn't like all the fuss, being as humble as he is. And he is quick to remind us that he's living in our culture and not the other way around. Namgyal is quite shy, so he won't be talkative at all, even though his English is better than Geshe-la's. Just put your offering in the donation box and have your intention set to benefit them both and that will suffice. If you were meeting His Holiness, I'd advise you to offer a khatak."

"What was it like meeting the Dalai Lama with Than and Andy?" he asked and leaned in with a big grin.

"We didn't meet him."

"What?" He sat back and lost his smile to a look of confusion. "I thought you three met him at the teachings in Indianapolis not long after you got back home?"

"We met each other at the teachings," I corrected. "I met His Holiness at his residence in Dharamsala just a few years ago on my third trip to India and then helped Geshe-la bring him to our center the following June."

"The Dalai Lama himself has been to your little center?" he asked with wonder in his eyes. "What was that like?"

"Surreal. Watching his limo and the Homeland Security entourage show up was unbelievable. I was in charge of the property and getting it ready in the last two months leading up to the visit. We had to keep it a secret until we knew for certain that His Holiness would be coming to our little house. When Geshe-la got the confirmation, I asked him if I could invite my Dad, knowing how proud he was that I had met the Dalai Lama at his residence in Dharamsala. He apparently printed the photos I emailed him after my audience and was showing them off to everyone in his office."

"It must have been pretty life-changing to meet him," Brock said, and I pulled out my cell phone to show him the pictures from that day. Brock slowly swiped through the photos and stopped at my favorite. "What's he holding in this one?"

"When I met him, I pulled out my wallet to show him Geshe-la's picture and express my gratitude for sending him to America. He took the wallet to look at the picture, then gently held my hand and said, 'Ah, yes! I know this man! Very learned scholar.'"

"That's got to be your favorite picture of all time!" he said as he marveled at the cell phone screen.

"It doesn't suck," I laughed. "We should go now. Geshe-la is probably finished and getting ready to fix lunch."

Brock followed me to the Indiana Buddhist Center and parked his car beside mine in the drive. He sat in the car for a few minutes looking in the mirror, preparing himself as though he were about to go inside for an interview. "I'm still really nervous," he said when he finally got out of the car.

"Like I said before, don't be. Just be yourself."

Namgyal opened the door and invited us inside. I motioned Brock to remove his shoes.

"Is that a custom thing?" he asked. I nodded.

Namgyal led us to the kitchen to sit at the table as he placed a large pot of water on the stove and started to make tea. "Geshe-la is still in his room," Namgyal said quietly. "Maybe still doing practice, I don't know."

"It's ok," I said. "Some days take longer than other days."

Just then, the door to Geshe-la's room creaked open and I could hear him repeating a mantra as he walked down the hall, into the living room, and rounded the corner to the kitchen. "Marc!" he exclaimed.

"Geshe-la!" I shot back with a huge smile.

"Who are you?" Geshe-la chuckled as he walked toward Brock,

reaching out his hand.

"My name is Brock."

"He's one of my former marching band kids, Geshe-la," I said, enjoying the sight of their handshake. Geshe-la didn't let go. He held it tenderly as he stepped closer to my young friend.

"You Buddhist?" Geshe-la asked. As Brock began to tell him about his growing interest in the Dharma, I stood up and quietly went into the living room where I grabbed a book from the wall of shelves and sat flipping through the pages.

After about ten minutes, Brock stepped into the living room and whispered, "What are you doing?"

"I know the man," I said as I stood, closed the book, and returned it to the shelves. "You don't. Go. Go spend some time with him. I'm going to leave."

Geshe-la stepped into the doorway of the kitchen. "You leaving?" he asked. "Have lunch!"

"No, Geshe-la. I'm supposed to meet my friend, Kathleen, at Fort Benjamin park for our weekly walk together. Brock will have lunch with you."

"No problem," Geshe-la smiled, then went back into the kitchen to help Namgyal.

Brock followed me to the door. "Do you have any advice for me?"

"Watch out for the hot sauce. They love spicy food."

"I mean, any words of wisdom about my journey into Buddhism?"

"There's plenty of time for us to talk again. And if you come to Geshe-la's teachings regularly, I'll be there, too. But..." I reached into my bag and pulled out a short Tibetan text wrapped in crimson brocade. "Here."

"What's this?" he asked as he took my gift.

"When I was in Nepal, a couple of weeks after I left Dawa-jojo's home, I was in Boudha feeding the pigeons one day when I looked up to see an old tantrika staring at me as a young man was speaking to him. A tantrika—*ngak-pa* in Tibetan—is like a Buddhist mystic. They're said to be practitioners who develop amazing powers, like being able to change the weather, clairvoyance, and mind-reading. As I looked at him, I said in my mind, 'Hello, there. Can you read my mind?' And then he started to walk away with the young man following him. I tried to speak to him with my mind and thought, 'If you can read my mind, give me a sign.' But they kept walking. Then

I concentrated all my mental energy and was shouting in my head, 'Give me something! Give me something!'"

"Well?" Brock stood staring at me, waiting for the end of the story.

"Nothing. They rounded the stupa and disappeared, and I went about wandering the streets and shops of Kathmandu. About forty-five minutes later, I went to see my friend, Tashi Lama—who owns a thangka shop in Boudha. As I stepped into the door, there was the old tantrika talking to Tashi! I was quite surprised. And then Tashi said, 'Oh, Marc. My friend has been here waiting for you for a short while.'"

"Wow!" Brock said.

"Oh, wait. It gets better," I chuckled. "I asked Tashi why he was waiting for me. The old tantrika told Tashi that he wanted to give me a sutra that he had with him, and as he gave it to me, my hands trembled. I opened the text and began to read the Tibetan title aloud, which made the old tantrika laugh. 'You speak Tibetan?' he asked me, and I told him that I can read and write but my conversation skills are lacking."

"What was the text?" Brock asked.

"It's called the Sutra of Boundless Life and Wisdom," I answered. "I slowly flipped through the pages, chanting the text with the old tantrika. When we finished, he patted me on the shoulder and reached in his bag and handed me... another. I looked at Tashi, waiting for him to translate what the old man was saying. 'He wants you to have another so you can give it to a friend, too.'

"You said 'give me something' twice, didn't you?" Brock asked with astonishment.

"Yep," I said, my eyes starting to tear up from the precious memory. "So, I make copies of this sutra and give it to new Dharma students from time to time. This one is for you."

"Thank you," he said, looking at the text in his hands. "I'll try to find some nice material to wrap it in."

"Good idea. Now, go in the kitchen and get to know that man." I pulled the door shut behind me, hopeful that I set into motion a relationship that would blossom for lifetimes to come. Now, their story is just beginning—just between the two of them. I played the role of introducing many prospective students to Geshe-la over the years, and I get out of the way as soon as I can. Seeing Brock's smile in the kitchen window as I passed on the way to my car gave me a good feeling that he would return, on his own, as often as he could.

For the record, Buddhism isn't about proselytizing and converting. The Dalai Lama has always encouraged his audiences to continue to follow their own religious tradition. I have merely been someone who offers another option when those I meet tell me that they have too many questions that their family's tradition cannot answer. Or, as in the case with young gay men like Brock, they find that they cannot reconcile with the doom that particular tradition claims to await them for being born in a way that does not accord with the narrow-minded views they espouse.

I don't disparage Christianity, the worldview that also surrounded me as a child. However, I do stand in opposition to those who continue to weaponize its doctrine and try to pass public policies that would force people like me to follow laws with which I disagree. Everyone is entitled to their own beliefs. But belief is just another word for opinion. Facts cannot be disputed, and thus our legislators should be more concerned with facts than the many varied opinions about who created the world and how best to show devotion.

I always say that I am an American first. If it weren't for the freedoms our forefathers established, Dharma would never have crossed the shores of this country and made its way to the Midwest, where a young gay man disenfranchised from the traditions of his community for being born a little different from the other boys found it and discovered that there was nothing wrong with him after all.

Buddhism is a spiritual science, and it reveals the true nature of consciousness to those who seek. There are many layers to our reality. Likewise, there are varied levels of students, each on their own path toward enlightenment. The Tibetans say, "*wang-tul de-pe je-drang, wang-nun-rig-pai je-drang,*" which means, "Those who follow out of faith have dull mental faculties; those who follow out of logic and reason are mentally sharp." The practices of Buddhism service the needs of seekers that fit in the spectrum between those two types of practitioner. If bumper stickers could indicate which type of person one was, Brock's many progressive messages on the back of his car shouted that he was the latter—a man of reason... and love.

When Brock was a drum major in high school, he saw my mala around my neck and asked if I would tell him more about the Dharma. "After you graduate and are an adult making your own decisions," I told him. Schools are no place for religious indoctrination, even for my life-saving spiritual practice, I believe. However, if my students are writing a paper on world religions and ask to interview me about my practice and my training, I will give them an interview for the purpose of answering those questions as there are many incorrect sources that their teachers often use in the classroom.

Brock has many attributes that remind me of myself, besides being gay. He is open-minded, intelligent, and diligent—three qualities that one master named Pabongkha Rinpoche said were necessary traits for a qualified student of the Dharma. Ray Kroc, the founder of McDonald's had a saying that was etched on bronze placards posted at almost all of their restaurants that is applicable here, too: "When you're green you're growing. When you're ripe you rot." It is my endeavor to remain a student of the Dharma until the last breath leaves my lungs.

Since the return home from my first trip to India and Nepal, the magic hasn't stopped happening. Making deliberate use of the Law of Attraction—which is merely a shortcut for effecting worldly change that is, as Karmapa told me, best used for enlightenment—has improved the lives of those who trusted me enough to give it a real try. I have hundreds of letters, emails, and cards from those who have unbelievable stories of mathematically impossible coincidences—like those between me and Andy, Than, and Yuri—thanking me for introducing them to a better worldview.

The Law of Attraction helped my Buddhist practice through the years. For one, seeing that it works in my life I am able to apply better understanding of the power of visualization toward my tantric practices in which visualization is key. Having the empowerment to visualize oneself as the meditational deity is what plants the impressions within the mindstream that eventually ripen and develop into the enlightened form of a Buddha. I certainly can't prove that this is true, but this is the only point in my life where faith plays a role for me—this is the faith in the authoritative words of the Buddha and every realized master throughout history in the Tibetan lineage.

Secondly, I know that like attracts like. The more I meditate on compassion for all beings, the happier I've become and the more I meet others who share the same attitude about the world and every single one of its inhabitants. Our first experiences in this world were the compassion and kindness from our own mothers. They sacrificed so much for us while we were in the womb and then fed us, cleaned us, protected us, and loved us after we were born. We innately know the beauty of compassion, but somehow, we have strayed away from spreading it in our communities, our governments, and our international affairs. The world will be a brilliant paradise if we teach our students about the importance of compassion and attend to their emotional intelligence as part of their educational upbringing. Thankfully, the Dalai Lama has been working tirelessly to institute a curriculum all around the world with just such a goal.

And finally, Law of Attraction helped me understand karma by showing me that every experience I have—good or bad—comes from my own consciousness. Whether knowingly or ignorant of the causal thoughts and actions that bring about their effects, I'm the one in the driver's seat. I'm either driving along carefully, paying attention to the road or asleep at the wheel, putting myself and others in danger. Only a Buddha is fully awake, and all of the rest of us should aspire to be, too. You see, life is like a great big role-playing game. The way to win isn't to have the most stuff or the highest status—it's how to find the way out of the game entirely.

The Law of Reflection—as I came to think of it and apply it with my own understanding of consciousness—is the final piece of a puzzle I sought for years. Everyone we meet is a reflection of something about ourselves. Should we see something negative or ugly about someone else, it's merely evidence that those little neurons that house information we've wired about that person are firing in our brains. Those little bits of negativity or ugliness are actually us—physically—and not the other person at all. The more we focus on the beauty of another—the more we find qualities in them that we can appreciate—the more our own good qualities develop and grow. This to me is a spiritual law.

Driving out of the parking lot of the IBC, leaving Brock alone, nervous, and trying to understand Geshe-la's broken English, I felt the same sense of satisfaction I felt after doing this to so many students in the past. Knowing how close to my heart my relationship with that wise and compassionate Ladakhi master is, I wish that everyone in the world may have such a bond with someone like him and that they experience transformation and healing in their own lives. The influence of such a master, one who understands your emotional and intellectual proclivities and can prescribe practices that will change your life and your direction is the reason the student-teacher relationship exists, not just in Buddhism, but in every avenue of learning.

The Buddha, Dharma, and Sangha are the doctor, the medicine, and the nurses. I referred to my early years before meeting Geshe Jinpa Sonam as practicing over-the-counter Dharma—pulling books from the shelves and seeking knowledge to heal myself much like someone going to the store to buy antacid or cough syrup. For those who find themselves in places where there are no teachers, temples, or Dharma centers their options are as similarly limited as mine were in Kokomo, Indiana. Though I could drive to Bloomington or Indianapolis, there are millions that don't have that luxury. Whenever I can, just as so many other lay practitioners, I give away books, explain mantras, give meditation instructions, or just be an ear to those who need some immediate relief. Though the laity are not Sangha, and though we cannot prescribe actual medicines from the doctor, we can help—and will—however we can. You can consider us your friendly neighborhood *Dharmacists*.

Acknowledgments

I would like to thank the following:

John Aylsworth, John Binkowski, Sharon Blanco, Kathy Buckley, Laura Conley, Sonam Drolma, Tenzin Drokar (and the entire Gorgotsang family), Robert E. Durham, Julia Jude, Nathaniel Jude, Tami McLaren, Yuri Medvedev, Christopher Moss, Evan Moss, Joel Preston Moss, Geshe Lobsang Namgyal, Tenam Namgyal, Jonathan Newcomb, Deana Sewell, Gina Shirley, Mary Ellen Silk, Shirley and Gary Smith, Geshe Jinpa Sonam, Alan Temby, Andrew Turley, Wyatt White

Also, thanks to the following:

Kirti Monastery of Dharamsala, India
Indiana Buddhist Center of Indianapolis Indiana
Tibetan Mongolian Buddhist Center of Bloomington, Indiana
Diamond Mountain University of Bowie, Colorado
Dorje Loppun Rinpoche Ngawang Tenzin

Special thanks to all contributors that helped during the pandemic as I wrote this:

Kristina Allen, Angela Anderson, Jennifer Anderson, Matt Arant, Antonio Argelles, Chris Arrick, Luke and Laura Aylsworth, Mellissa Ballard, Sandra Bertelle, Alden Blaho, Scott Bostwick, Shanon and Megon Briles, Charles Brock, Lucinda Brown, Aaron Cavinder, Michael Cavosie, Heidi Chestnut, Sean and Laura Conley, Quinn Connolly, Jeanne Coonan, Shannon Crosby, Tasha Davis, Benjamin Druffel, Pam Duenas, Toni Duncan, Lindsay Ecklund, Andreina Espinosa, William Fathauer, Jeremy Goltz, Benjamin Gordon, Paul Green, Mylissa Greenawalt, Bonnie Harmon, Robbi Hicks, Andrew Hoffman, Cindy Jackson, Jeff

Katt, Tanya Kelly, Justin Koszarek, Ryan Krapf, Jessica Lipman, Joshua Mansfield, Mark Martin, William Mathews, Trent Mason, Jason McDonald, Dianne McKinnon, Abigail Melendez, Andrea Moeller, Joel Preston Moss, Marisa Mullett, Evan Munn, Michelle (Holy Sheetz) Murphy, Jon Newcomb, Cheryl Nimz, Geoffrey Ong, Sharon Parr, Michelle Perry, Andrew Porter, Laura Reske, Bradley Sanker and family, Diane Sargeant, LeAnn Scacco, Devon and Kathleen Schonsheck, Carl Smith, Jo Smith, Whitney Stone, Doug Stout, Casey Szink, Rory Tasker, Marrisa Thompson, Julie Towle, Eileen Tucker, Shelba Waldron, Kat Webb, Wyatt White, Lee-Alison Wilson, Julie Yanda, Laura Zomboracz

•

About the Author

MARC PRESTON MOSS is the senior-most student of Geshe Jinpa Sonam, spiritual director of the Indiana Buddhist Center in Indianapolis, Indiana. He serves on the Board of Directors and teaches weekly introductory Buddhist philosophy courses. Marc also studied with Geshe Lobsang Tenzin, former spiritual director of the Tibetan Cultural Center and the Chamtse Ling Buddhist temple in Bloomington, Indiana. He also speaks publicly for the center around the state and has been a guest teacher of meditation and philosophy for many Dharma and wellness centers throughout the Midwest. As a student of Dharma, Marc's travels have led him to India four times, studying in Dharamsala, Himachal Pradesh, as well as in Mundgod, Karnataka, the seat of Drepung monastery.

When not engaged in Buddhist activities, Marc designs and choreographs for scholastic and Independent competitive marching arts programs across the country. He has worked with over three hundred and fifty schools in the past thirty years. Marc attended Ball State University from 1991-1993. Currently, he resides in Indianapolis, Indiana.

& Illustrator

SCOTT ALLEN is originally from Flushing, Michigan and received his BFA in graphic design from Central Michigan University with graduate studies in Georgia at the Savannah College of Art and Design. Scott spent many summers growing up at the family cottage on the water in northern Michigan and that environment was a major influence in his paintings. Scott's work is based on a combination of various styles: Abstract, Cubism, and Impressionism, but the one constant is color.

Instagram: @ScottAllenPaintings

Glossary of Buddhist Terms

Arya—literally "elevated" or "exalted;" refers to one who has reached a spiritually advanced state called the Path of Seeing, a direct perception of the ultimate state of reality.

Asana—a pose in yoga.

Avalokiteshwara—the name of a particular Bodhisattva, said to be the embodiment of the compassion of all the Buddhas.

Bodhicitta—the compassionate wish to become a Buddha oneself to help all other sentient beings.

Bodhisattva—one who has developed Bodhicitta and seeks to bring others to enlightenment, as well.

Bodhisattva Vow—a formal vow taken by Mahayana Buddhists to achieve enlightenment for the benefit of all beings (See Root Downfalls and Secondary Downfalls for more about the vow).

Buddha—one who has eliminated all the sufferings and the causes of suffering from their continuum and has achieved the omniscient mind.

Darshan—an opportunity for seeing or having an audience with a holy person.

Dependent Origination—all phenomena arise through the coming together of their own particular causes and conditions; cause and effect.

Dharma—refers to the teachings of the Buddha.

Empty/Emptiness—lack of inherent existence, or true existence, in all phenomena.

Four Noble Truths—(Four Arya Realities) The central theme of Buddha's first teaching after achieving enlightenment: Truth of Suffering, Truth of the Origins of Suffering, Truth of Cessations of Suffering, Truth of the Path to Cessations of Suffering.

Gelukpa—one of the four main traditions of Tibetan Buddhism; the Dalai Lama's sect.

Geshe—literally means "virtuous friend," a scholarly monastic degree awarded in the Gelukpa sect, like a Doctor of Divinity.

Hinayana—literally "lesser vehicle," refers to traditions or schools of Buddhism in which the basic motivation of practitioners is to be liberated from cyclic existence themselves.

Interdependence—See Dependent Origination.

Kagyu—one of the four main traditions of Tibetan Buddhism; the Karmapa's sect.

Karma—literally "action," refers to the process of cause and effect.

Karmapa—pinnacle teacher of the Kagyu tradition.

Khatak—an offering scarf.

Lama—a spiritual teacher.

Lamrim—literally "stages of the path," a method of practice and study common in the Gelukpa linage of Tibetan Buddhism which leads the practitioner through all the stages of the spiritual journey to full enlightenment.

Law of Attraction—a worldview that espouses that all things are created by mind and mental suggestion; "That which is like unto itself is drawn."

Mahayana—literally "great vehicle," refers to traditions or schools of Buddhism in which the basic motivation of practitioners is to achieve highest enlightenment to lead all sentient beings to the same state.

Meditation—a mental activity of mind training and discipline for focusing mental energy on a particular object or thought for training awareness to achieve clarity, stability, and intensity.

Nagarjuna—(c. 150–250 CE)—founder of the Middle Way School of Buddhism, referred to as one of the six great commentators on Buddha's teachings.

Nyingma—one of the four main traditions of Tibetan Buddhism; the followers of original translations of the Dharma into Tibetan carried out up until the late tenth century.

Renunciation—a definite and strong wish to be freed from cyclic existence.

Rinpoche—literally "precious," a title given most often to reborn lamas and senior teachers of Tibetan Buddhism.

Root Downfall—(of the Bodhisattva Vow) are 18 ways in which, when committed, the practitioner has broken their commitment to achieving enlightenment for all beings.

Sakya—one of the four main traditions of Tibetan Buddhism; The main teacher of this sect is Sakya Trizin.

Samsara—cyclic existence of birth, death, and rebirth.

Sangha—the spiritual community of practitioners who live by the Buddha's teachings.

Secondary Downfalls—(of the Bodhisattva Vow) 46 infractions to the vow to achieve enlightenment for all beings which, when committed, do not result in the breaking of the vow but a weakening of the intensity of the commitment.

Stupa—a reliquary for enlightened relics and a representation of the enlightened mind.

Tantra—esoteric practices in Mahayana Buddhism in which practitioners use mantra and visualizations of deities to develop total control of the consciousness and achieve enlightenment.

Thangka—a traditional Tibetan painting framed by embroidered fabric, depicting Buddhas, meditational deities, symbols, mandalas, or famous teachers.

Three Jewels—The Buddha, Dharma, and Sangha.

Vajrapani—a wrathful Buddha/Bodhisattva who represents inner strength.

Vajrayogini—in the practice of tantra, she is a meditational deity and spirit guide.

Yunchap—literally "water offerings," which are daily water bowl offerings made on Buddhist altars to the Three Jewels.

Further Reading

The XIVth Dalai Lama, *The Four Noble Truths* (London: Thorsons, 1997).

The XIVth Dalai Lama, *Essence of the Heart Sutra: The Dalai Lama's Heart of Wisdom Teachings*, trans. & ed. by Geshe Thupten Jinpa (Boston: Wisdom Publications, 2015).

Amit Goswami, *The Self-Aware Universe: How Consciousness Creates the Material World* (New York: Putnam's Sons, 1995).

Charles F. Haanel, *The Master Key System* (Mineola, New York: Ixia Press, 2018).

Jill Bolte Taylor, *My Stroke of Insight: A Brain Scientist's Personal Journey* (New York: Plume, 2009).

Joe Dispenza, *Evolve Your Brain: The Science of Changing Your Mind* (Health Communications, Inc., 2010).

Lama Thubten Yeshe, T*he Essence of Tibetan Buddhism: The Three Principal Aspects of the Path and an Introduction to Tantra*, ed. Nicholas Ribush (Boston: Lama Yeshe Wisdom Archive, 2001).

Lama Zopa Rinpoche & Geshe Tashi Tsering, *Relative Truth, Ultimate Truth: The Foundation of Buddhist Thought*, Vol. 2 (Boston: Wisdom Publications, 2008).

Matthieu Ricard & Xuan Thuan Trinh, *The Quantum and The Lotus: A Journey to the Frontiers where Science and Buddhism Meet* (New York: Crown Publishers, 2001).

Nagarjuna, *Fundamental Wisdom of the Middle Way*, trans. by Jay Garfield (New York: Oxford University Press, 1995).

Pabongka Rinpoche, *Liberation in the Palm of Your Hand: A Concise Discourse on the Stages of the Path to Enlightenment*, trans. by Michael Richards (Boston: Wisdom Publications, 1991).

Sogyal Rinpoche, *The Tibetan Book of Living and Dying*, eds. Patrick Gaffney and Andrew Harvey (San Francisco: Harper, 2002).

W.Y. Evans-Wentz & C. G. Jung, *The Tibetan Book of the Great Liberation* (New York: Oxford University Press, 2000).

www.ingramcontent.com/pod-product-compliance
Lightning Source LLC
Chambersburg PA
CBHW050853160426
43194CB00011B/2134